Readings in
Managerial Economics

Readings in Managerial Economics

W. Warren Haynes
Late of the State University of New York, Albany

Thomas Joseph Coyne
The University of Akron

Dale K. Osborne
State University of New York, Albany

1973

BUSINESS PUBLICATIONS, INC. Dallas, Texas 75231
IRWIN-DORSEY INTERNATIONAL London, England WC2H 9NJ
IRWIN-DORSEY LIMITED Georgetown, Ontario L7G 4B3

© BUSINESS PUBLICATIONS, INC., 1973

All rights reserved. No part of this publication may be reproduced, stored in a retrieval system, or transmitted, in any form or by any means, electronic, mechanical, photocopying, recording, or otherwise, without the prior written permission of the publisher.

First Printing, March 1973
Second Printing, October 1973
Third Printing, June 1974
Fourth Printing, April 1975

ISBN 0-256-01241-5
Library of Congress Catalog Card No. 72-95403
Printed in the United States of America

Preface

The articles in this volume of readings have been chosen and organized to supplement the small but growing number of textbooks used in courses in managerial economics. The main purpose of the volume is to increase the student's access to journal articles. The book may be valuable in microeconomic theory courses, but it is intended primarily for undergraduate students in managerial economics and students working toward the M.B.A. degree.

In addition to their articles reprinted here, we would have liked to borrow George Stigler's and Kenneth Boulding's Introduction to their American Economic Association volume, *Readings in Price Theory*—an introduction as elegant as the papers it precedes. But while this might give our collection a certain degree of poetic harmony, not to mention novelty, it would doubtless carry the anthologizing practice to indecent lengths. Besides, we want our hands to be visible by more direct means than the selections themselves.

"Presumably," say Stigler and Boulding, "an anthologist is maximizing something." And, we would add, like all economic agents he maximizes something subject to constraints. Our own constraints are those common to the practice—chiefly space, coverage, and balance—plus some we have set for ourselves. We have not reprinted material from books, since doing so would not have furthered the purpose of our book. We intended to avoid articles already available in other anthologies but found in a few cases that doing so would conflict with the more important constraints of coverage and balance. Thus we felt bound to include Working on statistical demand curves and Stigler on the oligopolistic kink, although these two articles appear in the Stigler and Boulding volume.

One constraint we have not adopted is that of uniformity in the level of abstraction. We did not hesitate to include rather abstract articles that develop important principles, or more elementary ones that illustrate them clearly. The resulting unevenness in the level of discourse seems to us an inherent feature of that mixture of tools and results which is managerial economics.

In our editing we have removed a number of footnotes and, in a few cases, textual material, which did not further the aims of the book. Overall, editorial changes are minor.

To assist users with their selections, we have provided a matrix of cross references between the subjects treated in this volume and specific chapters in several of the leading textbooks used in the field. In addition, these chapters are cross-referenced with specific articles in the Table of Contents.

We thank the authors and their publishers for permission to reprint these articles.

We have benefited from helpful comments and suggestions from a number of colleagues and students. We are particularly grateful to our students for their feedback concerning many of the articles we considered.

March 1973 T. J. COYNE
D. K. OSBORNE

Table of Contents
and
Text Cross-Reference*

PART I. THE SCOPE AND METHOD OF MANAGERIAL ECONOMICS

1. What Can Economic Theory Contribute to Managerial Economics? *William J. Baumol* 3

    Recommended for use with:
    > Brigham and Pappas—Chapter 1
    > Ferguson and Maurice—Chapter 1
    > Haynes—Chapter 1
    > Horowitz—Chapter 2

2. The Ethics of Rational Decision *Kenneth E. Boulding* 8

    Recommended for use with:
    > Haynes—Chapter 2

3. The Motives of Managers, Environmental Restraints, and the Theory of Managerial Enterprise *William L. Baldwin* 18

    Recommended for use with:
    > Horowitz—Chapter 11

---

*Textbooks referenced include:

Brigham, Eugene, and Pappas, James, *Managerial Economics* (Hinsdale, Illinois: Dryden Press, 1972).

Colberg, Marshall G., Forbush, Dascomb R., and Whitaker, Gilbert R., *Business Economics* (Homewood, Illinois: Irwin, 1970).

Ferguson, C. E., and Maurice, Charles, *Economic Analysis* (Homewood, Illinois: Irwin, 1970).

Haynes, W. Warren, *Managerial Economics* (Austin, Texas: Business Publications, 1969).

Horowitz, Ira, *Decision Making and the Theory of the Firm* (New York: Holt, Rinehart and Winston, 1969).

Spencer, Milton, *Managerial Economics* (Homewood, Illinois: Irwin, 1968).

Stokes, Milton, *Managerial Economics* (New York: Random House, 1968).

4. Theories of Decision Making in Economics and Behavioral Science *Herbert A. Simon* 32

    Recommended for use with:
        Brigham and Pappas—Chapter 1
        Ferguson and Maurice—Chapter 1
        Haynes—Chapter 1
        Horowitz—Chapters 1 and 10
        Spencer—Chapter 2
        Stokes—Chapter 2

PART II. DEMAND

5. What Do Statistical "Demand Curves" Show? *E. J. Working* 61

    Recommended for use with:
        Colberg, Forbush, Whitaker—Chapter 3
        Haynes—Chapter 3

6. New Evidence on Demand Elasticities *Hendrik S. Houthakker* 74

    Recommended for use with:
        Haynes—Chapter 3

7. Factors Affecting the Purchase Value of New Houses *L. J. Atkinson* 85

    Recommended for use with:
        Brigham and Pappas—Chapter 5
        Stokes—Chapter 3

8. The Price Elasticity of Liquor in the U.S. and a Simple Method of Determination *Julian L. Simon* 113

    Recommended for use with:
        Brigham and Pappas—Chapter 4
        Colberg, Forbush, Whitaker—Chapters 3 and 4
        Ferguson and Maurice—Chapter 2
        Haynes—Chapter 3
        Horowitz—Chapter 2
        Spencer—Chapter 5
        Stokes—Chapter 3

PART III. FORECASTING

9. Short-Term General Business Conditions Forecasting: Some Comments on Method *John P. Lewis* 127

Recommended for use with:
    Brigham and Pappas—Appendix B
    Colberg, Forbush, Whitaker—Chapter 2
    Haynes—Chapter 4
    Spencer—Chapter 3
    Stokes—Chapter 10

10. Alternative Approaches to Forecasting: The Recent Works of the National Bureau   *Robert A. Gordon* 144

    Recommended for use with:
        Brigham and Pappas—Appendix B
        Colberg, Forbush, Whitaker—Chapter 2
        Haynes—Chapter 4
        Spencer—Chapter 3
        Stokes—Chapter 10

11. Forecasting and Analysis with an Econometric Model   *Daniel B. Suits* 154

    Recommended for use with:
        Brigham and Pappas—Chapter 5
        Colberg, Forbush, Whitaker—Chapter 2
        Haynes—Chapter 4

12. Consumer Attitudes, Buying Plans, and Purchases of Durable Goods: A Principal Components, Time-Series Approach   *F. Gerald Adams* 183

    Recommended for use with:
        Brigham and Pappas—Chapter 5

PART IV. COSTS

13. Statistical Cost Functions: A Reappraisal   *J. Johnston* 199

    Recommended for use with:
        Brigham and Pappas—Chapter 9
        Haynes—Chapters 2, 5, and 6
        Horowitz—Chapter 5
        Spencer—Chapter 7
        Stokes—Chapter 4

14. Economies of Scale in Industrial Plants   *John Haldi and David Whitcomb* 219

x   Contents

    Recommended for use with:
        Brigham and Pappas—Chapter 8
        Colberg, Forbush, Whitaker—Chapter 6
        Haynes—Chapter 6
        Spencer—Chapter 6

15. The Economies of Scale   *George J. Stigler*   232

    Recommended for use with:
        Brigham and Pappas—Chapter 9
        Haynes—Chapter 6

16. Break-Even Analysis with Stepwise Varying Marginal Costs and Revenues   *M. C. Meimaroglou*   250

    Recommended for use with:
        Brigham and Pappas—Chapter 10
        Ferguson and Maurice—Chapter 6
        Haynes—Chapter 5
        Spencer—Chapter 4
        Stokes—Chapter 5

17. Economic Aspects of Broiler Production Density   *W. R. Henry and J. A. Seagraves*   264

    Recommended for use with:
        Brigham and Pappas—Chapter 9
        Colberg, Forbush, Whitaker—Chapter 5
        Ferguson and Maurice—Chapter 6
        Haynes—Chapters 5 and 6
        Horowitz—Chapter 5
        Spencer—Chapters 6 and 7
        Stokes—Chapter 4

PART V.   PRICING

18. The Kinky Oligopoly Demand Curve and Rigid Prices   *George J. Stigler*   281

    Recommended for use with:
        Brigham and Pappas—Chapter 10
        Colberg, Forbush, Whitaker—Chapter 12
        Haynes—Chapters 3 and 7
        Horowitz—Chapters 4 and 7
        Spencer—Chapter 9
        Stokes—Chapter 7

19. Pricing Objectives in Large Companies *Robert F. Lanzillotti* 300

   Recommended for use with:
   Brigham and Pappas—Chapter 11
   Colberg, Forbush, Whitaker—Chapter 12
   Ferguson and Maurice—Chapter 9
   Haynes—Chapter 7
   Horowitz—Chapters 10 and 11
   Spencer—Chapter 9
   Stokes—Chapter 5

20. Pricing Practices in Small Firms *W. Warren Haynes* 319

   Recommended for use with:
   Brigham and Pappas—Chapter 11
   Haynes—Chapters 2 and 7

21. Variations on the Full-Cost Theme *Martin Howe* 332

   Recommended for use with:
   Brigham and Pappas—Chapter 8
   Haynes—Chapter 5

22. Decentralization and Intracompany Pricing *Joel Dean* 343

   Recommended for use with:
   Brigham and Pappas—Chapter 11
   Colberg, Forbush, Whitaker—Chapters 11 and 12
   Haynes—Chapter 7
   Spencer—Chapter 9

23. On the Economics of Transfer Pricing *Jack Hirshleifer* 360

   Recommended for use with:
   Brigham and Pappas—Chapter 11
   Colberg, Forbush, Whitaker—Chapters 11 and 12
   Haynes—Chapter 8
   Spencer—Chapter 9

PART VI. CAPITAL BUDGETING

24. Depreciation, Market Valuations and Investment Theory
    Vernon L. Smith 375

Recommended for use with:
> Brigham and Pappas—Chapter 13
> Colberg, Forbush, Whitaker—Chapter 7
> Haynes—Chapters 9 and 10
> Spencer—Chapter 11
> Stokes—Chapter 11

25. A Misplaced Emphasis in Capital Budgeting
    W. Warren Haynes and Martin B. Solomon, Jr. 383

    Recommended for use with:
    > Brigham and Pappas—Chapter 3
    > Haynes—Chapter 9
    > Spencer—Chapter 11
    > Stokes—Chapter 11

26. Some New Views on the Payback Period and Capital Budgeting Decisions *H. Martin Weingartner* 393

    Recommended for use with:
    > Haynes—Chapter 9
    > Horowitz—Chapter 10

27. Uncertainty and Its Effect on Capital Investment Analysis
    Martin B. Solomon, Jr. 408

    Recommended for use with:
    > Haynes—Chapter 9

28. Measuring the Productivity of Investment in Persuasion
    Joel Dean 414

    Recommended for use with:
    > Colberg, Forbush, Whitaker—Chapter 13
    > Haynes—Chapters 2 and 5
    > Horowitz—Chapter 13
    > Spencer—Chapter 8
    > Stokes—Chapter 13

TEXT CROSS-REFERENCES

	Text Chapters					
Readings in This Book	Part I Scope and Method of Managerial Decisions	Part II Demand	Part III Forecasting	Part IV Costs	Part V Pricing	Part VI Capital Budgeting
Brigham and Pappas	1		4, 5	5, App. B	8, 9, 10	8, 10, 11	3, 13
Colberg, Forbush, Whitaker		3, 4	2	5, 6	11, 12	7, 13
Ferguson and Maurice	1	2		6	9	
Haynes	1, 2	3	4	2, 5, 6	2, 3, 5, 7, 8	2, 5, 9, 10
Horowitz	1, 2, 10, 11	2		5	4, 7, 10, 11	10, 13
Spencer	2	5	3	4, 6, 7	9	8, 11
Stokes	2	3	10	4, 5	4, 5, 7	11, 13

part ONE
The Scope and Method of Managerial Economics

INTRODUCTION

Managerial economics is economics applied to managerial decision making. It is a branch of economics bridging the gap between abstract theory and managerial practice. Its stress is on the use of the tools of economic analysis in clarifying problems, in organizing and evaluating information, and in comparing alternative courses of action. Though it is sometimes known as business economics, its methods and point of view are applicable not only in business but also in other institutions, such as government, universities, nonprofit foundations, etc., which allocate resources.

Economics is defined sometimes as the study of the allocation of scarce resources among unlimited ends. It follows that managerial economics is the study of the allocation of resources available to a firm or other decision-making institution among the objectives of the institution. Thus like all economics, managerial economics is concerned with choice; but among the various branches of economics it is supremely pragmatic. It cuts through many of the refinements of theory. While it seems to avoid some of the most difficult issues of abstract economic theory, it inevitably faces complications that are ignored in pure theory, for it must deal with the total situation in which decisions are made.

Managerial economics is therefore manifestly different from microeconomic theory; but it is somehow related. Just what this relation is has been a lively topic of debate. The extreme positions are, on the one hand, a naïve belief that the most abstract economic theories are applicable to the most complex of managerial problems, and on the other, an equally repugnant belief that no part of economic theory is applicable to even the simplest of them. From a large and admirable literature covering the question from one extreme to the other, we have selected articles that express what seem to us the more tenable views.

The well-known paper by William Baumol establishes a point of view for managerial economics; namely, that a managerial economist can make significant contributions as a member of the management group simply because he is an effective model builder. The economist's analytic tools and techniques help him to deal with the problems of the firm in a very rigorous and revealing manner.

Rather different issues are encountered in the article by Kenneth Boulding. Boulding's article is concerned with broader issues than are usually met in managerial economics. With his usual economy and lucidity Boulding places the question of rational decision making in a larger context. His article can be read with profit by that small but apparently growing body of persons who find themselves doubting the very possibility of a rational approach to problems in the modern world.

In the article by William Baldwin, it is argued that long-run profit maximization need not be dependent upon any one type of behavior; instead, target return pricing, incremental reasoning in pricing, full-cost pricing, pricing designed to maximize sales, and so on, are all theories that point ultimately to long-run total profit of the firm.

Herbet Simon, on the other hand, argues for the recognition of the numerous instances where applied price theory overlaps with areas of psychology and sociology. It must be realized that economic man—the consumer as well as the entrepreneur—is a compassionate person hoping to attain and then maintain a variety of objectives, only one of which happens to be profit maximization.

1. What Can Economic Theory Contribute to Managerial Economics?*

WILLIAM J. BAUMOL

What to me is one of the most significant aspects of economic theory for management science was brought out very clearly in a talk I had some time ago with a biologist friend of mine. This biologist is an eminent authority on clock mechanisms in animals. There is a remarkable and well-known periodicity in the behavior of a large variety of animal species—in fact, probably among all of them. To illustrate the point, the emergence of adult fruit flies from their pupae usually occurs shortly after dawn. Even if the flies are placed in a darkened room whose temperature, humidity, and other evidences of passage of time are carefully controlled, they will continue to emerge from the pupae at just about the same time day after day. However, if after being kept under these controlled laboratory conditions they are suddenly shown some light in order to produce the effect of a false dawn, there is a permanent shift of phase and, after some transient behavior, they will change the time at which they emerge from the pupae to that corresponding to the dawn which they were last shown. This suggests that there is a very definite way in which these animals can tell the time; that is to say, in which they can recognize when twenty-four hours are over, even though there is nothing conscious about it.

Of course a clock mechanism suggests periodicity, and periodicity, to any good cycle theorist, suggests difference or differential equations. And in fact, after this biologist had been working on the subject for some time, he became aware of this possibility and set out to find a mathematician who could help him to determine an appropriate equation. This was done, a relationship was fitted by statistical methods, and it turned out that it was appropriate to use a nonlinear differential equation. It was found that one such equation could fit a great variety of the data which this man had available. Not only could it do that,

---

American Economic Review, vol. 51, no. 2 (May 1961), pp. 142–46.

but with the aid of the equation he was able to make a number of interesting predictions which were subsequently very closely confirmed by data which he was able to collect.

Here is where we come to the point of the story—the contrast between the situation of the biologist and that of the economic theorist—for the biologist who had obtained a very nice relationship on the basis of empirical data was totally unable to give any sort of analytical explanation of what he had. He had absolutely no model on which he could base a derivation of his mathematical relationship. We may, perhaps, generalize by remarking that biologists, with some notable exceptions, have data without models, whereas we in economic theory have models which usually are created without data. And in this way we have summarized one of the economic theorist's greatest weaknesses and one of his greatest strengths.

I would now like to emphasize the latter, the more pleasant, side: the fact that the economist is an expert model builder. Indeed, there are very few disciplines which produce model builders with such practice and such skill. This, I think, is one of the most important things which the economic theorist can contribute to the work of management science. In management science it is important—in fact, absolutely essential—to be able to recognize the structure of a managerial problem. In order to be able to analyze it at all and to be able to do so systematically, it is necessary to do several things: first of all, to undertake a judicious simplification—an elimination of minor details which are peripheral to the problem and which, if included in the model, would prevent any successful and systematic analysis. Second, it is important to capture in a formal statement the essence of all the interrelationships which characterize the situation, because it is only after stating these interrelationships so explicitly that we can hope to use the powerful techniques of rigorous analysis in the investigation of a managerial problem. It is the model which incorporates both these features; it is the central focus of the entire analysis which must capture the essence of the situation which is being investigated.

Thus, in any of the complex situations which are encountered in the systematic analysis of management problems, model building is a critical part of the investigation. Problems as diverse as the optimal size and composition of a department store product line or the location of a company's warehouses have one thing in common: their complexity—which arises to a large extent out of the network of interrelationships among their elements. An increase in the number of items carried in a store reduces the capacity for carrying stocks of other items: on the one hand it makes it more likely that the customer will find what she wants when she enters the store; on the other she may find more often that although the store usually carries what she desires, it happens to be out of it temporarily. The length of time a customer must search for an item is affected by a change in product line; the likelihood of "impulse" purchases is also affected, etc. The drawing together of such a diversity of strands is the major function of the model, without which most of our tools will not function. Moreover, in my experience it is not atypical that nearly half of the time spent in the investigation of such a problem is devoted to model building—to capturing the essence of the situation in a set of explicit relationships. For there are no cut and dried rules in model building. It is essentially a matter of discovery, involving all of the intangibles of discovery—hunch, insight, and intuition, and no holds are barred. Only after the model has been built can the problem sometimes be reduced to a routine by use of standard rules of calculation.

To my knowledge there are few classroom courses in this critical skill of model building, and, because it has no rules, it cannot be taught like trigonometry or chemistry. But apparently it can be learned by experience. And, as I have said, the economic theorist has had a great deal of experience in the construction and use of such models. When he employs some differential equations, you can almost be certain that he has derived them from a model which he built, not, like the biologist, from some data which he has collected.

This, then, is one of the major contributions which the economic theorist can, in my opinion, make to managerial analysis. It is, however, a skill and a predisposition that he brings with him, not a series of specific results.

This takes me to the second major point that I wish to make: the other way in which I think economic theory can be helpful to management science. I believe the most important thing a managerial economics student can get out of a course in economic analysis is not a series of theorems but rather a set of analytical methods. And for that reason I think it is far more important for him to learn the basis of these theorems, their assumption and their methods of derivation, than to end up with a group of conclusions. I can say quite categorically that I have never encountered a business problem in which my investigation was helped by any specific economic theorem, nor, may I add, have I ever met a practical problem in which I failed to be helped by the method of reasoning involved in the derivation of some economic theorem.

One of the major reasons that the propositions of economic theory are not directly applicable to management problems is that the theory does not deal with the major concerns of the businessman. Product line, advertising, budgeting, sales force allocation, inventory levels, new product introduction are all relative strangers to the idealized firm of value theory whose major concern is price-output policy. Certainly there is little in the theoretical literature which refers directly to the warehouse location or the department store product line problems which were mentioned previously.

Even where more familiar theoretical matters, such as pricing problems, arise in practice, the results of the theory provide only limited help. This is because theorems in economic analysis deal with rather general abstract entities, with firms which have the peculiar and most interesting characteristics of actual companies eliminated from them in order to enable the analyst to draw conclusions which apply to the entire economy and not just to one or several particular firms. As a result, when attempting to apply these theorems, one finds that they have abstracted some of the features it is most essential to retain in order to analyze the specific situation with which one is faced in the market. The theory offers us fairly general admonitions, like the one which tells us that marginal cost must equal marginal revenue if we are to maximize profits—surely a statement which is not very much of a guide in application. I repeat that in my applied work I have never found any occasion to use either this theorem or any other such specific proposition of economic analysis.

But I have often found it absolutely essential to use the techniques of marginal analysis as it occurs in the theory of the firm, the theory of production, and in welfare economics. Several times I have even found it helpful to use the techniques and derivations of some of the elasticity theorems. This last illustration perhaps merits a little expansion. It may appear extraordinary that the elasticity theorems were of any use in application at all for they would seem to provide the ultimate illustration of tools whose use requires the availability of extensive data. However, the point I am making is that it was not the theorems but the methods of analysis and derivation which were employed. For example, an analogue of the elementary proposition that unit elasticity is the borderline between increasing and decreasing total revenue in response to a decrease in price can be applied in other situations. In fact, it is precisely because of the lack of data that it often becomes necessary to decide just where such break-even points occur, and in a number of cases I have found that the ability to prove that this critical point is sufficiently beyond what may reasonably be expected is an adequate substitute for the availability of data. Thus knowledge of the method of derivation of the theorems—and, indeed, of the spirit of the theorems themselves—often enables one to do things without data which otherwise would be pretty much out of the question.

But this is not the major point. If it is true—and it certainly has been true in my experience—that every firm and every managerial situation requires a model which is more or less unique, none of the standard theorems is going to fit in with it. It will be necessary, in effect, to derive special theorems which enable one to deal with that specific situation. Here one is helped, then, not by the generalized propositions which have been developed by the theorist, but by the methods which have enabled him to achieve his results which show us how analogous conclusions or analogous analyses can be conducted for the problems at hand. It is for this reason that I make my plea about the teaching of economics and economic theory to the managerial economist. This plea is not only that economic theory should be taught to the business student but that it should be presented to him pretty much as it is taught to the liberal arts student, with the emphasis not on a series of canned conclusions but on the methods of investigation on the derivations behind the results—on the analytic tools and methods.

There is a third way in which economic theory can help in managerial analysis—and, perhaps strangely, here the more elementary concepts of economics are primarily involved or, rather, concepts which though relatively sophisticated are used in a very elementary way. These elementary concepts can imbue the economist with habits of thought which enable him to avoid some significant pitfalls. For example, consider the case of external economies and diseconomies. How much can familiarity with this concept tell us about the dangers involved in directing one branch of an enterprise to maximize its profits in disregard of the effects of its actions on other parts of the firm! Similarly, we economists are made very sensitive by marginal analysis to the perils of resource allocation by average cost and profit—resource allocation rules of thumb which are so frequently encountered in business practice. Such bits of reasoning once led one of my colleagues, who was reviewing some of the cases cited in the literature of managerial analysis, to remark that he was amazed at how often this reading had forced him to recall his sophomore economics!

To summarize, then, I have suggested very little by way of concrete contribution from economic theory to managerial economics. With some exceptions, I have not said that this particular result or that particular body of discussion is essential or even particularly helpful for the managerial economist. I have been able to offer no illustrations of managerial problems in which I was able to use very specific pieces of the body of economic analysis. But this is right in line with the very nature of my major point: the assertion that a managerial economist can become a far more helpful member of a management group by virtue of his studies of economic analysis, primarily because there he learns to become an effective model builder and because there he acquires a very rich body of tools and techniques which can help him to deal with the problems of the firm in a far more rigorous, a far more probing, and a far deeper manner.

2. The Ethics of Rational Decision*

KENNETH E. BOULDING

In recent years a great deal of attention has been paid by social scientists and others to the problem of the theory of decisions. The decision is a basic concept of social systems, especially in social dynamics. It represents perhaps the most important single class of *events*, an event being defined as a kind of step function which separates one position of a social system from the next in point of time. Some events are not the result of human decision at all, such as aging or accidents; some are the results of previous decisions, such as depreciation of a previously created capital structure; but when all these are removed, there remains an important category of events which constitute a deliberate change in state of a social system as a result of human action.

The concept of a decision always implies that the change of state in question is not the only possible state, and that there is at least one other possibility. A decision, that is to say, involves choice. We imply that from any given present state, there is a number greater than one of possible alternative states in the future. We can simplify the problem by supposing that the condition that determines the future is contained in a given state, and hence the choice is among the possible "next" states of the system.

The problem of decision can then be broken down into two further problems. There is the problem of the definition of our knowledge of alternative possible states. In the initial state, we have to have some kind of image of possible future states, and it is a very interesting and quite difficult question as to how we acquire this image. There is more in this than meets the eye. Having now acquired an image of possible futures, by whatever means, in which each possible state includes what we have to do in order to attain it, the next question is how do we value these possibilities in a value ordering, so that we can choose the right one of them as superior to all the others. The principle known to economists as the principle of maximizing behavior simply states that when we are faced with a number of possibilities, we always choose that which seems to us to be best at the time. This seems like a principle

* *Management Science*, vol. 12, no. 6 (February 1966), pp. B-161–B-169.

of such extreme formality that it is a little surprising at first sight that it could have any use whatever. However, in the hands of economists it turns out to be quite surprisingly powerful, and it is indeed the foundation of operations research and management science, most of which consists in elaborate techniques for putting content into this otherwise contentless proposition.

The moment we state it in this way, it is clear that a decision is a process, to paraphrase a famous legal expression, "affected with the ethical interest." The ethical interest impinges on it at two points. It impinges even in the first stage when we ask ourselves, how do we come to know the range of possible alternatives, for there may be alternative ways of coming to know alternatives, and we have to make some kind of value judgment among them. At the second stage of the decision-making process, in which the alternatives are subjected to value ordering, the ethical interest is clearly implied, for one of the major concerns of ethics is the evaluation of value orderings themselves. Ethics, that is, is concerned with what might be called decision problems of the second degree, that is, decision about how decisions are going to be made, and according to what principles are they going to be made.

The very use of the word "rational" in the expression "rational decision making" has ethical implications, for the problem of whether the *rational* is to be identified as the *good* is by no means a simple one. The definition of rationality itself is also by no means simple. It is customary to define rationality in terms of a set of limitations on the nature of a value ordering. It is argued, for instance, that a value ordering is irrational if it is intransitive, that is, if we prefer A to B, B to C, and C to A, or even more, if we prefer A to B, we should not at the same time prefer B to A. Even these formal definitions of rationality frequently gets us into trouble. The plain fact is that intransitive orderings are observed in real life all the time, simply because comparing pairs of things two at a time is not the same kind of process as trying to make a rank ordering of a number of things simultaneously, even within the mind of a single individual. When we come to such things as committee and group decisions, the possibility of intransitive orderings increases substantially. In the famous voting paradoxes, for instance, those propounded by Duncan Black, and the whole set of problems associated with the name of Kenneth Arrow, it is suggested that such things as group decisions and committee decisions will often depend as much on the process or ritual by which the decision is reached as it does on the actual preferences of the individuals in the group. Even at this rather formal level, therefore, there are many difficulties in the concept of rationality.

If we take into account the cost of the decision-making process itself, the concept of rationality disintegrates even further. Here the theory of the dilemma is of some importance. If we have a weak ordering of the alternatives open towards us, so that for instance there are two possibilities at the top of our rank ordering of equal value to us, of which, however, we must choose one, we find ourselves in a difficult and painful position. If the possibilities are in fact absolutely equal in rank, then the rational decision is to be irrational and to make the selection by a random process, such as tossing a coin. Even if two possibilities are not identical but are very close to each other in our estimation, the difficulty and the cost of deciding between them may be so great that it again is rational not to be rational, and to decide the issue by random process. We could almost argue that this is what the American political system does, in the sense that where the two contending parties are really rather similar, the process of deciding between them turns out to be an almost random ritual.

A rather similar problem arises in the first part of the decision process, that is, the building up of the image of possibilities. Here, perfect knowledge is almost always too costly, and we have to be content with imperfect knowledge. This means, however, that we have the problem of search, that is, the investment of resources which might have alternative uses in expanding our image of the possibilities that are open to us. I know of no simple rational model of the process of search at all. How do we know when to stop looking for the needle in the haystack?—short of putting the whole haystack through a sieve! I recall the children's game of hide and seek, in which the group who have hidden an object tell the seeker whether he is "hot" or "cold." If there are indeed processes like this in the search procedure, we are very fortunate. Many times, however, there is nobody to shout "hot" or "cold." There may be no feedback whatever from the search until we find what we are looking for. This gets even more difficult when we are not even sure that what we are looking for exists, which is often the case in social systems. This suggests, incidentally, that existence theorems might have a profound effect on behavior because of their effect on the willingness to search. Even if we know what we are looking for, however, if we have not found it do we try, try again, or do we simply call it quits and try something else? Should we interpret failure as "too little and too late" and renew our efforts along the same lines, or should we interpret it as "too much and too soon" and divert our attention to other lines of endeavor altogether? Unfortunately there is often very little in the search situation which indicates which of these paths we should follow. One may perhaps hazard a guess that both in individual and organizational behavior, there is more tendency to beat our heads against a stone wall and to refuse to reverse the directions of search (pigheadedness) than there is to fail to persist in directions which are going to reward us at the next turn of the road (faintheartedness). I am not sure, however, that this proposition can be proved.

The problem of the calculus of probabilities when future outcomes are uncertain also presents us with a wide range of difficulties in regard to rational decision. In the first place, if we are dealing with stochastic systems, in which there are real random elements from the point of view of the observer, it is by no means easy to separate the random from the nonrandom elements in the system by simple observation of the sequence of events. Here we tend to fall into two opposite errors. We may interpret an event that is nonrandom, and is in fact built into some kind of a system, as if it were a random event, in which case we are in danger of failing to perceive the truly systematic nature of the world in which we are living. An even commoner, and perhaps more dangerous error, is the interpretation of random events as if they were in fact systematic. This results in building up an image of a system which in fact is untrue, that is, which does not correspond to the nonrandom, systematic character of the real world. If we add to this the fact that in social systems our images are quite often self-justifying, in the sense that they induce behavior on the part of the individual who holds them which tends to create the social system of his image, we see that rational decision making is a very precarious system indeed, and one is almost tempted to the cynical conclusion that people are not divided into *rational* and *irrational*, but into *lucky* and *unlucky*.

At this point, indeed, the ethical predispositions and images of the decision maker may have profound consequences, not only on the kinds of decisions he makes, but also on the kind of real world in which he lives. There is a famous Quaker story of a Friend who was asked by a newcomer to his community, what type of people lived there. He asked the newcomer, "What kind of people did thee live among before?" The newcomer replied, "Oh, I lived among a mean, suspicious, unfriendly, treacherous bunch of people," whereupon the Quaker replied, "Well, I am very sorry, friend, but thee will probably find the same type of people here." Going down the road, the Quaker meets another newcomer, of whom he asks the same question. "Oh," said the second man, "I lived among a fine group of people, friendly and honest, and I was sorry to leave them;" whereupon the Quaker said, "I am glad to say, friend, thee will find the same kind of people here."

Turning now to the problems involved in the selection of the value function itself, we face another interesting and difficult problem, which arises out of the development and use of what might be called value indexes. A value index, like money or money's worth, is a "measure of value," that is, it is a set of numbers arrived at by some well-defined process, which has the property that the higher the number, the higher the value of the state of the social system from which it is derived. In decision theory, we do not usually have to assume that the set of numbers of the value index represents a cardinal ordering of the underlying value function, for all we usually need is a rank ordering, that is, a set of ordinal numbers. However, every set of cardinal numbers is also at the same time a rank ordering. A value index which gives us such a set has all the properties we need, and we can easily neglect the implications of cardinality; that is, we do not have to assume that a value represented by an index of 200 is twice as great as one represented by an index of 100.

Problems arise, however, when the value index fails to maintain a one to one ordinal relation with the underlying value function, and this can also easily happen. We see this, for instance, in the familiar example of profit maximization. Profits are an extraordinarily useful value index, no matter how we measure them. Ten dollars is usually better than nine, and 10 percent better than 9 percent. The assumption of profit maximization, therefore, gives us a useful body of analysis in economics, the conclusions of which are certainly not wholly unrelated to the real world. Nevertheless, it is also clear that most firms do not maximize profits, mainly because at a certain point, profits tend to break down as a value index. For instance, it might well prefer a profit rate of 6 percent which gives it a quiet life, good public relations, good labor relations, and so on, to a profit rate of 7 percent which is less secure and which involves nonmonetary disadvantages in the shape of poor labor relations, poor public relations, and so on. If profit can be sacrificed for anything, however, it is clearly not maximized; hence it cannot be taken without qualification as a value index.

The problem of a value index is of crucial importance for operations research, for the solution of any operations research problem involves the selection of a value index, the establishment of its functional relation to other variables which describe the state of the system, and a definition of that state of the system at which the value index is a maximum. If the value index which is selected does not have an ordinal relation to the underlying value function, the solutions which are reached by operations research can be severely misleading. One sees the same problem even at less sophisticated levels in what might be called the subordinate ideals of various departments in an organization. There is a famous story of a production manager who said that all he wanted to do was to minimize costs, until it was pointed out that the easiest way to do this would be to shut down operations altogether, in which case the costs would be reduced to zero. Here the fulfillment of subordinate goals can easily be inimical to the fulfillment of the larger goals and the more ultimate value system. We see this in the necessity which every organization has for compromise among departmental goals;

we see it particularly acutely in the problems of the centrally planned economy; we also see it in the field of formal education, where the ultimate goal of producing educated people is often interfered with because we set up subordinate goals in the shape of grades, degrees, and so on, which are supposed to motivate people step by step towards the final goal. Thus, what might be called the subordination of subordinate goals emerges as one of the major problems of decision making in organizations.

The problem of the subordination of subordinate goals, however, also emerges as one of the major problems of ethics. One of the prime problems of ethics, as I have suggested earlier, is the evaluation of value functions themselves. This frequently takes the form of the criticism of the "insubordination" of subordinate goals, that is, a situation in which the subordinate goals become dominant and take the place of the more fundamental value function which they are supposed to represent. Even though ethical theory does not come out with any single formula for relating subordinate goals to ultimate goals, it can state with a high degree of certainty that given the complexity of the human organism, no single value index can ever serve without question as a measure of the ultimate goal. That is, in pursuing any particular subordinate goal, we must always get to the point at which we must ask ourselves, "Is a little more of this worth what we have to sacrifice in order to get it?" Obsession by single subordinate goals, whether this is money or sex or eating or even stamp collecting, is a sign of mental or at least ethical ill health. A person who is ethically mature will constantly be weighing subordinate goals against each other and making decisions about how far to pursue each one.

The quantification of value functions into value indices, whether this is money or whether it is more subtle and complicated measures of payoff, introduces elements of ethical danger into the decision-making process, simply because the clarity and apparent objectivity of quantitatively measurable subordinate goals can easily lead to a failure to bear in mind that they are in fact subordinate. The development of accounting is an interesting case in point. Before the development of double-entry bookkeeping and the fairly accurate recording of profit and loss, which began to take place in about the 14th or 15th century, presumably even merchants and still more landlords and farmers would only have very vague ideas about how profitable their operations might be. With the development of accounting, the measurement of profit became much more exact, but as a result also, certain other elements of the total value situation became less prominent and, therefore, neglected, such things for instance as morale, loyalty, legitimacy, and intimacy and complexity of personal relations. I suspect that the sociological weakness of the business community and its extraordinary inability to stand up, both to military ideologies, as witness the case of Japan, and also to socialist ideologies, arises from this fundamental deficiency. A subculture within which profit making becomes the only criterion for decisions either must be supported by a set of institutions from outside, which can develop something like an integrative structure, such as the church or the club or the school or the state, or else it will simply collapse because of its integrative weakness. I seem to recall saying somewhere else that the only thing that is wrong with capitalism is that nobody loves it. Schumpeter makes essentially the same point, that capitalism fails in spite of its spectacular economic success because the institutions of the market do not develop an integrative system sufficient to sustain it in the face of the kind of hatred, loss of legitimacy, and criticism which arise out of pure profit-oriented decisions. This illustrates a principle of very great importance, that decisions which may seem to be rational from the point of view of a single part of the social system may in fact turn out to be disastrous from the point of view of the continuance of the social system itself.

This principle becomes even more strikingly manifested when we look at the problem of rational decision in threat systems, that is, in social systems in which threats and counterthreats are used in the organization of roles and behavior. In systems which are dominated by exchange, such as business, especially where markets are reasonably perfect, the decision maker can assume with a modicum of security that he makes the decisions in the face of an environment which will not change because of the decisions which he makes. In the case of threat systems, this is rarely, if ever, true. There is practically no analog in threat systems of the economists' concept of the perfect market. All threat systems operate under conditions analogous to oligopoly. Under these circumstances there is a strong tendency for the system to degenerate into zero-sum and negative-sum games, whereas in the exchange system, positive-sum games are prominent. The main problem with negative-sum games, however, is not how to play them well but how to avoid playing them at all; that is, how to transform the system from a threat system into either an exchange system or an integrative system. Unfortunately, the people who operate the threat system and who are supported by it have a certain vested interest in maintaining it. Hence they concentrate on the problem of how to act rationally within the threat system when frequently this is a problem that has no real solution, and effort concentrated towards replacing the threat system by a more positive-sum kind of arrangement would have much higher payoffs.

The ethical matrix of behavior, which determines the predispositions out of which the decision maker evaluates the various value systems which are open to him is of great importance in determining the width of the agenda of the decision maker. There seems to be a fundamental disposition in mankind to limit agenda, often quite arbitrarily, perhaps because of our fears of information overload. We all suffer in some degree from agoraphobia, that is, the fear of open spaces, especially open spaces in the mind. As a result, we all tend to retreat into the cosy closed spaces of limited agendas and responsibilities, into tribalism, nationalism, and religious and political sectarianism and dogmatism. Nevertheless, ethical analysis puts out a warning flag at this point. Even though there may be good reasons for limiting agenda to prevent in formation overload, nevertheless, limiting the agenda is always costly and is sometimes very costly, and there is something about this process which prevents us from realizing how costly it is, simply because we cannot know the cost of limiting the agenda unless we widen it, which act, of course, the very process of limiting the agenda forbids. Hence what looks like rational decisions under limited agendas often turn out to be disastrous, whether this is in business, in politics, or even in religion, and for that matter, even in science, where the deliberate limiting of agendas is at the same time often the secret of present success and an obstacle to future progress.

On the other side of the coin, there is also a considerable relationship between the capacity of a decision maker to handle large quantities of information and his ability to widen his agenda. People who have narrow agendas, the bigots, the Birchers, the Marxists, the nationalists, and the schizophrenics, are by and large people whose information processing capacities are highly limited. They retreat into narrow agendas because they cannot bear the information overload which would seem to result from wide ones. Improvements in information processing, therefore, have profound ethical significance, because they remove obstacles to that widening of agendas which is one of the major components of most ethical systems. Preaching, which has been one of the main technologies of ethics, never seems to have been very effective, beyond a certain point, and it may be that the horizons of the power of ethical ideas may be substantially extended by the development of improved methods of information processing by the individual and by the organization.

Let me conclude by illustrating these principles in the particular case of an ethical system which is at least vaguely familiar to most people in our society, that is, the Christian ethic. I am aware, of course, that there is no such thing as a single Christian ethic, and that even in the Bible we find a complex, organic historical web of interacting and often inconsistent ethical systems. By way of illustration, however, I will just pick out two classical ethical statements: The first, the injunction, "Love one's neighbor as oneself" first comes in the Old Testament and is as much a part of the Judaic as of the Christian tradition; and the second, the injunction to love one's enemies, which is more distinctively Christian, even though it has usually been regarded as a "counsel of perfection," to be admired rather than observed.

The injunction to love one's neighbor as oneself has two major implications for decision theory: the first, often overlooked, that one should love oneself. In terms of economics this means that one should maximize utility rather than minimizing disutility, a distinction which is virtually unknown to economics, but which is very important to psychology. In other words, one should move towards the best rather than movng away from the worst. This, I have argued, is the essential key to mental health. The internal conflicts and dilemmas of the utility maximizer are all of the approach-approach variety, which are easily resolved, like the dilemma of the famous donkey between the two bales of hay. The disutility minimizer constantly gets into avoidance-avoidance conflicts like the donkey between two skunks, and hence gets into insoluble dilemmas in which all rational choice breaks down.

The injunction to love one's neighbor involves a widening of agendas on the one hand and the development of an integrative system on the other. It implies in the first place that we regard our decisions as involving the total social system, and not only that part of it which revolves around our own persons. It implies, that it is to say, a kind of Copernican Revolution and an abandonment of perspective. Instead of seeing the world through our own eyes from our own position, we make the imaginative leap, as Copernicus did, and in effect see ourselves from outside. This is an injection, therefore, which leads towards what might be called objective realism. It also, however, has profound implications for the kind of value system which we place over the world as viewed objectively. It involves a realistic appraisal of the self and its position in the world, rather than a self-denial, which I think is not really consistent with the Christian ethic, but creeps into it from the more negative religions of the East. In practice, of course, one must make concessions to perspective—the near are going to be dearer than the far, and the association of the near and dear is by no means unreasonable, especially in the light of the limits of one's power and responsibility. It is after all, the neighbor—that is, the near one—that one is advised to love.

The question, who is my neighbor, is of course the tricky one, and this is where the love of enemies, who are also near and, therefore, neighbors, becomes relevant. There are a good many different kinds of love of enemies. There is one kind that rises out of self-hatred, as William Blake saw so clearly ("He who loves his enemies hates his friends; surely that is not what Jesus intends"). There is also a certain kind of love of enemies which might be described as political rationality. A politician doesn't have to love his friends, as they will vote for him anyway. In his policies, therefore, he moves frequently towards the position of those who *just* did not vote for him, and if his friends are really friends, they will be dismayed but will continue to vote for him. Finally, there is the kind of love of enemies which might be described as integrative behavior, which is seldom recognized as such, but of which a great many examples can be found. This sometimes is done by those who are weak in the threat system, such as the joking behavior often remarked by anthropologists and observed in many classes which are subject to discrimination, such as Negroes, Jews, and traveling salesmen. The whole study of "disarming behavior"—politeness, the handshake, the bow, the form of address, likewise falls under this category. There can also, however, be integrative behavior on the part of those who are strong in the threat system, but who recognize the essential weakness and instability of the threat system itself, and who hence are concerned to replace it by something with larger horizons.

I would suggest, therefore, that it can be shown very easily that payoffs of an ethic of love are very large. Under universal benevolence, almost all social changes are good for everybody. Why then, in spite of all the preaching, is benevolence still so rare, and malevolence so common? The answer, as I have suggested earlier, may well be the defect in our information processing system. It is our attempt to defend ourselves against information overload which forces us into malevolence, prisoners' dilemmas, arms races, price wars, class wars, schisms, feuds, and divorces. Management science, however, is an alternative defense against information overload. It is not inconceivable, therefore, that techniques which perhaps were originally designed with extremely limited and abstract ends in view and which look at first sight very hostile to the subtle agendas of ethical behavior may ultimately bear fruit in the development of an ethical maturity beyond what all the efforts of the moralists and the preachers have hitherto been able to achieve. I suspect this will only happen, however, if ethical theory itself can respond in depth and maturity to the opportunities which the burgeoning sciences of man now seem to offer it.

3. The Motives of Managers, Environmental Restraints, and the Theory of Managerial Enterprise[*]

WILLIAM L. BALDWIN

I. INTRODUCTION

Recent additions to the large and rapidly growing body of literature analyzing the modern corporation reject, almost without exception, earlier concepts of the business firm in which the firm was treated as an organization designed to implement the economic objectives of an individual or group who were both its owners and managers. Yet in spite of this obvious common source of dissatisfaction among students of the business firm, as well as widespread agreement on the conceptual challenge posed by today's giant corporation, critical reactions to the owner-entrepreneur as an abstraction have led to distinct and not entirely harmonious lines of investigation.

One major line, which may be described as attempts to develop a theory of managerial enterprise, assumes the separation of ownership and control in large, widely owned corporations and recognizes the fact that most of these corporations operate in oligopolistic markets where their managers are free enough from the pressures of competition to choose among alternative courses of action. Theories of managerial enterprise deal primarily with the objectives of professional managers, the external restraints under which these objectives are carried out in oligopolistic markets, and the business behavior which results from the assumed managerial objectives and restraints. The common assumptions underlying this line of work are that management, emancipated from control by owners, formulates the objectives of the firm and that managerial goals may differ from those of the stockholders.

It would be a caricature of the theories of managerial enterprise,

[*] *The Quarterly Journal of Economics,* vol. 78, no. 2 (May 1964), pp. 238–56.

and grossly unfair to a number of discerning writers, to state that the theories assume that managers' objectives alone motivate the market behavior of giant corporations. Certainly, the literature recognizes restraints on managers other than the actions of oligopolistic rivals. Yet I consider it a fair criticism to observe that there is a distinguishable body of work in which attention has been directed almost exclusively to management as the group which impresses its goals on the corporation in the process of both making and carrying out basic corporate decisions. This emphasis leads to assumptions that frequently ignore and are occasionally inconsistent with the findings of recent studies which deal with the corporate organization, its environment, and the nature of power in the modern business world. Some of these studies threaten to make models based on managerial autonomy appear nearly as simplistic and inapplicable to modern corporate reality as are earlier models based on the owner-entrepreneur.

The purpose of this paper is to argue that further development of the theory of managerial enterprise, if it is to become of increasing value for descriptive, normative, and policy-formulating purposes, must place greater emphasis on the varied types of nonmarket as well as market restraints within which managerial functions are performed. I maintain that only after examining a number of significant contributions to our understanding of managerial goals and functions and placing these contributions within an appropriate framework of restraints, is it possible to assess the effect of the elimination of the owner-entrepreneur on the usefulness of a revised theory of the firm. The restraints appear to be of such nature that it is inadvisable to substitute managerial goals for the traditionally assumed business orientation toward profits.

II. BEHAVIORAL ASSUMPTIONS UNDERLYING THEORIES OF MANAGERIAL ENTERPRISE

The most important distinguishing assumptions behind the concept of managerial enterprise as the central role of managers in determining the purposes for which the large, widely owned corporation is operated, and the relatively unhindered power of managers to make the decisions necessary to carry out these purposes. In the late 1940s and early 1950s, works concerned with various aspects of managerialism typically treated a high degree of managerial control over business property as a phenomenon to be discussed but as one whose existence could be assumed to have been demonstrated by earlier writers. It was further recognized that the motives of managers would differ from those of the profit-maximizing owner-entrepreneur. Motives such as personal vanity, desire to control the largest possible industrial empire, maximization of personal remuneration, and recognition of widespread professional responsibilities have not only been attributed to management but also treated as the forces which underlie and explain corporate behavior.

Theories of managerial enterprise, explicitly or tacitly accepting the dominance of managers, have focused on the formulation of managerial objectives which can be treated as the motivational forces in various descriptive and predictive models. It should be noted that the essence of a theory and of a broadly applicable model is abstraction. Thus, it is no valid criticism of a motivational assumption to provide one or a few scattered counterexamples from the real world. Yet in a theory of the firm which claims current relevance we can hope for simplifying assumptions which in description or effect approximate important aspects of modern corporate reality. The most significant among assumptions in recent literature which appear to meet reasonable standards of realism and relevance can be grouped into three general types: target rate of return, maximization of sales or growth subject to a profit constraint, and managerial mediation of the claims made by various groups on what has been called the "Responsible Corporation." All three types have two things in common. They are supported by logic or by respectable evidence based on observation or testimony, and they reject profits maximization as a useful or realistic abstraction.

Pricing to yield a predetermined target rate of return on investment might be viewed as a behavioral assumption developing with some logic out of earlier studies of full-cost pricing, or out of the organizational theory concept of "satisficing" which March and Simon describe as looking for a sharp enough needle in the haystack, rather than the sharpest. Cyert and March apply the concept to the business firm by assuming the firm's objective is an acceptable level of profit rather than the maximum attainable. Satisficing has been tested in experimental goal-seeking and problem-solving situations and appears to be a verifiable type of human behavior.

However, the most important recent contribution which stresses target rate of return pricing is the 1958 study made under the auspices of the Brookings Institution by Kaplan, Dirlam, and Lanzillotti, which relies primarily on the direct evidence of actual pricing practices of large firms as reported in interviews with business executives. The Brookings researchers carefully qualified their findings, noting difficulties inherent in the interview technique and warning readers that their findings should not be interpreted as contradictory to the assumption of profits maximization. They regard profits maximization as of little if any operational usefulness, rather than as incorrect. "For the most part," they observed, "the companies doubted that by changing their pricing policies they could raise their profits in the long run." Kaplan, Dirlam, and Lanzillotti concluded, "There has been, as already noted, some clustering around a norm of target return pricing. But the discussions of policy also disclosed that among those that could be characterized in general as following an administered, stabilized, cost-plus system of pricing, the degree of precision and of compliance ranged too widely to make target return a master key to pricing."

Both target rate of return and satisficing models treat some form of profits as an objective. Thus Lanzillotti, referring to the Brookings findings, states, "The foregoing data, above all, make it clear that management's approach to pricing is based upon *planned* profits." Cyert and March argue for the use of an "acceptable-level profit norm" in place of profits maximization as a motivational assumption warranted by current knowledge of both individual and organizational behavior.

In contrast to target rate of return and satisficing, recent models presented by Baumol and Marris make a more fundamental break with traditional assumptions by treating the need for profits as a restraint on managers who are maximizing other variables. Although rejection of the role of profits as an objective is a basic change in *assumptions*, the *methods* employed by Baumol and Marris are in accord with traditional economic analysis of maximization or minimization, unlike theories assuming some given level of profits as a goal. In *Business Behavior, Value and Growth,* Baumol offers the hypothesis that oligopolistic firms seek to maximize sales revenue subject to a restraint in the form of a minimum necessary rate of profit. Baumol argues that the hypothesis is more realistic than profits maximization and that it can be used to explain certain aspects of observed behavior that are inconsistent with the older assumption. In defending the greater realism of his assumption, Baumol draws convincingly on his personal experiences as a business consultant. In his later article, Baumol suggests that maximization of the rate of growth of sales, which implies an optimum rather than a maximum profit rate, is an appropriate motivational assumption for a dynamic model of an oligopolistic firm. Marris, who assumes maximization of the rate of growth of corporate capital limited by a desire for security against bankruptcy and take-over raids, does not regard his model as contradictory to Baumol's. He notes in respect to indicia of size of the firm that "maximizing the long-run growth rate of any one indicator can reasonably be assumed equivalent to maximizing the growth rate of most others."

Some defenders of giant firms and of the resulting concentration of industry have drawn support from the separation of ownership and control. Management, it is claimed, is becoming a profession; and professional managers tend to regard themselves as trustees of corporate property, exercising their powers for the benefit of virtually all those who come into contact with the corporation and adjudicating conflicting claims of such beneficiaries as stockholders, employees, customers, suppliers, communities, and the general public. This concept of managerial motivation may be described by Herrymon Maurer's phrase, "the Responsible Corporation." Pronouncements by corporate executives and their public relations departments indicating firm and undeviating adherence to corporate responsibility may be regarded with deep skepticism, but we cannot dismiss as merely naïve the acceptance of the importance of these goals by several students of the corporation. Berle, for example, sees corporate recognition of public responsibilities as a response to an observed need for justifying or giving legitimacy to managerial power. Legitimacy may well be recognized as a necessary condition for continued possession of power. Further, if the doctrine of the Responsible Corporation is repeated frequently and fervently enough, executives who expound it, and more importantly their successors, may come to believe in or at least live by what was originally a mere rationalization. It is almost as hard to believe that all claims of recognition of public responsibility are examples of self-seeking hypocrisy as it is to believe in the absolute truth of all. At least some of the verbiage ought to be accepted as a genuine search for a *raison d'être* among business executives.

Thus, managerial enterprise has been described as driven by at least three fundamental motivational forces. Behavioral hypotheses based on all three can be justified on grounds of both a priori logic and substantial degrees of empirical evidence. However, those wishing to develop or apply a theory of managerial enterprise are not necessarily forced into a difficult or arbitrary selection and rejection of motivational assumptions. Two other alternatives are open. First, one could argue that among a diverse business population motivational forces would differ with size of the firm, form of organization, nature of product, various aspects of market structure, and other environmental influences. Lanzillotti, who found target rate of return pricing the most frequently stated objective, but only one among several within the firms interviewed, advocates such an approach. Baumol defends the realism of his sales maximization hypothesis only in application to models of oligopolistic firms. Cyert and March state, in presenting a model of an oligopolistic decision-making process, "It is believed that decision rules must have an empirical basis and that they cannot be derived by deduction." Therefore they refrain from positing any general method for determining an acceptable profit level. But this alternative appears to be a counsel of despair, threatening to reduce the theory of managerial enterprise to a chaotic state in which each firm is examined as a unique entity and in which theorizing about oligopolistic markets involving a number of dissimilar firms with various objectives seems nearly hopeless. Before accepting such a sacrifice of simplicity, neatness, and generality of the theory as inevitable, a second alternative should be explored. The three types of behavioral assumptions mentioned above may be examined for consistency among themselves and for the extent of their inconsistency with profits maximization. Hopefully they can be fitted into a single meaningful motivational framework. The remainder of this paper is primarily devoted to this task.

III. TARGET RATE OF RETURN PRICING AS A MANAGERIAL TOOL

There is no question but that prices are frequently calculated on the basis of a predetermined rate of return on business assets. Yet if the objective of management is viewed as earning a certain percentage yield on total invested capital, whether supplied by stock purchases, borrowing, or retained earnings, obvious elements of indeterminacy arise. A specified target rate might be achieved by setting prices to yield that rate on a given volume of assets, or additional capital might be invested until the target rate is earned with a given set of prices, or both prices and the level of investment might be varied with numerous combinations leading to the target rate. In order to yield determinate prices and levels of investment, additional assumptions are necessary. One might, for example, assume that managers desire the largest possible volume of sales or of assets under their control consistent with the target rate.

Another use of target rate of return is as a device for determining increments of investment. Under this test, a potential project is undertaken only if the estimated yield on the required investment is equal to or exceeds a predetermined rate. But a yield on investment can be computed only after prices and associated outputs are estimated. One cannot use a predetermined yield to set prices and evaluate an investment proposal simultaneously. Also, it should be noted that target rate of return as a criterion for limiting investment is fundamentally inconsistent with pricing to yield a target rate of return, as the former is an incremental or marginal concept implying an average rate of return above the target, whereas the latter implies an average rate of return equal to the target rate.

A final objection to target rate of return pricing as an objective is that simply assuming a target rate avoids the question which is most important both in the decision-making process and in any attempt to use the theory of managerial enterprise for normative purposes: i.e., what determines or limits the target rate?

It would appear that although a target rate of return is in fact frequently utilized in corporate planning and decision making, it cannot be regarded as a true goal of management. Rather, it seems far more reasonable to assume that a target rate of return is a tool, used to assist in the attainment of other goals. Chamberlain, on the basis of an extensive review of managerial and accounting literature and a questionnaire survey of his own, concludes that both standard markup on fully allocated costs and pricing to yield a target rate of return on investment are "simply useful instruments in its [management's] objective of making a profit." The observation of Kaplan, Dirlam, and Lanzillotti, that most of the firms they interviewed did not believe they could increase their long-run profits by changing their pricing procedures, is consistent with Chamberlain's conclusion. A. E. Kahn, in a perceptive comment on Lanzillotti's article, emphasizes the significance of the firms' belief. "The misconstruction," he noted, "is in confusing *procedures* with '*goals*.' Actually, the target return seems above all to reflect what the executives think the company can get; and to the extent actual earnings diverge from the target, it is because the market turns out to allow more or less."

One of the most interesting possibilities relates target rate of return pricing to barriers to entry. Means has suggested that if a firm is concerned with maintaining a level of profit above the competitive rate, "the price maker starts with an estimate of the highest rate of profits which will not induce new entrants and then works back to determine the prices which will just yield this rate of profit when operating at a reasonable proportion of capacity. This procedure has come to be known as pricing for a target rate of return on investment or, more simply, as *target pricing*."

Bain has developed a classification of barriers to entry based on the influence of potential entrants on price policy. Bain describes entry as "blockaded" when the price that would attract new entrants is above the profit-maximizing price of the most favored firms now in the industry and is hence irrelevant. Entry is "effectively impeded" if the entry-forestalling price is lower than the price which would exist in the absence of concern over possible entrants but is far enough above the competitive price to make the present value of profits associated with the entry-forestalling price greater than the present value of those which could be gained by charging higher prices and attracting entrants. Entry is "ineffectively impeded" when the entry-forestalling price is so slightly above the competitive level that it is more profitable to charge higher, entry-inducing prices. Bain's second case, of "effectively impeded" entry would appear to coincide with the conditions described by Means.

In addition, Bain classified 20 industries in terms of the height of barriers to entry rather than degree of impedance. A comparison of this latter classification with Lanzillotti's list of primary pricing objectives of 20 firms yields results suggesting consistency with Means' statement. Very crudely, we should expect to find a positive correlation between the height of barriers to entry and use of target rate of return pricing unless entry is blockaded. For each of his industries, Bain lists the four largest firms; and nine of Lanzillotti's firms appear on these lists. Of the nine, four indicated target rate of return as their primary pricing objective. One of these four is in an industry classified by Bain as having very high entry barriers, and the other three are in industries whose barriers are classified as substantial. Of the five firms reporting other primary objectives (maintenance of market share, stabilization of price, and meeting competitors), three are in industries with substantial barriers to entry, and the remaining two are in industries classified as having moderate to low entry barriers.

Thus, use of a target rate of return is consistent with a profit motivation, with or without the restraining condition of potential entry. If the objective is assumed to be profits and the target rate determined either by the maximum rate attainable or the highest rate which will not attract entrants, the outcome is determinate and the target rate becomes a workable planning device.

The use of a target rate of return is also consistent with objectives other than profit. Baumol's minimum necessary rate of return, which acts as a constraint on the maximization of sales revenue, may be viewed as a target, determined in his model by the prices set for securities in a competitive capital market and by a firm's need for capital. Similarly, Marris regards the rate of profit necessary to ensure an adequate degree of security against bankruptcy and take-over raids as a constraint on the growth rate when the profit rate associated with maximum growth is deemed too low to furnish such security. But in the models of Baumol and Marris, as in those treating profits as an objective, a determinate result is obtained only when the determinants of the target rate are specified and a variable to be maximized is posited.

Finally, a "just," "fair," or "traditional" target rate of return might be assumed by the proponents of the Responsible Corporation as a necessary, but not sufficient, condition to balance management's responsibilities to stockholders against responsibilities to other groups.

Target rate of return pricing, in summary, should be viewed as a tool rather than as an objective. As such, it is in no way inconsistent with the hypothesized objectives still to be discussed.

IV. MANAGEMENT GOALS AND RESTRAINTS ON MANAGERIAL AUTONOMY

Theories of managerial enterprise, such as those of Baumol and Marris and the literature of the Responsible Corporation, have two things in common. First, they deny that profits maximization is a reasonable assumption to make about managerial goals; and second, they focus on managerial goals they regard as more plausible, assuming that since management controls the business property, these goals best explain the motive force behind the actions of the firm. In order to assess the import of these critical modifications of the traditional theory of the firm, while granting that an attempt to resurrect the owner-entrepreneur would be retrogressive, it is necessary to consider the extent of the conflict between profits and the assumed goals of managers and to examine the actual amount of freedom managers have to impose their goals on the firm.

Managers, taken as individuals engaged in an organizational activity, clearly have numerous goals of their own such as personal financial rewards, security, power and prestige within the organization, desire to be liked, human sympathy, the urge to create, and perhaps occasionally the desire for an easy life. But all employees bring a complex of personal objectives to the organizations in which they participate. Indeed, one central concern of modern organization theory is with the methods by which organizations induce members to join and to participate in achieving the goals of the organization and in the process resolve conflicts between personal and organizational goals. Thus it is recognized that organizations have goals of their own and that a certain degree of fulfillment of participants' personal goals is a necessary cost incurred in channeling individual actions towards achievement of the organization's purpose. In this respect, individual managers are no different from other employees. The use of committees as decision-making units, requirements that proposals be justified by estimated rates of return, decentralization of authority and responsibility, salary and promotion boards, the inability of any one man to comprehend all aspects of a giant firm, and the philosophy and traditions embodied in the "corporate personality," to say nothing of the much publicized pressures towards conformity among "organization men," all serve to prevent any individual from imposing his will on the corporate organization. The managerial motives which should concern us, therefore, are those which are common to management as a group or suborganization. Sales revenue and growth maximization can both be defended on the ground that the salaries and very probably prestige of the entire managerial group are more dependent on the scale of operation than on profit. Acceptance of social corporate responsibility has been regarded as a necessary defense of the position and perquisites of management as a whole.

To some extent, achievement of the goals ascribed to managers enhances profitability. Baumol notes that maximizing sales revenue helps long-run profits in several ways. Consumers may favor products they consider growing in use, credit may be positively related to sales volume, a firm's market power may decline if it loses distributors or market share, and employee relations are better in firms which are hiring than in those which are firing. In Marris' model, once the financial policy dealing with retention of earnings, dividends, and reinvestment is given, maximizing the rate of growth implies maximization of the rate of profit. Virtually all of the writers who emphasize management's responsibilities to various groups note that the corporate property must be managed efficiently in order to carry out the responsibilities properly. But the meaning of efficiency is elusive. Mason has raised a crucial question as to what criteria managers are supposed to use in setting prices and remunerating factors when they are trying to do the best they can for society, laborers, customers, and owners. "I can find no reasoned answer," he notes, "in the managerial literature." One partial answer, and as Mason observes it is only partial, is that efficiency implies the most profitable price and resource use. The profits might then be distributed among various claimants in accordance with some concept of social justice or fairness, perhaps using rebates to reimburse customers.

The managerial motives under discussion are not fully consistent with profits maximization. In the absence of a profit restraint, Baumol's sales revenue maximizer will aim for the price and output combination at which the demand curve facing it is of unitary elasticity and its marginal revenue is zero, implying a price below and an output above that of a profits maximizer with positive marginal costs. Marris notes that when the financial policy assumed in his model is permitted to vary, the associated maximum growth and profit rates vary in opposite directions from each other. Maximizing the profit which then may be distributed is not an appropriate strategy for managers concerned with "fairness" to groups who cannot be identified or reimbursed. If managers with the motives assumed by Baumol or Marris or a group managing a Responsible Corporation were free to run a firm as they saw fit, the results would not be those of a profit-maximizing firm.

Nevertheless, the same decisions would often be made under profits maximization and some other criterion; and it would appear that if managers were under certain types of constraints their motives could be utilized as incentives in directing their activities towards an organizational goal of profits. For example, a nonmanagement group such as an outside board of directors or dominant stockholders could impose some form of profit-maximizing financial policy on a firm and then leave a group of Marris' managers free to maximize the growth rate subject to that policy. Profits maximization, alone, is not sufficient to determine the precise financial policy which should be adopted. The policy, of course, will also depend on the extent of the controlling group's preference for present over future income and the degree of their aversion to risk.

Lilienthal and Kaplan, in 1952 and 1954 respectively, noted the rise of important institutional investors as alert and knowledgeable stockholder groups. In the decade since they wrote, institutional investment has continued to grow. In 1959 books, both Berle and Father P. P. Harbrecht explored the extent and significance of the phenomenon. Harbrecht found that financial institutions controlled the voting rights of 27 to 30 percent of all corporate stocks outstanding and found ample reason to believe that these institutions will continue their net stock purchases. Although many pension and trust funds have policies against acquiring a controlling interest in any one firm, the funds are concentrated in a few major New York banks who, as trustees, vote the stocks of funds they are managing and who may be unable to avoid positions of control. Further, institutional purchases are concentrated in "blue chip" securities which are predominantly those of giant corporations. Harbrecht's conclusions deserve to be quoted at some length:

It may not be too much to say that the center of influence in our economy, having left the Wall Street of the 1920s and migrated in the 1930s and 1940s to the provincial centers of corporate power, has now returned to New York financial circles. What is more, the financial strength now building up in the New York banks is of a different character. The power position that was consolidated in the 1920s was deliberately sought by the financiers and had no stable institutional character. But, as we have already noted, the present concentration of financial power is not so much the result of a drive for power as it is of (1) social demands which require the aggregation of great wealth to provide security, and (2) the fortunate presence of the financial institutions as apt media for administering this wealth. The alignment of forces now taking shape is of an institutional and permanent character which will be part of our economic and social structure for some time to come. What we are witnessing is a genuine evolutionary development rather than a temporary consolidation of power resulting from personal acquisitiveness.[1]

Harbrecht's findings strongly imply that the managerial literature of the 1930s, 1940s, and early 1950s may have been valid at the time of writing, but of only transitory importance. The group which predominates in shaping the objectives of giant corporations may prove to be managers of banks, mutual funds, and insurance companies rather than those managing the actual corporate property. The institutional investors, like other stockholders, should be primarily interested in profits; and unlike many small individual investors, however sophisticated, the institutions should find it a rational allocation of staff and executive time to devote much observation and study to the policies and prospects of firms in which they have invested or may invest. It may be argued that institutional trust officers have individual and group objectives similar to those of corporate management, but, even if this contention is granted, their attitudes towards corporations whose securities they acquire should be as objective and profit oriented as the attitudes of corporate managers towards specific machines or tools.

Harbrecht and others have pointed out that even if institutions refrain from exercising their control through voting power or support existing

---

[1] Paul P. Harbrecht, S. J., *Pension Funds and Economic Power* (New York: Twentieth Century Fund, 1959), pp. 249–50.

management as a matter of policy, their investment decisions will have an important influence on security prices and the availability of capital. Scattered small shareholders have, as a group, a similar power to influence management by sale of their holdings when they are dissatisfied, since the sale of a small fraction of an outstanding security issue may depress the price severely.

Other restraints on management which tend to direct their activities toward profits maximization may be mentioned. First, there is the threat of a proxy fight. Corporate raiding has become almost a profession, or more accurately a full-time highly skilled occupation. In all probability the very largest corporations are quite immune from raids—at least I find it difficult to imagine a successful attack on General Motors or U.S. Steel—but those most invulnerable to the raider are those Harbrecht finds most attractive to the institutional investor. And it seems clear from the work of Karr and others that in the firms which we might call middle-sized giants, perhaps among the nation's largest 500 but below the top 50, the position of inefficient or self-serving management is far from secure against proxy attacks. Second, the law still presumes that directors have a fiduciary relation to stockholders and are trustees for them. Stockholders' derivative suits, as difficult as they may be to win, possess a substantial nuisance value. Finally, Earley's studies of accounting and budgeting practices show increasing adoption of managerial techniques utilizing marginal principles. In one article Earley concludes, "Undoubtedly the new techniques of business management make it advisable to change somewhat the simpler models of the business firm and its behavior. But the postulate that the typical firm searches vigorously for larger profits and has impressive means to conduct this search should be retained." Use of sophisticated and profit-oriented methods of financial reporting and control should be regarded, in part, as a managerial response to external pressures but also as an additional organizational restraint imposed on the present management.

In summary, we have reviewed only those motives ascribed to management which appear logically reasonable and in accord with available evidence. These motives are apparently such that, under appropriate external and organizational restraints, the activities of a managerial group can be directed towards an organizational goal of profits without undue conflict. None of the writers cited in this paper assumes that managers have absolute autonomy in their control of corporate property. But it does appear that the managerial literature, taken as a whole, has failed to recognize the full range and significance of internal and external restraints in limiting the ability of managers to translate their objectives into organizational purposes. The cumulative effect of these restraints would appear to be such as to cast grave doubts on the wisdom of substituting managerial goals for profits.

V. IMPLICATIONS FOR THE THEORY OF THE FIRM

We have noted two arguments in support of throwing profits maximization onto the same scrap pile of obsolete tools where the owner-entrepreneur now rests, in order to develop a realistic theory of managerial enterprise. First, the assumption is said to be unrealistic for the modern giant corporation with which the theory is concerned; and second, even if some form of long-run profits maximization is regarded as the ultimate objective, the concept is considered too vague to be useful.

It is not contended here that the external and organizational restraints just reviewed are sufficient to compel all corporate managers to make all of their decisions exclusively on the basis of maximization of organizational profits. But if we want a theory of managerial enterprise which assumes a single organizational objective subject to maximization or minimization, profit does appear to be more realistic than any of the alternatives offered. The advantages of such a unified theory are substantial if we want to apply theoretical analysis to markets involving a number of firms, to prediction and evaluation of industrial performance, and to problems of public policy. The findings reviewed in this paper strongly suggest, although the contention is in no way definitively proven, that profit maximization is a fairly close approximation to actual motives of the typical large corporation and that any losses suffered by abstracting from the complexity of interplay among real-world motives will be relatively minor.

The fact remains that the theory of the firm is in an inadequate state. Even if profits maximization is the most accurate single motivational assumption we can make in dealing with the modern corporation, it may be virtually useless as a basis for determination of a single most rational solution to many problems. The core of the difficulty lies in the fact that often a course of action which could not be predicted can be explained in terms of long-run profits maximization after the fact, if and only if certain *ex post* assumptions are made about the internal organization of the firm and about how its environment affected its views on risk aversion, the probabilities of future developments, and the appropriate rate at which to discount future earnings. It is a valid criticism that the concept of long-run profits maximization is vague. Individuals and, presumably, organizations differ in their time preferences and degrees of aversion to risk. Even if the rate for discounting future income is assumed, there is no generally accepted formulation of rational behavior under conditions of uncertainty. Modigliani and Miller have recently made effective use of maximization of the present market value of the firm's outstanding shares as the criterion for investment and financing decisions under conditions of uncertainty, thus throwing the ascertainment of appropriate risk and time-preference functions back to a market-determined consensus of present and potential investors. In the absence of a refined and undoubtedly complex theory of securities market behavior, profits maximization will continue to yield ambiguous results in many cases. But this empty box should not preclude us from assuming, in the numerous problems where relative profitabilities can be compared, that the most profitable course of action will be chosen.

The defense of profits maximization embodied in this paper amounts only to an argument that the trouble with the existing body of theory is inadequacy instead of error. But it also implies that the remedy lies in further exploration of the relevant characteristics of modern giant corporations and of their environments, rather than new motivational assumptions. Baumol, for example, notes as an advantage of and justification for his assumption of sales revenue maximization that the resulting model can be used to explain observed patterns of behavior which are inexplicable in traditional theory, such as price changes in response to changes in fixed overhead costs and the actual shifting of taxes which have been regarded as unshiftable. But these and similar shortcomings of traditional theory need not be blamed on the assumption of profit-maximizing behavior. Rather, the error may lie in neglect of the constraints to which such behavior is subject. In Bain's analysis, for one, changes in such items as fixed costs and lump-sum or percentage-of-profit taxes will influence even the short-run equilibrium of a profit-maximizing firm if the changes affect conditions of potential entry and thus the entry-barring price.

The literature already includes valuable pioneering contributions to greater understanding of crucial characteristics of the corporate world. Managerial decisions are made and profits earned in an environment which includes the market for corporate securities, conditions of entry such as noted by Bain, the external institutional influences analyzed by Harbrecht, accounting and budgetary checks and guides described by Chamberlain and Early, and aspects of organizational and communications systems being developed into a meaningful theory by students such as Simon, March, and Cyert. If the argument of this paper is correct, the descriptive and predictive value of the theory of the firm will be enhanced and more relevant models will be developed as a result of further such work on the conditions under which decisions that may be assumed to be profit maximizing are made in today's giant, widely owned and professionally managed corporations.

4. Theories of Decision Making in Economics and Behavioral Science*

HERBERT A. SIMON

Recent years have seen important new explorations along the boundaries between economics and psychology. For the economist, the immediate question about these developments is whether they include new advances in psychology that can fruitfully be applied to economics. But the psychologist will also raise the converse question—whether there are developments in economic theory and observation that have implications for the central core of psychology. If economics is able to find verifiable and verified generalizations about human economic behavior, then these generalizations must have a place in the more general theories of human behavior to which psychology and sociology aspire. Influence will run both ways.

I. HOW MUCH PSYCHOLOGY DOES ECONOMICS NEED?

How have psychology and economics gotten along with little relation in the past? The explanation rests on an understanding of the goals toward which economics, viewed as a science and a discipline, has usually aimed.

Broadly speaking, economics can be defined as the science that describes and predicts the behavior of several kinds of economic man—notably the consumer and the entrepreneur. While perhaps literally correct, this definition does not reflect the principal focus in the literature of economics. We usually classify work in economics along two dimensions: (a) whether it is concerned with industries and the whole economy (macroeconomics) or with individual economic actors (microeconomics); and (b) whether it strives to describe and explain economic behavior (descriptive economics), or to guide decisions either at the level of public policy (normative macroeconomics) or at the level of the individual consumer or businessman (normative microeconomics).

The profession and literature of economics have been largely preoc-

---

American Economic Review, vol. 49, no. 3 (June 1959), pp. 253-80.

cupied with normative macroeconomics. Although descriptive macroeconomics provides the scientific base for policy prescription, research emphases have been determined in large part by relevance to policy (e.g., business cycle theory). Normative microeconomics, carried forward under such labels as "management science," "engineering economics," and "operations research," is now a flourishing area of work having an uneasy and ill-defined relation with the profession of economics, traditionally defined. Much of the work is being done by mathematicians, statisticians, engineers, and physical scientists (although many mathematical economists have also been active in it).

This new area, like the old, is normative in orientation. Economists have been relatively uninterested in descriptive microeconomics—understanding the behavior of individual economic agents—except as this is necessary to provide a foundation for macroeconomics. The normative microeconomist "obviously" doesn't need a theory of human behavior: he wants to know how people *ought* to behave, not how they *do* behave. On the other hand, the macroeconomist's lack of concern with individual behavior stems from different considerations. First, he assumes that the economic actor is rational, and hence he makes strong predictions about human behavior without performing the hard work of observing people. Second, he often assumes competition, which carries with it the implication that only the rational survive. Thus, the classical economic theory of markets with perfect competition and rational agents is deductive theory that requires almost no contact with empirical data once its assumptions are accepted.

Undoubtedly there is an area of human behavior that fits these assumptions to a reasonable approximation, where the classical theory with its assumptions of rationality is a powerful and useful tool. Without denying the existence of this area, or its importance, I may observe that it fails to include some of the central problems of conflict and dynamics with which economics has become more and more concerned. A metaphor will help to show the reason for this failure.

Suppose we were pouring some viscous liquid—molasses—into a bowl of very irregular shape. What would we need in order to make a theory of the form the molasses would take in the bowl? How much would we have to know about the properties of molasses to predict its behavior under the circumstances? If the bowl were held motionless, and if we wanted only to predict behavior in equilibrium, we would have to know little, indeed, about molasses. The single essential assumption would be that the molasses, under the force of gravity, would minimize the height of its center of gravity. With this assumption, which would apply as well to any other liquid, and a complete knowledge of the environment—in this case the shape of the bowl—the equilibrium is completely determined. Just so, the equilibrium behavior of a perfectly adapting organism depends only on its goal and its environment; it is otherwise completely independent of the internal properties of the organism.

If the bowl into which we were pouring the molasses were jiggled rapidly, or if we wanted to know about the behavior before equilibrium was reached, prediction would require much more information. It would require, in particular, more information about the properties of molasses: its viscosity, the rapidity with which it "adapted" itself to the containing vessel and moved towards its "goal" of lowering its center of gravity. Likewise, to predict the short-run behavior of an adaptive organism, or its behavior in a complex and rapidly changing environment, it is not enough to know its goals. We must know also a great deal about its internal structure and particularly its mechanisms of adaptation.

If, to carry the metaphor a step farther, new forces, in addition to gravitational force, were brought to bear on the liquid, we would have to know still more about it even to predict behavior in equilibrium. Now its tendency to lower its center of gravity might be countered by a force to minimize an electrical or magnetic potential operating in some lateral direction. We would have to know its relative susceptibility to gravitational and electrical or magnetic force to determine its equilibrium position. Similarly, in an organism having a multiplicity of goals, or afflicted with some kind of internal goal conflict, behavior could be predicted only from information about the relative strengths of the several goals and the ways in which the adaptive processes responded to them.

Economics has been moving steadily into new areas where the power of the classical equilibrium model has never been demonstrated, and where its adequacy must be considered anew. Labor economics is such an area, oligopoly or imperfect competition theory another, decision making under uncertainty a third, and the theory of economic development a fourth. In all of these areas the complexity and instability of his environment becomes a central feature of the choices that economic man faces. To explain his behavior in the face of this complexity, the theory must describe him as something more than a featureless, adaptive organism; it must incorporate at least some description of the processes and mechanisms through which the adaptation takes place. Let us list a little more concretely some specific problems of this kind:

(a) The classical theory postulates that the consumer maximizes utility. Recent advances in the theory of rational consumer choice have shown that the existence of a utility function, and its characteristics, if it exists, can be studied empirically.

(b) The growing separation between ownership and management has directed attention to the motivations of managers and the adequacy of the profit-maximization assumption for business firms. So-called human relations research has raised a variety of issues about the motivation of both executives and employees.

(c) When, in extending the classical theory, the assumptions of perfect competition were removed, even the definition of rationality became ambiguous. New definitions had to be constructed, by no means as "obvious" intuitively as simple maximization, to extend the theory of rational behavior to bilateral monopoly and to other bargaining and outguessing situations.

(d) When the assumptions of perfect foresight were removed, to handle uncertainty about the environment, the definition of rationality had to be extended in another direction to take into account prediction and the formation of expectations.

(e) Broadening the definition of rationality to encompass goal conflict and uncertainty made it hard to ignore the distinction between the objective environment in which the economic actor "really" lives and the subjective environment that he perceives and to which he responds. When this distinction is made, we can no longer predict his behavior—even if he behaves rationally—from the characteristics of the objective environment; we also need to know something about his perceptual and cognitive processes.

We shall use these five problem areas as a basis for sorting out some recent explorations in theory, model building, and empirical testing. In section II, we will examine developments in the theory of utility and consumer choice. In section III, we will consider somewhat parallel issues relating to the motivation of managers. In section IV, we will deal with conflict of goals and the phenomena of bargaining. In section V, we will survey some of the work that has been done on uncertainty and the formation of expectations. In section VI, we will explore recent developments in the theory of human problem solving and other higher mental processes, and see what implications these have for economic decision making.

II. THE UTILITY FUNCTION

The story of the reestablishment of cardinal utility, as a consequence of the introduction of uncertainty into the theory of choice, is well known. When Pareto and Slutsky had shown that the theory of consumer demand could be derived from the properties of indifference curves, without postulating a cardinal utility function underlying these curves, it became fashionable to regard utility as an ordinal measure—a ranking of alternatives by preference. Indeed, it could be shown that only ordinal utility had operational status—that the experiments that had been proposed, and even tried in a couple of instances, to measure an individual's utilities by asking him to choose among alternatives could never distinguish between two cardinal utility functions that were ordinally equivalent—that differed only by stretchings and contractions of the unit of measurement.

It was shown by von Neumann and Morgenstern, as a by-product of their development of the theory of games, that if the choice situation were extended to include choices among uncertain prospects—among lottery tickets, say—cardinal utilities could be assigned to the outcomes in an unequivocal way. Under these conditions, if the subject's behavior was consistent, it was possible to measure cardinally the utilities that different outcomes had for him.

A person who behaved in a manner consistent with the axioms of choice of von Neumann and Morgenstern would act so as to maximize the expected value—the average, weighted by the probabilities of the alternative outcomes of a choice—of his utility. The theory could be tested empirically, however, only on the assumption that the probabilities assigned to the alternatives by the subject were identical with the "objective" probabilities of these events as known to the experimenter. For example, if a subject believed in the gamblers' fallacy, that after a run of heads an unbiased coin would be more likely to fall tails, his choices might appear inconsistent with his utility function, while the real difficulty would lie in his method of assigning probabilities. This difficulty of "subjective" versus "objective" probability soon came to light when attempts were made to test experimentally whether people behaved in accordance with the predictions of the new utility theory. At the same time, it was discovered that the problem had been raised and solved thirty years earlier by the English philosopher and mathematician Frank Ramsey. Ramsey had shown that, by an appropriate series of experiments, the utilities and subjective probabilities assigned by a subject to a set of uncertain alternatives could be measured simultaneously.

Empirical Studies

The new axiomatic foundations of the theory of utility, which show that it is possible, at least in principle, to determine empirically whether people "have" utility functions of the appropriate kind, have led to a rash of choice experiments. An experimenter who wants to measure utilities, not merely in principle but in fact, faces innumerable difficulties. Because of these difficulties, most experiments have been limited to confronting the subjects with alternative lottery tickets, at various odds, for small amounts of money. The weight of evidence is that, under these conditions, most persons choose in a way that is reasonably consistent with the axioms of the theory—they behave as though they were maximizing the expected value of utility and as though the utilities of the several alternatives can be measured.

When these experiments are extended to more "realistic" choices—choices that are more obviously relevant to real-life situations—difficulties multiply. In the few extensions that have been made, it is not at all clear that the subjects behave in accordance with the utility axioms. There is some indication that when the situation is very simple and transparent, so that the subject can easily see and remember when he is being consistent, he behaves like a utility maximizer. But as the choices become a little more complicated—choices, for example, among phonograph records instead of sums of money—he becomes much less consistent.

We can interpret these results in either of two ways. We can say that consumers "want" to maximize utility, and that if we present them with clear and simple choices that they understand they will do so. Or we can say that the real world is so complicated that the theory of utility maximization has little relevance to real choices. The former interpretation has generally appeared more attractive to economists trained in classical utility theory and to management scientists seeking rules of behavior for normative microeconomics; the latter to behavioral scientists interested in the description of behavior.

Normative Applications

The new utility theory has provided the formal framework for much recent work in mathematical statistics—i.e., statistical decision theory. Similarly (it would be accurate to say "synonymously"), this framework provides the basis for most of the normative models of management science and operations research designed for actual application to the decision-making problems of the firm.[1] Except for some very recent developments, linear programming has been limited to decision making under certainty, but there have been far-reaching developments of dynamic programming dealing with the maximization of expected values of outcomes (usually monetary outcomes) in situations where future events can be predicted only in terms of probability distributions.

Again, there are at least two distinct interpretations that can be placed on these developments. On the one hand, it can be argued: "Firms would like to maximize profits if they could. They have been limited in doing so by the conceptual and computational difficulties of finding the optimal courses of action. By providing powerful new mathematical tools and computing machines, we now enable them to behave in the manner predicted by Alfred Marshall, even if they haven't been able to in the

---

[1] This work relates, of course, to profit maximization and cost minimization rather than utility maximization, but it is convenient to mention it at this point.

past." Nature will imitate art and economic man will become as real (and as artificial) as radios and atomic piles.

The alternative interpretation rests on the observation that, even with the powerful new tools and machines, most real-life choices still lie beyond the reach of maximizing techniques—unless the situations are heroically simplified by drastic approximations. If man, according to this interpretation, makes decisions and choices that have some appearance of rationality, rationality in real life must involve something simpler than maximization of utility or profit. In section VI, we will see where this alternative interpretation leads.

The Binary Choice Experiment

Much recent discussion about utility has centered around a particularly simple choice experiment. This experiment, in numerous variants, has been used by both economists and psychologists to test the most diverse kinds of hypotheses. We will describe it so that we can use it as a common standard of comparison for a whole range of theories and empirical studies.

We will call the situation we are about to describe the *binary choice* experiment. It is better known to most game theorists—particularly those located not far from Nevada—as a two-armed bandit; and to most psychologists as a partial reinforcement experiment. The subject is required, in each of a series of trials, to choose one or the other of two symbols—say, plus or minus. When he has chosen, he is told whether his choice was "right" or "wrong," and he may also receive a reward (in psychologist's language, a reinforcement) for "right" choices. The experimenter can arrange the schedule of correct responses in a variety of ways. There may be a definite pattern, or they may be randomized. It is not essential that one and only one response be correct on a given trial: the experimenter may determine that both or neither will be correct. In the latter case the subject may or may not be informed whether the response he did not choose would have been correct.

How would a utility-maximizing subject behave in the binary choice experiment? Suppose that the experimenter rewarded "plus" on one third of the trials, determined at random, and "minus" on the remaining two thirds. Then a subject, provided that he believed the sequence was random and observed that minus was rewarded twice as often as plus, should always, rationally, choose minus. He would find the correct answer two thirds of the time, and more often than with any other strategy.

Unfortunately for the classical theory of utility in its simplest form, few subjects behave in this way. The most commonly observed behavior is what is called *event matching*. The subject chooses the two alternatives (not necessarily at random) with relative frequencies roughly proportional to the relative frequencies with which they are rewarded. Thus, in the example given, two thirds of the time he would choose minus, and as a result would make a correct response, on the average, in five trials out of nine (on two thirds of the trials in which he chooses minus, and one third of those in which he chooses plus).[2]

All sorts of explanations have been offered for the event-matching behavior. The simplest is that the subject just doesn't understand what strategy would maximize his expected utility; but with adult subjects in a situation as transparent as this one, this explanation seems farfetched. The alternative explanations imply either that the subject regards himself as being engaged in a competitive game with the experimenter (or with "nature" if he accepts the experimenter's explanation that the stimulus is random), or that his responses are the outcome of certain kinds of learning processes. We will examine these two types of explanation further in sections IV and V respectively. The important conclusion at this point is that even in an extremely simple situation, subjects do not behave in the way predicted by a straightforward application of utility theory.

Probabilistic Preferences

Before we leave the subject of utility, we should mention one recent important development. In the formalizations mentioned up to this point, probabilities enter only into the estimation of the consequences that will follow one alternative or another. Given any two alternatives, the first is definitely preferable to the second (in terms of expected utility, or the second to the first, or they are strictly indifferent. If the same pair of alternatives is presented to the subject more than once, he should always prefer the same member of the pair.

One might think this requirement too strict—that, particularly if the utility attached to one alternative were only slightly greater or less than that attached to the other, the subject might vacillate in his choice. An empirical precedent for such vacillation comes not only from casual observation of indecision but from analogous phenomena in the psychophysical laboratory. When subjects are asked to decide which of two weights is heavier, the objectively heavier one is chosen more often than the lighter one, but the relative frequency of choosing the heaviest approaches one half as the two weights approach equality. The probability that a subject will choose the objectively heavier weight depends, in general, on the ratio of the two weights.

Following several earlier attempts, a rigorous and complete axiom

---

[2] Subjects tend to choose the more highly rewarded alternative slightly more frequently than is called for by event matching. Hence, the actual behavior tends to be some kind of average between event matching and the optimal behavior.

system for a utility theory incorporating probabilistic preferences has been constructed recently by Duncan Luce. Although the theory weakens the requirements of consistency in preference, it is empirically testable, at least in principle. Conceptually, it provides a more plausible interpretation of the notion of "indifference" than does the classical theory.

III. THE GOALS OF FIRMS

Just as the central assumption in the theory of consumption is that the consumer strives to maximize his utility, so the crucial assumption in the theory of the firm is that the entrepreneur strives to maximize his residual share—his profit. Attacks on this hypothesis have been frequent. We may classify the most important of these as follows:

(a) The theory leaves ambiguous whether it is short-run or long-run profit that is to be maximized.

(b) The entrepreneur may obtain all kinds of "psychic income" from the firm, quite apart from monetary rewards. If he is to maximize his utility, then he will sometimes balance a loss of profits against an increase in psychic income. But if we allow "psychic income," the criterion of profit maximization loses all of its definiteness.

(c) The entrepreneur may not care to maximize, but may simply want to earn a return that he regards as satisfactory. By sophistry and adept use of the concept of psychic income, the notion of seeking a satisfactory return can be translated into utility maximizing, but not in any operational way. We shall see in a moment that "satisfactory profits" is a concept more meaningfully related to the psychological notion of aspiration levels than to maximization.

(d) It is often observed that under modern conditions the equity owners and the active managers of an enterprise are separate and distinct groups of people, so that the latter may not be motivated to maximize profits.

(e) Where there is imperfect competition among firms, maximizing is an ambiguous goal, for what action is optimal for one firm depends on the actions of the other firms.

In the present section we shall deal only with the third of these five issues. The fifth will be treated in the following section; the first, second, and fourth are purely empirical questions that have been discussed at length in the literature; they will be considered here only for their bearing on the question of satisfactory profits.

Satisficing versus Maximizing

The notion of satiation plays no role in classical economic theory, while it enters rather prominently into the treatment of motivation in psychology. In most psychological theories the motive to act stems from *drives*, and action terminates when the drive is satisfied. Moreover, the conditions for satisfying a drive are not necessarily fixed, but may be specified by an aspiration level that itself adjusts upward or downward on the basis of experience.

If we seek to explain business behavior in the terms of this theory, we must expect the firm's goals to be not maximizing profit, but attaining a certain level or rate of profit, holding a certain share of the market or a certain level of sales. Firms would try to "satisfice" rather than to maximize.

It has sometimes been argued that the distinction between satisficing and maximizing is not important to economic theory. For in the first place, the psychological evidence on individual behavior shows that aspirations tend to adjust to the attainable. Hence in the long run, the argument runs, the level of aspiration and the attainable maximum will be very close together. Second, even if some firms satisficed, they would gradually lose out to the maximizing firms, which would make larger profits and grow more rapidly than the others.

These are, of course, precisely the arguments of our molasses metaphor, and we may answer them in the same way that we answered them earlier. The economic environment of the firm is complex, and it changes rapidly; there is no a priori reason to assume the attainment of long-run equilibrium. Indeed, the empirical evidence on the distribution of firms by size suggests that the observed regularities in size distribution stem from the statistical equilibrium of a population of adaptive systems rather than the static equilibrium of a population of maximizers.

Models of satisficing behavior are richer than models of maximizing behavior, because they treat not only of equilibrium but of the method of reaching it as well. Psychological studies of the formation and change of aspiration levels support propositions of the following kinds: (a) When performance falls short of the level of aspiration, search behavior (particularly search for new alternatives of action) is induced. (b) At the same time, the level of aspiration begins to adjust itself downward until goals reach levels that are practically attainable. (c) If the two mechanisms just listed operate too slowly to adapt aspirations to performance, emotional behavior—apathy or aggression, for example—will replace rational adaptive behavior.

The aspiration level defines a natural zero point in the scale of utility—whereas in most classical theories the zero point is arbitrary. When the firm has alternatives open to it that are at or above its aspiration level, the theory predicts that it will choose the best of those known to be available. When none of the available alternatives satisfies current aspirations, the theory predicts qualitatively different behavior: in the short run, search behavior and the revision of targets; in the longer run, what we have called above emotional behavior, and what the psychologist would be inclined to call neurosis.[3]

Studies of Business Behavior

There is some empirical evidence that business goals are, in fact, stated in satisficing terms. First, there is the series of studies stemming from the pioneering work of Hall and Hitch that indicates that businessmen often set prices by applying a standard markup to costs. Some economists have sought to refute this fact, others to reconcile it—if it is a fact—with marginalist principles. The study of Earley belongs to the former category, but its evidence is suspect because the questions asked of businessmen are leading ones—no one likes to admit that he would accept less profit if he could have more. Earley did not ask his respondents how they determined marginal cost and marginal revenue, how, for example, they estimated demand elasticities.

Another series of studies derived from the debate over the Keynesian doctrine that the amount of investment was insensitive to changes in the rate of interest. The general finding in these studies has been that the rate of interest is not an important factor in investment decisions.

More recently, my colleagues Cyert and March, have attempted to test the satisficing model in a more direct way. They found in one industry some evidence that firms with a declining share of market strove more vigorously to increase their sales than firms whose shares of the market were steady or increasing.

Aspirations in the Binary Choice Experiment

Although to my knowledge this has not been done, it would be easy to look for aspiration-level phenomena in the binary choice experiment. By changing the probabilities of reward in different ways for different groups of subjects, we could measure the effects of these changes on search behavior—where amount of search would be measured by changes in the pattern of responses.

Economic Implications

It has sometimes been argued that, however realistic the classical theory of the firm as a profit maximizer, it is an adequate theory for

---

[3] Lest this last term appear fanciful, I should like to call attention to the phenomena of panic and broken morale, which are well known to observers of the stock market and of organizations but which have no reasonable interpretation in classical utility theory. I may also mention that psychologists use the theory described here in a straightforward way to produce experimental neurosis in animal and human subjects.

purposes of normative macroeconomics. Mason, for example, in commenting on Papandreou's essay on "Problems in the Theory of the Firm" says, "The writer of this critique must confess a lack of confidence in the marked superiority, *for purposes of economic analysis,* of this newer concept of the firm over the older conception of the entrepreneur." The italics are Mason's.

The theory of the firm is important for welfare economics—e.g., for determining under what circumstances the behavior of the firm will lead to efficient allocation of resources. The satisficing model vitiates all the conclusions about resource allocation that are derivable from the maximizing model when perfect competition is assumed. Similarly, a dynamic theory of firm sizes, like that mentioned above, has quite different implications for public policies dealing with concentration than a theory that assumes firms to be in static equilibrium. Hence, welfare economists are justified in adhering to the classical theory only if: (a) the theory is empirically correct as a description of the decision-making process; or (b) it is safe to assume that the system operates in the neighborhood of the static equilibrium. What evidence we have mostly contradicts both assumptions.

IV. CONFLICT OF INTEREST

Leaving aside the problem of the motivations of hired managers, conflict of interest among economic actors creates no difficulty for classical economic theory—indeed, it lies at the very core of the theory—so long as each actor treats the other actors as parts of his "given" environment, and doesn't try to predict their behavior and anticipate it. But when this restriction is removed, when it is assumed that a seller takes into account the reactions of buyers to his actions, or that each manufacturer predicts the behaviors of his competitors—all the familiar difficulties of imperfect competition and oligopoly arise.[4]

The very assumptions of omniscient rationality that provide the basis for deductive prediction in economics when competition is present lead to ambiguity when they are applied to competition among the few. The central difficulty is that rationality requires one to outguess one's opponents, but not to be outguessed by them, and this is clearly not a consistent requirement if applied to all the actors.

Game Theory

Modern game theory is a vigorous and extensive exploration of ways of extending the concept of rational behavior to situations involving

---

[4] There is by now a voluminous literature on the problem.

struggle, outguessing, and bargaining. Since Luce and Raiffa have recently provided us with an excellent survey and evaluation of game theory, I shall not cover the same ground here. I concur in their general evaluation that, while game theory has greatly clarified the issues involved, it has not provided satisfactory solutions. Not only does it leave the definition of rational conduct ambiguous in all cases save the zero-sum two-person game, but it requires of economic man even more fantastic reasoning powers than does classical economic theory.

Power and Bargaining

A number of exploratory proposals have been put forth as alternatives to game theory—among them Galbraith's notion of countervailing power and Schelling's bargaining theory. These analyses draw at least as heavily upon theories of power and bargaining developed initially to explain political phenomena as upon economic theory. They do not lead to any more specific predictions of behavior than do game-theoretic approaches, but place a greater emphasis upon description and actual observation, and are modest in their attempt to derive predictions by deductive reasoning from a few "plausible" premises about human behavior.

At least four important areas of social science and social policy, two of them in economics and two more closely related to political science, have as their central concern the phenomena of power and the processes of bargaining: the theory of political parties, labor-management relations, international politics, and oligopoly theory. Any progress in the basic theory applicable to one of these is certain to be of almost equal importance to the others. A growing recognition of their common concern is evidenced by the initiation of a new cross-disciplinary journal, *Journal of Conflict Resolution*.

Games against Nature

While the binary choice experiment is basically a one-person game, it is possible to interpret it as a "game against nature," and hence to try to explain it in game-theoretic terms. According to game theory, the subject, if he believes in a malevolent nature that manipulates the dice against him, should "minimax" his expected utility instead of maximizing it. That is, he should adopt the course of action that will maximize his expected utility under the assumption that nature will do her worst to him.

Minimaxing expected utility would lead the subject to call plus or minus at random and with equal probability, regardless of what the history of rewards has been. This is something that subjects demonstrably do not do.

However, it has been suggested by Savage and others that people are not as interested in maximizing utility as they are in minimizing regret. "Regret" means the difference between the reward actually obtained and the reward that could have been obtained with perfect foresight (actually, with perfect hindsight!). It turns out that minimaxing regret in the binary choice experiment leads to event-matching behavior. Hence, the empirical evidence is at least crudely consistent with the hypothesis that people play against nature by minimaxing regret. We shall see, however, that event matching is also consistent with a number of other rules of behavior that seem more plausible on their face; hence we need not take the present explanation too seriously—at least I am not inclined to do so.

V. THE FORMATION OF EXPECTATIONS

While the future cannot enter into the determination of the present, expectations about the future can and do. In trying to gain an understanding of the saving, spending, and investment behavior of both consumers and firms, and to make short-term predictions of this behavior for purposes of policy making, economists have done substantial empirical work as well as theorizing on the formation of expectations.

Empirical Studies

A considerable body of data has been accumulated on consumers' plans and expectations from the Survey of Consumer Finances, conducted for the Board of Governors of the Federal Reserve System by the Survey Research Center of the University of Michigan. These data, and similar data obtained by others, begin to give us some information on the expectations of consumers about their own incomes, and the predictive value of their expenditure plans for their actual subsequent behavior. Some large-scale attempts have been made, notably by Modigliani and Brumberg and, a little later, by Friedman to relate these empirical findings to classical utility theory. The current empirical research on businessmen's expectations is of two main kinds:

1. Surveys of businessmen's own forecasts of business and business conditions in the economy and in their own industries. These are obtained by straightforward questionnaire methods that assume, implicitly, that businessmen can and do make such forecasts. In some uses to which the data are put, it is also assumed that the forecasts are used as one basis for businessmen's actions.

2. Studies of business decisions and the role of expectations in these decisions—particularly investment and pricing decisions. We have already referred to studies of business decisions in our discussion of the goals of the firm.

Expectations and Probability

The classical way to incorporate expectations into economic theory is to assume that the decision maker estimates the joint probably distribution of future events. He can then act so as to maximize the expected value of utility or profit, as the case may be. However satisfying this approach may be conceptually, it poses awkward problems when we ask how the decision maker actually estimates the parameters of the joint probability distribution. Common sense tells us that people don't make such estimates, nor can we find evidence that they do by examining actual business forecasting methods. The surveys of businessmen's expectations have never attempted to secure such estimates, but have contended themselves with asking for point predictions—which, at best, might be interpreted as predictions of the means of the distributions.

It has been shown that under certain special circumstances the mean of the probability distribution is the only parameter that is relevant for decision—that even if the variance and higher moments were known to the rational decision maker, he would have no use for them. In these cases, the arithmetic mean is actually a certainty equivalent, the optimal decision turns out to be the same as if the future were known with certainty. But the situations where the mean is a certainty equivalent are, as we have said, very special ones, and there is no indication that businessmen ever ask whether the necessary conditions for this equivalence are actually met in practice. They somehow make forecasts in the form of point predictions and act upon them in one way or another.

The "somehow" poses questions that are important for business cycle theory, and perhaps for other problems in economics. The way in which expectations are formed may affect the dynamic stability of the economy, and the extent to which cycles will be amplified or damped. Some light, both empirical and theoretical, has recently been cast on these questions. On the empirical side, attempts have been made: (a) to compare businessmen's forecasts with various "naïve" models that assume the future will be some simple function of the recent past, and (b) to use such naïve models themselves as forecasting devices.

The simplest naïve model is one that assumes the next period will be exactly like the present. Another assumes that the change from present to next period will equal the change from last period to present; a third, somewhat more general, assumes that the next period will be a weighted average of recent past periods. The term "naïve model" has been applied loosely to various forecasting formulae of these general kinds. There is some affirmative evidence that business forecasts fit such models. There is also evidence that elaboration of the models beyond the first few steps of refinement does not much improve prediction. Arrow and his colleagues have explored some of the conditions under which forecasting formulae will, and will not, introduce dynamic instability into an economic system that is otherwise stable. They have shown, for example, that if a system of multiple markets is stable under static expectations, it is stable when expectations are based on a moving average of past values.

The work on the formation of expectations represents a significant extension of classical theory. For, instead of taking the environment as a "given," known to the economic decision maker, it incorporates in the theory the processes of acquiring knowledge about that environment. In doing so, it forces us to include in our model of economic man some of his properties as a learning, estimating, searching, information-processing organism.

The Cost of Information

There is one way in which the formation of expectations might be reincorporated in the body of economic theory: by treating information gathering as one of the processes of production, so to speak, and applying to it the usual rules of marginal analysis. Information, says price theory, should be gathered up to the point where the incremental cost of additional information is equal to the incremental profit that can be earned by having it. Such an approach can lead to propositions about optimal amounts of information-gathering activity and about the relative merits of alternative information-gathering and estimating schemes.

This line of investigation has, in fact, been followed in statistical decision theory. In sampling theory we are concerned with the optimal size of sample (and in the special and ingenious case of sequential sampling theory, with knowing when to stop sampling), and we wish to evaluate the efficiencies of alternative sampling procedures. The latter problem is the simpler, since it is possible to compare the relative costs of alternative schemes that have the same sampling error, and hence to avoid estimating the value of the information. However, some progress has been made also toward estimating the value of improved forecast accuracy in situations where the forecasts are to be used in applying formal decision rules to choice situations.

The theory of teams developed by Marschak and Radner is concerned with the same problem. It considers situations involving decentralized and interdependent decision making by two or more persons who share a common goal and who, at a cost, can transmit information to each other about their own actions or about the parts of the environment with which they are in contact. The problem then is to discover the optimal communication strategy under specified assumptions about communication costs and payoffs.

The cost of communication in the theory of teams, like the cost of observations in sampling theory, is a parameter that characterizes the economic actor, or the relation of the actor to his environment. Hence, while these theories retain, in one sense, a classical picture of economic man as a maximizer, they clearly require considerable information about the characteristics of the actor, and not merely about his environment. They take a long stride toward bridging the gap between the traditional concerns of economics and the concern of psychology.

Expectations in the Binary Choice Experiment

I should like to return again to the binary choice experiment, to see what light it casts on the formation of expectations. If the subject is told by the experimenter that the rewards are assigned at random, if he is told what the odds are for each alternative, *and if he believes the experimenter*, the situation poses no forecasting problem. We have seen, however, that the behavior of most subjects is not consistent with these assumptions.

How would sequential sampling theory handle the problem? Each choice the subject makes now has two consequences: the immediate reward he obtains from it, and the increment of information it provides for predicting the future rewards. If he thinks only of the latter consequences, he is faced with the classical problem of induction: to estimate the probability that an event will occur in the future on the basis of its frequency of occurrence in the past. Almost any rule of induction would require a rational (maximizing) subject to behave in the following general manner: to sample the two alternatives in some proportion to estimate the probability of reward associated with each; after the error of estimate had been reduced below some bound, always to choose the alternative with the higher probability of reward. Unfortunately, this does not appear to be what most subjects do.

If we give up the idea of maximization, we can make the weaker assumption that the subject is adaptive—or learns—but not necessarily in any optimal fashion. What do we mean by adaptation or learning? We mean, gradually and on the basis of experience responding more frequently with the choice that, in the past, has been most frequently rewarded. There is a whole host of rules of behavior possessing this characteristic. Postulate, for example, that at each trial the subject has a certain probability of responding "plus," and the complementary probability of responding "minus." Postulate further that when he makes a particular response the probability of making the same response on the next trial is increased if the response is rewarded and decreased if the response is not rewarded. The amount of increment in the response probability is a parameter characterizing the learning rate of the particular subject. Almost all schemes of this kind produce asymptotic behaviors, as the number of trials increases, that are approximately event matching in character.

Stochastic learning models, as the processes just described are usually called, were introduced into psychology in the early 1950s by W. K. Estes and Bush and Mosteller and have been investigated extensively since that time. The models fit some of the gross features of the observed behaviors—most strikingly the asymptotic probabilities—but do not explain very satisfactorily the fine structure of the observations.

Observation of subjects in the binary choice experiment reveals that usually they not only refuse to believe that (or even to act as if) the reward series were random, but in fact persist over many trials in searching for systematic patterns in the series. To account for such behavior, we might again postulate a learning model, but in this case a model in which the subject does not react probabilistically to his environment, but forms and tests definite hypotheses about systematic patterns in it. Man, in this view, is not only a learning animal; he is a pattern-finding and concept-forming animal. Julian Feldman has constructed theories of this kind to explain the behavior of subjects in the binary choice experiment, and while the tests of the theories are not yet completed, his findings look exceedingly promising.

As we move from maximizing theories, through simple stochastic learning theories, to theories involving pattern recognition, our model of the expectation-forming processes and the organism that performs it increases in complexity. If we follow this route, we reach a point where a theory of behavior requires a rather elaborate and detailed picture of the rational actor's cognitive processes.

VI. HUMAN COGNITION AND ECONOMICS

All the developments we have examined in the preceding four sections have a common theme: they all involve important modifications in the concept of economic man and, for the reasons we have stated, modifications in the direction of providing a fuller description of his characteristics. The classical theory is a theory of a man choosing among fixed and known alternatives, to each of which is attached known consequences. But when perception and cognition intervene between the decision maker and his objective environment, this model no longer proves adequate. We need a description of the choice process that recognizes that alternatives are not given but must be sought; and a description that takes into account the arduous task of determining what consequences will follow on each alternative.

The decision maker's information about his environment is much less than an approximation to the real environment. The term "approximation" implies that the subjective world of the decision maker resembles the external environment closely, but lacks, perhaps, some fineness of detail. In actual fact the perceived world is fantastically different from the "real" world. The differences involve both omissions and distortions, and arise in both perception and inference. The sins of omission in perception are more important than the sins of commission. The decision maker's model of the world encompasses only a minute fraction of all the relevant characteristics of the real environment, and his inferences extract only a minute fraction of all the information that is present even in his model.

Perception is sometimes referred to as a "filter." This term is as misleading as "approximation," and for the same reason: it implies that what comes through into the central nervous system is really quite a bit like what is "out there." In fact, the filtering is not merely a passive selection of some part of a presented whole, but an active process involving attention to a very small part of the whole and exclusion, from the outset, of almost all that is not within the scope of attention.

Every human organism lives in an environment that generates millions of bits of new information each second, but the bottleneck of the perceptual apparatus certainly does not admit more than 1,000 bits per second, and probably much less. Equally significant omissions occur in the processing that takes place when information reaches the brain. As every mathematician knows, it is one thing to have a set of differential equations, and another thing to have their solutions. Yet the solutions are logically implied by the equations—they are "all there," if we only knew how to get to them! By the same token, there are hosts of inferences that *might* be drawn from the information stored in the brain that are not in fact drawn. The consequences implied by information in the memory become known only through active information processing, and hence through active selection of particular problem-solving paths from the myriad that might have been followed.

In this section we shall examine some theories of decision making that take the limitations of the decision maker and the complexity of the environment as central concerns. These theories incorporate some mechanisms we have already discussed—for example, aspiration levels and forecasting processes—but go beyond them in providing a detailed picture of the choice process.

A real-life decision involves some goals or values, some facts about the environment, and some inferences drawn from the values and facts. The goals and values may be simple or complex, consistent or contradictory; the facts may be real or supposed, based on observation or the reports of others; the inferences may be valid or spurious. The whole process may be viewed, metaphorically, as a process of "reasoning," where the values and facts serve as premises, and the decision that is finally reached is inferred from these premises. The resemblance of decision making to logical reasoning is only metaphorical, because there are quite different rules in the two cases to determine what constitute "valid" premises and admissible modes of inference. The metaphor is useful because it leads us to take the individual *decision premise* as the unit of description, hence to deal with the whole interwoven fabric of influences that bear on a single decision—but without being bound by the assumptions of rationality that limit the classical theory of choice.

Rational Behavior and Role Theory

We can find common ground to relate the economist's theory of decision making with that of the social psychologist. The latter is particularly interested, of course, in social influences on choice, which determine the *role* of the actor. In our present terms, a role is a social prescription of some, but not all, of the premises that enter into an individual's choices of behavior. Any particular concrete behavior is the resultant of a large number of premises, only some of which are prescribed by the role. In addition to role premises there will be premises about the state of the environment based directly on perception, premises representing beliefs and knowledge, and idiosyncratic premises that characterize the personality. Within this framework we can accommodate both the rational elements in choice, so much emphasized by economics, and the nonrational elements to which psychologists and sociologists often prefer to call attention.

Decision Premises and Computer Programs

The analysis of choice in terms of decision premises gives us a conceptual framework for describing and explaining the process of deciding. But so complex is the process that our explanations of it would have remained schematic and hypothetical for a long time to come had not the modern digital computer appeared on the scene. The notion of decision premise can be translated into computer terminology, and when this translation has been accomplished, the digital computer provides us with an instrument for stimulating human decision processes—even very complex ones—and hence for testing empirically our explanations of those processes.

A fanciful (but only slightly fanciful) example will illustrate how this might be done. Some actual examples will be cited presently. Suppose we were to construct a robot incorporating a modern digital computer, and to program (i.e., to instruct) the robot to take the role of a business executive in a specified company. What would the program look like? Since no one has yet done this, we cannot say with certainty, but several points are fairly clear. The program would not consist of a list of prescribed and proscribed behaviors, since what an executive does is highly contingent on information about a wide variety of circumstances. Instead, the program would consist of a large number of *criteria* to be applied to possible and proposed courses of action, of routines for *generating* possible courses of action, of computational procedures for *assessing* the state of the environment and its implications for action, and the like. Hence, the program—in fact, a role prescription—would interact with information to produce concrete behavior adapted to the situation. The elements of such a program take the form of what we have called decision premises, and what the computer specialists would call instructions.

The promise of constructing actual detailed descriptions of concrete roles and decision processes is no longer, with the computer, a mere prospectus to be realized at some undefined future date. We can already provide actual examples, some of them in the area of economics.

1. *Management Science.* In the paragraphs on normative applications in section II, we have already referred to the use of such mathematical techniques as linear programming and dynamic programming to construct formal decision processes for actual situations. The relevance of these decision models to the present discussion is that they are not merely abstract "theories" of the firm, but actual decision-making devices. We can think of any such device as a simulation of the corresponding human decision maker, in which the equations and other assumptions that enter into the formal decision-making procedure correspond to the decision premises—including the role prescription—of the decision maker.

The actual application of such models to concrete business situations brings to light the information-processing tasks that are concealed in the assumptions of the more abstract classical models.

(1) The models must be formulated so as to require for their application only data that are obtainable. If one of the penalties, for example, of holding too small inventories is the loss of sales, a decision model that proposes to determine optimal inventory levels must incorporate a procedure for putting a dollar value on this loss.

(2) The models must call only for practicable computations. For example, several proposals for applying linear programming to certain factory scheduling problems have been shown to be impracticable because, even with computers, the computation time is too great. The task of decision theory (whether normative or descriptive) is to find alterna-

tive techniques—probably only approximate—that demand much less computation.

(3) The models must not demand unobtainable forecast information. A procedure that would require a sales department to estimate the third moment of next month's sales distribution would not have wide application, as either description or prescription, to business decision making.

These models, then, provide us with concrete examples of roles for a decision maker described in terms of the premises he is expected to apply to the decision—the data and the rules of computation.

2. *Engineering Design.* Computers have been used for some years to carry out some of the analytic computations required in engineering design—computing the stresses, for example, in a proposed bridge design. Within the past two years, ways have been found to program computers to carry out synthesis as well as analysis—to evolve the design itself. A number of companies in the electrical industry now use computers to design electric motors, transformers, and generators, going from customer specifications to factory design without human intervention. The significance of this for our purpose here is that the synthesis programs appear to simulate rather closely the processes that had previously been used by college-trained engineers in the same design work. It has proved possible to write down the engineers' decision premises and inference processes in sufficient detail to produce workable computer programs.

3. *Human Problem Solving.* The management science and engineering design programs already provide examples of simulation of human decision making by computer. It may be thought that, since in both instances the processes are highly arithmetical, these examples are relevant to only a very narrow range of human problem-solving activity. We generally think of a digital computer as a device which, if instructed in painful detail by its operator, can be induced to perform rather complicated and tedious arithmetical operations. More recent developments require us to revise these conceptions of the computer, for they enable it to carry out tasks that, if performed by humans, we would certainly call "thinking" and "learning."

Discovering the proof of a theorem of Euclid—a task we all remember from our high school geometry course—requires thinking and usually insight and imagination. A computer is now being programmed to perform this task (in a manner closely simulating the human geometer), and another computer has been successfully performing a highly similar task in symbolic logic for the past two years. The latter computer is programmed to learn—that is to improve its performance on the basis of successful problem-solving experience—to use something akin to imagery or metaphor in planning its proofs, and to transfer some of its skills to other tasks—for example, solving trigonometric identities—involving completely distinct subject matter. These programs, it should be observed, do not involve the computer in rapid arithmetic—or any arithmetic for that matter. They are basically nonnumerical, involving the manipulation of all kinds of symbolic material, including words.

Still other computer programs have been written to enable a computer to play chess. Not all of these programs, or those previously mentioned, are close simulations of the processes humans use. However, in some direct attempts to investigate the human processes by thinking-aloud techniques and to reproduce in computer programs the processes observed in human subjects, several striking simulations have been achieved. These experiments have been described elsewhere and can't be reviewed here in detail.

4. *Business Games.* Business games, like those developed by the American Management Association, International Business Machines Corporation, and several universities, represent a parallel development. In the business game, the decisions of the business firms are still made by the human players, but the economic environment of these firms, including their markets, are represented by computer programs that calculate the environment's responses to the actions of the players. As the games develop in detail and realism, their programs will represent more and more concrete descriptions of the decision processes of various economic actors—for example, consumers.

The games that have been developed so far are restricted to numerical magnitudes like prices and quantities of goods, and hence resemble the management science and engineering design programs more closely than they do those we have described under the heading of human problem solving. There is no reason, however, to expect this restriction to remain very long.

Implications for Economics

Apart from normative applications (e.g., substituting computers for humans in certain decision-making tasks) we are not interested so much in the detailed descriptions of roles as in broader questions: (1) What general characteristics do the roles of economic actors have? (2) How do roles come to be structured in the particular ways they do? (3) What bearing does this version of role theory have for macroeconomics and other large-scale social phenomena?

Characterizing Role Structure. Here we are concerned with generalizations about thought processes, particularly those generalizations that are relatively independent of the substantive content of the role. A classical example is Dewey's description of stages in the problem-solving process. Another example, of particular interest to economics, is the hypothesis we have already discussed at length: that economic man is a *satisficing* animal whose problem solving is based on search activity to meet certain aspiration levels rather than a *maximizing* animal whose problem solving involves finding the best alternatives in terms of specified criteria. A third hypothesis is that operative goals (those associated with an observable criterion of success, and relatively definite means of attainment) play a much larger part in governing choice than nonoperative goals (those lacking a concrete measure of success or a program for attainment).

Understanding How Roles Emerge. Within almost any single business firm, certain characteristic types of roles will be represented: selling roles, production roles, accounting roles, and so on. Partly, this consistency may be explained in functional terms—that a model that views the firm as producing a product, selling it, and accounting for its assets and liabilities is an effective simplification of the real world, and provides the members of the organization with a workable frame of reference. Imitation within the culture provides an alternative explanation. It is exceedingly difficult to test hypotheses as to the origins and causal conditions for roles as universal in the society as these, but the underlying mechanisms could probably be explored effectively by the study of less common roles—safety director, quality control inspector, or the like—that are to be found in some firms, but not in all.

With out present definition of role, we can also speak meaningfully of the role of an entire business firm—of decision premises that underlie its basic policies. In a particular industry we find some firms that specialize in adapting the product to individual customer's specifications; others that specialize in product innovation. The common interest of economics and psychology includes not only the study of individual roles, but also the explanation of organizational roles of these sorts.

Tracing the Implications for Macroeconomics. If basic professional goals remain as they are, the interest of the psychologist and the economist in role theory will stem from somewhat different ultimate aims. The former will use various economic and organizational phenomena as data for the study of the structure and determinants of roles; the latter will be primarily interested in the implications of role theory for the model of economic man, and indirectly, for macroeconomics.

The first applications will be to those topics in economics where the assumption of static equilibrium is least tenable. Innovation, technological change, and economic development are examples of areas to which a good empirically tested theory of the processes of human adaptation and problem solving could make a major contribution. For instance, we know very little at present about how the rate of innovation depends on the amounts of resources allocated to various kinds of research and development activity. Nor do we understand very well the nature of "know-how," the costs of transferring technology from one firm or economy to another, or the effects of various kinds and amounts of education upon national product. These are difficult questions to answer from aggregate data and gross observation, with the result that our views have been formed more by armchair theorizing than by testing hypotheses with solid facts.

VII. CONCLUSION

In exploring the areas in which economics has common interests with the other behavioral sciences, we have been guided by the metaphor we elaborated in section I. In simple, slow-moving situations, where the actor has a single, operational goal, the assumption of maximization relieves us of any need to construct a detailed picture of economic man or his processes of adaptation. As the complexity of the environment increases, or its speed of change, we need to know more and more about the mechanisms and processes that economic man uses to relate himself to that environment and achieve his goals.

How closely we wish to interweave economics with psychology depends, then, both on the range of questions we wish to answer and on our assessment of how far we may trust the assumptions of static equilibrium as approximations. In considerable part, the demand for a fuller picture of economic man has been coming from the profession of economics itself, as new areas of theory and application have emerged in which complexity and change are central facts. The revived interest in the theory of utility, and its application to choice under uncertainty, and to consumer saving and spending is one such area. The needs of normative macroeconomics and management science for a fuller theory of the firm have led to a number of attempts to understand the actual processes of making business decisions. In both these areas, notions of adaptive and satisficing behavior, drawn largely from psychology, are challenging sharply the classical picture of the maximizing entrepreneur.

The area of imperfect competition and oligopoly has been equally active, although the activity has thus far perhaps raised more problems than it has solved. On the positive side, it has revealed a community of interest among a variety of social scientists concerned with bargaining as a part of political and economic processes. Prediction of the future is another element common to many decision processes, and particularly important to explaining business cycle phenomena. Psychologists and economists have been applying a wide variety of approaches, empirical and theoretical, to the study of the formation of expectations. Surveys of consumer and business behavior, theories of statistical induction, stochastic learning theories, and theories of concept formation have all been converging on this problem area.

The very complexity that has made a theory of the decision-making process essential has made its construction exceedingly difficult. Most approaches have been piecemeal—now focused on the criteria of choice, now on conflict of interest, now on the formation of expectations. It seemed almost utopian to suppose that we could put together a model of adaptive man that would compare in completeness with the simple model of classical economic man. The sketchiness and incompleteness of the newer proposals has been urged as a compelling reason for clinging to the older theories, however inadequate they are admitted to be.

The modern digital computer has changed the situation radically. It provides us with a tool of research—for formulating and testing theories—whose power is commensurate with the complexity of the phenomena we seek to understand. Although the use of computers to build theories of human behavior is very recent, it has already led to concrete results in the simulation of higher mental processes. As economics finds it more and more necessary to understand and explain disequilibrium as well as equilibrium, it will find an increasing use for this new tool and for communication with its sister sciences of psychology and sociology.

part TWO
Demand

INTRODUCTION

Demand analysis is important to decision making in two ways: (1) it provides the basis for analyzing market influences on the firm's products and thus helps the firm to adapt to the influences; and (2) it provides guidance in the manipulation of demand itself. Some decisions require a passive adaptation to market forces while others require the active shifting of those forces.

If the theoretical foundations of demand analysis are useful to the managerial economist, it would seem that empirical studies of demand are, too. Unfortunately, however, the results of very few empirical demand studies have stood up. The classic article by E. J. Working tells, inferentially why. To provide reliable estimates of elasticities, an empirical study must follow a simultaneous equations approach, and deal with such well-known econometric problems as identification and multicollinearity; but even all the trimmings of grand econometric method are only necessary, not sufficient, conditions for reliable demand estimates, as experience so sadly shows. Nevertheless, the subject is important. Accordingly, Hendrik Houthakker's article should be taken as an example of the serious study given to price elasticities, and of the commonsense informal checks which economists often use in this area. Though like all demand studies its results must be used with caution, the evidence it surveys appears to be among the best we have.

L. J. Atkinson's article is a good example of the cross-sectional approach to demand analysis, using many social and personal as well as economic variables. It may perhaps be read more for its exemplary use of a particular method than for its substantive results. We have no particular reason to doubt the results. But even good results can become dated; good methods do not.

Good methods of estimating demand are mandatory if demand studies are to be useful in predicting the effects of changes in the independent variables. But a frequently used alternative to the statistical approaches surveyed here is one of the traditional forecasting methods. The material in Part III, therefore, is pertinent to this section as well.

Because of the problems that hinder demand estimation by statistical techniques, economists are always looking for alternative methods. "Quasi-experimental techniques are feasible for some products. If enough other variables can be held constant, observations on prices and purchases can give quite a lot of information about price elasticities." An application of this method to liquor is reported on in the article by Julian Simon.

5. What Do Statistical "Demand Curves" Show?[*]

E. J. WORKING

Many questions of practical importance hinge upon the elasticity of demand, or of demand and supply. The economist can answer them only in a vague and indefinite manner, because he does not know the nature of the demand curve. What will be the effect of a five-million-bushel increase in the corn crop upon the price of corn and of hogs? What will be the effect of a tariff on imports and prices; on the protected industry; on the balance of international payments? How large an indemnity can Germany pay? The answers all depend in greater or less measure upon the elasticity of demand of the various commodities in question.

Such are the needs of the theorist, and in recent years a great deal of attention has been turned to the construction of statistical demand curves. Beef, corn, cotton, hay, hogs, pig iron, oats, potatoes, sweet potatoes, sugar, and wheat are on the list of commodities for which we have statements of the "law of demand." Many economists have been skeptical, while others have been enthusiastic, on the significance of such demand curves. In consequence of this divergence of opinion, it may be well to consider some of the theoretical aspects of what the demand curves constructed by our statistical experts may be expected to show. Do they correspond to the demand curves of economic theory? If so, it would seem that they represent something tangible by which our theories may be tested and turned to better account.

Among the statistical studies of demand that have been made, there are cases in which the same commodity has been studied by more than one investigator, and their results indicate varying degrees of elasticity of demand. But despite this, in all but one of the cases the demand curves have been negatively inclined—they have been in accord with Marshall's "one general *law of demand.*"

In the case of pig iron, however, Professor H. L. Moore finds a "law

---

[*] *The Quarterly Journal of Economics*, vol. 41, no. 2 (February 1927), pp. 212–35.

of demand" which is not in accord with Marshall's universal rule. He finds that the greater the quantity of pig iron sold, the higher will be the prices. If this is the nature of the statistical demand curve for pig iron, surely statistical demand curves must be of a very different sort from the demand curves of traditional economic theory!

Professor Moore holds that the statistical "law of demand" at which he arrives is a *dynamic* law, while that of theory is a *static* law. He says in part: "The doctrine of the uniformity of the demand function is an idol of the static state—the method of *cæteris paribus*—which has stood in the way of the successful treatment of dynamic problems." If it be true that statistical demand curves and the demand curves of theory differ so utterly from each other, of what value is statistical analysis to the theorist—of what value is economic theory to the statistical analyst? It would seem that so far as the study of demand is concerned, the statistical analyst and the economic theorist are on paths so divergent as to be wholly out of touch with each other. Before we accede to such a discouraging thought, let us examine a little more closely the nature of statistical demand curves as they may be viewed in the light of economic theory.

Let us first consider in what way statistical demand curves are constructed. While both the nature of the data used and the technique of analysis vary, the basic data consist of corresponding prices and quantities. That is, if a given quantity refers to the amount of a commodity sold, produced, or consumed in the year 1910, the corresponding price is the price which is taken to be typical of the year 1910. These corresponding quantities and prices may be for a period of a month, a year, or any other length of time which is feasible; and, as has already been indicated, the quantities may refer to amounts produced, sold, or consumed. The technique of analysis consists of such operations as fitting the demand curve, and adjusting the original data to remove, in so far as is possible, the effect of disturbing influences. For a preliminary understanding of the way in which curves are constructed, we need not be concerned with the differences in technique; but whether the quantities used are the amounts produced, sold, or consumed is a matter of greater significance, which must be kept in mind.

For the present, let us confine our attention to the type of study which uses for its data the quantities which have been sold in the market. In general, the method of constructing demand curves of this sort is to take corresponding prices and quantities, plot them, and draw a curve which will fit as nearly as possible all the plotted points. Suppose, for example, we wish to determine the demand curve for beef. First, we find out how many pounds of beef were sold in a given month and what was the average price. We do the same for all the other months of the period over which our study is to extend, and plot our data with quantities as abscissas and corresponding prices as ordinates. Next we draw a curve to fit the points. This is our demand curve.

In the actual construction of demand curves, certain refinements necessary in order to get satisfactory results are introduced. The purpose of these is to correct the data so as to remove the effect of various extraneous and complicating factors. For example, adjustments are usually made for changes in the purchasing power of money, and for changes in population and in consumption habits. Corrections may be made directly by such means as dividing all original price data by "an index of the general level of prices." They may be made indirectly by correction for trends of the two time series of prices and of quantities. Whatever the corrections and refinements, however, the essence of the method is that certain prices are taken as representing the prices at which certain quantities of the product in question were sold.

With this in mind, we may now turn to the theory of the demand-and-supply curve analysis of market prices. The conventional theory runs in terms substantially as follows. At any given time, all individuals within the scope of the market may be considered as being within two groups—potential buyers and potential sellers. The higher the price, the more the sellers will be ready to sell and the less the buyers will be willing to take. We may assume a demand schedule of the potential buyers and a supply schedule of the potential sellers which express the amounts that these groups are ready to buy and sell at different prices. From these schedules supply and demand curves may be made. Thus we have our supply and demand curves showing the market situation at any given time, and the price which results from this situation will be represented by the height of the point where the curves intersect.

This, however, represents the situation as it obtains at any given moment only. It may change; indeed, it is almost certain to change. The supply and demand curves which accurately represent the market situation of today will not represent that of a week hence. The curves which represent the average or aggregate of conditions this month will not hold true for the corresponding month of next year. In the case of the wheat market, for example, the effect of news that wheat which is growing in Kansas has been damaged by rust will cause a shift in both demand and supply schedules of the traders in the grain markets. The same amount of wheat, or a greater, will command a higher price than would have been the case if the news had failed to reach the traders. Since much of the buying and selling is speculative, changes in the market price itself may result in shifts of the demand and supply schedules.

If, then, our market demand-and-supply curves are to indicate conditions which extend over a period of time, we must represent them as shifting. A diagram such as the following, Figure 1, may be used to indicate them. The demand and supply curves may meet at any point within the area a, b, c, d, and over a period of time points of equilibrium will occur at many different places within it.

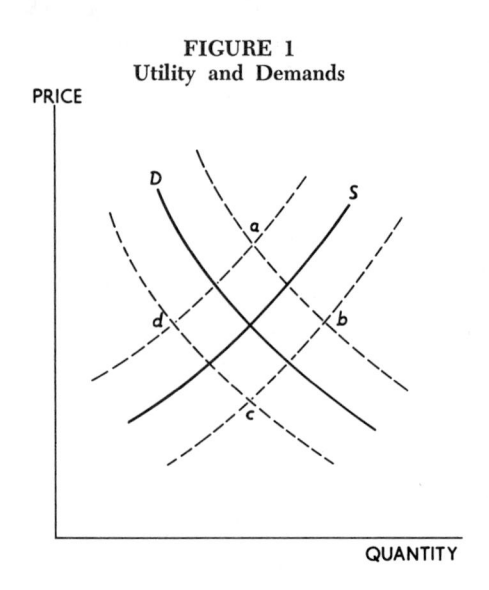

FIGURE 1
Utility and Demands

But what of statistical demand curves in the light of this analysis? If we construct a statistical demand curve from data of quantities sold and corresponding prices, our original data consist, in effect, of observations of points at which the demand and supply curves have met. Although we may wish to reduce our data to static conditions, we must remember that they originate in the market itself. The market is dynamic and our data extend over a period of time; consequently our data are of changing conditions and must be considered as the result of shifting demand and supply schedules.

Let us assume that conditions are such as those illustrated in Figure 2, the demand curve shifting from D_1 to D_2 and the supply curve shifting in similar manner from S_1 to S_2. It is to be noted that the chart shows approximately equal shifting of the demand and supply curves.

Under such conditions there will result a series of prices which may be graphically represented in Figure 3. It is from data such as those represented by the dots that we are to construct a demand curve, but evidently no satisfactory fit can be obtained. A line of one slope will give substantially as good a fit as will a line of any other slope.

But what happens if we alter our assumptions as to the relative shift-

5. What Do Statistical "Demand Curves" Show?

FIGURE 2

FIGURE 3
What Do Statistical "Demand Curves" Show?

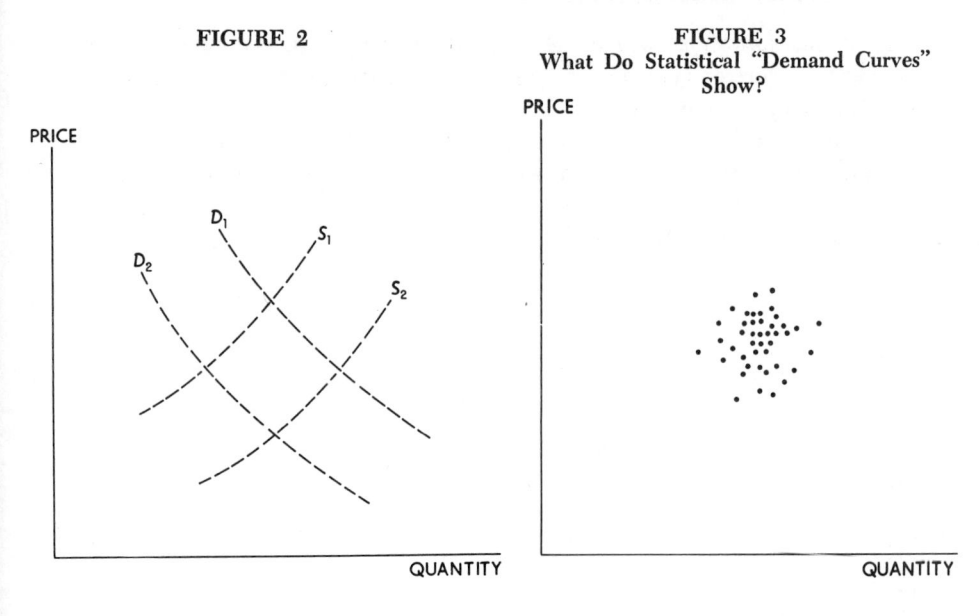

ing of the demand and supply curves? Suppose the supply curve shifts in some such manner as is indicated by Figure 4, that is, so that the shifting of the supply curve is greater than the shifting of the demand

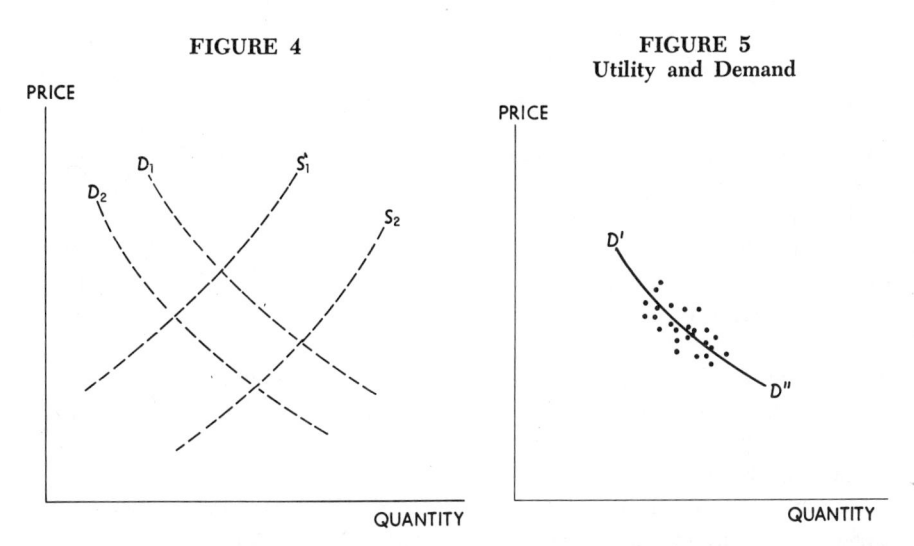

FIGURE 4

FIGURE 5
Utility and Demand

curve. We shall then obtain a very different set of observations—a set which may be represented by the dots of Figure 5. To these points we may fit a curve which will have the elasticity of the demand curve that we originally assumed, and whose position will approximate the central position about which the demand curve shifted. We may consider this to be a sort of typical demand curve, and from it we may determine the elasticity of demand.

If, on the other hand, the demand schedules of buyers fluctuate more than do the supply schedules of sellers, we shall obtain a different result. This situation is illustrated by Figure 6. The resulting array of prices and quantities is of a very different sort from the previous case, and its nature is indicated by Figure 7. A line drawn so as most nearly

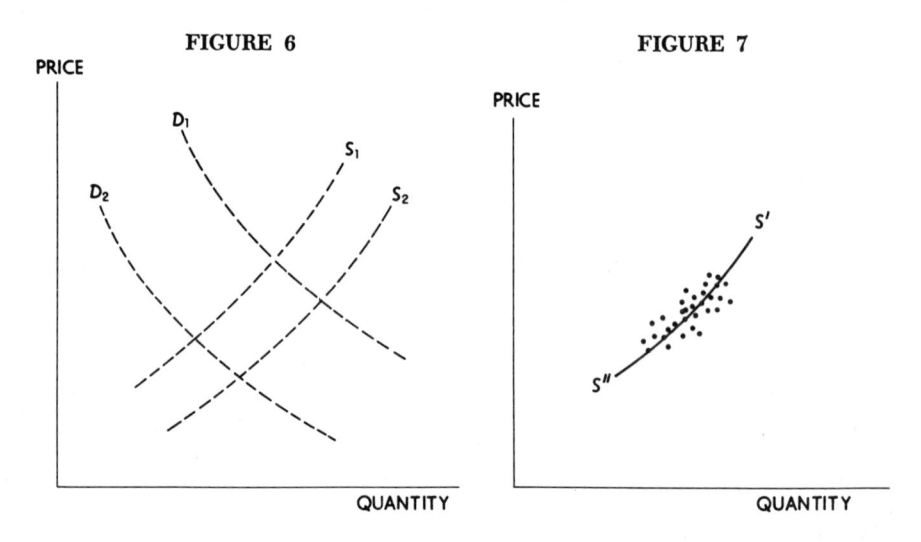

FIGURE 6

FIGURE 7

to fit these points will approximate a supply curve instead of a demand curve.

If this analysis is in accord with the facts, is it not evident that Professor Moore's "law of demand" for pig iron is in reality a "law of supply" instead? The original observations of prices and corresponding quantities are the resultant of both supply and demand. Consequently, they do not necessarily reflect the influence of demand any more than that of supply. The methods used in constructing demand curves (particularly if the quantity data are of quantities sold) may, under some conditions, yield a demand curve, under others, a supply curve, and, under still different conditions, no satisfactory result may be obtained.

In the case of agricultural commodities, where production for any given year is largely influenced by weather conditions, and where farmers sell practically their entire crop regardless of price, there is likely to be a much greater shifting of the supply schedules of sellers than of the demand schedules of buyers. This is particularly true of perishable commodities, which cannot be withheld from the market without spoilage, and in case the farmers themselves can under no conditions use more than a very small proportion of their entire production. Such a condition results in the supply curve shifting within very wide limits. The demand curve, on the other hand, may shift but little. The quantities which are consumed may be dependent almost entirely upon price, so that the only way to have a much larger amount taken off the market is to reduce the price, and any considerable curtailment of supply is sure to result in a higher price.

With other commodities, the situation may be entirely different. Where a manufacturer has complete control over the supply of the article which he produces, the price at which he sells may be quite definitely fixed, and the amount of his production will vary, depending upon how large an amount of the article is bought at the fixed price. The extent to which there is a similar tendency to adjust sales to the shifts of demand varies with different commodities, depending upon how large overhead costs are and upon the extent to which trade agreements or other means are used to limit competition between different manufacturers. In general, however, there is a marked tendency for the prices of manufactured articles to conform to their expenses of production, the amount of articles sold varying with the intensity of demand at that price which equals the expenses of production. Under such conditions, the supply curve does not shift greatly, but rather approximates an expenses-of-production curve, which does not vary much from month to month or from year to year. If this condition is combined with a fluctuating demand for the product, we shall have a situation such as that shown in Figures 6 and 7, where the demand curves shift widely and the supply curves only a little.

From this, it would seem that, whether we obtain a demand curve or a supply curve, by fitting a curve to a series of points which represent the quantities of an article sold at various prices, depends upon the fundamental nature of the supply and demand conditions. It implies the need of some term in addition to that of elasticity in order to describe the nature of supply and demand. The term "variability" may be used for this purpose. For example, the demand for an article may be said to be "elastic" if, at a given time a small reduction in price would result in a much greater quantity being sold, while it may be said to be "variable" if the demand curve shows a tendency to shift markedly. To be called variable, the demand curve should have the tendency to shift back and forth, and not merely to shift gradually and consistently to the right or left because of changes of population or consuming habits.

Whether a demand or a supply curve is obtained may also be affected by the nature of the corrections applied to the original data. The corrections may be such as to reduce the effect of the shifting of the demand schedules without reducing the effect of the shifting of the supply schedules. In such a case the curve obtained will approximate a demand curve, even though the original demand schedules fluctuated fully as much as did the supply schedules.

By intelligently applying proper refinements, and making corrections to eliminate separately those factors which cause demand curves to shift and those factors which cause supply curves to shift, it may be possible even to obtain both a demand curve and a supply curve for the same product and from the same original data. Certainly it may be possible, in many cases where satisfactory demand curves have not been obtained, to find instead the supply curves of the articles in question. The supply curve obtained by such methods, it is to be noted, would be a market supply curve rather than a normal supply curve.

Thus far it has been assumed that the supply and demand curves shift quite independently and at random; but such need not be the case. It is altogether possible that a shift of the demand curve to the right may, as a rule, be accompanied by a shift of the supply curve to the left, and vice versa. Let us see what result is to be expected under such conditions. If successive positions of the demand curve are represented by the curves D_1, D_2, D_3, D_4, and D_5 of Figure 8, while

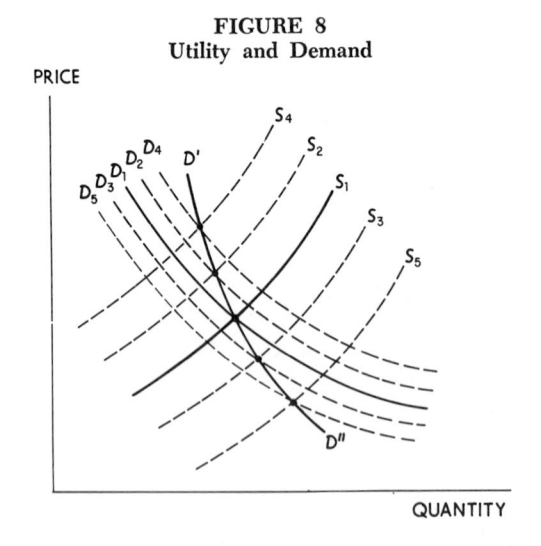

FIGURE 8
Utility and Demand

the curves S_1, S_2, S_3, S_4, and S_5 represent corresponding positions of the supply curves, then a series of prices will result from the intersection of D_1 with S_1, D_2 with S_2, and so on. If a curve be fitted to these points, it will not conform to the theoretical demand curve. It will have a smaller elasticity, as is shown by $D'D''$ of Figure 8. If, on the other hand, a shift of the demand curve to the right is accompanied by a shift of the supply curve to the right, we shall obtain a result such as that indicated by D'D'' in Figure 9. The fitted curve again fails to conform to the theoretical one, but in this case it is more elastic.

Without carrying the illustrations further, it will be apparent that similar reasoning applies to the fitted "supply curve" in case conditions are such that the demand curve shifts more than does the supply curve.

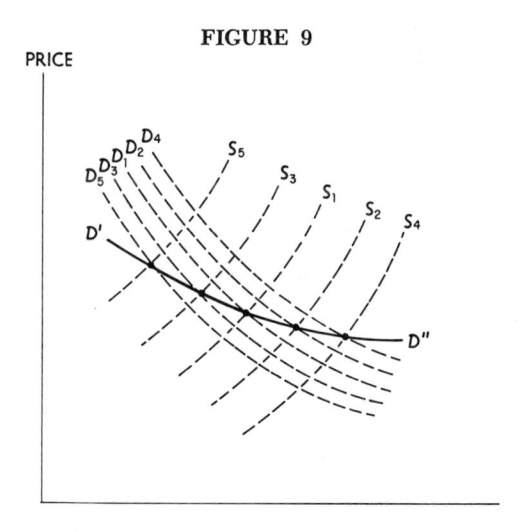

FIGURE 9

If there is a change in the range through which the supply curve shifts, as might occur through the imposition of a tariff on an imported good, a new fitted curve will result, which will not be a continuation of the former one—this because the fitted curve does not correspond to the true demand curve. In case, then, of correlated shifts of the demand and supply curves, a fitted curve cannot be considered to be the demand curve for the article. It cannot be used, for example, to estimate what change in price would result from the levying of a tariff upon the commodity.

Perhaps a word of caution is needed here. It does not follow from the foregoing analysis that, when conditions are such that shifts of the supply and demand curves are correlated, an attempt to construct a demand curve will give a result which will be useless. Even though shifts of the supply and demand curves are correlated, a curve which is fitted to the points of intersection will be useful for purposes of price forecasting, provided no new factors are introduced which did not affect the price during the period of the study. Thus, so long as the shifts of the supply and demand curves remain correlated in the same way, and so long as they shift through approximately the same range, the curve of regression of price upon quantity can be used as a means of estimating price from quantity.

In cases where it is impossible to show that the shifts of the demand and supply curves are not correlated, much confusion would probably be avoided if the fitted curves were not called demand curves (or supply curves), but if, instead, they were called merely lines of regression. Such curves may be useful, but we must be extremely careful in our interpretation of them. We must also make every effort to discover whether the shifts of the supply and demand curves are correlated before interpreting the results of any fitted curve.

. . . . .

In assuming that we are dealing with quantities actually sold in the market, and in disregarding the fact that for many commodities there is a whole series of markets at various points in the marketing chain, we have simplified our problem. But it has been more than mere simplification, for the interpretation which is to be placed on statistical demand curves depends in large measure upon these matters. Whether the demand curve is a "particular" or a "general" demand curve, depends upon whether or not we use quantities sold. Whether it represents consumer or dealer demand, depends upon the point in the marketing chain to which the quantities sold refer.

Most theorists are acquainted with the concept of the general demand curve as it is presented by Wicksteed and Davenport. Briefly, the idea is that demand should be considered as including not merely the quantities that are bought, but rather all those in existence. The general demand curve, then, includes the possessors of a commodity as having a demand for it at any price below their reservation price, even if they are prospective sellers. Instead of showing the amounts that will be bought at various prices, it shows the marginal money valuation which will be placed upon varying quantities of an existing supply.

Wicksteed even indicates that the supply curve ought not to be considered at all. The following gives an intimation of his viewpoint:

But what about the "supply curve" that usually figures as a determinant of price, coördinate with the demand curve? I say it boldly and baldly: There is no such thing. When we are speaking of a marketable commodity, what is usually called a supply curve is in reality a demand curve of those who possess the commodity; for it shows the exact place which every successive unit of the commodity holds in their relative scale of estimates. The so-called supply curve, therefore, is simply a part of the total demand curve.[1]

Thus the general demand curve is an expression of the relation between the supply of a commodity and its valuation.

. . . . .

---

[1] P. H. Wicksteed, "The Scope and Method of Political Economy in the Light of the 'Marginal Theory of Value,'" *Economic Journal* (March, 1914) p. 1.

The amount of a commodity sold at one point in the marketing chain may differ from that sold at another in much the same way that the amount produced may differ from the amount sold. This is particularly true if monthly data are used. A case in point would be the demand for eggs. The amount of eggs sold by farmers in the spring of the year is greatly in excess of the amount sold by retail dealers, while in the winter months it is much less. Since differentials between the prices received by farmers and those received by retail dealers remain fairly constant, very different demand curves would be obtained. The consumers' demand curve would be very much less elastic than that of the dealers who buy from farmers.

Differences between dealer demand and consumer demand are largely dependent upon whether we are considering short or long periods. Over long periods of time, dealer demand tends to conform to consumer demand. This difference, however, is not a thing which depends upon the length of period over which the data extend, but of the length of period to which the individual observations of prices and quantities refer. In the case of eggs, if yearly data were used, the principal difference which would be found between the elasticity of consumer and dealer demands would be due to price differentials alone.

The question whether statistical demand curves are static or dynamic is a perplexing one and rather difficult to deal with. This is largely due to uncertainty as to just what is meant by the terms "static" and "dynamic." Moore holds that his "laws of demand" are dynamic, and that this is an eminently desirable feature. Schultz, while considering it most desirable to obtain both a static and a dynamic law by means of multiple correlation, holds that the statistical devices of relative changes and of trend ratios give a static "law of demand."

Conditions are often defined as being static or dynamic on two different grounds. They may be called static if they refer to a point of time; or else they may be said to be static if all other things are held equal. Statements such as these, however, lack much in clarity and accuracy. How can a statement be made as to prices at which different quantities of a commodity will sell at a *point* of time? Is it really supposed that *all* other things must be held equal in order to study the demand of the commodity? Rather, the real supposition, though it may not be accurately expressed, is that the relationships between the various economic factors should be the same as those which exist at a given point of time, or that the relationships between these factors should remain constant.

The data used in a statistical study of demand must, of course, extend over a period of time, but they may in effect conform to conditions at a point of time if trend is removed and if there is no other change in the relationship between quantity and price. Of course, the shifting of the demand and supply curves constitutes a change in the relationship between the quantity and price, but the process of curve fitting corresponds to that of averaging. Consequently, the fitted curve may be considered to depict the average relationship between quantity and price. This amounts to the same thing as representing the relationship at a point of time which is typical for the period studied. In this sense, then, of relating to a point of time, Moore's "laws of demand" are static instead of dynamic.

Holding "all other things equal," however, is a different matter. Schultz states the difficulty in the following manner:

> In *theory* the law of demand for any one commodity is given only on the assumption that the prices of all other commodities remain constant (the old *ceteris paribus* assumption). This postulate fails in the case of commodities for which substitutes are available. Thus when the price of beef is changed markedly, the prices of such rival commodities as mutton, veal, and pork cannot be supposed to remain constant. Likewise, the price of sugar cannot be increased beyond a certain point without affecting the prices of glucose, corn sugar, and honey.[2]

Marshall makes similar restrictions as to the need for other things to be held equal, and suggests that in some cases it may be best to "group together commodities as distinct as beef and mutton," in order to obtain a demand curve which will not be too restricted because of other things being equal.

The question arises, however, whether it is desirable to hold all other things equal in any case. Is it not better to have a demand curve for beef which expresses the relation between the price and quantity of beef while the prices of pork, mutton, and veal, vary as they normally do, with different prices of beef? Furthermore, may not this be called a static condition? The point can perhaps be made clearer if we take an extreme example. If we are studying the demand for wheat, it would be almost meaningless to get the demand curve for No. 2 Winter wheat while holding the price of all other grades of wheat constant. Other grades of wheat can be so readily substituted that the demand would be almost completely elastic. The difference between this and holding the prices of pork, mutton, and veal constant, while the price of beef varies, is only one of degree—a difference which depends upon the ease with which substitutes can be used in place of the article whose demand is being studied.

All other things being held equal is not a condition represented by a statistical law of demand or, strictly interpreted, of any useful demand curve theory. Some of the things that are correlated with the price of the commodity in question may be held equal, but it is impossible for

---
[2] Henry Schultz, "The Statistical Law of Demand," *The Journal of Political Economy* (October and December 1925). See pp. 498–502 of October issue.

all things to be held equal. However, a statistical law of demand represents a condition under which the relationships between factors may be considered to have remained the same, or, to put it more accurately, a condition which is an average of the relationships during the period studied.

In conclusion, then, it is evident that the mere statement that the demand for a commodity has a given elasticity is meaningless. As with the results of all other statistical analysis, statistical demand curves must be interpreted in the light of the nature of the original data and of the methods of analysis used. There are four questions, the answers to which it is particularly important to know. They concern (1) whether the supply or demand curve is more variable, (2) the market to which the price and quantity data refer, (3) the extent to which "other things are held equal," and (4) whether the shifting of the supply and demand curves is correlated or random.

For precision, it is preferable that the data of price and quantity should refer to the same market. Yet this may be out of the question. In a study of the demand for wheat, for example, if we want to obtain a demand curve of the quantity demanded by the entire country, we cannot use prices for all different points and for all different grades. Instead, the price at one market and for one grade may be used as representative, and the demand of the entire country determined for various prices at the one marketplace. If the price at any other market or for any other grade were used, the elasticity of demand might be different.

Furthermore, the point in the market chain must be specified and the results interpreted accordingly. As is the case with geographical points, it is preferable that the quantities and prices should refer to the same stage in the marketing process. If this is not the case, the interpretation should be made with the situation in view.

It is to be expected that the methods used in constructing statistical demand curves should be such as to give a demand curve which represents a point of time, that is, that trends in both quantities and prices are removed, or else multiple correlation is used to effect the same result. If, in addition to this, other things are held constant, the fact should be noted and the elasticity of demand should be stated as referring to a condition where these other things are held constant.

The matter of correlation between shifts of the demand and supply curves is a more difficult problem to deal with. Every effort should be made to discover whether there is a tendency for the shifting of these to be interdependent. In case it is impossible to determine this, it should be carefully noted that the demand curve which is obtained is quite likely not to hold true for periods other than the one studied, and cannot be treated as corresponding to the demand curve of economic theory.

6. New Evidence on Demand Elasticities*

H. S. HOUTHAKKER

The increased statistical activity of international organizations is now providing econometricians with large bodies of data, usually in the form of more or less standardized time series for a number of countries. By appropriate techniques these data can be used to mitigate what has always been the main difficulty in the analysis of economic time series, namely the short time span they cover. A single time series of ten observations is barely worth analyzing; when used in combination, however, ten series of ten observations each may yield not only useful estimates, but also theoretical and methodological insights not easily obtainable otherwise.

There are also obvious arguments against the use of data from different countries, namely the implication that basically all countries are the same, an idea repugnant to those who believe that institutions and social conditions are a cause rather than an effect of long-run economic conditions. Actually, "structural" differences among countries can to a large extent be taken care of by randomly distributed error terms and similar devices, provided the number of countries is not too small. In fact there is no reason to postulate that differences among countries are of a more fundamental type than differences among aggregates for the same country in different years, or differences among households in the same country. The latter differences are not usually regarded as insuperable obstacles in time-series or cross-section analysis. Consequently, we should not hesitate to attempt combining time series from several countries, if only to see what difficulties arise.

The data analyzed in the present paper refer to household consumption and were published by the Organization for European Economic Cooperation (since transformed into the Organization for Economic Cooperation and Development) in its *General Statistics* as part of the National Accounts tables. The data refer to five catagories of consumers' expenditures—food, clothing, rent, durables, and miscellaneous—a break-

---

* *Econometrica*, vol. 33, no. 2 (April 1965) pp. 277–88.

down which makes good sense for most purposes. There are annual figures in local currencies in both current and constant (1954) prices, from which prices can be derived as implicit deflators. Judging from the frequency with which they are revised, these data are compiled with considerable care, though complete accuracy is hardly to be expected.

The following calculations, unless noted otherwise, are based on *General Statistics* of January 1961 and March 1961. They cover all or part of the 12 years 1948–59; all observations that were in some way incomplete or significantly nonstandard were disregarded. The sample consisted of 140 annual observations from 13 countries (Austria, Belgium, Denmark, France, Greece, Italy, Luxemburg, the Netherlands, Norway, Sweden, the United Kingdom, Canada, and the United States) for each of the five categories of consumption and for total expenditure. All aggregates were converted to per capita figures.

Most of the demand equations tested are variants of the double-logarithmic formula.

$$\log q_{ijt} = \alpha_i + \beta_i \log \mu_{jt} + \gamma_i \log p_{ijt} + \delta_i t + u_{ijt}, \tag{1}$$

where q_{ijt} is per capita expenditure in constant prices on commodity i ($i = 1, \ldots, 5$) in country j ($j = 1, \ldots, 13$) in year t ($t = 0, 1, \ldots, 11$); μ_{jt} is total consumers' expenditure at constant prices per capita in country j in year t; p_{ijt} is the relative price of commodity i (that is, the implicit deflator for commodity i divided by the implicit deflator for total consumption) in country j in year t; and u_{ijt} is an error term, normally distributed with zero mean, whose variance is further specified below.

Despite its well-known defects, especially that of nonadditivity, this function remains without serious rivals in respect of goodness of fit, ease of estimation, and immediacy of interpretation. It is especially suitable in the combination of data from different countries because in most cases no exchange rate adjustment is necessary. On the other hand it does not lend itself easily to the dynamic modifications suggested by some of the results of this paper.

Variants of the basic equation (1) were obtained by the following three devices: (a) use of first differences; (b) separate regressions "within" and "between" countries (analysis of covariance); and (c) different assumptions about time trends, which are sometimes suppressed altogether.

The first of these is well known in econometrics; it has commonly been applied to avoid serial correlation in the residuals, but the results of this paper suggest that its implications are not merely statistical but also economic. The second technique is not new either, but it is particularly suitable for the combined use of contemporaneous time series because it permits a segregation of long-run and short-run effects. The "between" regressions take into account only the means over time of the variables for each country, whereas the "within" regressions are based on the annual deviations from each country's means. Trends are an old standby in econometrics; in the present context they are introduced not for their own merit (which is slight) but to clarify the meaning of the other estimates.

In all the regressions each annual observation has been weighted by the population of the country in the year concerned, on the assumption that the variance of u_{ijt} is proportional to the population of country j in year t; in other words, each observation has been regarded as the mean of a sample whose size is equal to the population. In the "between" regressions, therefore, the weight of each observation equals the total population of the country in all the years together. No attempt has been made to adjust for differences in reliability among the series for the several countries, since there is no basis for such an adjustment. Least squares estimation has been used throughout.

FIRST-DIFFERENCE ESTIMATION

We shall begin with the equations in first differences. The "within countries" version of (1) is

$$\Delta \log q_{ijt} - \overline{\Delta \log q_{ij}} = \beta_{iw} (\Delta \log \mu_{jt} - \overline{\Delta \log \mu_j}) \\ + \gamma_{iw} (\Delta \log p_{ijt} - \overline{\Delta \log p_{ij}}), \quad (2)$$

where the Δ's indicate first differences (thus $\Delta \log \mu_{jt} = \log \mu_{jt} - \log \mu_{j,t-1}$), and the barred terms are the means over all the years of the first differences for each country. These means themselves appear in the "between countries" equation

$$\overline{\Delta \log q_{ij}} = \beta_{ib} \overline{\Delta \log \mu_j} + \gamma_{ib} \overline{\Delta \log p_{ij}} + \delta_i. \quad (3)$$

It is to be noted that the barred terms correspond to the average rates of growth of the variables in each country during the period of observation.

The intercept α_i in (1) disappears when first differences are taken and the trend coefficient δ_i disappears upon subtracting the country means; however, δ_i appears as an intercept in (3) to allow for the possibility of a "general trend," common to all countries. There may not be any such trend, so (3) has also been fitted with $\delta_i = 0$. The β_i and γ_i need not be the same in equations (2) and (3) and therefore have distinguished subscripts b and w. Equation (2) has been estimated from 127 sets of annual deviations from the country means (13 sets were lost by differencing), and (3) has been estimated from the 13 sets of country means. The results are given in Table 1 (standard errors in brackets).

Most of the estimates in Table 1 look reasonable enough (for goodness of fit, see Table 2); they are usually many times as large as their

TABLE 1
Elasticities and Intercepts for First-Difference Model

Equation: Variable:	Within Countries Total Exp.	Within Countries Price	Between Countries Intercept	Between Countries Total Exp.	Between Countries Price	Between Countries ($\delta_i = 0$) Total Exp.	Between Countries ($\delta_i = 0$) Price
Food	.351 (.070)	−.161 (.075)	−.0044 (.0011)	1.145 (.111)	.277 (.122)	.744 (.071)	.234 (.183)
Clothing	1.574 (.132)	−.282 (.085)	−.0064 (.0023)	1.050 (.180)	−.476 (.262)	.713 (.177)	−.052 (.284)
Rent	.029 (.067)	−.114 (.106)	.0069 (.0038)	.753 (.486)	−.257 (.111)	1.545 (.221)	−.362 (.102)
Durables	3.919 (.266)	−.502 (.236)	.0012 (.0052)	1.831 (.628)	−1.397 (.765)	1.946 (.371)	−1.371 (.766)
Miscellaneous	.755 (.053)	−.388 (.086)	−.0011 (.0012)	1.035 (.130)	.424 (.185)	.934 (.060)	.455 (.181)

standard errors, and all but four of the price elasticities have the right sign.[1] There are considerable differences between the corresponding elasticities in the three equations, but before we discuss these a word should be said about the intercepts in the "between" equations. Two of these (for durables and miscellaneous) are not significant by any standard, and their omission does not change the other estimates substantially. The other three intercepts are more influential.

During the period of observation, total expenditure per capita rose nearly everywhere in nearly every year and was therefore correlated with time, so the intercept may have picked up some of the effect of changes in total expenditure. We see, in fact, that where the intercept is negative (in food, clothing, and miscellaneous), the elasticity with respect to total expenditure falls upon omission of the intercept; conversely, in the other two cases it rises. From this it would seem that the effect of total expenditure is more completely captured by the "between" equations without an intercept, which therefore merit primary interest.

An exception to this conclusion, however, may have to be made in the case of rent. In many countries rents have been strictly controlled, and the resulting housing shortage is alleviated only by building in excess

---
[1] It must be admitted, however, that the "within" price elasticities may be biased in the negative direction by the use of implicit deflators as prices. Thus, if in a particular year the data sources estimated the expenditure on food at current prices correctly but the expenditure at constant prices at a higher figure than it really was, then the implicit deflator will be too low, and the regression will attribute the spuriously high constant-price figure to price elasticity. The same result follows if the constant-price expenditure has been underestimated. On the other hand, if the current-price expenditure is too high and the constant-price figure correct, the implicit deflator will be too high, but since the current-price figure does not appear in the regression, this does not provide an offset to the bias due to errors in the constant-price figure.

of population growth. Expenditure on rent, therefore, cannot be adequately explained by total expenditure and price only; the intercept may serve to represent other determinants. This also means, of course, that the estimates for rent deserve less confidence than those for the other categories of consumption.

The most meaningful comparisons are those between the left-hand and the right-hand parts of Table 1. The elasticities with respect to total expenditure are greater in the "within" equation for clothing and durables, and in the "between" equation for food and miscellaneous (a category consisting mostly of services). Are these differences significant? The standard errors strongly suggest that they are, and this is borne out by the analysis of covariance in Table 2.

TABLE 2
Original and Residual Sums of Squares, with Analysis of Covariance for First-Difference Equations

	Degrees of Freedom	Food	Clothing	Rent	Durables	Misc.
Original s.s. total	127	.4359	1.7609	.7084	10.3738	.7677
Original s.s. within countries	114	.2043	1.4877	.1849	7.4504	.2914
Original s.s. between countries	13	.2316	.2732	.5235	2.9234	.4763
Residual s.s. total	125	.1983	.8152	.5027	3.1348	.1453
Residual s.s. within countries	112	.1552	.6061	.1687	2.4959	.1011
Residual s.s. between countries	11	.0185	.0388	.0801	.1693	.0086
Residual s.s. due to different regressions	2	.0247	.1702	.2539	.4696	.0356
Mean square within countries		.00139	.00542	.00151	.02225	.00090
Mean square due to different regressions		.01233	.08512	.12697	.23482	.01780
F-ratio		8.9	15.7	84.3	10.6	19.7

In this simple case the analysis of covariance reduces to an analysis of variance on the residuals from three equations: (2), (3), and a "total" equation in which it is assumed that $\beta_{iw} = \beta_{ib}$ and $\gamma_{iw} = \gamma_{ib}$ ($i = 1, \ldots, 5$); this amounts to treating the annual deviations from the country means in the same way as the country means themselves. By subtracting the residual sums of squares in the "within" and "between" equations from the residual sum of squares in the "total" equations, we find the reduction in residuals attributable to the differences in the regression coefficients. An F-test is then applied, with the residual sum of squares in the "within" equations as the basis for comparison. All the sums of squares are weighted as indicated previously, but, except for the "within" figures, they are not adjusted for the mean because there are no intercepts. Table 2 also gives the "original" sums of squares (i.e., the sums of squares of the q_{ijt}) so as to permit an evaluation of the goodness of fit.

For 2 and 112 degrees of freedom, F will exceed 7.3 only once in 1000 trials, so the observed F-ratios are all highly significant, and the "within-between" split in the equations is vindicated. Comparison of the original and residual sums of squares reveals that the fit is quite satisfactory in the "between" equations (except for rent), but much less so in the "within" equations.

Although it is conceivable that the differences between the "within" and "between" elasticities with respect to total expenditure have a purely statistical origin, their pattern suggests that they can also be explained in economic terms. Still disregarding rent (which actually fits the pattern too), we note that in both durables and clothing, consumers' inventories are likely to be important, whereas in food and services habit formation probably plays a part. Now consider the following demand equation:

$$q_i = a_i + b_i\mu + k_i s_i, \qquad (4)$$

where s is a measure of inventories or of the accumulated force of habit, and prices are ignored for simplicity. If the commodity concerned is a durable, k_i will be negative: the larger the initial stock s_i, the smaller new purchases q_i. Conversely, in the case of habit formation, k_i will be positive. The coefficient b_i is the short-run derivative with respect to total expenditure; it is a short-run coefficient because s_i is held constant. Equation (4) needs to be supplemented by the dynamic identity

$$\dot{s}_i = q_i + w_i s_i, \qquad (5)$$

where $\dot{s}_i$ is a derivative with respect to time, and w_i is a depreciation rate (normally negative). In long-run equilibrium, $\dot{s}_i = 0$ and hence

$$-w_i \tilde{s}_i = a_i + b_i\mu + k_i \tilde{s}_i, \qquad (6)$$

where the tilde indicates long-run equilibrium values. Together with (5), this implies

$$\tilde{q}_i = \frac{a_i w_i}{k_i + w_i} + \frac{b_i w_i}{k_i + w_i} \mu, \qquad (7)$$

which may be written more briefly as

$$\tilde{q}_i = \tilde{a}_i + \tilde{b}_i \mu. \qquad (8)$$

On comparing the short-run coefficient b_i and the long-run coefficient $\tilde{b}_i$, we see, assuming $w_i < 0$, that $b_i < \tilde{b}_i$ if $k_i < 0$, that is, if the ith commodity is durable; and $b_i > \tilde{b}_i$ if $k_i > 0$, that is, if the ith commodity is habit forming.

These remarks suggest that the "within" equations, being based on annual deviations from mean rates of change for each country, capture primarily short-run effects, and that the "between" equations are of a longer-run nature. We conclude that in demand analysis it is essential to specify the period of adjustment. *It is vain to search for "the" elasticity of demand.*

So far we have talked only about elasticities with respect to total expenditure. Actually, there is not much to say about the estimated price elasticities, some of which have the wrong sign in any case. They do not display any clear pattern.

ESTIMATION FROM ORIGINAL OBSERVATIONS

The basic equation (1) has also been estimated without the use of first differences, again "within countries" and "between countries," but without the trend coefficient δ_i. The "within" equation is identical with equation (2) except for the suppression of the Δ sign everywhere. The "between" equation, however, presents a new problem because the basic data are expressed in each country's national currency. This did not matter when first differences of logarithms were used because in that case the "between" equations involved only rates of change that are independent of the units of measurement. In the "within" equations without first differences but with logarithms, the units of measurement appear only in the country means and not in the deviations from these means. But in the "between" equations with logarithms, the problem cannot be sidestepped: we have to put the data in common units.

In international comparisons the use of official exchange rates, distorted though they often are, cannot always be avoided. Fortunately, for the data used in this paper, there is a more satisfactory solution. For 12 of the 13 countries in the sample, the German Statistical Office has calculated purchasing power parities by means of detail price comparisons (Statistisches Bundesamt, 1960). These parities are available not only for consumption as a whole, but also for nine categories of expenditure, which can be aggregated into the five categories used here. They are available for both the consumption pattern of the country concerned and for the German consumption pattern; the figures actually used were the geometric means of these two parities.

The purchasing power parities for individual categories of consumption have been calculated only for one year, which in every case was a year within the period of observation. This year was consequently used to translate the national currency figures into German marks of 1954; the remaining years were obtained from the national price data that have been used throughout the analysis.

We may point out, in passing, that the differences between official exchange rates and purchasing power parities are often substantial. To mention two extreme cases: when price comparisons were made in 1953, the U.S. dollar was overvalued by 30 percent and the Dutch guilder undervalued by 25 percent, both in relation to the German mark. In individual categories of consumption the deviations are sometimes even greater. Despite the general overvaluation of the dollar, for instance, such items as durables are relatively cheap in the United States.

After the conversion into German marks, the form of the "between" equations is identical to (1), except that all the variables are now means over the period of observation. The results will be found in Table 3,

TABLE 3
Elasticities and Correlations Coefficient for Model Without First Differences

Equation: Elasticity or R^2:	Within Countries			Between Countries		
	Total Exp.	Price	R^2	Total Exp.	Price	R^2
Food.............	.717	.076	.910	.452	−.399	.941
	(.021)	(.048)		(.040)	(.222)	
Clothing..........	.712	.028	.580	.890	−.532	.953
	(.102)	(.136)		(.159)	(.588)	
Rent.............	1.261	−.274	.715	1.686	−.586	.906
	(.085)	(.041)		(.201)	(.135)	
Durables..........	2.471	−.012	.873	1.739	−1.107	.968
	(.137)	(.220)		(.383)	(.766)	
Miscellaneous......	1.001	.297	.954	1.102	−.936	.989
	(.026)	(.077)		(.043)	(.380)	

together with the corresponding. R^2. The intercepts in the "between" equations have been left out of the table. The "within" equations are based on 134 sets of annual deviations from country means and the "between" equations on 12 sets of country means.

Except for three of the "within" price elasticities, the estimates of Table 3 again look very reasonable.[2] The "between" results are especially satisfactory, which may be attributed to the wide range of incomes and prices covered by the 12 countries. As noted earlier, the results for rent do not merit much attention and are given only for the sake of completeness.

---

[2] The remarks about bias in footnote 1 apply here as well. The fact that in this case three of the "within" price elasticities are positive suggests that the bias may not be too serious. It should not be forgotten, however, that all equations have been fitted by (weighted) least squares. Since prices are almost certainly more influenced by supply factors than are total expenditures, least-squares bias may also account for the unacceptable results. The principal obstacle to the use of more sophisticated estimation procedures in demand analysis is the lack of a well-developed theory of supply. A wrongly specified supply equation may be worse than none at all.

82   Readings in Managerial Economics

Confining our comparison to the elasticities with respect to total expenditure, we see that the "within" elasticities are not as different from the "between" elasticities as they were in Table 1. The standard errors suggest that, except for food, the differences are not very significant. Moreover, the pattern of the differences agrees only partly with that of Table 1, the exceptions being provided by food and clothing. Interestingly enough, nearly all the total expenditure elasticities in Table 3 are closer to the "between" elasticities in Table 1 than to the "within" elasticities. If our interpretation of the first-difference estimates is correct, therefore, the estimates of Table 3 are of a relatively long-run nature, the "within" estimates perhaps less so than the "between" estimates. Food, however, presents a rather puzzling exception.[3]

ESTIMATES FOR SEPARATE COUNTRIES

To conclude this essay we present some evidence on the heterogeneity of demand functions among countries. The importance of this question to the combined use of time series from different countries was noted at the beginning of this paper.

The data used are the same as in Table 3, except that Greece is now again in the sample since there is no need for conversion to a common currency. A "within" equation has been calculated for each of the 13 countries and for all combined. The results, with the total weight for each country, are given in Table 4, and the analysis of covariance in Table 5.

As one would expect, the elasticities for individual countries in Table 4 show considerable variation. The price elasticities in particular show no uniformity at all; the elasticities with respect to total expenditure are rather more consistent. Some of the very peculiar estimates (e.g.,

---

[3] The "within" equations have also been supplemented with a time trend, thus providing a counterpart to the middle part of table I. As before, the intercorrelation between total expenditure and time is high ($r = .90$), casting considerable doubt on the results, which are briefly as follows:

Coeff. of:	Total Exp.	Price	Time
Food	.875	.099	−.0183
Clothing	1.096	−.329	−.0613
Rent	.157	−.136	.1016
Durables	2.830	−.183	−.0571
Miscellaneous	1.046	.231	−.0044

The time coefficients are conceptually comparable to the intercepts in table I; both show the annual increase in the logarithm (to the base 10) of q_i ($i = 1, \ldots, 5$). Those given in this footnote are all implausibly large, but their signs agree for the most part with those in table I.

TABLE 4
Elasticities for Individual Countries and for All Countries Combined

Country	Total Weight	Food Total Exp.	Food Price	Clothing Total Exp.	Clothing Price	Rent Total Exp.	Rent Price	Durables Total Exp.	Durables Price	Miscellaneous Total Exp.	Miscellaneous Price
Austria	77	.742	−.535	.636	.017	.450	−.199	2.428	−.943	1.114	−.580
Belgium	106	.917	−.686	.055	.323	.330	.053	2.233	.438	1.126	−.106
Denmark	53	.482	−.529	.347	.029	.847	.522	3.676	.346	.868	−.078
France	474	.677	−.156	1.469	.531	.871	−.165	2.531	−.146	1.041	−.061
Greece	51	.729	−.344	1.168	−.876	1.666	−.119	1.804	−1.132	−1.283	−.941
Italy	525	.782	−.262	.593	−.193	.695	−.102	2.722	.413	1.343	−.319
Luxemburg	2	1.147	−1.020	.153	−.106	.592	5.689	1.812	−.807	1.063	−.286
Netherlands	117	.574	.595	1.810	.466	.322	.357	1.992	−2.188	.850	−.292
Norway	37	.779	−.198	1.378	−.168	1.992	−.277	.801	−2.209	.562	.439
Sweden	86	.381	.060	−.944	−1.810	1.567	−.332	2.867	.521	1.276	−.860
United Kingdom	612	.728	.124	1.035	−.091	.658	−.188	3.005	−1.456	.811	.245
Canada	182	.689	−.292	−.086	−.376	1.266	−.091	3.438	.964	.902	−.355
United States	1937	.319	−.339	.779	.422	1.667	.076	2.026	1.088	1.108	−.059
Combined	4258	.714	.083	.705	−.103	1.285	−.288	2.363	−.124	1.006	.238

TABLE 5
Analysis of Covariance on "Within" Regressions (Without First Differences) for Separate Countries and Combined

	Degrees of Freedom	Food	Clothing	Rent	Durables	Misc.
Original s.s.	140	2.83463	4.17313	5.53382	35.45320	6.05435
Residual s.s. combined	125	.25123	1.08811	1.41257	4.92819	.24742
Residual s.s. separate	101	.10765	.55165	.56933	2.63335	.15081
Residual s.s. due to different regressions	24	.14358	.53646	.84324	2.29484	.09661
Mean square separate		.00107	.00546	.00564	.02607	.00149
Mean square due to different regressions		.00598	.02235	.03514	.09562	.00403
F-ratio		5.6	4.1	6.2	3.7	2.7

for clothing in Sweden) are due to multicollinearity, which is more likely to be a problem in individual time series than in a combination of time series. It is somewhat disconcerting to find, however, that the estimates for the combined series are not always more reasonable than the majority of the individual estimates. Thus the combined price elasticities for food and miscellaneous are positive, even though for each commodity nearly all individual price elasticities are negative.

The analysis of covariance in Table 5 indicates that by and large the differences among the elasticities in the individual countries are statistically significant. The percent significance level for F with 24 and 101 degrees is about 1.95, and the observed F's are well above this, though they are not as strikingly significant as in Table 3.

Should we infer from this that the combined use of time series from different countries is unjustified? I do not think so. While it may be true that for individual countries more accurate estimates can often be obtained by using only that country's data, there is also a considerable risk of arriving at nonsensical results, as Table 4 amply demonstrates, at least for the elasticities with respect to total expenditure. For many purposes (for instance, when elasticities are needed, but no good data are available) it is useful to have estimates that reflect a wide range of evidence. The situation is similar in cross-section analysis.

It is also true, on the other hand, that the methods demonstrated in this paper need improvement. The difficulty of obtaining good estimates of price elasticities is especially challenging. The dynamic considerations mentioned earlier also require further elaboration.

7. Factors Affecting the Purchase Value of New Houses[*]

L. JAY ATKINSON

SECTION I—INTRODUCTION AND SUMMARY

Why do some families pay more than others for their new homes? Income is obviously an important reason but what other factors are also important? Are the age, occupation, and education of the household head—to cite a few characteristics—of any significance? If so, how are they related to the amount a family pays for a new home? And how do changes over time in relative prices and credit conditions affect the amount paid?

. . . . .

Given the number of units that may be demanded in the future, it becomes necessary to determine average value per unit if projections of aggregate value are required. Although projections of average unit value were obtained by extending past trends, this technique did not provide much in the way of analytical content. This report analyzes unpublished data and yields a number of insights into the demand factors that give rise to variations in the purchase price of new houses. No projections are shown.

Cross-Section Data

Except in the last section, which is concerned with a time series analysis, most of the data for the present report are cross-sectional and are from the 1960 Census of Housing. The data, which are based on a large sample of buyers of new homes, include an extensive list of characteristics pertaining to the structure and to the household.

The article provides several cross-tabulations that show how the value of a newly built house varies by income class and by other characteristics of the household. Although the sample is a good-sized one, with many

---

[*] *The Survey of Current Business,* vol. 46, no. 8 (August 1966), pp. 20–34.

cells containing a fairly large number of observations, there are obvious limits to the number of cross-classifications that can be shown and readily interpreted. In order to lay bare the net relationships—that is, the relationship between house value and each of several characteristics of the household, with all other factors held constant—the individual household data have been analyzed by means of multiple regression. The regression analysis is the heart of this report. The basic regression took this general form: The value of a newly built house acquired by a family or individual depends upon the current income of the household; the age, sex, race, education, occupation, and marital status or length of time married of the household head; and the location of the housing unit. Some modifications of this regression were also explored.

A feature of this study is its treatment of a large number of nonincome variables, for which data have not ordinarily been available until recently. The use of such data in statistical analysis had been limited not only because they were scarce but also because many of the variables were nonnumerical. The development in the last few years of new statistical techniques involving the use of "dummy" variables and the availability of large computers have overcome these obstacles.

In addition to the analysis of nonincome influences, this article puts considerable emphasis on the estimation of income elasticity—the percentage change in purchase price or value associated with that in income. Tests were made to determine if income elasticity is constant throughout the full range of income.

Limitations of Cross-Section Estimates

Although the analysis is based on a rich body of statistical data, the cross-section study has certain limitations:

(1) It applies to a single period. The stability of the relationships shown can be tested only with observations for other periods.

(2) The analysis omits a number of variables that on a priori grounds would appear to be significant in accounting for variation in house value. Some of these omitted variables, such as changes over time in prices and financing terms (including downpayments, amortization period, and interest rates), are for all practical purposes inherent limitations of a single-period cross-sectional approach. For others, such as assets held by the household and the prices of comparable accommodations afforded by used houses, the data were not available.

(3) Although the estimated regression coefficients are statistically significant at the 1 percent level, they have sizable errors; this reflects both sampling variability and intercorrelation among the independent variables.

(4) Certain biases are characteristic of regression computations from

cross-section data, as has been widely noted. One type of bias is related to the concept of income that is appropriate for calculating elasticity.[1]

Time Series Analysis

The final section of this paper uses time series data to analyze the factors influencing house value. Ideally, the results of time series analysis could serve as a check on the cross-section results and would permit the introduction of variables such as price and credit terms that were necessarily excluded in the cross-section approach.

In practice, the time series analysis has serious shortcomings. The various nonincome factors (age, education, etc.) used in the cross-section analysis are not available in usable time series. The few series that are available—on house value, price, income, and credit terms—are deficient in many respects. Moreover, there is a high degree of correlation among the independent variables, so that it is difficult to isolate and appraise their separate relationship to house value. An important characteristic of the available time series is that they are highly aggregative—annual averages for the United States—in contrast to the cross-section data, which are on a household basis.

In the analysis of many other types of problems—consumption functions, for example—estimates based on aggregated time series have usually been considerably different from those derived from cross-section data, and the two types of estimates have seldom been reconciled. In this study, such differences are encountered, and no reconciliation has been achieved.

Principal Findings

Points 1 through 5 apply to the cross-section analysis.

(1) All of the independent variables accounted for about half of the total variation in the price paid for new homes.

(2) As was expected, income was the single most important variable, accounting for almost 50 percent of the explained variation in house value.

(3) With all of the other explanatory variables held constant and with the highest and lowest income groups excluded, the cross-section estimates of income elasticity ranged from 0.41 to 0.47. This means

---

[1] Such possible biases have been discussed in numerous publications. Many of these are cited by Margaret G. Reid in *Income and Housing* (University of Chicago Press, 1963). This study and others suggest that estimates of income elasticity for housing derived from cross-section data may be too low. See also R. F. Muth, "The Demand for Nonfarm Housing," in A. C. Harberger (ed.), *The Demand for Durable Goods* (University of Chicago Press, 1960).

that a difference of 10 percent in income was associated with a difference of around 4.1 to 4.7 percent in the value of a newly purchased house. These net regression results were not much different from the simple regression estimate of income elasticity when only income was related to the value of a new house.

(4) The income elasticity estimate was found to be constant over an extremely wide range of income. Other investigations of income elasticity have often found that elasticity declined as income increased.

(5) Several nonincome variables had an important influence upon the variation in house values in the cross-section analysis. For example, with all other factors held constant, an increase in age, years married, or amount of education of the household head raises the value of new homes acquired. Again, with all other factors held constant, homes acquired by white household heads have a higher value than those acquired by nonwhites, and homes in the North and West have a higher value than those in the South.

The following points are from the time series analysis:

(6) When house value was related to family income in a simple relationship based on aggregated data, the estimate of income elasticity was around 0.8. The (net) income elasticity rose to approximately 1.0 when variables for credit terms and prices were added to the estimating equation.

(7) The price elasticity for new houses was estimated to be less than unity, with the usual inverse relationship between price and real value of house purchased. An inverse relationship was also found between house value and a credit variable in the form of monthly mortgage payments, i.e., the lower the monthly payments, the higher the value of house acquired.

The remainder of this article is organized as follows: Section II presents the cross-section data and some preliminary cross-section relationships. In the third and longest section, the data are analyzed by means of multiple regression to show how the value of new houses is related to the income of the household and a series of nonincome characteristics. The fourth section deals with the constancy of the estimated income elasticity throughout the income range and also modifies the cross-section estimate of income elasticity. The fifth and final section is an analysis, based on time series, of income elasticity and the effect of changes in prices and credit on house value.

SECTION II—THE DATA AND THEIR TREATMENT

Most of the basic data used in this study were part of a systematic 1-in-1,000 sample of the 53 million U.S. households enumerated in the 1960 Census. For each sample household, the Census Bureau made avail-

7. Factors Affecting the Purchase Value of New Houses

able on magnetic tapes about 100 characteristics, of which 15 were selected as the most relevant for this analysis. Information from Census tabulations and housing studies was utilized in selecting the most appropriate characteristics.

For most of the characteristics except house value and income (e.g., age, education, years married), the Census designations are self-explanatory. The value of the house is that reported to the Census Bureau in answer to the question "What is the current [spring 1960] market value of your house?" Although a householder's appraisal of value may be rather imprecise, especially for older houses, it seemed reasonable to suppose that for newly acquired houses the respondent would give the purchase price. An independent check confirmed this assumption.

Income is measured as the total money income of all members of the household in the preceding year (1959) as reported to the Census Bureau.

As the first step in this study, the entire Census sample of 53,000 households was classified according to "tenure type." Tenure type desig-

TABLE 1
Number of Households Classified by Tenure Type, April 1960
(thousands)

	Number	Percent distribution
Total households	**52,875**	**100.0**
Owners	**32,742**	**61.9**
Buyers, 1955–60:		
Houses built 1959–60	1,398	2.6
Houses built 1955–58	4,677	8.9
Houses built before 1955	6,457	12.2
Other owners	20,210	38.2
Renters	**20,133**	**38.1**
In one-to-two-family houses	12,458	23.6
Built 1955–60	883	1.7
Built before 1955	11,575	21.9
In three-or-more-family structures	7,675	14.5
Built 1959–60	159	.3
Built 1955–58	392	.7
Built before 1955	7,124	13.5

Source: U.S. Department of Commerce, Office of Business Economics. Universe estimates based on tabulations from 1-in-1,000 sample of households, U.S. Census of Housing, 1960.

nates certain features of the housing unit—whether it is owner-occupied or rented, when it was built, and the number of units in the structure. The various tenure-type classifications, which were derived from the 1960 Census data, are shown in table 1. The portion of the sample that had recently bought new homes constitutes the main set of (cross-section) data analyzed in this article. There were 1,398 observations in this group, of which 1,155 had complete records.

. . . . .

Some Characteristics of New House Buyers

Although this paper does not analyze the factors that influence the decision to buy (or not to buy) a new house, some background information on this subject may be of interest. Chart 1 illustrates the relationship between the purchase of a new home and a few of the characteristics considered here. It shows a percentage distribution of buyers of new houses according to each of three characteristics—age, education, and region. For comparison, similar data are presented for all households in the United States as of April 1960.

Among those households that had recently bought new homes, the 10-year age brackets 25 to 34 and 35 to 44 accounted for 70 percent of the total. Those under 25 and those 55 or older accounted for only a small portion of buyers. The age distribution of buyers was quite different from the age distribution of all households. Relative to all household heads (male), buyers were more common for each of the age groups under 45 and less common for each of the older groups.

The amount of education of the household head was directly related to the probability that he would buy a new house. Those whose education did not exceed seven years were only half as likely to be new buyers as all household heads; those who graduated from college were twice as likely to be new buyers.

As of 1960, the South and the West had higher-than-average proportions of new house buyers relative to all households; the North Central region was a little below average and the Northeast considerably below average.

Some Preliminary Relationships

Chart 2 suggests some of the ways that house value is related to income and nonincome factors. The top panel shows the relationship between house value and income for three broad age classifications. It indicates three main points: There is a direct relationship between value and income for each of the three classifications; the slopes of the three lines are about the same; and for any given income, there is some difference in the average house value for the different age groups.

The middle panel, in which households are classified by educational attainment of the household head, also illustrates the direct relationship between house value and income. There is less uniformity in the slopes of the lines than there was for the age classifications. Finally, at any

CHART 1
Percent Distribution of Buyers of New Houses Built 1959—First Quarter 1960 Compared with All Households

AGE OF MALE HEAD OF HOUSEHOLD

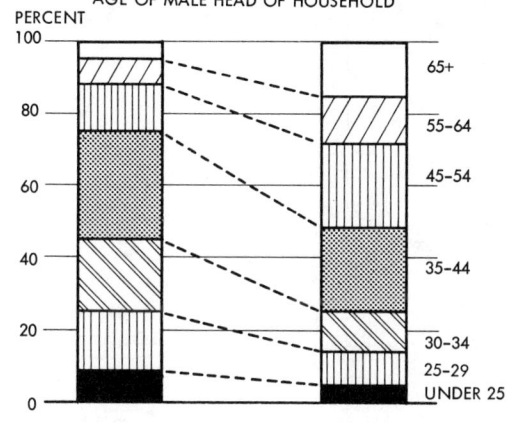

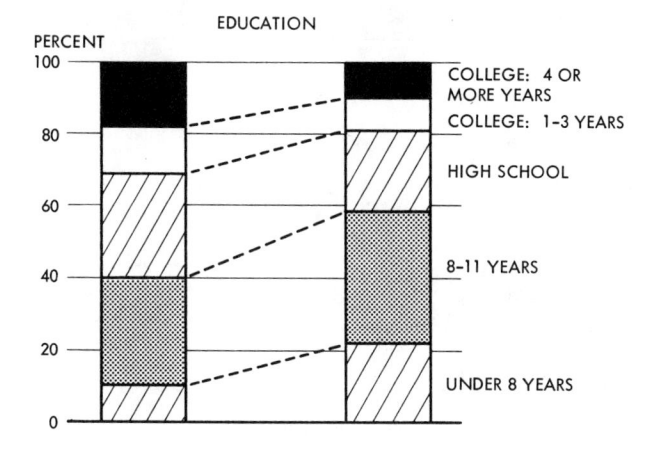

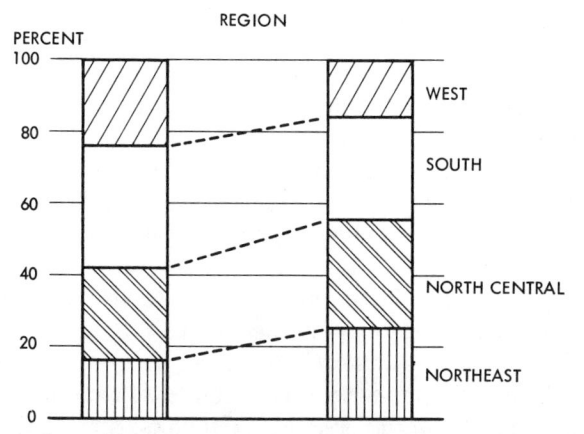

- 65+
- 55-64
- 45-54
- 35-44
- 30-34
- 25-29
- UNDER 25

EDUCATION

- COLLEGE: 4 OR MORE YEARS
- COLLEGE: 1-3 YEARS
- HIGH SCHOOL
- 8-11 YEARS
- UNDER 8 YEARS

REGION

- WEST
- SOUTH
- NORTH CENTRAL
- NORTHEAST

Source: U.S. Department of Commerce, Office of Business Economics; Basic Data: Census 66-8-7.

CHART 2
Relationship between House Value and Income, Buyers of New Houses Built 1959—First Quarter 1960

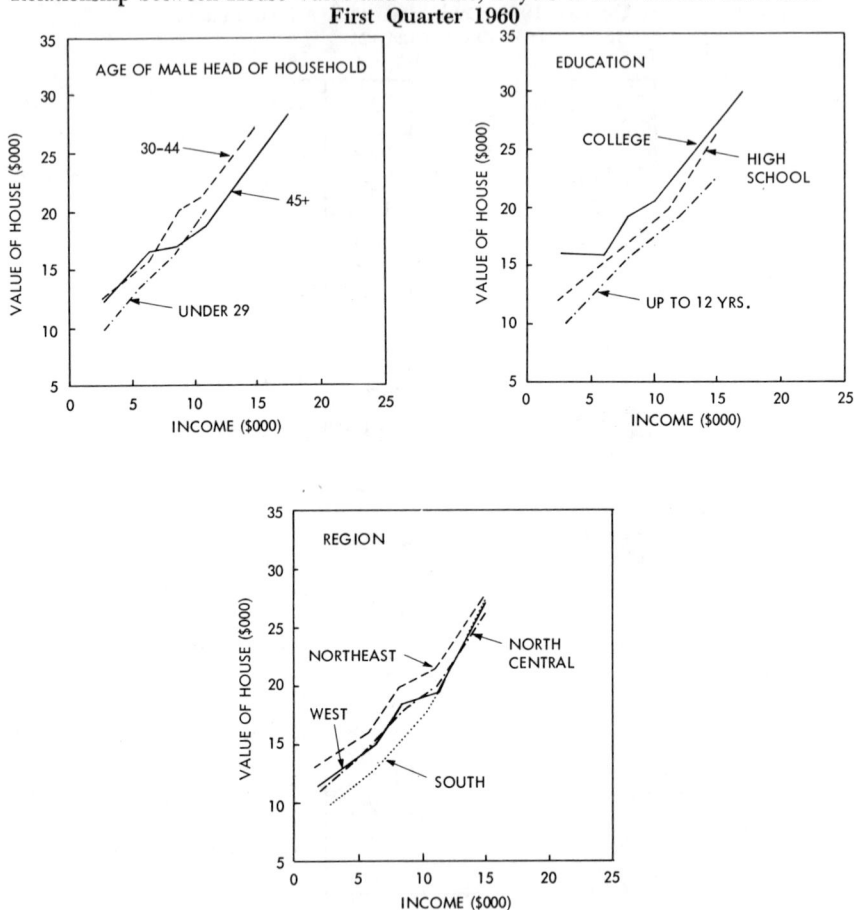

Source: U.S. Department of Commerce, Office of Business Economics; Basic Data: Census 66-8-8.

given income level, house value appears to vary directly with the level of education of the household head.

The direct value-income relation also shows up when the data are classified by region. However, some clearcut regional differences are apparent with respect to both the slope of the lines and their level. The slope is greatest in the South and least in the Northeast. Throughout most of the income range, house values for any given income level are highest in the Northeast and lowest in the South.

As was indicated earlier, these relationships between house value and income, with one other characteristic held constant, have been presented only to give a taste of the discussion that follows. Their interpretation is deferred to the section dealing with the comprehensive regression analysis, in which both gross and net relationships are considered.

SECTION III—REGRESSION ANALYSIS

. . . . .

Form of Relationship

In the general form of the regression, the value of the house (dependent variable) is a function of income and eight other characteristics of the household or the household head: region, size of place, size of Standard Metropolitan Statistical Area (SMSA) and location within the area, age and sex, length of time married, race, education, and finally, occupation.

In the regression equation shown in this section, the value of the house and income are numerical variables. All the other variables are classified in nonnumerical categories and are treated in the regressions as "dummy" variables, even though some, such as years of education, were originally reported by the household in numerical form.

As would be expected, there was a question as to the appropriate form of the relationship between house value and income. On the basis of past studies, there seemed to be some preference for a log form—i.e., relative differences in income are related to relative difference in house value. However, four forms were calculated: log-log, linear-linear, log-linear, and linear-log. The two mixed forms yielded no improvement in fit and are not shown in the article. There was little difference between the results calculated by the log form and those calculated by the linear form, although the log form accounted for somewhat more of the variation in house value (significant at the 1 percent level).

Summary results of the log equation (#3) are presented first. Then, for the sake of simplicity, a systematic explanation will be made for the linear equation (#1).

Summary of Results: Log Equation (#3)

Table 2 gives summary results for the log equation (#3) and shows the relative importance of each of the nine characteristics in explaining the variation in house value. Together, the nine independent variables in the equation accounted for 47 percent of the relative variation in the value of new house acquired. ($R^2 = 0.47$). For time series correlations of highly aggregated data, an R^2 with this value would be unacceptable, but for cross-section data in which the unit of observation

TABLE 2
Analysis of Variation in Value of New Houses
Log Equation (#3)

	Sum of squares	Percent of total	Percent of total explained
Total.	56.480	100	...
Variation explained by regression.	26.683	47	100
Variation attributable to:			
Location.	(6.570)	(12)	(25)
Region.	4.511	8	17
Size of place.	.141	(*)	1
Size of SMSA.	1.918	3	7
Age and sex.	2.124	4	8
Marital status.	.842	1	3
Race.	.495	1	2
Education.	4.304	8	16
Occupation.	.966	2	4
Income.	11.382	20	43
Variation not explained by regression.	29.797	53	...

* Less than ½ of 1 percent.
Note: Detail may not add to totals because of rounding.

is the household, these results appear to be very satisfactory by the usual standard of generally comparable analyses.

Income was by far the most important variable and accounted for 20 percent of the total variation. Each of the other characteristics also made a significant contribution (at the 1 percent level). Large influences upon variation in house value were exerted by two of the three location variables—region and size of SMSA—as well as by education and age and sex of the head. Smaller but important effects were associated with occupation, length of time married, and race. However, the size of the urban area in which the home was located was not very important. As a group, the nonincome variables accounted for 27 percent of the total variation in the value of new houses or over half of that explained by the regression. On the basis of results obtained from similar studies, it is surprising that the nonincome variables accounted for so much variation.

Income Effects

As has already been indicated, income was the most important explanatory variable. In the simple regression between value and income, income accounted for 30 percent of the variation in the value of new houses. As the nonincome variables were introduced into the regression equation, they lowered the net variation explained by income because of the correlation between income and the other "independent" variables. When all the variables were included in the regression equation, the contribution of income was reduced by one third, from 30 to 20 percent. Although the correlation among the independent variables is substantial, as was expected, the explanatory influence of income still remaining is considerable.

In the log form of the equation, the regression coefficient for income is an estimate of the income elasticity for new house value. In the gross or simple regression, the income coefficient was 0.42; that is, differences of 10 percent in income were associated with difference of 4.2 percent in house value. This result is consistent with a large number of estimates that have been made in similar analyses of cross-section data. As each of the other significant variables was introduced into the equation, all previously calculated regression coefficients were affected to some extent. The regression coefficient on income declined (with only an insignificant exception), reaching a terminal value of 0.28 when all the variables had been included. A modification of the regression calculation, which is discussed in section IV, results in an increase in the estimate of the net income elasticity to the 0.41–0.47 range mentioned in the introduction.

The Linear Multiple Regression (#1)

The preceding discussion has shown the relative importance of each of the nine independent variables in accounting for the variation in the value of new houses, and has given one estimate of the income elasticity coefficient. The next step is the consideration of the regression coefficients for the nonincome characteristics, using the results of the linear equation.[2] Each of the variables is discussed in turn. For each characteristic or variable, the coefficients are shown as deviations from the mean, so that for a characteristic as a whole the weighted sum of the deviations is zero. Chart 3 provides a general view of the results. It shows gross differences in house value (expressed as deviations from the mean) for each of several nonincome variables and then gives the corresponding net differences obtained from equation #1. These gross and net differences are discussed in detail in the rest of this section.

Location

Data from the cross-classifications suggest that region may have an important influence on the average value of new houses. For each region, column 1 of the summary table shows the gross difference from the U.S. average house value. Average value is least in the South and highest

[2] In the linear equation, the independent variables account for 42 percent of the variation in the dependent variable.

96   Readings in Managerial Economics

CHART 3
Gross and Net Difference in House Value from U.S. Average New Houses Built 1959-First Quarter 1960

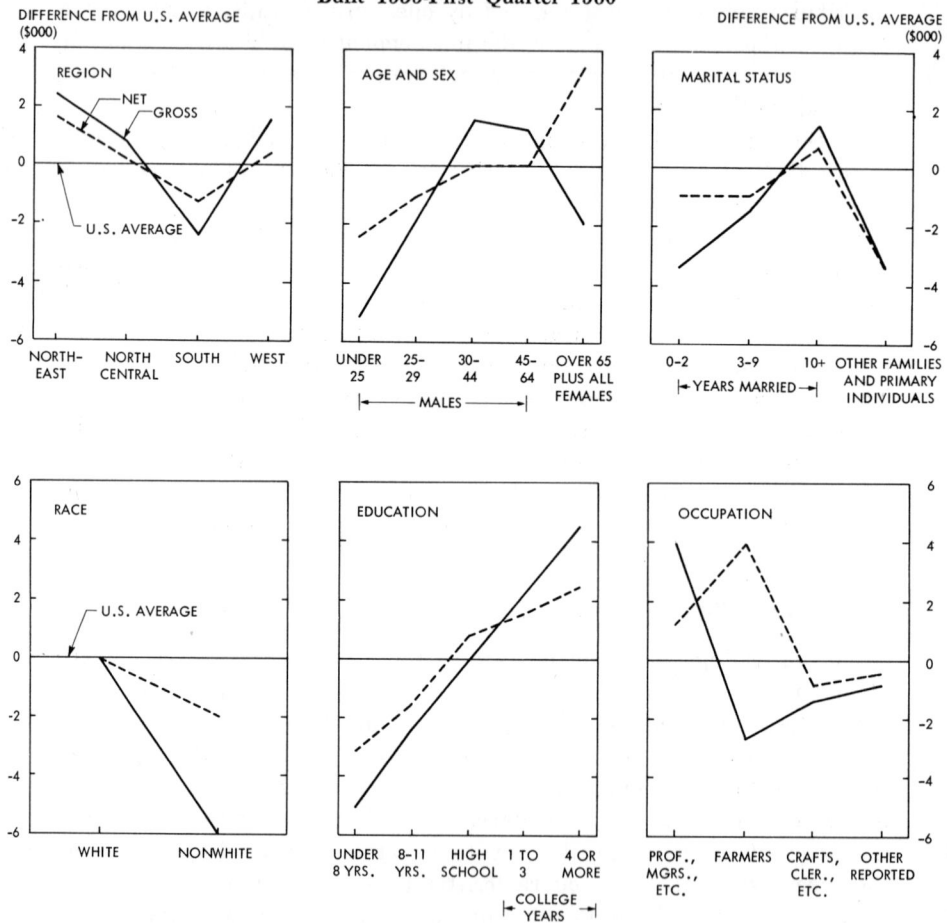

Note: Net based on linear regression equation (#1).
Source: U.S. Department of Commerce, Office of Business Economics; Basic Data: Census 66-8-9.

in the Northeast and West, with the North Central not far above the U.S. average. However, these gross differences in value may reflect not only purely regional differences but also differences associated with regional variations in income, size of city, and age, race, education, and occupation of the household head, as well as factors not included in the regression equation. The net differences among regions, with the influence of all other characteristics included in the regression equation held constant, are shown in column 4. Because income has an important influence on house value and because there are major regional differences in income, the adjustment for income is shown separately in column 2; gross differences adjusted for income are shown in column 3.

Influence of Region on Variation in Average Value of New Houses

Region	Gross Differences from U.S. Average	Adjustment for Differences Attributable to Income	Gross Differences Adjusted for Differences in Income	Net Differences from U.S. Average
	Col. 1	Col. 2	Col. 3 = Col. 1 + Col. 2	Col. 4
Northeast	$2,336	−$166	$2,170	$1,790
North Central	596	−77	519	565
South	−2,384	510	−1,874	−1,406
West	1,726	−664	1,062	486

Part of the gross variation in each of the four regions is obviously attributable to regional differences in income. The adjustment for income difference is largest for the West, where incomes are well above the national average, and nearly as large (in the opposite direction) for the South, where incomes are below average; for the other two regions, the income adjustment is small. When adjustment is made for the differences among regions in all of the other characteristics, there remain fairly sizable net differences in house value that are associated with region. On a net basis, average value is also least in the South and highest in the Northeast; however, the West, like the North Central region, is only moderately above the U.S. average.

There may be several reasons for the large net differences in house value in the South and Northeast. In the South, they may reflect lower construction costs for a house of specified characteristics, less elaborate heating systems needed because of the milder climate, and lower land values. The opposite conditions may give rise to deviations in the opposite direction in the Northeast.

Two other locational factors were considered in the regression equation and are mentioned very briefly here. First, classification was made according to "size of place"—into rural nonfarm areas, small urban areas, and large urban areas. The net differences in house value for these classifications were rather small, although the variance of the three as a group was statistically significant (at the 1 percent level). A more elaborate classification pertaining to Standard Metropolitan Statistical Areas (SMSAs) was more successful. For households located outside SMSAs, net values were considerably below average (−$1,443). Net differences above the U.S. average were largest for central cities in SMSAs of over 1 million population ($4,273) and well above the U.S. average in suburban (noncentral city) locations in such SMSAs ($1,488).

They were only a little above average in SMSAs of less than 1 million, both in the central city ($171) and in the suburbs ($206).

Age and Sex

It was apparent from the cross-tabulations that the value of new houses purchased by households with male heads increased directly with age in the younger age groups (under age 35), reached a maximum in the intermediate age groups, and declined for the oldest age groups. A similar pattern prevailed for income in relation to age. Therefore, the question posed was whether there was a net association between age and value of house, that is, one not attributable to differences in income or in other nonincome variables.

The adjustment for income (column 2) is fairly sizable (on a relative basis) for the first three age groups in the table and very large for the two oldest groups. Still, the broad pattern that can be seen in column 1 is evident after the income adjustment (column 3). When allowance is made for all of the other explanatory variables, appreciable net differences in house value associated with age remain only for the two youngest groups and the oldest age group, which also includes all female household heads. On a net basis, the gross differences virtually disappear for the two intermediate age groups, 30–44 and 45–64, and are considerably reduced for the two youngest age groups. For the remaining group (males 65 and over and all females), house value is substantially above

Influence of Age and Sex on Variation in Average Value of New Houses

Age and Sex of Household Head	Gross Differences from U.S. Average	Adjustment for Differences Attributable to Income	Gross Differences Adjusted for Differences in Income	Net Differences from U.S. Average
	Col. 1	Col 2	Col. 3 = Col. 1 + Col. 2	Col. 4
Male under 25 years	-$5,194	$1,340	-$3,854	-$2,361
25–29 years	-2,094	673	-1,421	-1,139
30–44 years	1,367	-349	1,018	-4
45–64 years	1,047	-995	52	138
65 years and older and all females	-2,053	1,729	-324	3,373

average on a net basis—just the reverse of the pattern evident on a gross basis.

Why, after allowance is made for income and other factors, do young household heads buy houses that are less expensive than average while the oldest heads acquire more expensive houses? If it were mainly a question of anticipated family needs and income expectations, one might have looked for just the opposite results: relatively high house values for the young and relatively low values for the old. An influence more powerful than income prospects and anticipated family needs appears to be at work here. Net asset holdings may explain the net results observable in the table. Recent studies have shown a strong positive correlation between net asset holdings and age. Thus, the effect of asset holdings, a variable that could not be directly measured in the present study, may be indirectly reflected in the net variation associated with age.

Marital Status

In the consideration of marital status, comparisons were made for couples married for various lengths of time and for the small number of other households (families with only one spouse present and primary individuals) that had acquired new homes. These "other households" are not discussed because they are a rather small group and contain several different household types.

For married couples, the gross data show a positive association be-

Influence of Marital Status on Variation in Average Value of New Houses

Marital Status of Household Head	Gross Differences from U.S. Average	Adjustment for Differences Attributable to Income	Gross Differences Adjusted for Differences in Income	Net Differences from U.S. Average
	Col. 1	Col. 2	Col. 3 = Col. 1 + Col. 2	Col. 4
Husband-wife married:				
0–2 years	−$3,244	$975	−$2,269	−$983
3–9 years	−1,374	526	−848	−948
10 years and over	1,473	−595	878	994
Other families and primary individuals	−3,201	1,733	−1,468	−3,165

tween years married and purchase price. Differences in income account for roughly one third of the differences in house value. When all other factors are allowed for, a further sizable reduction is made in the large negative deviation for the group married two years or less, but little change occurs for the other two groups. On a net basis, those married less than 10 years buy houses about $1,000 below average and those married longer about $1,000 above average.

It was recognized that the length of time married would be correlated with the age of the household head. Nevertheless, a significant reduction in the variation in house value was accounted for by the length of time married, although the reduction was considerably smaller than that associated with age and sex of the head. It may well be that the years-married variable, like the age variable, reflects the influence of asset holdings on the purchase price of a house.

Race

Nonwhites acquired homes that were valued at $5,000 less than the U.S. average. Of this difference, one fourth was associated with lower income, and nearly one half (in addition) with other nonincome factors in the equation; the remaining portion was associated with race, as is shown below. The net difference may reflect the effects of the less advantageous financing terms available to Negro house buyers or the other difficulties Negroes face in buying houses in line with their incomes and assets.

Influences of Race on Variations in Average Value of New Houses

Race	Gross Differences from U.S. Average	Adjustment for Differences Attributable to Income	Gross Differences Adjusted for Differences in Income	Net Differences from U.S. Average
	Col. 1	Col. 2	Col. 3 = Col. 1 + Col. 2	Col. 4
White	$246	$11	$257	$75
Nonwhite	−5,824	1,453	−4,371	−1,804

Education

The education of the household head was an important influence on value. The net variation associated with education accounted for one sixth of the variance explained by all the variables.

As the table shows, gross differences in value varied directly and widely with differences in education. The corresponding variation in income accounted for about one fourth of the gross variation. The other nonincome variables brought about a similar reduction in variation for those with the least and the most education but were not important for those who had some high school or one to three years of college education.

Influence of Education on Variations in Average Value of New Houses

Education of Household Head	Gross Differences from U.S. Average	Adjustment for Differences Attributable to Income	Gross Differences Adjusted for Differences in Income	Net Differences from U.S. Average
	Col. 1	Col. 2	Col. 3 = Col. 1 + Col. 2	Col. 4
Under 8 years	−$4,944	$1,113	−$3,831	−$3,092
8-11 years	−2,124	623	−1,501	−1,503
High school	246	−96	150	628
College, 1-3 years	2,216	−586	1,630	1,455
College, 4 or more years	4,646	−1,154	3,492	2,352

The net differences in house value associated with education may well reflect different income prospects. As compared with the less educated, household heads who have graduated from college are likely to acquire homes that are more expensive in relation to their incomes because they have better prospects for rising income throughout their working lives. Lending institutions are likely to take account of such different prospects.

Occupation

Two general points may be made regarding occupation: First, this variable is obviously related to education; second, the classification system leaves something to be desired. It includes two small and poorly identified groups: Those not reporting occupation and "farmers" living in nonfarm areas. In addition, it includes a heterogeneous "other reported" group, which contains laborers, service workers, and salesmen.

The findings for the three groups will not be discussed, mainly because they are not significant.

Influence of Occupation on Variation in Average Value of New Houses

Occupation of Household Head	Gross Differences from U.S. Average	Adjustment for Differences Attributable to Income	Gross Differences Adjusted for Differences in Income	Net Differences from U.S. Average
	Col. 1	Col. 2	Col. 3 = Col. 1 + Col. 2	Col. 4
Professional, managerial, etc.	$3,960	−$1,423	$2,537	$1,064
Craftsmen, operatives, clerical	−1,442	333	−1,109	−805
Farmers	−2,635	780	−1,855	4,039
Other reported	−983	517	−466	−356
Not reported	−1,283	−136	−1,147	−808

The highest skilled group, which embraces professionals, managers, officials, and proprietors, acquired new houses valued at nearly $4,000 above the average; one third of the gross deviation was associated with higher income, and one third was attributable to other nonincome factors in the regression. The group classified as craftsmen, operatives, and clerical workers acquired houses valued below the national average; a little less than one fourth of this deviation was attributable to below-average income. The nonincome influences brought about a similar reduction, and the net deviation for this class was still below the average (−$800).

The prospect of rising income is probably one factor that explains the above-average house value for the professional and managerial group. Another is that lenders may be favorably disposed toward persons in this occupational group because they experience little unemployment.

Use of Regression Coefficients: An Example

The preceding discussion of net regression coefficients has indicated how house value would vary if all explanatory variables (income, region, age and sex, education, etc.) except the one under consideration were

7. Factors Affecting the Purchase Value of New Houses 103

held constant. This section is a digression that illustrates an interesting use of the coefficients.

Suppose one wished to estimate house value for a hypothetical household with a series of specified characteristics. The regression coefficients can be thought of as building blocks to be combined in various ways to yield an estimate of house value. Subject to certain limitations, table 3, which is based on data for 1959 and the first quarter of 1960, illustrates the procedure to be followed.

TABLE 3
Calculated House Value for a Hypothetical Household

Average, based on households reporting house value....................	....	**$17,662**
Income...............................	$7,000......................	....
As deviation from mean...........	−$1,340....................	−614
Region............................	South.......................	−1,406
Location..........................	Suburb of small SMSA..........	206
Age and sex.......................	25–29, male..................	−1,139
Years married.....................	3–9.........................	−948
Race..............................	White.......................	75
Education.........................	High school..................	628
Occupation........................	Craftsman....................	−805
Equals: calculated total........	....	**13,659**

Source: Equation #1.

The left-hand column of table 3 gives the general characteristics and the next column the specific values assumed for the household. The third column gives the regression coefficient taken from the tables just discussed.

It should be remembered that the net coefficients have been shown as deviations from the mean; thus, the calculated house value will be the net result of additions to and subtractions from the grand average house value for the entire sample—$17,662.

In the example, it is assumed that the household has an income of $7,000. Since the average for all households in the sample was $8,340, the income coefficient (.4584) is multiplied by the difference ($7,000 − $8,340) to yield the adjustment in value (−$614) corresponding to the assumed income. The rest of the adjustments in the illustration are taken directly from the tables. The example chosen yields a house value of $13,659. Similar computations may be made for any set of specified characteristics.

Such a calculation makes use of the assumption that the variables are independent in their influence upon the dependent variable and that their effects are additive in the manner shown. However, this is unlikely to be strictly true, as was indicated earlier. Age and number of years married are obviously related, as are other independent variables. In addition, all of the coefficients are subject to error. Because of these limitations, the results shown must be used with caution; however, they should be of some value to those interested in analyzing housing markets.

SECTION IV—MODIFICATION OF ESTIMATED INCOME ELASTICITY

The importance of income in the preceding regression analysis has already been made clear. In the four equations that were calculated (two of which have been shown), income accounted for 40 to 45 percent of the explained variation in house value—more than any other single variable.

The next step involves a more intensive analysis of the net regression coefficient on income and an analysis of the constancy of the income coefficient throughout the income range. A straight line fitted to the logs of house value on the logs of income, as in equation #3, assumes that the income elasticity is constant for all income levels.[3] Although it could be ascertained in advance by simple graphic methods that the gross value-income relationship was approximately logarithmic, no such simple expedient permitted the establishment of the net relationship after the influence of the other variables (age and sex, education, etc.) had been accounted for. The usual supposition is that the elasticity would be higher in the lower part of the income range and would decline at upper income levels, as has been reported for many consumption goods in family budget studies.

This section produces a modification of the estimate of income elasticity and tests for constancy in a broad range of income. The test is made possible by extending the dummy variable technique—previously employed only with nonincome characteristics—to the income variable. The modification of the estimated income elasticity comes about chiefly through the omission of the two open-end income classes.

Initially, equations #1 and #3 were recalculated (and designated 1A and 3A); for the specific income of each household, 1 of 12 dummy variables representing the 12 income classes was substituted. An advantage of this technique is that it does not require the analyst to specify in advance the form of the relationship between house value and income. As is indicated below, with the dummy variable technique, each income class has its own regression coefficient. Once these have been calculated, it can then be determined whether they show constant, decreasing, or increasing elasticity.

---

[3] Each of the other equations involves a specific implication concerning income elasticity. Equation #1 (linear) implies that elasticity rises with rising income; one linear-log combination implies increasing elasticity as income rises and the other implies decreasing elasticity.

7. Factors Affecting the Purchase Value of New Houses

The results of the recalculations are shown in chart 4. The 12 points connected by the heavy black line represent calculated house value based on equation 3A. If a least squares straight line is now fitted through these calculated values, the slope of this line (0.31) turns out to be

CHART 4
House Value-Income Net Regression, Buyers of New Houses Built 1959—
First Quarter 1960
(when open-end income classes are included, the slope of the net regression line is reduced)
RATIO SCALE

REGRESSION LINE FITTED TO CALCULATED VALUES FROM EQ. 3A

EQUATION: LOG Y = 2.96 + .31(LOG X)
BASED ON WEIGHTED DATA

(when open-end classes are excluded, the slope is increased—the equation shows constant elasticity throughout the income range from $4,000 to $25,000)

REGRESSION LINE FITTED TO CALCULATED VALUES FROM EQ. 3A EXCLUDING OPEN END CLASSES

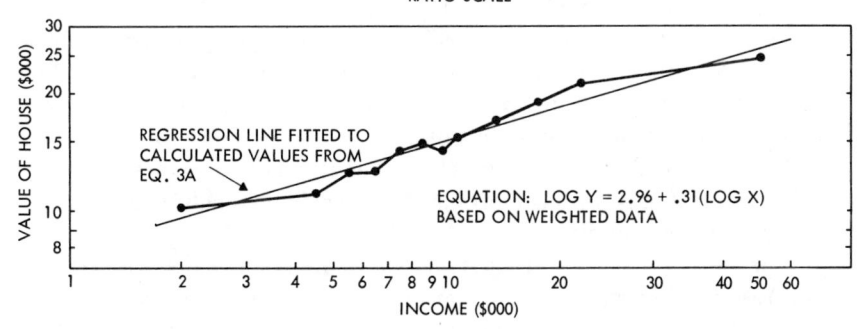

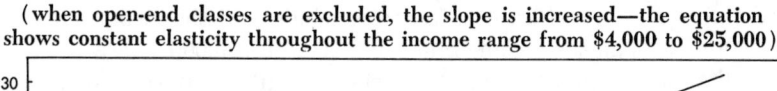

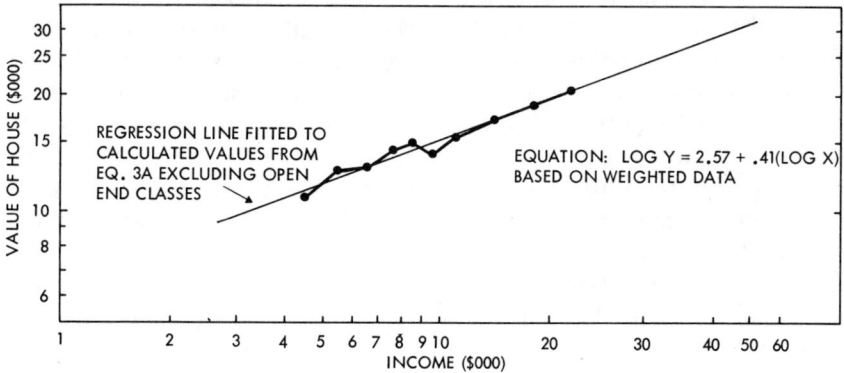

EQUATION: LOG Y = 2.57 + .41(LOG X)
BASED ON WEIGHTED DATA

Source: U.S. Department of Commerce, Office of Business Economics; Basic Data: Census 66-8-10.

only a little larger than that of the line of net regression on income from equation #3 (0.28). The points for the lowest and highest income classes appear out of line; the inclusion of these two extreme points reduces the slope of the line, as may be seen in the chart.

There seemed to be some merit in establishing a relationship between house value and income with the two extreme income groups omitted. The lowest income group accounted for about 15 percent of the new house sample; the highest group, about 2 percent. The principal reason for excluding the $25,000-and-over income group is that the data do not have a solid basis, since specific income and value data were not available for income above $25,000 and house values above $35,000.

For households with incomes under $4,000, influences other than current income appear to be much more important in affecting the price paid for new housing. This group is unusual in many respects. One fourth of these household heads did not work at all in the preceding year; it seems very likely that most of these were retired persons, since one sixth of the group were 65 years of age or older. Such households draw upon accumulated saving from past incomes for house purchases. About one-sixth were female household heads, a much higher proportion than in the total sample; many of these were widows using the proceeds from insurance or inheritance to purchase a house. The group was also probably overweighted with household heads whose incomes were too low to obtain funds through ordinary financial channels and who obtained family loans or gifts.

In the bottom part of chart 4, a least squares line has been fitted to the results (logarithms) of equation 3A, excluding the two open-end classes; it yields an income elasticity of 0.41, as compared with 0.31 based on all the income classes. It can be seen, moreover, that the line fits the points well, so that it is fair to conclude that the income elasticity is constant through the income range of $4,000 to $25,000.

Results based on equation 1A (which is like equation #1, except for the substitution of dummy variables) also tend to confirm the finding that income elasticity is essentially constant throughout the income range of $4,000 to $25,000. The slope of the line based on equation 1A is 0.47, somewhat above the slope based on equation 3A.[4]

These adjusted estimates of income elasticity based on net regression are about the same as the simple regression estimates derived from the relationship between house value and income for all income classes. They are also within the fairly narrow range reported by other investigators using cross-section data of fairly recent vintage and only one or a very few independent variables.

SECTION V—TIME-SERIES ANALYSIS

If time-series data on income and nonincome characteristics of house buyers were available, it would be possible, through the use of the coefficients obtained in the cross-section analysis, to make estimates of house value over time. This approach would permit one to take account

---

[4] The Durbin-Watson values for the two equations are 2.54 for equation 3A and 1.44 for equation 1A. These are nonsignificant values at the 5 percent level, and (for a cross-section regression) they indicate no significant departure from linearity for the log variables fitted.

of shifts in the various characteristics that were shown to be important in influencing the value of new house acquisitions. For example, there have been trends toward increased education and a higher degree of occupational skills of employed persons. To the extent that these trends exist among new home buyers, the average unit value of new house purchases would tend to rise.

In principle, such estimates would also reflect the inherent deficiencies of the cross-section analysis. For example, they would ignore changes in average unit value that were due to changes in relative prices, credit terms, or asset holdings. At any particular point in time, the variations observed in average unit value among households may reflect the influence of the prevailing structure of prices, credit terms, and asset holdings, as well as other unspecified factors. Changes in such factors over time could give rise to changes in average house value from one period to another.

In practice, time series are not available for the nonincome characteristics of house buyers, so that an estimating procedure like the one outlined cannot be employed. Nevertheless, a time-series analysis was made, using aggregative data on prices, credit, and income. Such an analysis does not explicitly provide for variables that, according to the cross-section analysis, affect average unit value. However, it may shed some light on the effect of variables previously ignored in this study.

The available time-series data have serious shortcomings. Our main interest is in changes in the average U.S. value of all new nonfarm houses in real terms, but a suitable series is not available even on a current dollar basis, much less on a constant dollar basis. The available price series (for deflation purposes) have major deficiencies. Moreover, there are no credit data applicable to all purchasers of new houses in the nation as a whole.

The only consistent set of time series available for new single-family houses is the group insured by FHA, and it was decided to use these in an attempt to explain changes over time in the average value of new houses. Consistency of data is a considerable advantage in any statistical analysis; it may yield results that are biased with respect to the entire nation but provide analytical insights that might otherwise be obscured by faulty data. The following discussion will therefore be in terms of new houses insured by FHA. Afterwards, an attempt will be made to explain the variation over time in the construction cost of all new single-family houses in the United States, using data from a variety of sources.

FHA Data

Annual data on average acquisition price for new single-family homes with mortgages insured by FHA under section 203 are available from

1947 to 1964. The data are broken down into value of site and value of house. To deflate value of house excluding site, a special cost index, based mainly on FHA cost estimates of a standardized house, was used. This index rose about half as fast as the Boeckh index over the postwar period. No price series was available to deflate the market value of the site. It was assumed that the change in market value reflected price change only. The addition of the site value for a single year (1958) to each of the annual estimates of deflated construction cost for the house itself (in 1958 dollars) yields a deflated series on average value including site. It should be noted that this deflated series, following a general rise throughout the earlier postwar period, declined slightly after 1957 and then edged upward.

The income series used is the "effective income" of purchasers of new FHA houses. This is estimated by FHA to be the mortgagor's earning capacity (before deduction for Federal income taxes) that is likely to prevail during approximately the first third of the mortgage term. Current earnings are adjusted by FHA if they are considered to be partly of a nonpermanent character. Ordinarily, future increases that may be anticipated by the mortgagor are not included in the FHA estimate of effective income. The income series was deflated by OBE's implicit price deflator for personal consumption expenditures to obtain real income in 1958 dollars.

The price index is derived by combining the separate indexes for house and site. Since the values of residential building lots have shown a considerably larger relative rise than construction costs over the postwar period, it may be noted that their inclusion results in a more rapid rise for the combined cost of a house and lot in the years 1957–64 than for the construction cost of a house exclusive of lot. The combined price index was divided by the deflator for personal consumption expenditures to yield a series on the relative price of new houses of fixed specifications.

In general, it was thought that credit would influence house value in two main ways: by its effect on the downpayment and by its effect on the monthly payment on interest and principal. The monthly payment is a composite that reflects the size of the mortgage, the rate of interest, and the length of the amortization period. Other things being equal, the lower the downpayment or monthly payment, the more expensive the house the purchaser may be expected to buy. There are complications, however. In some cases, a given change in credit conditions may affect both monthly payments and downpayment, and in opposite directions. For example, a change in the downpayment requirement will change the size of the mortgage and thus the monthly payments. In other cases, a change in credit conditions—e.g., a change in interest rates—will affect monthly payments but not the downpayment.

Considerable information on downpayment, length of mortgage term, and mortgage interest rates is available from FHA. An attempt was made to introduce these factors explicitly as separate independent variables; because of intercorrelations, the results were not satisfactory. In particular, the coefficients for the downpayment ratio and for the mortgage interest rate usually had the wrong sign. Accordingly, it was decided to combine the separate credit elements into a composite credit factor that would reflect changes in monthly payments.[5]

Several ordinary least squares equations were fitted to the data for the years 1947–64, using deflated average annual acquisition price as the dependent variable and real income, relative price, credit terms, and a time trend as independent variables. All variables were expressed in logs. Generally speaking, the results yielded high coefficients of determination. Results of the equation with income, price, and the composite credit variable just cited are shown immediately below.

$$\tilde{V}FHA = 1.63 + 1.15 \text{ Inc.} - .74P - .34 \text{ CCF}$$
$$(.002) \quad (.09) \qquad (.40) \quad (.07).$$
$$\bar{R}^2 = .982; \text{ D.W.} = 1.38.$$

where

$\tilde{V}FHA$ = log of deflated value ("acquisition cost") of FHA new one-family houses in 1958 dollars.

Inc. = log of deflated "effective income" (in 1958 dollars) of FHA home buyers.

P = log of deflated price index for a standardized FHA house (1958 = 100).

CCF = log of composite credit factor.

As can be seen from the $\bar{R}^2$, the fit was quite good. The intercorrelation between the independent variables was high, as is usually the case in such regressions, and the Durbin-Watson test (D.W.) indicates that serial correlation was significant at the 5 percent level. Coefficients of the three independent variables all have the expected signs. The coefficients for income and credit are several times their respective standard errors, and the price coefficient is 1.85 times its standard error.

---

[5] The composite credit factor is based on an index of monthly payments on interest and principal. It was derived by multiplying an index of the amount of the mortgage by an index of cost per dollar of mortgage. Cost per dollar of mortgage was computed from the standard formula for level (equal) monthly payments, based in the interest rate and the length of the amortization period.

At any given time, downpayment ratios vary directly with house value. A shift over time toward more expensive houses would therefore tend to raise downpayment ratios in the absence of any change in credit conditions. In the derivation of the composite credit factor, it was necessary to exclude the influence of such shifts in order that the credit factor might reflect only changes in credit over time.

For interest rate, mortgage yield rather than nominal interest rate was used in all calculations.

The income elasticity coefficient is above unity (1.15). This estimate based on annual averages of new FHA houses is substantially higher than the cross-section elasticity estimate based on the household data in section II.

The price-elasticity coefficient of −0.74 is about midway in the range of estimates reported by others.[6] The price index data for houses, however, are of such limited quality that comparisons are not completely valid. The standard error for the price coefficient is relatively larger than the errors associated with the two other coefficients, and as is illustrated below, the price elasticity coefficient was rather unstable. The standard error at 0.4 means that a range of one standard error about the coefficient extends from −0.34 to −1.14.

The final variable in the equation is the composite credit factor, which reflects the combined influence of shifts in downpayment and mortgage ratios, mortgage yield, and length of amortization period on monthly payments. According to the equation, a 10 percent reduction in monthly payments as a result of a change in credit terms is associated with a 3.4 percent increase in the value of house acquired.

When a time trend was added to the equation, it was not statistically significant and had little effect on the value of the other coefficients; it is omitted in the equation shown. Other options were also tried. For example, the use of the Boeckh index as a deflator for house value in place of the FHA series for the cost of a standardized house resulted in little change in the coefficients, except that the income elasticity estimate was reduced to less than unity. The equation in logs is:

$$\bar{v}_{bk} = 1.97 + .90 \text{ Inc.} - .73 P_{bk} - .46 \text{ CCF}$$
$$\phantom{\bar{v}_{bk} = 1.97 + }(.002)(.12)(.30)(.10)$$
$$\bar{R}^2 = .933 \quad \text{D.W.} = 1.42$$

The symbols are the same as above, with the subscripts bk referring to the Boeckh index. The equation containing the Boeckh index did have a time trend, which was not quite significant at the 5 percent level. The inclusion of the time trend in the Boeckh equation reduced the price elasticity coefficient so that it was no longer statistically significant. Finally, an equation was also fitted using the previous year's house value as an independent variable. The results were similar to

---

[6] The range of estimates of price elasticity for housing is extremely wide, varying from −0.08 by James S. Duesenberry and Helen Kistin ("The Role of Demand in the Economic Structure," in Wassily Leontieff [ed.], *Studies in the Structure of the American Economy* [Oxford University Press, 1953], p. 467), to more than −1.0 by R. F. Muth ("The Demand for Nonfarm Housing," in A. C. Harberger [ed.], *The Demand for Durable Goods* [University of Chicago Press, 1960], pp. 72–3), and −1.4 by Tong Hun Lee ("The Stock Demand Elasticities for Nonfarm Housing," *Review of Economics and Statistics*, February 1964, pp. 82–9).

those shown in the equation above, with an insignificant contribution of the lagged variable.

Other Time-Series Regressions

Since one would like to know how the value of all new houses—rather than FHA houses only—is related to income, price, and credit influences, a similar set of time-series regressions was attempted for all single-family houses in the nation. The series on house value was based on the regular Census series on the construction cost of one-family nonfarm houses. The income series is the OBE personal income data divided by number of households; this average for all households is used rather than a series on the income of buyers of new houses. The deflations were carried out in the way described earlier. For the deflated house price series, alternatives based on FHA and Boeckh cost indexes were employed. The credit series was the same as that used in the FHA regression.

The results were less satisfactory than those obtained in the FHA equations. The income elasticity estimate was about the same, i.e., around unity. The credit term variable taken from the FHA data had a coefficient about the same size as in the FHA regression, but the standard error was much larger than before and not quite significant at the 5 percent level. For the price elasticity coefficient, no meaningful results were obtained with either the FHA cost for a standardized house or the Boeckh series. Finally, the use of lagged variables resulted in little change in the estimates of elasticity.

Evaluation of Results

A major contribution of the time-series analysis is the fact that credit terms appear to have significant and important effects on house value and that relative prices are important in some formulations. The extent to which the various net regression coefficients derived from the 1960 cross-section household data were affected by the particular pattern of prices and credit terms prevailing at that time cannot be determined, as was already indicated.

The net coefficient on income from the FHA time-series data (after the introduction of price and credit variables) turned out to be considerably greater than the cross-section estimates based on individual household data. The two sets of data are, of course, not comparable in terms of coverage. Conceivably, the use of "effective income" in the FHA data rather than actual income could account for some of the difference in the two estimates of income elasticity, but a limited test suggests otherwise. For six years—1958–64—both "effective" and actual income data were available from FHA reports. For the years 1959–63, the ratio of actual to effective income varied by only 1 percent; only in 1964 did actual income increase much more sharply than effective income.

There may be nonincome influences that are not included in the time-series regression and that partially account for the difference in the two estimates of income elasticity. One such influence may be education, as was suggested in the introduction to this section. Differences of this kind are by no means unique to this study. More comprehensive data are clearly needed before a start can be made in resolving the differences between the two basic approaches.

8. The Price Elasticity of Liquor in the U.S. and a Simple Method of Determination*

JULIAN L. SIMON

1. INTRODUCTION AND LITERATURE SURVEY

The price elasticity of demand for liquor is of considerable practical importance to the American community because it is the basis for calculations of the effect of liquor taxes upon total tax revenue and upon liquor industry sales and profits. Estimates of liquor elasticity affect the judgments of legislators when they consider tax bills and, hence, the estimates affect the levels of taxes.

At this time we do not have a satisfactory elasticity estimate for the United States. These are the studies that bear on the matter.

(1) Richard Stone developed estimates from time series in England covering the period 1920–38. His best estimates were —0.57 for price and 0.60 for income. Stone's work is sufficiently well known so that we need not evaluate it here. The major drawback for our purposes is that the elasticity in the United States may differ from that in England for a host of cultural and economic reasons.

(2) A. R. Prest developed price elasticity estimates from time series in England, 1870–1938, using a method similar to Stone's. He obtained —0.57 using a logarithmic function and —0.031 using a linear function.

(3) Using a time-series technique for the years 1923–39 in Sweden, S. Malmquist estimated a price elasticity of —0.2 to —0.4. Liquor was rationed in Sweden during that period, which introduced great complexities into Malmquist's analysis, and thus reduces the comparability to the United States. Also, the price of liquor was extremely stable over the measured period.

(4) As part of an exhaustive institutional study of the liquor industry, Harold Wattell regressed sales linearly on price and income in Pennsylvania from 1935 to 1951. His estimate was that price was decidedly inelastic.

---
*Econometrica, vol. 34, no. 1 (January 1966), pp. 193–205.

(5) William A. Niskanen developed a structural equation system of linear demand and supply functions for the U.S. beer, wine, and liquor markets. His endogenous variables were total consumption of each beverage type and price indices for each beverage type. His exogenous variables were demand deposits, time trend (last two digits of year), and average tax revenues for beverage types. Prices and taxes were deflated to 1947. He estimated the structural parameters indirectly by least squares from the reduced form equations.

For the period 1934–54, Niskanen estimated the price elasticity of liquor to be −1.74. In a longer and later work, he estimates that for 1934–41 and 1947–60 the "price elasticity is around −2.0 . . . ," and this was the estimate on which he relied. Before further adjustment, however, the elasticity estimate of his most-relied-on regression is −1.420.

2. RELEVANT PROBLEMS OF CONVENTIONAL METHODS

There are two basic methods of evaluating elasticities: time-series and cross-sectional analysis. The two methods are sometimes used in combination, cross section for income and time series for price.

The difficulties in *time-series* analysis pertinent to liquor-elasticity determination are:.

(1) Over time, changes in taste occur with a vengeance in liquor consumption. Per capita consumption in the United States has been as high as 3.25 gallons in 1860, compared to 1.14 gallons in 1949. And there is considerable fluctuation from year to year even when income and price are held constant. The year-to-year changes are more than large enough to obscure the effect of even a very large price change, as is the case with the federal excise increase in 1951.

It should not surprise us that liquor consumption is more variable and more subject to general cultural influences in the short run than is food, say. Liquor's major psychological function is to reduce fear and inhibition, and the tension level of our society varies with various external stimuli. And in the long run, shifts in religious beliefs and general style of life also affect drinking behavior.

(2) Changes in relative income, relative price, price levels, and other variables also cause trouble.

(3) Price indices are hard to create.

(4) Typically, the current price of liquor changes very infrequently; and it changes only slightly when it changes at all, because of government regulation and the nature of the commodity. This means that the time series has few observations to work with, scattered over long periods of time during which other variables can change radically. None of the studies mentioned above had data meeting the requirement of a time-series sample that has a wide representation of experiences.

These difficulties with time-series analysis are sufficiently great that investigators of liquor price elasticity have indicated little confidence in their estimates.

The main difficulty with *cross-sectional* analysis is that the population of the various states—which would be the appropriate price-change units for a U.S. study—have very different tastes for liquor. Nor are the differences explained by income. Compare the four states in which the price of Seagrams 7 Crown was $4.85 in January 1962 as shown in table I.

TABLE I

State	January 1962 Price of Seagrams 7 Crown	Per Capita Liquor Consumption in 1961	Gallons of Liquor Consumed per $1 Million of Income
Indiana	4.85	1.26	350
Massachusetts	4.85	2.76	681
Minnesota	4.85	2.22	613
New Mexico	4.85	1.75	506

Source: *Liquor Handbook*, 1962.

These variations in taste render useless a simple cross-sectional correlation of consumption and price in the various states. Furthermore, even if states were far more numerous than they are, we probably could not expect random differences in state tastes to wash out because of the likely association between state price and state taste.

3. DESCRIPTION OF METHOD

This investigation uses a method that has features of both the cross section and the time series. Though it has not been used by economists, to my knowledge, it is very similar to designs used for experiments in psychology and the natural sciences and to sociological paradigms. Because this method is not an experiment, though similar to one, I call it the "quasi-experimental" method.

. . . . . .

The essence of the method is to examine the "before" and "after" sales of a given state, sandwiched around a price change and standardized with the sales figures of states that did not have a price change. The standardizing removes year-to-year fluctuations and the trend. We then pool the results of as many quasi-experimental "trial" events as are available.

When it can be used, this method avoids the important difficulties of time series and cross section and introduces no major new difficulties. Moreover, it has some special advantages which we shall discuss later.

This is the procedure:
1. Select as quasi-experimental events each state price increase of 2 percent or more from 1950 to 1961. Exclude states where moonshine is an important part of liquor consumption. Exclude price change events that occur within 18 months before or after a federal tax change.
2. Notation: "−1" is the month preceding a state price change, "+1" is the month following a price change.
3. Compute the per capita consumption for the 12-month periods, −14 to −3 and +5 to +16. Find the percent of change in consumption between "before" and "after." The periods before and after the tax change are timed to avoid the stock-up that occurs before a price change and the liquidation of stock-up.
4. Compare each monopoly-state trial with other monopoly states, private license states with other private license states. (The two groups differ in consumption measurements and in the structure of liquor retailing.) Compare each trial state against other states in its group, excluding (a) states that themselves had price changes between −18 and +18, (b) states that had sales tax changes, (c) moonshine states, (d) the District of Columbia and two anomalous states. Data for the comparison states were combined (i) by simple averaging of the per capita consumption figures of the individual states, (ii) by totaling the consumption and population figures and computing per capita estimates from the totals, and (iii) where applicable, computing total estimates with and without Pennsylvania. Elasticity estimates were generated for all three sets of data.

The index used for comparison is:

$$\frac{\text{Trial state, per capita consumption ``after'' } - \text{ Trial state, per capita consumption ``before''}}{\text{Trial states, per capita consumption ``before''}}$$

minus

$$\frac{\text{Comparison states, p.c. consumption ``after'' } - \text{ Comparison states, p.c. consumption ``before''}}{\text{Comparison states, per capita consumption ``before''}}$$

5. Estimate the percent price change in the test state. In most monopoly state tax changes in our sample, the price increase actually is a change in the markup percentage, perfectly appropriate for our purposes. In a few monopoly state cases, there was the complication that part of the state's pricing formula included flat per gallon taxes. In those cases the writer made *ad hoc* adjustments somewhat similar to the license state situation below, in order to arrive at a point estimate.

The usual form of a tax change in license states is a change in the flat gallonage excise tax. This causes the same *absolute* change in the wholesale, and subsequently the retail, prices of all brands of liquor. The percent price change for low-priced liquors is therefore greater than for high-priced liquors. A percentage estimate of price change for the state as a whole therefore depends implicitly upon the distribution of liquor in each price range sold in the state, data which are not available.

The license state estimate was made in this fashion. Assuming customary retail markups, the increase in the retail price of a fifth was calculated. This price change was then expressed as a percent of the retail price of a fifth of a medium-priced liquor before the tax change. The calculated change was then compared against the actual change in Seagrams 7 Crown and other large selling brands, to the extent that these data were available.[1]

6. Divide the index in paragraph 4 by the percent price change in paragraph 5 to get an estimate of price elasticity.

7. As in all statistical investigations, there were exceptions that required special handling. For example, one state changed its price structure in two steps spaced three months apart. The "before" and "after" periods therefore required special adjustment.

4. PROBLEMS WITH THIS METHOD

Most of the difficulties that arise in this investigation also plague other techniques. They include.

1. Consumption figures in private license states refer to wholesale rather than retail purchases. The wholesale purchases lead retail purchases by weeks or months. Wholesale purchases are also subject to greater fluctuation from period to period than are retail sales, one cause of which is changes in brand prices not associated with general price changes and business anticipations. Monopoly state consumption, on the other hand, is measured by actual retail sales.

2. The accuracy of population figures is unexpectedly crucial. We used interpolated yearly adjusted census figures, but they are far from perfect. This is a major source of variability in the elasticity estimates.

3. As discussed above, there are flaws in the estimates of price changes. Individual brand price changes during the before and after

---

[1] Seagrams 7 Crown was used as an index of a medium-priced brand, based on *Liquor Handbook* estimates of quantities sold at various prices in the U.S. Seagrams 7 Crown is by far the largest selling brand in the United States, selling 2.5 times as much as the next biggest seller, and accounting for more than 7 percent of total U.S. liquor consumption. Its price is commonly used as a standard in the liquor industry and its price to the retailer practically never changes execpt in response to tax level changes.

We may gain some reassurance from the fact, inherent in the relative sizes of the quantities with which we are working, that the percent estimate of price change is quite insensitive to errors in the choice of index of the central tendency of the distribution.

periods will also affect consumption. But the remarkable stability of most liquor prices, in large part a result of fair trade and state control, renders this source of error very minor.

4. Bar and carry-out sales are differentially affected by price changes. Carry-out sales account for 70–75 percent of the total, and we used carry-out prices as an index of all prices. Different states have different laws controlling or limiting bar sales.

5. Price changes can affect interstate purchase traffic.

5. RESULTS: AN ESTIMATE OF PRICE ELASTICITY

The median of the elasticity estimates for the nonmoonshine trial states shown in column 6 of table II is —0.79. This median, adjusted upwards somewhat to take account of the moonshine states but still closer to —0.79 than to —1.0, is perhaps our best estimate of elasticity for the United States as a whole, subject to the following considerations:

1. The median was chosen as an estimate of the central tendency of the data because (a) it is not affected by the extremity of the extreme observations, and (b) it has no conceptual difficulty with positive elasticity estimates. If we were to compute a mean it would be reasonable, but theoretically uncomfortable, to include the positive estimates as being positive.

2. We may say with .965 probability that the mean of the population from which this sample of elasticity estimates was drawn is between —0.03 and —0.97.

3. The variation among elasticity estimates for the various states in the sample may be due to true variation among the states as well as to random error. Variation among the states may result from different states' elasticities, or from different trends in consumption, or both.

If there is true variation among the states, the accuracy of our overall elasticity estimate depends upon how fair a sample of the states (with respect to the characteristic under consideration) that we actually obtained. We can only hope that the states that fell into our sample were not self-selected in some biased fashion.

. . . . . .

In light of the extremely small price changes with which we worked, the amount of variation in the elasticity estimates is not surprising.

4. Inclusion of two observations for some states is a questionable practice. It is done because of the fewness of observations. The paired observations are in the center of the distribution, however, which suggests that they do not cause a serious bias.

5. The extreme states are small states, which increases our confidence in the median estimate. Nevada might well be eliminated from the sam-

ple on the same ground that the District of Columbia was, namely, that its liquor clientele is heavily transient, which would induce an artificially high elasticity estimate. And Idaho's price change was only 2 percent which makes the elasticity estimate unduly sensitive to random error.

6. Some liquor traffic among states is possible. The estimate for the United States as a whole therefore must be less elastic than for the individual states, just as an industry elasticity must be lower than the mean elasticity for the firms in the industry.

7. The states in table II do not include those states in which important quantities of moonshine are made. table III shows estimates for price changes in moonshine states. We had hypothesized that estimates of elasticity would be higher in moonshine states. There is an indication in the skimpy data of a somewhat higher elasticity. However, more than 90 percent of moonshine production takes place in states that consume less than 9 percent of legal U.S. consumption.

8. This method ignores substitution effects of beer and wine. In some cases, wine prices are changed along with liquor prices; in other cases they are not. The amount of wine sold (measured in alcohol) is small compared to liquor consumption. Therefore, the shift to wine will not be very important in affecting liquor consumption even if wine is very elastic with respect to liquor prices. . . .

9. This method estimates price elasticity by way of estimating the change in quantity sold, and assuming the mean price-paid-per-bottle changes as the price index changes. This estimate must be more elastic than an estimate based upon the total revenue before and after the price change, because the price change will shift some purchases to relatively cheaper brands. Investigation shows, however, that the switch to cheaper brands as a result of product price changes is slight, even when the trend to higher priced brands is taken into account.

10. It is not immediately clear what the length-of-run nature of these elasticities is. Because the "after" time period begins four months after the price change, the estimate is certainly not a very-short-run elasticity of the usual type. . . .

After an initial unsettled period, theory would lead us to expect that demand would become progressively less elastic as liquor drinkers retool their tastes and stomachs and switch to beer, wine, and other liquor substitutes. To test for this effect, I broke the "after" period into two six-month segments and developed elasticity estimates for the second six-month segments, as shown in column 11.

The signs of the differences between the 6-month period and the 12-month period are thoroughly mixed. In 13 cases the late-period estimate is higher, and in 10 cases it is lower. There is no reason to think that the elasticity was falling during the "after" period, or that the longer run estimate should be less elastic.

TABLE II

State	Date of Price Change (1)	Price of Seagram 7 Crown Fifth Before Price Change (2)	Relative Price Change (Price "After" Minus Price "Before" Divided by Price "Before") (3)	For the Trial State: Per Capita Consumption "After" Minus Per Capita Consumption "Before" Divided by Per Capita Consumption "Before" (4)	For the Comparison States Totaled: Per Capita Consumption "After" Minus Per Capita Consumption "Before" Divided by Per Capita Consumption "Before" (5)
Rhode Island	6/1/58	4.60	.033	+.073	+.041
Idaho	5/1/61	4.45	.020	+.035	+.018
Ohio	6/6/55	3.46	.061	+.083	+.033
Washington	4/15/61	4.80	.052	+.031	+.018
Oregon	5/11/59	4.35	.035	+.053	+.051
Washington	4/1/59	4.58	.048	+.059	+.058
Oregon	7/1/61	4.60	.033	+.017	+.018
Maine	7/1/61	4.15	.024	+.015	+.018
Montana	12/1/58	4.25	.071	+.036	+.047
Nevada	5/1/61	4.55	.039	+.041	+.047
Vermont	8/1/57	(3.60) est.	.143	−.046	+.034
Missouri	5/1/61	(4.70) est.	.028	+.025	+.047
Idaho	3/16/55	4.05	.086	−.047	+.025
Maine	1/2/59	4.05	.025	+.040	+.061
California	7/1/55	4.38	.048	+.039	+.085
Oregon	5/2/55	4.10	.061	−.025	+.036
Iowa	7/1/61 & 4/1/59	4.03	.030	−.013	+.018
Connecticut	7/1/61	(4.50) est.	.066	−.031	+.054
Ohio	7/1/59	3.67	.100	−.081	+.051
Iowa	4/2/55	(3.78) est.	.050	−.070	+.025
Illinois	8/1/59	4.19	.036	−.018	+.053
Montana	7/1/57	(4.09) est.	.040	−.182	−.033
Alaska	7/1/61	5.85	.026	−.059	+.054

It is worth noting, however, that if there *had* been differences between long- and short-run elasticities, this method could have detected the differences. The time-series method alone cannot compare long- and short-run elasticities. Indeed, the interpretation of the length-of-run nature of elasticities derived from cross-section methods, and from time series, including the various transformations of time series, is far from clear-cut. Nor can we claim a perfectly straightforward interpretation for quasi-experimental elasticities either, because the world in which the price changes play out their effect is not an otherwise static world, even after we standardize with the comparison states. Nevertheless, the interpretation would seem to be less difficult than for other methods, the biggest advantage being that the periods during which we examine

TABLE II
(*Continued*)

Price Elasticity (Comparison States Totaled): Col. 4 − Col. 3 (6)	For the Comparison States Totaled without Pennsylvania 1959 Tax Change: Per Capita Consumption "After" Minus Per Capita Consumption "Before" Divided by Per Capita "Before" (7)	Price Elasticity (Comparison States Totaled without Pennsylvania): Col. 4 − Col. 3 (8)	For the Means of the Comparison States: Per Capita Consumption "After" Minus Per Capita Consumption "Before" Divided by Per Capita "Before" (9)	Price Elasticity (Means of Comparison States): Col. 4 − Col. 3 (10)	Price Elasticity Using Total Comparison States, and as the "After" Period the Six Months from +11 to +16 (11)
+0.97		+0.97	+.051	+0.67	−0.24
+0.85	+.009	+1.30	+.020	+0.75	+1.65
+0.82		+0.82	+.029	+0.88	+0.28
+0.25	+.009	+0.42	+.020	+0.21	+1.02
+0.06	+.063	−0.29	+.060	−0.20	−0.20
+0.02		+0.02	+.061	−0.04	+0.04
−0.03	+.009	+0.24	+.036	−0.58	+0.51
−0.12	+.009	+0.25	+.036	−0.88	+4.63
−0.15		+0.15	+.049	−0.18	−0.48
−0.15		−0.15	+.038	+0.08	+2.95
−0.56		−0.56	+.014	−0.42	−5.38
−0.79 [median]		−0.72 [median]	+.038	−0.46	−2.07
−0.84		−0.84	+.023	−0.81	−0.98
−0.84	+.071	−1.24	+.065	−1.00	−5.72
−0.96		−0.96	+.077	−0.79 [median]	−2.00
−1.00		−1.00	+.029	−0.88	−0.92
−1.03	+.009	−0.73	+.036	−1.53	−1.30
−1.29		−1.29	+.046	−1.17	−1.02
−1.32	+.063	−1.44	+.059	−1.40	−1.39
−1.90		−1.90	+.024	−1.88	−1.94
−1.97		−1.97	+.039	−1.58	−2.39
−3.73		−3.73	−.025	−3.93	−3.23
−4.35		−4.35	+.046	−4.04	−0.08

the effect of particular price changes are exactly defined in length and are the same in each case, which is not true of the time-series method.

Elasticities may not be the same for a price decrease as for a price increase. Though we have not done so here, the quasi-experimental method would make possible the comparison of down-side and up-side elasticities, as time series and cross-sectional methods will not.

11. Informal inspection suggests no relationship between elasticity estimates and (a) amount of price change, (b) absolute price of liquor, or (c) secular date of price change. But if such relationships did exist, this method could reveal them. This is an important advantage over time series, which can estimate only *an* elasticity, whether or not it is constant over the range of prices.

. . . . . .

TABLE III

State	Date of Price Change (1)	Price of Seagram 7 Crown Fifth Before Price Change (2)	Relative Price Change (Price "After" Minus Price "Before" Divided by Price Before) (3)	For the Trial State: Per Capita Consumption "After" Minus Per Capita Consumption "Before" Divided by Per Capita Consumption "Before" (4)	For the Comparison States Totaled: Per Capita Consumption "After" Minus Per Capita Consumption "Before" Divided by Per Capita Consumption "Before" (5)
Georgia	6/6/55	(4.80) est.	.069	+.127	+.085
Alabama	12/1/59	4.20	.101	−.075	+.019
Virginia	7/1/60	3.65	.100	−.140	0
West Virginia	7/1/57	3.85	.065	−.086	+.021
Virginia	7/1/58	3.55	.028	−.013	+.050

6. EVALUATION OF METHOD

1. All the cited time-series studies take explicit account of income changes, and some take account of taste trends and changes in general price level, as devices to reduce the variability in the universe and to isolate the effect of price changes. By comparison, the method used in this study not only takes out the long-term trends, but also the period-to-period variability, to the extent that income and taste changes affect the various states in the same way. Furthermore, the use of a sample of trial states must help wash out the idiosyncratic movements of given states with reference to all other states. On balance, I think this method has vast advantages over the time series in accounting for variations and trends in income, price level, and taste.

2. The method of this study is limited by the paucity of data. There are only 25 price changes to be considered. But no other method can develop *more* information than is provided by this number of price changes. And, in fact, the regression method tends to *lose* information where there are changes in consumption when prices do not change, if the consumption changes are not completely explained by the other variables—as, of course, they cannot be. It is true that a regression approach using a composite price index gains some information from brand price changes that take place in addition to tax-induced price changes. But liquor prices are remarkably sticky, so this is not a great advantage.

TABLE III
(*Continued*)

Price Elasticity (Comparison States Totaled) Col. 4 − Col. 5 / Col. 3 (6)	For the Comparison States Totaled without Pennsylvania 1959 Tax Change: Per Capita Consumption "After" Minus Per Capita Consumption "Before" Divided by Per Capita "Before" (7)	Price Elasticity (Comparison States Totaled without Pennsylvania): Col. 4 − Col. 7 / Col. 3 (8)	For the Means of the Comparison States: Per Capita Consumption "After" Minus Per Capita Consumption "Before" Divided by Per Capita "Before" (9)	Price Elasticity (Means of Comparison States): Col. 4 − Col. 9 / Col. 3 (10)	Price Elasticity Using Total Comparison States, and as "After" Period the Six Months from 11 to 16 (11)
+0.61	+.049	+0.61	+.077	+0.72	+1.17
−0.93	−.023	−1.23	+.042	−1.16	−0.77
−1.40	+.032	−1.17	+.012	−1.52	−1.36
−1.65	+.061	−1.82	+.020	−1.63	−1.66
−2.25		−1.71	+.053	−2.36	−2.14

Furthermore, composite indices of liquor prices must be extremely crude, because of the multiplicity of brands and the lack of knowledge about individual brand sales, especially if the regression is for the United States as a whole.

3. The quasi-experimental method has in common with true experimental methods that causation is clearly established, because we can be reasonably sure which is the exogenous variable. This is a great advantage over time series.

4. A major advantage of this method is that it permits the critical reader to test it with his intuition at every step of the way to see if the method and results are reasonable. Complex econometric techniques are too often black boxes even to adepts; their complexity makes it impossible to *understand* the relationships, and consequently they leave one with a sense of unease. Such is not the case with the quasi-experiment. It does not demand faith for one to have belief in its results.

5. The method used in this study would seem to be useful in investigations where there are several divisible and independent economic units *within* which prices (or other sales-influencing variables) move together, but *among* which prices change independently. As an example, this author is presently using the same method in an investigation of the elasticities of retail and local advertisers with respect to newspaper advertising rates.

part THREE
Forecasting

INTRODUCTION

The general subject of forecasting may be divided in two ways: (1) according to the forecast period, whether short-run or long, and (2) according to the forecasting method, whether "subjective" (judgmental) or "objective" (based on economic relationships and statistical techniques). The article by John Lewis rather cuts across this classification, concerning itself with method in short-run forecasts. Lewis argues that many of the short-run methods are complementary, that a good combination of subjective and objective methods can achieve better forecasts than either when used alone.

The objective methods are subdivided further into several approaches. The "leading indicators" method of the National Bureau of Economic Research is evaluated by Robert Gordon, who concludes that on balance the indicators can be valuable tools of analysis. The "econometric" method, usually based on a more or less complete economic model, is lucidly explained and illustrated by Daniel Suits.

These are the most commonly used methods. An alternative, based on the statistical techniques known as principal components and factor analysis, is still somewhat rudimentary—in terms of experience if nothing else. The method is used in the article by F. G. Adams, who analyzes the value of consumer attitudes and buying plans in forecasting. He concludes that this approach warrants further exploration.

9. Short-Term General Business Conditions Forecasting: Some Comments on Method[*]

JOHN P. LEWIS

The assignment that gave rise to this paper stipulated that I should first establish some kind of classification of general short-term forecasting techniques and then evaluate the several techniques on the basis of their showings during the past two or three years. What follows, however, does not really attempt the second of these tasks. One's impulse to construct batting averages is forestalled, for one thing, by the near impossibility of defining the universe from which a sample of representative forecasts might be drawn. Moreover, it is far harder to classify forecasters than forecasting techniques; few of us in practice are willing to stick exclusively to a particular technique, no matter how partisan to it we may be (and in this habit of mixed practice, I shall be saying, we are very wise.) Furthermore, insofar as one *can* associate particular forecasters or forecasting groups or exercises with particular techniques, the variance in recent performance is much greater between the best and worst records within particular categories than it is among the best performances in the several categories. Finally, as one who must sometimes practice the art himself, I feel, in any event, that there is a certain basic indecency about displaying forecasters' comparative batting average publicly. To do so is too much like reading a paper to an open meeting of a county medical society in which one undertakes to spell out which local doctors lost the most patients last year.

Accordingly, my purpose here will be to dwell, rather than upon batting averages, upon the potentialities for complementarity among the several major forecasting approaches. In doing so, I hope largely to avoid contentiousness, of which we have already had altogether too much with respect to short-term forecasting methodology. The central, if pious, thesis of the paper is that all of us who find ourselves engaged in the

[*] *Journal of Business,* vol. 35, no. 4 (October 1962), pp. 343–56. © Copyright 1962, The University of Chicago Press.

forecasting enterprise rather urgently need every bit of quasi-respectable help we can get from one another.

I. SOME GROUND CLEARING

I propose to focus my discussion on five varieties of forecasting techniques that currently constitute the professional economic core of the activity—(1) leading indicators of the National Bureau of Economic Research (NBER) variety, (2) the leading monetary indicators that have been pioneered by Professor Milton Friedman and his associates, (3) use of those surveys of spenders' intentions and of other compilations of advance plans and commitments that, I believe, Martin Gainsbrugh was the first to label collectively as "foreshadowing indicators," (4) econometric model building, and (5) that looser, less elegant, but more comprehensive variety of model building that has been called many things, which I prefer to label "opportunistic."

These techniques have certain common characteristics. They share a certain professional respectability and orthodoxy; they are not, within the trade, regarded as crackpot approaches (although this, if one looks at the history of the art, is not necessarily a cause for reassurance). They all invite some use of the economists' trained skills; thereby they implicitly assume that a systematic marshalling of such skills can yield insights into the near-term economic future that an intelligent layman would be likely to miss. In this sense they are not diffident techniques. Finally, they all are genuinely professional techniques in that they are regimens for arriving by mainly dispassionate, quasi-objective procedures at technically honest answers to the question of what the unfolding condition of the economy is likely to be. They are not the best techniques, in other words, for telling bosses, Presidents, congressmen, and other decision makers what they want to hear. All of these techniques, to be sure, can be twisted to yield preconceived answers, but at least they create tensions—they set up conflicts of loyalties—in any conscientious professional when he is called upon to abuse them in this fashion.

By concentrating on these five varieties of technique—the two kinds of leading-indicator analysis, the foreshadowing indicators, and the two kinds of model building—we shall be leaving out of account a fair part of the total methodological terrain. We shall pass over, for example, those analytical cults whose basic forecasting hypothesis is that inexorable, rhythmical cycles in activity are so deeply rooted in the laws of the economy that all the forecaster needs to do is, first, identify the relevant cycles by penetrating the cunning veil which nature seems to cast over them; second, locate the present position of the economy in the identified cycle or cycles; and then, third, proceed to read future business conditions right off the calendar. It would be presumptuous to say that the rhythmical cycle hypothesis has no place at all in sensible forecasting practice—it has certain, although limited, uses, for example, in the inventory field—but those who retain it as their principal general forecasting doctrine have, by now, been consigned to the crackpot category, and I think deservedly so.

We also shall be passing over a rather mixed bag of forecasting practices that I have labeled elsewhere as the "agnostic techniques"—meaning by that those more or less self-evidently weak methods for probing the future to which people resort when they doubt their capacity to do anything better. They may, for example, adopt a no-change hypothesis, projecting the latest period's level to the coming period, or, if they want to be a bit more sophisticated, they may extrapolate the recent trend to future periods. In the very best contemporary forecasting, of course, there are a number of points at which practitioners still fall back on precisely this procedure. However, if no-change extrapolations were the craft's universal methodology, it would be professionally bankrupt.

General expectations surveys also belong in the "agnostic" category. I am referring now to surveys, not of respondents' spending intentions or even of their own sales expectations, but of their anticipations of general business conditions. Such general expectations surveys may provide the forecaster with some useful data of a psychological sort, but if they are viewed as producing self-contained forecasts in their own right, their use rests on the hypothesis that the blind can lead the blind—if they do it collectively, that is. Then there is that variety of forecaster whom we might call "the parasitical agnostic"—the fellow who relies, via the Joe Livingston type of survey, upon the consensus of the experts. This, of course, is a fairly sensible, if unambitious, procedure, and, in fact, such surveys are of great utility to the experts themselves. For if there is any quality that ill suits a practicing forecaster it is arrogant indifference to what others in the trade are saying. All the same, the surveying of expert expectations obviously is a derivative forecasting methodology at best; it would cease to exist if the only experts were those who were expert in surveying experts' expectations.

Gerhard Colm has suggested to me one other methodological category that ought to be included in the list, but it too I shall largely pass over here. Colm's suggestion is the "cynical" forecast, and his example is the curious inability of the Council of Economic Advisers late in the Eisenhower Administration to detect the approach or even the start of the recession of 1960–61. I would prefer a slightly less harsh label—say, the "contrived" or "ulterior-motive" forecast—and, to balance things up politically, suggest as another example the present Administration's forecast of a $570 billion GNP for 1962. This last has not entailed any violent wrenching of professional standards, but Administration economists rather plainly have been looking on the bright side for a reason.

Having brought the matter up, I want to make a couple of quick comments on central-government forecasting, particularly that done within the executive office of the president. Two separable problems are involved. One is simply the feedback problem that besets any highly influential forecaster, public or private: Shall he allow himself to be deflected by the fact that his prognostications are likely, themselves, to have some impact upon business conditions in the forecast period? The accepted answer to this question, it seems to me, is "No." An agency like the Council of Economic Advisers should do the most accurate job it can of identifying the prospects likely to emerge under existing policies. But then when, by following this no-nonsense procedure, it finds itself about to release a pessimistic forecast, it also should do what it can to see that there comes, packaged with the forecast, a program of policies whose adoption would tend to make the disappointing forecast become untrue.

The other, and much stickier, problem under which official forecasters labor is that of occasional but stubborn direct political constraints. At least two economic-policy changes presently under discussion in Washington would relax the political inhibitions under which government forecasters lately have been working. One is the proposed delegation of increased standby stabilization powers to the president. This would weaken the presently inhibiting assumption that the tempo of adjustments in fiscal policy directed by business conditions necessarily should match the tempo of our congressional and electoral calendars. The second—and, in this context, the more important—reform may occur in the field of budgeting practice. Moves are under way to deflate further the traditional administrative budget concept and, in particular, to inject some sort of business-style distinction between capital and current outlays into federal accounting. Such a change, which would parallel the standard practice in most West European countries, could, as one of its by-products, greatly ease the constraint that the balanced-budget fetish has been imposing on responsible forecasters.

But I stray too far afield. For the ulterior-motive type, like the agnostic and rhythmical-cycle types, of forecasting lies beyond the boundaries to which I want to confine the burden of this discussion.

II. SOME LIMITATIONS OF THE TECHNIQUES USED SINGLY

As for the central core of professional short-term forecasting techniques, a commentator at this juncture, I think, must deliberately choose what the mood of his commentary is going to be. One could readily take a very bullish view of things, for the state of the art plainly is greatly improved from its condition a generation or even a decade ago. It would be equally legitimate, however, to adopt a thoroughly bearish stance and enlarge on the theme that, when you come right down to it, we are still practicing alchemy, not chemistry. So long as two intelligent persons or groups practicing the "same" techniques can come out with radically different forecasting answers, our scientific pretensions do not become us very well.

As indicated already, however, my own choice of a theme is neither gloom nor buoyancy but, rather, synthesis. I want to emphasize the complementarity of the several techniques we have under inspection, and this can best be done in two stages. First, I want to suggest some of the weaknesses that each of the five conventionally respectable techniques exhibits as a self-sufficient, go-it-alone device. But then, second, I want to underscore the contribution that each of these techniques can make to a properly comprehensive and synthesized forecasting exercise.

A. NBER Leading Indicators

The point has been rather widely made by now that the National Bureau of Economic Research type of leading indicator analysis constitutes a good bit less than a complete set of forecasting tools. This comes as no shock to the more responsible users and proponents of leads-and-lags analysis. However, a brief summary of the limitations of the method may still be in order. They seem to me to be these:

In the first place, the NBER leading indicators are inherently weak devices for detecting the *magnitude* of coming changes in business conditions. Their purpose is the detection of coming turning points, but, despite the improvements that Julius Shiskin lately has attempted in this regard, they have little capacity for disclosing how sharp the turn will be or how high or deep the upswing or downswing will go.

In the second place, the leading indicators as a group are quite short-range devices. Even if there were no problem of garbled signals, they would, as a group, give us no more than six months' advance notice of a coming downturn in the economy—and far less than that in the case of upturns.

In the third place, there *is* a problem of garbled signals. Looked at individually the leading indicators series run jagged courses. When any given wiggle occurs it usually takes two or three months to tell whether the leading indicator really has turned a significant corner or not, and by then, of course, much of its lead has been eaten up. Moreover, the leads of the particular indicators are not consistent from cycle to cycle, making it difficult to guess how soon a signaled change may occur. More important, the several leading indicators almost never all point in the same direction, especially in months just prior to general turns in business conditions. And while the "diffusion indexes" represent a natural and probably necessary attempt to cope with this last problem, they suppress most of the illuminating detail in the series that underlie them; typically they give no weight to the magnitudes of the expansions and contractions in the component series; they weight all of the components together as if they were of equal intrinsic importance; and, despite all of this, the diffusion indexes themselves are highly irregular in their movements.

Finally, as a self-sufficient technique, the leads-and-lags approach has this major limitation: it implicitly assumes a very high degree of structural rigidity in the economy. It has no adequate way of coping, for example, with major changes in the structure of demand. It is in such terms, I think, that one must explain the few past occasions—in 1951, 1956, and in 1959—on which the leading indicators have given concerted and prolonged false signals.

B. The Leading Monetary Indicators

The rest of us are much indebted to Friedman and his colleagues for emphasizing in recent years the degree to which the rate of change in the money supply tends to lead changes in general business activity, and changes in monetary reserves lead the money supply, and changes in central bank policy lead monetary reserves. The efforts to marshal the evidence underlying these assertions, to establish a format for the presentation of pertinent indicators, and to interest some of our reserve banks and other financial institutions in their publication have been all to the good.

Despite my reading of some of Friedman's writings on the subject and several lucid papers by Beryl Sprinkel, however, I confess to some confusion as to how far the proponents of the leading monetary indicators mean to go in claiming self-sufficiency for them as forecast devices. This confusion is rooted, in turn, in my confusion about the theoretical debate from which advocacy of the leading monetary indicators seems to emerge.

I am rather puzzled by the alleged contest between so-called modern quantity theory and the better contemporary versions of what is called income and expenditure theory. It seems to me just as evident that early Keynesian theory went much too far in underrating the role of money as a determinant of general economic activity even as the quantity theorists of the twenties went too far in overrating it. Surely it was a mistake to believe that the frail stem of the money rate of interest could bear the full burden of the impact of finance and financial institutions on investment activity, just as it was a mistake to talk as if monetary and credit conditions had a direct impact only on investment and not also upon such other sectors as consumer buying of durables and state and local government outlays. I should have supposed that today just about any journeyman analyst of the so-called income and expenditure persuasion, and certainly any sensible forecaster working in that tradition, is, therefore, vitally concerned with monetary prospects. That, indeed, is precisely why such analysts are very *much* interested in the current posture of the Federal Reserve and are sometimes critical of it. And that is why they prize the help Friedman et al. are giving us in identifying the time linkages that seem to relate changes in monetary policy to changes in the availability and cost of finance.

But to go beyond this to the opposite extreme and accept the leading monetary indicators as *sufficient* tools for predicting general business conditions would seem to me a most bizarre procedure. It would rest on the hypothesis that, for predictive purposes, the economy could be treated as if central bank decision making were the only significant independent variable in the system. For better or worse, things are more complicated than this. The capacity for influential autonomous decision making is far more widely dispersed. Considerable quantities of it lodge also, for example, in the Congress, in the White House, in the Finance Committee of the United States Steel Corporation, in Detroit, in all the great industrial houses and major labor organizations in the country and, even, in fifty million households. The responsible general forecaster must, somehow or other, directly concern himself with all of this pivotal decision making, not just with a particular slice of it. Academically, it is an interesting exercise to imagine that one had to settle for a single, go-it-alone set of predictive indicators and then debate the question of which would be the more reliable—the monetary set or some other? But this is a good deal like the question with which good book would you most like to be cast on a desert isle? Neither question has much practical relevance. As a practical matter, there seems to be no reason for the general forecaster to confine himself to so spare and oversimplified a predictive hypothesis as sole reliance upon the leading monetary indicators would imply.

I do not mean to accuse Friedman and his associates of actually advocating exclusive reliance upon their wares, but some of their arguments have seemed to me susceptible to such a misinterpretation. The leading monetary indicators also have two more specific limitations.

First, the series on changes in monetary reserves and in the money supply, even after seasonal adjustment, are, like many of the NBER leading indicators, subject to rather violent gyrations. Thus it is much harder to detect, from the current data, a change of direction in the smoothed trends of these series than might first appear when one looks at the dramatic shifts in the ex post multimonth averages that the published charts of these series typically display.

Second, I would make the strange-sounding complaint that the average lead that the rate of change in the money supply is alleged to have over general cyclical downturns—namely, some twenty months since the mid-twenties, is really too *long* to be very useful for forecasting purposes. Recent cyclical fluctuations in the American economy have appeared more or less to have followed a three-phase format. In a recession phase activity falls away from its long-term growth trend. In a second, recovery phase, it moves back up toward the long-term trend. But then, in a third, normal-growth or normal-prosperity phase, it moves *along* the trend. And this is the key point: most of us would say that it is impossible to predict at the time it starts how long this third, along-the-trend phase of the cycle is likely to be. There are certain internal dynamics within the system that may tend roughly to govern the durations of most recession and recovery phases. But the duration of the prosperity phase probably is another matter; it appears to depend upon the particular sequence of demands—first, in autos, for example, then in plant and equipment or national defense, and then perhaps in state and local government—that happens to emerge as a result of the particular combination of decision making that occurs in a particular field.

Thus to tell me—as in effect the monetary change indicator does—that these prosperity, along-the-trend phases of cycles since the 20s have *averaged* about 20 months really does not help very much. It gives me no confidence at all that such will be the case this particular time. Especially it gives me no such confidence if I believe, as I do, that there is nothing inevitable or immutable about cyclical rhythms and that deliberate discretionary changes in federal fiscal and monetary policies often decisively affect the duration of prosperity periods.

C. Foreshadowing Data

If it is jousting with a straw man to disprove the self-sufficiency of the leading indicators as forecast devices, it would be still worse to belabor the point that foreshadowing data—the spenders' intentions surveys, the federal budget, contract construction awards, new orders of durable goods manufacturers, and so on—do not in themselves constitute a full kit of forecasting tools. For I know of no serious developer or advocate of such data who has ever hinted that they can single-handedly generate a forecast. On the contrary, there has from the beginning been an alliance between the assemblers of foreshadowing data and model builders, especially of the less elegant, looser persuasion, with the former, of course, supplying much of the latter's inputs. For the sake of the present record, however, and because one still does occasionally encounter people who seem to think that if we could only finish the job of blanketing the GNP with intentions surveys, we would have the forecasting problem licked, let me venture just a few comments on the limitations of the foreshadowing series.

In the past the approach has been constrained by sheer problems of technique—for one thing, in the area of sampling and survey methods, and for another thing, with respect to the interpretation of the sequences of decreasingly tentative expectations and decreasingly conditional decisions into which the surveys from time to time dip. Franco Modigliani, however, has made sense of this latter matter, and certainly our better sampling and survey technology has become highly sophisticated. It is my layman's impression, therefore, that technical problems no longer are the real roadblocks in the area.

However, the coverage of the foreshadowing series is not yet all that it might be. There are some gaps—notably in the case of state and local government outlays—where spenders do indeed make advance plans, commitments, or conditional spending decisions (in the case of state and local governments they are a matter of public record) but where we simply have no agency yet that has assumed the task of systematically collecting or sampling and collating them.

But there are major segments of the GNP—notably in the area of consumer soft goods and services—that are destined, I should think, to remain effectively immune to intentions surveys, no matter how willing the surveyors may be, for the simple reason that buyers in these fields do not do enough coherent advance planning so that they themselves can recognize and report it.

Finally, there is the familiar but important point that the existence of plans, even strongly intentioned plans, offers no assurance that they will be carried out. The forecaster must convert the finding of an intentions survey into a forecast at his own peril. In particular when he makes such a conversion he must assume that the general economic developments that the expenditure planner does *not* foresee are not going to thwart his spending intentions. Modigliani has supplied us with a very intriguing refinement of this point—namely, that if the survey can canvass a respondent's sales or income expectations at the same time it canvasses his spending intentions and if it can be shown that past discrepancies between intended and actual outlays have been related to the discrepancies between expected and actual sales or incomes, it may be possible systematically to "correct" the intentions figure for forecasting purposes—*if* the forecaster is in a position to second-guess respondents' reported sales or income expectations. This approach seems to me to have considerable promise: perhaps even more in the fields of consumer intentions and of business inventory intentions, than in the plant and equipment sector where Modigliani first experimented with it. But as he emphasizes it must be used within the framework of a general model-building exercise. For only in such a context would the forecaster have any real basis for judging that spenders' expectations of future sales or incomes are unlikely to be realized. Modigliani's point, in other words, only underscores the conclusion that foreshadowing series are not go-it-alone devices.

D. Econometric Models

I shall focus my remarks about the limitations of general short-term econometric forecasting upon the single example of the present version of the original Klein-Goldberger model over which Daniel Suits now presides at the University of Michigan. This is one of the oldest econometric forecasting exercises with a continuous work record. It would appear to be fairly representative of its genus. And, for our purposes, it has the overwhelming advantage of just having been laid out for all of us to see in Suits's lucid article in the March 1962 *American Economic Review*.

Judging from this sample of one, we can draw the happy conclusion that econometric forecasting has been in process recently of getting constructively corrupted. In the course of drafting my book on *Business Conditions Analysis* about five years ago, I was casting about for a sharp distinction to be drawn between econometric model building and the less rigorous varieties that I call "opportunistic." I hit on these propositions. A true econometrician was a man, first, who insisted on cranking his forecast out of his explicit simultaneous-equation model without hedging or judgmental adjustment. He insisted, second, upon selecting all of the independent variables in his equations and deriving all of their parameters from an analysis of historical time series. By this definition, Suits no longer is an econometrician—which is to say, the definition is out of date.

There are two striking concessions that Suits's present methodology makes to the "practical" considerations espoused by opportunistic model builders. First, he now freely plugs in—instead of a rather lame investment function that makes business fixed capital spending wholly dependent on last year's profits and last year's growth in plant-and-equipment stock—an intentions-survey result (in this case, the McGraw-Hill) as his business fixed-investment input. (Incidentally, he has not yet, so far as I can tell, adopted the Modigliani proposal for making a systematic correction in the intentions figure to compensate for the "error" in investors' sales expectations.) Second, the Michigan team now evidently feels free to tinker with the "a" constants in any or all of its linear equations to make allowance for judgmental considerations regarding the particular year at hand that it feels the formal model does not adequately encompass. In short, you might say that the Michigan group has become nothing but a bunch of elegant opportunists—and with good results. Its forecast record since it began corrupting its model in this considered fashion is a good bit better than it was in the early and middle fifties.

As it is represented by the present Michigan exercise, therefore, econometric model building already has gone a long way toward overcoming limitations with which I would have charged it a few years ago. But it is still far short of having surmounted its basic problem of excessive rigidity—that is, in effect, excessive simplification. To attempt to cram the myriad complexity of the economy into even a thirty-two-equation model entails, as Suits is careful to emphasize, an heroic abstraction. This is evident if one considers the model's lack of nimbleness in adjusting to the sort of temporary and significant but unusual development that is forever cropping up and of which the looser model builder routinely takes account. For example, most opportunistic model builders, I should suppose, added a bit extra to their inventory investment estimates for the first quarter of 1962 to allow for some steel stockpiling and then shaved their second and/or third quarter estimates a compensating amount. The Suits model has no explicit, untinkered-with capacity for handling such refinements. Its limitations become most evident if one considers the stark simplicity of the theories of sector-demand determination that underlie some of its expenditure equations.

Indeed, I would urge sector-demand specialists who have not already done so to look carefully in Suits' March 1962, article in the *American Economic Review* at the demand functions for their own particular sectors—at the equations, for example, for automobiles, for other consumer durables, and for housing starts. They are apt to find themselves a bit amazed that a forecasting technique that indulges in such gross oversimplifications with respect to the particular sectors in which they are expert can produce such generally good GNP forecasts as the Michigan model has done in recent years. That it can, of course, is dramatic testimony to the importance in general forecasting of that quality which is econometric model building's particular strength—namely, the quality of internal consistency. Even when many of its sector legs rest on quite mushy foundations, a model of the economy whose income-distribution and receipts, expenditures, and savings relationships all are internally consistent, judged by past experience, has a pretty fair chance of hitting the aggregates. But this does not mean that mushy sector forecasting and an incapacity for encompassing the idiosyncrasies of a particular period are admirable qualities in their own right.

E. Opportunistic Model Building

It is almost a contradiction in terms to imagine the looser forms of model building as being self-sufficient with respect to the other techniques. For the very essence of this approach—the reason I call it "opportunistic"—is its scavenging quality. Opportunistic model building is a procedure for gathering data, information, and insights of just about any conceivably relevant kind and for assembling them, in some orderly manner, into a coherent and quantified statement of prospects. I already have mentioned this approach's particularly heavy dependence upon inputs of foreshadowing data; in addition, sensible practitioners have ravenous appetites for help of other kinds.

Nevertheless, as a kind of horrible example, one can conjure up an imaginary forecaster who might take some pleasure in thinking of himself as a model builder and would indeed express his outlook judgments in the form of a GNP breakdown. But his would be strictly a laundry-list style of forecasting. He would simply go down the sector list, making up forward estimates, one by one, by some intuitive process out of whatever mix of past data, current gossip, and recent comments in the business press he happened to have at hand. He would not even bother to avail himself of the foreshadowing data systematically. He would ignore the insights that the NBER leading indicators might give him into the timing of coming changes in general activity and the help that the leading monetary indicators could supply as to prospective money and credit conditions. He would simply put down his sector forecasts, tot them up, and call the sum his forecast. The entire theory of aggregate demand determination underlying his analysis would consist of the national-income accounting identity that the GNP equals the sum of its parts. His analysis would contemplate no intersectoral, no income-expenditure, and no asset-expenditure interactions. The only internal-consistency test to which it would submit would be one to make sure that the GNP components did, indeed, add up to the total. And his mathematical requirements would be limited, not just to arithmetic, but to addition and subtraction.

Although I have called the foregoing an imaginary horrible example, a good bit of the actual short-term forecasting being done today comes uncomfortably close to fitting this description. This serves only to prove that something fairly close to go-it-alone opportunistic model building is, indeed, possible. But it also, it seems to me, is almost self-evidently foolish.

III. THE OPPORTUNITY FOR SYNTHESIS

So much for my argument that none of our five major short-term forecasting techniques is an island—at least not a very successful island when a consolidation of the five is perfectly feasible. The case for consolidation already has been anticipated considerably in the case against separatism. Thus I propose to enlarge on it only briefly, and shall do so in a moment.

A. A Few Substantive Comments on Opportunistic Model Building

First, by way of an aside, I want to get in a few somewhat more explicit licks on the craft of opportunistic model building. These are intended mainly as discussion provokers; I shall put my points very sketchily and, in a couple of cases, vulnerably.

The Usefulness of a Capacity Concept. The most controversial of the points I want to make about model-building practice is that such analysis can be greatly assisted by the incorporation of an explicit capacity concept. One must grant, of course, that capacity is a fuzzy, ambiguous, imprecise, not directly measured variable. But it generalizes about characteristics of the economy that are objective, dated, and vitally important. In one guise or another it is an essential concept for the general forecaster if he is going to discharge his ultimate function, which is to predict the basic healthiness of economic activity in a coming period. For that healthiness will depend most pivotally not on the absolute level of output but on the relationship between output and normal productive capacity. Such is plainly the crucial consideration, for one thing, in the case of general price prospects. For it is quite impossible to formulate any working hypothesis about the price-output relationships that changes in demand will encounter during a forecast period without formulating, at least implicitly, some assumption about the level and growth rate of capacity during the period.

The prospective relationship of capacity to output, adjusted for cyclical variations in output per man-hour, in the labor force, and in average working hours, likewise is the pivotal consideration for unemployment forecasting. Thus, although a model-building group may keep its capacity estimates invisible to the naked eye, as, for example, Suits's group does at Michigan, implicitly they are present in one form or another if the group is attempting to do a comprehensive forecasting job. The best procedure, I think, is to bring the capacity estimates out into the open where they can be seen and be argued about.

The Need for Explicit Sector Income Estimates. A second practice that I would urge upon opportunistic model builders is the construction of a model that forces the analyst to make explicit the breakdown of the gross national income into net receipts of governments, net foreign transfers by government, gross retained earnings of business, and disposable personal income that he is setting over against his final-demand breakdown. For only by this means does one have a framework that facilitates allowance for the impacts of expenditures in one sector upon those in others and that permits very much of the internal-consistency testing that is model building's greatest potential advantage.

If I read him rightly, Friedman may raise an eyebrow at this suggestion on the ground that I am asking for models with built-in multipliers, and that it can be shown that in this economy during the past several decades "investment multipliers," or "autonomous sector" multipliers have in fact been highly unreliable phenomena. With Friedman's findings of fact I heartily agree; indeed, they are what I would expect since I believe that the stability characteristics of the economy have been considerably improved during the past generation, with most of that improvement taking the form of just such a weakening of the intersectoral cumulative mechanisms as Friedman's findings suggest. In particular, we beneficently have managed, partly thanks to the so-called built-in stabilizers, greatly to reduce the sensitivity of disposable personal income (DPI) to declines in the GNP.

However, the inference for forecasting practice that I draw from all this is not that multiplier effects therefore should be banned from outlook models but rather than they require considerably more elaborate treatment than our simplified textbook theories of a few years back seemed to suggest. In a little semiannual forecast exercise that we run at Indiana, for example, we do three things. First, we separate consumer durables from the rest of consumption and treat them as a quasi-autonomous sector of the same sort as housing or plant and equipment. This is on the thesis that the aggregate of consumer soft goods and services is a much more stable function of DPI than is total consumption. Second (and this is the newest wrinkle of the three in our practice) we nevertheless treat the relation between soft goods and services consumption as being cyclically variable within fairly narrow limits. Third, and most important, we explicitly forecast the ratios of DPI to personal income and of personal income to GNP, treating both of these also as being cyclically variable.

Thus, in effect, we systematically incorporate into the model a rather highly variable multiplier that, in particular, takes explicit account of the tax-less-transfers and retained-earnings leakages between GNP and DPI. Rightly or wrongly, we attribute most of the very good luck that we have had with the exercise the last two or three times around to the more careful efforts we have been making along these lines.

Inventories and Net Exports. My other two substantive comments are far narrower in scope, and I shall no more than mention them. Both concern matters rather urgently in need of further investigation. First, it appears to me that our forecasting doctrines for inventory investment presently are in a state of some theoretical disarray. Having become rather thoroughly disenchanted with the practical usefulness of inventory-sales ratios as guides for inventory forecasting, many of us have become rather excited about the greater utility of new orders and order backlogs as indicators of prospective changes in manufacturers' inventories. In this we have followed the lead, for example, of the Duesenberry-Eckstein-Fromm model of a few years ago. The trouble, however, is that this new doctrine really makes sense only for those industries that produce to order, not to stock, and have little or no finished-goods inventory. Consequently, for improved inventory forecasting I suspect that we need a considerably more disaggregated approach than is now customary; we need to know a good bit more than published data presently reveal of the differing degrees to which different manufacturing sectors rely, on the one hand, upon order backlogs and, on the other, upon finished-goods inventories for cushioning the lags of their output behind their demand; knowing this, we need to forecast changes in manufacturing inventories by fabrication stages; and, I suspect, in the case of manufacturers' finished stocks as well as trade inventories we need to hark back to inventory-sales ratios but with renewed attention to inventory-cycle models.

The other point is simply that net-export forecasting is in a bad way because of the average forecaster's or forecasting group's inability to make any closely reasoned prediction of exports. With the passing of the dollar shortage it no longer is legitimate to assume that the volume of United States exports will be determined simply by the volume of dollars that the United States supplies to the rest of the world through its imports and its transfers abroad of public and private capital. But lacking this short cut, the general forecaster is left with an apparent but impossible need to predict demand developments the world over if he is to make a considered estimate of United States exports. Because of the comparatively narrow limits with which net exports move, the problem is not a particularly serious one for the aggregate domestic forecast. But if anyone can come up with a new legitimate short cut to export prediction, he certainly at least will ease the consciences of many of us.

B. Joining the Techniques Together

By way of conclusion, let me indicate how the five forecasting techniques upon which we have been focusing can sensibly complement one another. Perhaps this can be conveyed most succinctly by describing what I would regard as an ideal short-term forecasting exercise.

In the first place, this would be a group exercise. Outlook analysis is an activity, I think, in which the group has an inherent advantage over the lone wolf, partly because it benefits from a division of labor, partly because it must be considerably judgmental and gains from an effort to achieve a consensus. Second, it would be a continuing exercise.

I frankly would become bored as a member of a staff that gave its uninterrupted attention to the business outlook, and there are comparatively few organizations that could afford a fairly elaborate staff that had this single function. However, we are conjuring up an ideal, and there is no denying the expertise that comes with daily immersion in the outlook problem. Third, it would be a rather highly structured exercise. The free-wheeling virtuosity of gifted seat-of-the-pants analysts always is impressive, but it also is commonly overrated, and it has very little transferability. One quality of an ideal forecasting organization would be a considerable ability to maintain continuity despite changes in personnel. Well-defined tasks, procedures, and analytical doctrines would all contribute to this end.

I would place at the head of such a staff a seasoned opportunistic model-builder with a good measure of forecasting experience, theoretical sophistication, and executive ability. I would associate with him three deputy directors, each of whom would have cognizance of the whole operation. One Friedman would be asked to nominate; one Geoffrey Moore or Arthur F. Burns would nominate; and the third would be a first-class econometrician whose professional sensibilities, however, did not bruise too easily. The balance of the staff would be composed mainly of specialists who were immersed in the lore and data of particular demand and/or industry sectors.

The format of my idealized exercise would be a simultaneous equation model—indeed, a far more elaborate model than that presently employed at Michigan—and all members of the staff would require the limited command of mathematics necessary for translating their views into the terminology of such a model and for comprehending its manipulation. The point here would be for the exercise to avail itself of the maximum internal-consistency insurance, and its feasibility would depend upon ready and continuing access to adequate electronic computer services.

The equations in the model, however, would be subject to constant tending. Variables (and, as necessary, equations) would be added or subtracted and parameters would be altered as fast as, and for whatever reason, the staff judged such changes appropriate. In fact, each equation would constitute a summary statement of the staff's presently operative forecasting doctrine for the particular demand sector or the particular income relationship involved. It would be the responsibility of each sector forecaster to keep his equation(s) in a continuing state of repair so that at any given moment the most accurate forecast of which the staff currently was collectively capable, with the help of a computer, could be cranked out of the model with minimum delay.

Foreshadowing data with built-in adjustments, where appropriate, along the lines that Modigliani suggests would figure very prominently as inputs into the model. Monetary and credit variables would be more explicitly knit into the model than has been customary with econometric models to date, with the leading monetary indicators being incorporated as lead devices for signaling later changes in the money supply and credit availability. Moreover, despite the realistic complexity that would be built into the model, the forecasting staff would not consider its findings to be inexorably bound to the model results. In particular, the NBER leading indicators would be used as an independent aid for timing prospective changes of course in the economy, a feat at which opportunistic model building is notoriously clumsy.

This, perhaps, is enough to convey the gist of what I have in mind. Few of us, probably, ever will work in circumstances that closely parallel the conditions just sketched. But at least we can strive for whatever intertechnique collaboration fits our particular scale of operations. We can recognize that not merely should the several respectable short-term forecasting techniques be able to coexist; they have far more to gain from outright alliance than they do from internecine bickering.

10. Alternative Approaches to Forecasting: The Recent Work of the National Bureau[*]

R. A. GORDON

I

The appearance of *Business Cycle Indicators* provides a good opportunity to review some of the National Bureau's recent work on business cycles and forecasting. It is more than a decade since the bureau published Moore's *Statistical Indicators of Cyclical Revivals and Recessions*, a paper which "attained a degree of popularity unusual for National Bureau publications." Since then, Moore's list of indicators has been kept up to date and widely used. The papers brought together in the present volume represent a comprehensive report on the recent work of Moore and his colleagues on cyclical indicators.

Business Cycle Indicators consists of two volumes, the second of which is an appendix which describes and gives the monthly or quarterly data for a long list of series. Volume I is in three parts. The first and most important includes excerpts from annual reports of the National Bureau by Fabricant and Burns, Moore's earlier "Occasional Papers" on statistical indicators and several other papers by Moore, the original paper by Mitchell and Burns on indicators published in 1938, a paper by Frank Morris on the predictive value of the leading series, and one by W. A. Beckett reporting on a set of indicators for Canada. Moore's revised list of 26 series is presented in chapter 3.

Part II contains six papers, some previously unpublished, on individual leading indicators—profits, business failures, new incorporations and new business firms, manufacturers' new orders, hours worked, and other labor-market series. Of these, the paper by Zarnowitz on new orders will probably be of greatest interest. None of these chapters is likely to excite the reader; they are all essentially descriptive; and some are outright stodgy in their style and treatment of their subject matter.

---

[*] *Review of Economics & Statistics*, vol. 44, no. 3 (August, 1962), pp. 284–91.

Part III is concerned with methods of using the individual indicators and diffusion indices on a current basis. Two papers by Shiskin report on the work he has done with the indicators at the Census Bureau. Two others are by Moore. One describes an amplitude adjustment for the leading indicators, and the other deals with the "average duration of run" as a way of summarizing the current behavior of a group of series.

I shall make no attempt to review each of these papers. Instead, in the rest of this article, I shall (1) compare the National Bureau's approach to business-cycle research with that which rests on the use of aggregative models and (2) attempt a general evaluation of the usefulness of economic indicators in short-run forecasting.

II

As Moore points out in his introduction, the Bureau's work on indicators is a byproduct of its overall research program on business cycles, which is aimed at identifying empirical patterns and relationships that will help us to understand why and how business cycles occur. The indicator series and diffusion indices represent examples of such empirically determined patterns and relationships. Moore and his colleagues maintain that these empirical findings are of value even though they have not yet been fitted into an elaborate theoretical structure and though many of them do not involve the particular economic variables most emphasized in recent theoretical literature.

This has left the economic theorists and econometricians unhappy and a bit suspicious. In another context, Koopmans referred to the Bureau's methods of measuring cyclical behavior as "Measurement Without Theory." Do we have here a case of forecasting without theory—and, whether we do or not, does it matter?

It may help us to answer this question if we consider the two methods of short-term forecasting most widely used in this country—the "barometric" method and the method of GNP projections. The first looks for economic barometers or indicators which in the past have regularly heralded a new phase of the cycle. Such are the statistical indicators that the National Bureau has painstakingly sifted out of the hundreds of series in its files. Such also are the diffusion indices which tend to lead the turning points in general economic activity.

Forecasting from GNP models is quite different. Whatever variant is used, this method begins with the Keynesian identity for aggregate demand: $Y = C + I + G$. In the more common static forecasting models, in which the attempt is made to predict a single future value of GNP, I and G are treated as exogenous variables, and their future values are estimated on the basis of data relating to investment expectations, anticipated government expenditures, and the like. Then a consumption function is introduced in order to derive a multiplier to apply to the sum of $I + G$.[1] As often as not, the empirically derived consumption function is "adjusted" to allow for special circumstances.

The use of dynamic models, as exemplified by the work of Lawrence Klein, is much less common. In this case, lagged relationships are introduced so that future values of C and I are derived from present and past values of these and other variables. It is the investment function (or functions) that has caused the chief trouble. No one has yet found an investment function that regularly gives as good predictions of, for example, plant and equipment expenditures as can ordinarily be derived by relying on the SEC Commerce surveys of planned expenditures.

The rationale behind Moore's recent work is best understood if we contrast the analytical foundations underlying these two general approaches to economic forecasting and to the study of business fluctuations. It seems to me that four major points of difference need to be emphasized.

1. First of all, the National Bureau starts with the assumption that the business cycle itself should be taken as the basic unit of measurement. Economic behavior is to be studied during specific phases of the cycle in economic activity. Thus we have the elaborate techniques for measuring "reference" and "specific" cycles described by Burns and Mitchell in *Measuring Business Cycles*. This same emphasis on the business cycle as the unit of experience helps to explain the work that has gone into Moore's indicators. If we start with the fact that the business cycle itself is the basic unit of experience with which we should be concerned, then what is more natural than that we seek to determine empirically what sequences reveal themselves at the most important stages of the business cycle—namely, the turning points? Another illustration is Moore's study of ways of estimating the prospective severity of a contraction at an early stage in the decline. To find out how the severity of past contractions has been related to what happened in their early stages involves first marking off these contractions as units of experience to be studied.

This emphasis on the cycle as the unit of observation helps to explain the fact that the National Bureau has largely eschewed regression analysis in its business-cycle studies. Instead, it has been concerned with (1) empirically establishing important characteristics of past cycles in business activity, (2) discovering and comparing systematic patterns of behavior, in particular economic variables during past business cycles, and (3) testing whether these cyclical patterns have changed in significant ways over time.

---

[1] It is now common practice to do this in two steps: to estimate first the relation between disposable income and GNP and then that between the former and consumers' expenditures.

The bureau's work along these lines resulted first in the elaborate toolbox which Burns and Mitchell presented in *Measuring Business Cycles*. Outside the National Bureau, few students of economic fluctuations have made use of these tools; and even the bureau's workers have not made as extensive use of them as one might have expected. In particular, this apparatus has not yet been used to summarize in any comprehensive way what typically has happened in past business cycles.

Moore's new kit of tools consists primarily of three sets of measurements. One has to do with the timing of individual series at cyclical turning points. The second set consists of the diffusion indices—which, in effect, measure the extent to which the individual members of a group of series move in step during the course of the cycle. And the third set of measurements is concerned with the way in which the total amplitude of movement during a cycle phase (for example, recession) is related to amplitude during the early part of that phase. All of these statistical tools have the same objective: to facilitate systematic observations on the complex of unseen or imperfectly perceived interrelationships that constitute the business cycle.

All of this is in marked contrast to econometric studies involving GNP models. Neither the construction and testing of these models nor their use in forecasting requires that we first identify and mark off individual business cycles or business-cycle phases. The econometrician's standard analytical tool in business-cycle research is regression analysis. In setting up his equations and estimating the necessary parameters, he tends to view time as a continuum which provides a succession of undifferentiated observations on the relationships among the variables in which he is interested. Ordinarily, the phase of the cycle in which these observations fall does not matter. Empirical GNP models do not assume that a cycle corresponding to that of experience necessarily exists. One has to experiment to discover whether a given model does, in fact, generate a cycle.

2. The second major difference to be emphasized is illustrated by the bureau's insistence that business cycles represent fluctuations "occurring at about the same time in *many* economic activities."[2] Mitchell's eclectic approach encompassed a wide range of variables and a considerable degree of disaggregation. The bureau has reflected faithfully this comprehensive and eclectic approach. In contrast, most GNP models concentrate on a few, usually highly aggregated, variables—consumption, investment, disposable income, etc. The influence of both neo-Keynesian theory and national income accounting is obvious. Some of these models are so simplified that they suggest a world in which there are no prices, costs, or profits, and no money.

---

[2] The quotation, with italics added, is from Burns and Mitchell's widely quoted definition in *Measuring Business Cycles*.

Mitchell's emphasis on the many different facets of economic activity leads fairly directly to the notion of diffusion indices. A cyclical expansion becomes gradually diffused through the economy; and, as the expansion proceeds, some individual series begin to contract while aggregative measures of economic activity are still rising. As Burns puts it, there is an " 'unseen' cycle in the relative distribution of expansions and contractions of specific activities. . . ."

This suggests that there is a "horizontal" dimension to the bureau's conception of the cyclical process that is lacking in aggregative models. Disturbances spread laterally through the economy, but with time lags—not only from one type of economic process to another (ordering, producing, selling, investing, etc.) but also from industry to industry, from firm to firm, and from region to region.

3. The third point of difference is related to the second. The National Bureau has thus far refused to work with comprehensive models which are both highly simplified and specify in advance the variables to be included. Instead, the bureau has adhered to Mitchell's conception of a dynamic, Walrasian-type system consisting of a vast multiplicity of interrelationships *which cannot be completely specified in advance*. While common observation and accepted theory suggest that some variables are likely to be particularly important, we cannot say in advance precisely how these variables are related, how the relationships may change over time, or what other variables may also turn out to have causal significance. These uncertainties are to be resolved, not by *a priori* theorizing, but by systematic observation and measurement.

In contrast, GNP forecasting starts with a simple and self-contained analytic framework, with all variables specified at the outset. The value of the GNP being predicted will be the sum of the components of aggregate demand; the number of components is small; and one or more of these components is estimated from predetermined functional relationships involving relatively few additional variables. Determination of these relationships may involve any degree of theorizing as an initial step. They may also represent empiricism in an extreme form, as when I, as well as G, is treated exogenously, to be predicted on the basis of whatever information is available. Whatever the limitations in practice, however, forecasting from GNP models does have a theoretical rationale, and the final forecast must meet the test of consistency as defined by the specified relationships in the model being used.

4. Finally, the National Bureau's indicators are not intended to forecast absolute levels, whereas this is the purpose of a GNP forecasting model. The tools described in *Business Cycle Indicators* can be used to help identify the current phase of the business cycle and, by inference, to predict whether or not a new phase is about to begin; but they do not lead directly to an explicit forecast of the absolute value of the

GNP (or any other variable) at some future date. In contrast, GNP models permit us to predict future values of particular variables at specified future times, but without explicit consideration of what will be the course of the cycle between the present and the selected future date. If the forecast, for example, is that the GNP a year from now will be $10 billions higher than at present, and a cyclical expansion is currently under way, this "point forecast" is consistent with either uninterrupted expansion or with a turning point some time during the year. Thus, Moore's indicators help to call the cyclical turns but do not directly and explicitly predict absolute levels; GNP models attempt to predict absolute levels but do not identify turning points (except by inference from a succession of future forecasts).

III

Table 1 presents Moore's revised list of 26 indicators, together with a summary of their record at the 1960 and 1961 turning points. On the basis of this recent evidence and the information available for earlier years, how well have the indicators performed in predicting postwar cyclical turns?

It is easier to ask than to answer this question. Much depends on how the indicators are used, and what criteria of success one wants to impose. The indicators may be examined separately, or they may be combined into some sort of index. One may use various devices to allow for irregular fluctuations. And one can ask much or relatively little of the indicators. He asks much if he expects a clear signal in advance of precisely when a cyclical phase will end. His request is more modest if he asks that the indicators tell whether a cyclical phase *has* ended within the past few months. Despite the use of the past tense, this test represents forecasting success in a significant sense, for it permits one to predict with a modest lag that the recent reversal heralds a new cumulative movement.

Space does not permit a detailed evaluation of the postwar record for these indicators. My overall judgment would be that their judicious use does provide a valuable addition to the forecasters' tool box. The indicators have been of some help in every postwar cyclical turn, but have been more helpful in some than in others. They have also given some false signals. The leading indicators clearly signaled in advance the upturn in 1949 and the end of the decline in 1954. There was less of a concensus in 1958, but on balance they indicated the end of the contraction by the time it occurred. Tabel 1 suggests that they did a good job in marking promptly the 1961 low point. Eight of the 12 leading series had reached their lows by December 1960, and this would have begun to be evident by February 1961, which marked the end of the 1960–61 contraction. Five of the nine coincident indicators had reached

TABLE 1
List of Moore's Indicators and Summary of Their Average Timing and of Their Timing at 1960–61 Turning Points[a]

Indicator	Median Lead (−) or Lag (+) Through 1958 (months)	Lead or Lag at May 1960 Peak	Lead or Lag at Feb. 1961 Through
LEADING GROUP			
Sensitive employment indicators			
Average hours worked per week, mfg.	−6	−12	−2
Gross accession rate, mfg.	−4	−14	−4
Layoff rate, mfg., inverted.	−6	−12	−2
New investment commitments			
New orders, durable goods.	−5	−11	−1
Housing starts.	−6	−13	−2
Commercial and industrial building contracts	−2	c	c
Net change in number of businesses (Q)	−4	0	−3
Profits, business failures, and stock prices			
Business failures, liabilities, inverted	−7	−12	−8
Corporate profits after taxes (Q)	−2	−12	0
Common stock price index	−4.5	−10	−4
Inventory investment and sensitive commodity prices			
Change in business inventories (Q)	−10	−12	0
Industrial materials spot market price index.	−2	−6	−2
ROUGHLY COINCIDING GROUP			
Employment and unemployment			
Nonagricultural employment	0	+2	+1
Unemployment rate, inverted.	0	−3	+6[b]
Production			
Industrial production index	0	−4	0
Gross national product, current prices (Q).	0	0	0
Gross national product, constant prices (Q)	−2	0	0
Income and Trade			
Bank debits outside NYC	−1	c	c
Personal income.	−1	+5	0
Sales by retail stores	+0.5	−1	−1
Wholesale prices			
Wholesale prices, excl. farm prod. & foods	+1	−1	+8[b]
LAGGING GROUP			
Plant and equipment expenditures (Q).	+1	0	+3
Wage & salary cost per unit of output, mfg.	+6.5	+10	+6
Manufacturers' inventories, book value, end of month	+2.5	+1.5	+1.5
Consumer instalment debt, end of month	+4.5	+8.5	+5.5[b]
Bank interest rates on business loans, last month of quarter	+5	−5	+4[b]

[a] List of indicators and median leads and lags are taken from Moore, *Business Cycle Indicators*, vol. I, pp. 56–7. The timing in 1960–61 is based on the data in Julius Shiskin, *Signals of Recession and Recovery*, N.B.E.R. Occasional Paper 77. Geoffrey Moore has been kind enough to check these leads and lags for me, and, in a few cases of doubt, I have substituted his suggested turning points for those I had originally chosen. (For a list of current entries see a recent issue of *Business Conditions Digest*.)

[b] Based on lowest value reached in data shown in *Business Cycle Developments*, October 1961.

[c] No cyclical contraction.

their low by February; this would have begun to be known by, say, April.

The record at postwar peaks is somewhat less impressive. On the whole, the leading series called the turn in 1953 fairly well. They performed poorly in 1957. Their performance in 1960 was better than in 1957 but not as good as in 1953. The trouble in 1957 was that too many of the leading indicators turned down too early. Table 1 indicates that there were also a number of very long leads at the 1960 peak.

In this case the situation was confused by the effects of the steel strike in 1959.

The indicators have also given some false signals—most notably in 1951–52 and again, as already suggested, in 1956. The indicators, like diffusion indices, reflect cross-currents that develop in the economy. In a sense, this is one of their functions. But when, as in 1951–52, we have a "divided economy" reflecting expansionary forces stemming from defense expenditures and at the same time moderate deflationary forces in the civilian sector, the indicators may do a poor job of indicating whether on *net balance* the economy is likely to move in one direction or the other. Something similar happened in 1956–57.

IV

Let us now turn to the diffusion indices, the rationale for which has already been described. If an aggregate series shows cyclical fluctuations, then a diffusion index which records what percentage of the components of that aggregate are currently expanding will tend to display a lead in comparison with the aggregate series.[3] Thus, for example, a diffusion index based on the industry components of the index of industrial production will lead the total index.

Skeptics challenge the use of diffusion indices on two grounds in particular. First, a diffusion index behaves very much like a rate-of-change series computed from the aggregate to which the diffusion index is related. Why bother with a diffusion index, in which we have to count the direction of change in all the components, if essentially the same results can be obtained by computing simple first-differences from the aggregate series?[4]

The second objection applies to the use of both diffusion indices and rates-of-change as forecasting devices. Both types of series, unless severely smoothed, tend to be highly erratic, and therefore they give too many false signals to be reliable predictors.

Several writers have investigated the relations between a diffusion index and a series representing the first differences of the corresponding aggregate. Empirically, there is almost always a very close relation, and one is a good proxy for the other. There are, however, a number

---

[3] This is not a mathematical necessity but an empirical fact. It would not be true in the case in which all of the components reached their peaks and troughs at exactly the same time. Neither would it be true if the distribution of peaks and troughs among the component series were such that the diffusion index showed no cycle, while the aggregate did show a cycle because of the heavy weight given to one or a few components.

[4] For a balanced discussion of the relative merits of diffusion and rate-of-change series, see Sidney Alexander, "Rate of Change Approaches to Forecasting: Diffusion Indexes and First Differences," *Economic Journal*, vol. 68 (June 1958), pp. 288–301. Other references will be found in chapter 9 of *Business Cycle Indicators*, in which Moore replies to his critics.

of reasons for computing diffusion indices rather than relying on rates of change in aggregates. Moore offers one important reason in Chapter 9 of *Business Cycle Indicators*. Diffusion indices represent direct observation of the "unseen cycle" in one or another set of dynamic interrelationships which can only be inferred from rates of change in aggregates. If a rate-of-change series turns down considerably before the aggregate does, we cannot be sure to what extent this happens because all of the components are still increasing but at a declining rate and to what extent it is because an increasing number of the components are showing absolute declines. For some purposes this might make a significant difference.

Those who criticize the National Bureau for "measurement without theory" should give Moore his due. The National Bureau's conception of the business cycle makes the diffusion index an appropriate tool for measuring directly certain phenomena (dispersion in patterns of behavior during the cycle) which preliminary hypothesizing (based on Mitchell's earlier work) suggests are causally significant—and in a way that is not true of a rate-of-change series.

Diffusion indices are turning out to be useful tools in economic analysis, entirely apart from their use in forecasting. They have, for example, been used to study disparities in the cyclical behavior of profits, employment, and new orders in different firms or industries. . . . I suspect that econometricians might well find it useful to include a diffusion index in some of their equations. Thus, a reasonable hypothesis is that investment depends not only on the level of current or lagged profits or output (among other things) but also on the extent to which the number of firms experiencing higher profits or output is changing. In this case, the diffusion index acts as an expectational variable that has a good deal of rationale behind it.

Now we come to the practical objection that diffusion indices behave too erratically to be useful in forecasting. For use in short-run forecasting, current diffusion indices must be computed from the actual current changes in a series, over monthly or longer spans; and such current indices tend to behave quite erratically. While this is a serious problem, it is not an insuperable one. Various smoothing procedures can be used with time spans short enough so that the smoothed series is not seriously out of date. It is worth observing in this connection that diffusion indices tend to be somewhat less erratic than rate-of-change series derived from the corresponding aggregates (when both are subjected to the same degree of smoothing), and this is the more true the larger the number of components included in the diffusion index.

Data presented by Shiskin suggest that sole reliance on the diffusion indices he presents would have enabled one to compile a moderately good, but by no means perfect, record in predicting postwar cyclical turns. It is true that his comprehensive diffusion indices led at every postwar turn by varying periods from two to 29 months. But they also gave a number of false signals—in some cases so frequently that it was difficult to say when a true cyclical turn was being predicted. Shiskin's diffusion indices did well in calling the downturn in 1948 and all of the postwar upturns. The record at the peaks in 1953, 1957, and 1960 is somewhat spotty. In all three cases, the chief trouble was that the diffusion indices had given sufficient false signals during the preceding year or two that one might have hesitated to call the true turns when they did come. Even so, the diffusion indices would have helped one to conclude fairly early in the downswings that followed that a true cyclical peak had passed. Further improvements in smoothing techniques and more experience in the use of various sorts of confirmatory evidence should permit us to improve on this record.

V

Frank Morris has expressed a judgment regarding the forecasting value of Moore's recent work which seems to me to be fully supported by the brief evaluation presented in the preceding paragraphs.[5]

In conclusion, the National Bureau's statistical indicators, like most other tools of economic analysis, probably have considerably more merit than their most uninformed critics see and probably more limitations than some of their most ardent advocates like to recognize.

The difficulties in applying the indicators to forecasting on a current basis . . . should demonstrate that these indicators do not provide a certain and easy method of forecasting. They have not brought automation to forecasting; and they do not threaten the professional judgment of economists with technological unemployment. However, I believe that the postwar experience does show that, properly used, the indicators can be a very valuable tool for the forecaster.

---
[5] Moore, *Business Cycle Indicators*, p. 119.

11. Forecasting and Analysis with an Econometric Model[*]

DANIEL B. SUITS

Although an econometric model is the statistical embodiment of theoretical relationships that are every economist's stock in trade, its discussion has largely been kept on a specialized level and confined to the more mathematical journals. Models are rarely explored from the point of view of their usefulness to the profession at large, yet there is nothing about their nature or their application—aside, again, from a solid grasp of economic theory—that requires anything more than an elementary knowledge of school algebra. The compilation of an econometric model requires a certain degree of technical specialization, but once constructed, any competent economist can apply it to policy analysis and economic forecasting.

The purpose of this article is to present an actual econometric model of the U.S. economy, to demonstrate its use as a forecasting instrument, and to explore its implications for policy analysis. To minimize the technical background required, the presentation is divided into two main parts. Part I deals with the general nature of econometric models, and, using a highly simplified schematic example, illustrates how forecasts are made with a model, how a model can be modified to permit the introduction of additional information and judgment, and how short-run and long-run policy multipliers are derived from the inverse of the model. Part II presents the 32-equation econometric model of the U.S. economy compiled by the Research Seminar in Quantitative Economics. This model is the most recent product of a research project whose initial output was the well-known Klein-Goldberger model. In part III the outlook for 1962, as calculated and published in November 1961, is studied as an example of an actual forecast; and earlier forecasts of this kind that have been prepared by the Research Seminar annually since 1953 are compared with actual events as a demonstration of the potential of the method.

In part III the inverse of the model is also presented and its application to policy evaluation is reviewed. Short-run and long-run multipliers

[*] *American Economic Review*, vol. 52, no. 1, (March 1962), pp. 104-32.

are calculated for selected policy variables. Part III also includes a digression on deficit financing, covering an interesting and important theoretical implication of the model.

I. ECONOMETRIC MODELS AND THEIR APPLICATIONS

The science of economics can be variously defined, but for the present purpose it is useful to think of it as the study of the relationships among a system of observable and essentially measurable variables: prices, costs, outputs, incomes, savings, employment, etc. These relationships derive from the complex behavior and interaction of millions of households, millions of firms, and thousands of governmental units, producing and exchanging millions of products. The relationships can be represented by a system of mathematical equations, but unfortunately a theoretically complete representation (e.g. a Walrasian system) would involve trillions of equations—surely millions for each household and firm. Moreover these equations would be individually as complex as human behavior, and involve the elaborate interaction of numberless variables.

We have neither the time nor the resources to deal with such a vast system of equations; to proceed at all we must simplify and condense. Millions of individual households become a single "household sector," millions of products become a single item of expenditure, e.g., "durable goods." Moreover, complex mathematical relationships among thousands of variables become simple linear approximations involving two or three aggregates. An econometric model of the economy is obtained by confronting these highly simplified equations with data arising from the historical operation of the economic system and, by appropriate statistical techniques, obtaining numerical estimates for their parameters.

The minimum number of equations necessary for an adequate representation of the economic system depends on a number of considerations, but clearly the fewer the equations the greater must be the level of aggregation and the less accurate and useful the result. On the other hand, the larger the number of equations and the greater the detail shown in the variables, the more complicated it is to derive the individual equations, to manipulate the resulting system, and to see the implications of the model. Where modern computing facilities can be used the mere size of the model is no longer a serious barrier to its effective application, but for purposes of exposition the smaller and simpler the model the better.

A. A Simple Illustrative Example

To illustrate the principles of application, let us suppose that the statistical procedure gave rise to the following, purely schematic, model of four equations.

$$C = 20 + .7(Y - T) \quad (1)$$
$$I = 2 + .1Y_{-1} \quad (2)$$
$$T = .2Y \quad (3)$$
$$Y = C + I + G \quad (4)$$

According to equation (1), consumption (C) depends on current disposable income ($Y - T$). In equation (2), investment (I) depends on income lagged one period. The third equation relates taxes (T) to income, while the last defines income as the sum of consumption, investment and government expenditure G.

While this model is small, it illustrates most of the properties of the larger model. The single consumption function in equation (1) corresponds to the set of four equations (01), (02), (03), and (04) that describe the behavior of the consumer sector in part II. The investment behavior represented in (2) corresponds to equations (05), through (10). The single tax equation (3) corresponds to a combination of the eleven tax and transfer equations, while the relationship of production to income embodied in equation (4) is indicated in much greater detail by equations (11) through (20).

This econometric model approximates the economy by a system of equations in which the unknowns are those variables—income, consumption, investment, and tax yield—whose behavior is to be analyzed. The "knowns" are government expenditure and lagged income. When projected values for the "knowns" are inserted in the equations, the system can be solved to forecast the values of the unknowns.

Quotation marks are used advisedly in the word "knowns." For, while some economic variables move so slowly along secular trends that their future values can be projected with considerable accuracy, others—for example new government expenditures—are unknown in advance of their occurrence, even in principle. Moreover, even the values of lagged variables are unknown at the time of the forecast, since a useful forecast must be made some months before the end of the preceding year. For example, each of the forecasts shown in table 3 was made during the first week of November of the preceding year. To make such forecasts, lagged variables are estimated from data for the first three quarters of the year, with the third quarter given double weight.

At any rate, suppose we expect next year's government expenditure to be 20, and the preliminary estimate of this year's income is, say, 100. Substituting $G = 20$ and $Y_{-1} = 100$ into the equations above and solving gives $C = 86.2$, $I = 12$, $T = 23.7$, $Y = 118.2$.

B. Introducing Outside Information

It may appear from the foregoing that this kind of forecasting is a blind, automatic procedure; but while an econometric model looks like a rigid analytical tool, it is actually a highly flexible device, readily modifiable to bring to bear additional information and judgment. For example, the investment equation in our little model is surely an unreliable predictor of capital formation. If no other information were available the equation would have to serve the purpose. But suppose we have available a survey of investment intentions reported by business. An estimate derived from such a survey is clearly superior to any that equation (2) could produce. To introduce the information into the forecast we simply remove equation (2) from the model and, in the remaining equations, set I equal to the survey value. Forecasts made from the Research Seminar model have frequently involved use of a figure for gross investment in plant and equipment derived from the McGraw-Hill Survey of Investment Intentions rather than from equation (05) of the model.

Information can also be used to modify individual relationships short of replacing them entirely. For example a prospective improvement in consumer credit terms—a variable that does not appear in our schematic model—would be expected to stimulate consumption expenditure. It is often possible to set an upper limit to this stimulating effect, and by increasing the constant term in the consumption function by this amount, to set an upper limit to the forecast economic outlook. An adjustment of this kind was applied to equation (01) to allow for the probable influence of the compact car on the outlook for automobile sales during 1960. For the same forecast, a similar modification of the housing starts equation (06) was made in anticipation of activity of the Federal National Mortgage Association.

Using the flexibility to full advantage permits the forecaster to explore any desired number of alternative sets of projections and modifications, and to bring to bear all information and judgment he possesses. The econometric model is not, therefore, a substitute for judgment, but rather serves to focus attention on the factors about which judgment must be exercised, and to impose an objective discipline whereby judgment about these factors is translated into an economic outlook that is consistent both internally, and with the past observed behavior of the economic system.

C. The Inverse Matrix

In principle, the exploration of a range of alternative projections and other modifications of the model consists of inserting each set of alternatives in turn as "knowns" in the equations and solving for the resulting forecast. The process is greatly expedited by further simplifying the model and by the use of the inverse matrix. Simplification of the model is made possible by the fact that one of the unknowns, I, depends only on knowns. I helps to determine the current values of C, T, and Y, but the latter do not, in turn, feed back into the determination of the current value of I. As a result, once the knowns are given, I can be directly calculated from (2) without reference to any other part of the model, and hence, as far as the remaining equations are concerned, I can be treated as a known in the sense used above. (Indeed it is this fact that enables us to replace equation (2) with survey values for I.)

The process of solving the system of equations can then be divided into two parts. First: using the values of the knowns, calculate the value of I. Second: substitute the knowns (now including I) into the remaining equations, and solve for the other unknowns.

The inverse matrix facilitates the second step. For those unfamiliar with matrix manipulations the following will help clarify the nature and use of this table. Since I is now considered as known, the model is reduced to the system of three equations (1), (3) and (4) above. By transferring all unknowns to the left side, and representing the right sides by P_1, P_3, and P_4, these equations can be expressed as:

$$C - 0.7Y + 0.7T = 20 = P_1 \quad (1)$$
$$-.2Y + 1.0T = 0 = P_3 \quad (3)$$
$$-C + Y = I + G = P_4 \quad (4)$$

Now using any convenient method to solve this system for C, Y, and T in terms of P_1, P_3, and P_4 will yield:

$$C = 2.273P_1 - 1.591P_3 + 1.273P_4$$
$$T = .445P_1 + .682P_3 + .455P_4$$
$$Y = 2.273P_1 - 1.591P_3 + 2.273P_4$$

That is, the value of each unknown is obtained as a specified weighted total of P_1, P_3, and P_4. Where a large number of equations is used, and a lot of calculating is to be done, it is convenient to display the weights used for each unknown as a column of numbers in a table, with the detail of the P's shown in a separate column at the right:

C	T	Y	P	
2.273	.455	2.273	20	(1)
−1.591	.682	−1.591	0	(3)
1.273	.455	2.273	$I + G$	(4)

To make a forecast we first substitute Y_{-1} into equation (2) and solve for I. Then I and G are substituted in the P column of the table and the values of P_1, P_3 and P_4 calculated. These values, weighted by the numbers shown in the C column of the inverse and summed, give the forecast value of consumption; use of the weights of column Y gives the forecast for income, etc.[1] For example if we set $Y_{-1} = 100$ and $G = 20$, we first find from (2) $I = 12$. Substituting these values in column P of the table gives the forecast values: $C = 86.2$, $T = 23.7$, $Y = 118.2$.

D. Short-Run Policy Multipliers

It is an obvious step from economic forecasting to short-run policy analysis. To investigate any specified set of prospective government actions, we insert them in the proper place in column P and solve for the forecast implied by these assumptions. The analysis is expedited if we first calculate short-run multipliers for the individual components of government action. These can then be applied in any desired policy mixture.

Short-run multipliers for any policy variable are readily calculated by inserting $+1$ for the variable everywhere it appears in column P, and then (ignoring all terms that do not contain the variable in question) extending a forecast using the columns of the inverse. For example, to calculate the government expenditure multiplier, set $G = 1$ in row (4) of column P. This makes $P_4 = 1$. To find the effect of this value of G on, say, income, multiply this value of P_4 by the weight in row (4) of the Y column to get $Y = 1 \times 2.273 = 2.273$. That is, the income multiplier on government expenditure is 2.273. Likewise, $T = 1 \times .455 = .455$. That is, the tax-yield multiplier on government expenditure is .455. In other words, for every dollar of additional government expenditure, tax receipts rise by nearly 46 cents. A corollary is that—according to our schematic model—an increase in government expenditure of 1 with no change in tax legislation will generate an increase in deficit of only:

$$G - T = 1 - .46 = .54$$

In addition to changing the value of exogenous variables like government expenditure, government policy can produce changes in the equations themselves. An extensive change—e.g. a substantial alteration in tax rates—can only be studied by replacing the old tax equation by a new one, but less extensive changes can be studied as shifts in the levels of existing equations, the coefficients being unaltered.

Multipliers for such shifts are easily determined by placing $+1$ in the row of column P that corresponds to the equation being shifted.

---

[1] As those familiar with matrix algebra will recognize, the inverse matrix is tabulated here in its transposed form, and goes into the P vector at the right column by column.

The extensions are then made as before. For example, to calculate the multipliers on a $+1$ shift in the level of the tax equation, we put $+1$ in the row marked (3) of column P, since the tax equation is (3). The multiplier effect of this shift is then calculated by multiplying this 1 by the weight in the corresponding row of the appropriate column, as shown above. For example for income:

$$Y = 1 \times (-1.591) = -1.591$$

For consumption:

$$C = 1 \times (-1.591) = -1.591$$

In other words, the multipliers associated with the shift of an equation are merely the weights in the row of the inverse corresponding to that equation.

Note that according to our simplified model, the tax-yield multiplier is .682. That is, an upward shift of $1 billion in the tax *schedule* actually increases *yield* by only $682 million. The difference is due to the decline in income arising from the shift in the tax schedule.

The small size of our illustrative model limits the policy variables to government expenditure and the level of taxes. In the more extensive model below, policy is given considerably more scope; a number of individual tax and transfer equations can be shifted, and a number of different kinds of expenditure altered. The number of possible combinations of action is correspondingly very large; but one important advantage to a linear system lies in the fact that once multipliers for the individual components have been calculated, the economic implications of a complete policy "package" can be estimated by summing the effects of the individual components.

For example, an increase of $1 in government expenditure coupled with an upward shift of $1 in the tax schedule would generate a change in income given by the sum of the two individual multipliers:

$$Y = 2.273 - 1.591 = .682$$

This is what might be called an "*ex ante*-balanced" government expenditure multiplier. That is, the change in the law is such as to increase tax yield at the *existing* level of income by enough to balance the planned expenditure, but the budget will not necessarily be balanced *ex post*. The tax and expenditure program will alter income, and hence will change tax yields. Analysis of the complete fiscal impact of the operation requires the examination of all revenue and outlay items combined.

Adding together the two tax-yield multipliers we find that the additional expenditure of $1 is offset by a tax yield of:

$$.682 + .455 = 1.137$$

That is, the *ex ante*-balanced expenditure of $1 billion would, in our example, be accompanied by an increase of $1.137 billion in tax yield and give rise to an *ex post* surplus of $137 million.

E. Dynamics and Long-Run Multipliers

An increase in government expenditure of 1.0 will increase income by 2.273 the same year. But the long-run effect of expenditure sustained at this level will differ from this. According to equation (2), an increase in income this year will generate an increase in investment next year. This will again raise income and add further stimulus the following year, etc. Once the inverse has been tabulated, however, the sequence can easily be calculated by inserting the forecast values of one year as the "knowns" of the next. Thus an initial increase in G of 1 will raise Y by 2.273. This will raise I by $.2 \times 2.773 = .455$ the following year. The value of P_4 is then $G + I = 1.455$ and the second year income rises to 3.307 above its initial value, etc. The five-year sequence of values would be:

Year	1	2	3	4	5
Income	2.273	3.307	3.775	3.989	4.078

This means, for example, that if government expenditure is increased by 1 in 1961, and sustained at that new level, the level of income in 1965 will—other things equal—be 4.087 higher than it was in 1960.

Similar sequences can be worked out for other policy variables. For example a shift of 1 in the tax schedule in year 1 would imply the following sequence of annual income values:

Year	1	2	3	4	5
Income	−1.591	−2.314	−2.643	−2.793	−2.862

Like short-run multipliers, these long-run multipliers can be combined by simple addition. For example, a permanent rise of 1 in government expenditure coupled with an *ex-ante* shift of 1 in the tax schedule would raise income by $2.273 - 1.591 = .682$ the first year. After five years, however, income would be $4.087 - 2.862 = 1.225$ higher than its initial level.

Although the discussion has been focused on a highly simplified example, the principles developed apply equally to any linear econometric model. The presentation of the actual Research Seminar model in part II will follow the same pattern as the illustration of part I.

II. THE MODEL OF THE U.S. ECONOMY

The model developed by the Research Seminar in Quantitative Economics consists of 32 equations, most of them least-squares linear regressions fitted to annual first differences in the variables.[2]

Five advantages are gained by the use of first differences. In the first place, the autocorrelation of residuals from time series regressions causes a downward bias in calculated standard errors, giving an exaggerated appearance of precision to the result. The use of first differences serves to reduce this bias. Secondly, many of the equations—e.g. the demand for consumer durables—involve stocks for which data are not currently available. The increase in a stock is composed of current acquisitions less retirements. Since the latter tends to be a smooth series, exhibiting little year-to-year variation, the first difference in stock is well represented by acquisitions, a figure readily available on a current basis. Thirdly, in short-run analysis and forecasting, the present position is known, and *ceteris paribus* will continue. The important question is what change from that position will result from projected changes in other factors. The use of first differences serves to focus the power of the analysis on these changes. Fourthly, the use of first differences minimizes the effect of slowly moving variables such as population, tastes, technical change, etc., without explicitly introducing them into the analysis. The net effect of changes in these factors is represented in the constant term of the equation. Finally, use of first differences minimizes the complications produced by data revision when the model is applied. Revisions usually alter the level at which variables are measured, rather than their year-to-year variation.

In calculating the equations, the prewar and postwar periods were explored separately to determine whether there was any indication of a change in the coefficients. Except for institutional relationships—tax laws, transfers, etc.—no important shifts were discovered. Nevertheless the final equations are fitted only to data drawn from the period 1947–1960 to maximize their applicability to current problems.

The equations of the model are presented and discussed below by sectors, and the symbol for each variable is explained the first time it appears. In general the variables correspond to the magnitudes as given in the national accounts, measured in billions of 1954 dollars. In calculat-

---

[2] The exceptions are definitional equations, and those approximating tax laws. Use of least squares is unnecessary for the former, and inappropriate to the latter. The frequency of change in tax laws makes past data irrelevant to their current analysis. Tax equations were fitted by eye through a few relevant points.

ing the equations, however, all imputations were removed from the Department of Commerce figures for consumer expenditure and disposable income. These imputations, mainly associated with services rendered by financial institutions and by owner-occupied dwellings, are added back in after a forecast is made to maintain comparability with the national accounts. First differences are indicated throughout by prefixing Δ to the symbol of the variable. Note, however, that lagged undifferenced values of certain variables appear at some points (e.g. in the automobile demand equation [01] below). These undifferenced values serve as proxy variables for first differences in stocks are explained above. Figures in parentheses are the standard errors of the regression coefficients.

A. Aggregate Demand

1. Consumption.
Automobiles and Parts:

$$\Delta A = .177 \, \Delta(Y - X_u - X_f - X_s) - .495 \, A_{-1} \quad (01)$$
$$(.086) \qquad\qquad\qquad\qquad (.168)$$
$$+ .260 \, \Delta L_{-1} + 4.710$$
$$(.082)$$

Consumer expenditure for new and net used automobiles and parts (ΔA) depends on disposable income (Y), net of transfers for unemployment compensation (X_a), and other federal (X_f) and state (X_s) transfers. These transfers are deducted on the ground that they are unlikely to find their way into the automobile market. Servicemen's insurance dividends (X_{GI}) are not deducted from disposable income. In addition, automobile demand depends on the stock of cars on the road (A_{-1}) and on the real value of consumer liquid assets at the end of the preceding year (ΔL_{-1}). For this purpose liquid assets are defined as household holdings of currency and demand deposits plus fixed-value redeemable claims as estimated by the Federal Reserve Board. The sizeable constant term in the equation probably reflects replacement demand.

Demand for Other Durables:

$$\Delta D = .176 \, \Delta Y - .0694 D_{-1} + .0784 \, \Delta L_{-1} + .262 \quad (02)$$
$$(.015) \qquad (.029) \qquad (.016)$$

This equation relates ΔD, consumer expenditure for durables (other than automobiles and parts) to diposable income (ΔY), the accumulating stock of durables (D_{-1}) and liquid assets.

Demand for Nondurable Goods:

$$\Delta ND = .224 \, \Delta Y + .205 \, \Delta ND_{-1} + .143 \, \Delta L_{-1} - .149 \quad (03)$$
$$(.060) \qquad (.135) \qquad (.059)$$

Nondurable expenditure depends on disposable income, liquid assets, and last year's nondurable expenditure (ΔND_{-1}). Notice the difference between this and the foregoing equations. In (01) and (02) the lagged values were undifferenced representing accumulation of stock. In this equation the difference itself is lagged, representing a dynamic adjustment in nondurable expenditure: an initial rise in level is followed by a subsequent secondary rise.

Demand for Services:

$$\Delta S = .0906\ \Delta Y + .530\ \Delta S_{-1} + .0381\ \Delta L_{-1} + .363 \qquad (04)$$
$$(.029) \qquad (.170) \qquad (.029)$$

This equation is similar to (03) and relates expenditure for services (ΔS) to disposable income, liquid assets, and lagged service expenditure. It should be remembered that service expenditure is here defined to exclude imputed items.

These four equations constitute the demand sector. Note that the aggregate marginal propensity to consume can be estimated by summing the income coefficients in the four equations. The sum, .67, is an estimate of the marginal propensity to consume, at least as an initial impact. The lagged terms in the individual equations, however, generate a dynamic response of consumption to income. As the equations show, the long-run response of nondurables and services tends to be greater, and that of automobile and durable less, than the initial impact. The implications of this fact for the calculation of multipliers will appear below.

2. Gross Capital Expenditure.

Plant and Equipment Expenditure:

$$\Delta PE = .605\ \Delta(P^*_{-1} - T_{fc-1} - T_{sc-1}) - .124\ PE_{-1} + 4.509 \qquad (05)$$
$$(.238) \qquad\qquad\qquad\qquad (.216)$$

ΔPE, expenditure for new plant and equipment, includes producers' durables, nonfarm nonresidential construction, and all farm construction. It is related to the preceding year's corporate profits (P^*_{-1}) after federal (T_{fc}) and state (T_{sc}) corporate income taxes and to its own lagged, undifferenced value (PE_{-1}). The latter represents growth in the stock of plant and equipment. As in (01) above, the large constant term probably represents replacement.

Housing Starts:

$$\Delta HS = 19.636\ \Delta \left(\frac{FHA + VA}{2} - Aaa\right) - .702\ HS_{-1} + 66.147 \qquad (06)$$
$$(17.0) \qquad\qquad\qquad\qquad (.312)$$

This equation, which applies only to the postwar period, relates the number of nonfarm residential housing starts (ΔHS), measured in thousand of units per month, to the gap between the simple average of the FHA and VA ceiling interest rates on the one hand, and the Aaa bond yield on the other (both expressed in percentage points). This interest rate differential reflects the substantial influence of credit availability on the volume of FHA and VA financed residential construction. It can function, however, only in the presence of a strong underlying housing demand. With the accumulation of a large stock as a consequence of construction in recent years, this interest rate differential may lose its role in the model. The term HS_{-1}, the lagged undifferenced value of housing starts, only partially represents the effect of this accumulation, and equation (06) is probably due for revision.

Housing Expenditure:

$$\Delta H = .125\ \Delta HS + .024\ \Delta HS_{-1} + 6.580\ \Delta C + .083 \quad (07)$$
$$(.013) \qquad (.012) \qquad (5.42)$$

Expenditure on housing, (ΔH), depends on the rate at which residential construction is carried forward, and thus on current and lagged starts. In addition it depends on construction costs. The term ΔC is the ratio of the index of construction costs to the GNP deflator.

Durable Goods Inventory:

$$\Delta ID = .291\ \Delta(A + D) + .591\ \Delta PD + .305\ \Delta M_{+1} - .669\ ID_{-1} \quad (08)$$
$$(.100) \qquad\qquad (.157) \qquad (.085) \qquad (.109)$$

Accumulation of durable inventories, ΔID, depends on sales of consumer durables, producers durables ΔPD, and the stock of inventory already accumulated ID_{-1}. In addition an important component of inventory is associated with government military orders. Production on such orders appears in the national accounts as goods in process, and exerts a strong impact on the economy long before delivery of the finished product materializes as government expenditure. A wide variety of arrangements and lead times are involved in this process. As a proxy for such orders in any given year, we use ΔM_{+1}, federal military purchases from private industry the following year.

The equilibrium sales-inventory ratio implied by this equation compares favorably with that observed from other data.

Nondurable Goods Inventory:

$$\Delta IND = .427\ \Delta ND - 1.121\ IND_{-1} \quad (09)$$
$$(.111) \qquad\quad (.248)$$

Accumulation of nondurable inventory, ΔIND, depends on consumer sales of nondurables and the stock already on hand, IND_{-1}.

Imports:

$$\Delta R = .0602\ \Delta G^* + .369 \quad (10)$$
$$(.03)$$

This relates the aggregate level of imports to the private $\text{GNP}(G^*)$.

3. Private Gross National Product

$$\Delta G^* = \Delta(A + D + ND + S) + (\Delta F - \Delta R) + \Delta ID + \Delta IND \quad (11)$$
$$+ \Delta PE + \Delta H + \Delta g$$

Private GNP is defined as the sum of its parts including net exports $(\Delta F - \Delta R)$ and government purchases from private firms (Δg).

B. Income and Employment

Wage and Salary Workers, Private Sector:

$$\Delta E = .068 \, \Delta G^* \quad (12)$$

This production function, relating ΔE, the number of full-time equivalent employees in the private sector (measured in millions of persons) to the private GNP, applies specifically to the forecast of 1962 and is based on the first three quarters recovery experience during 1961.

Unemployment:

$$\Delta U = \Delta LF - \Delta E_0 - \Delta E_G - \Delta E \quad (13)$$

Unemployment is the difference between labor force (ΔLF) on the one hand, and the number of self-employed and unpaid family workers, (ΔE_0), government workers, including armed services (ΔE_G) and employees of private industry (ΔE).

Average Annual Earnings:

$$\Delta w = -.0216 \, \Delta U + .00436 P^*_{-1} - .0743 \quad (14)$$
$$(.0076) (.0025)$$

Δw, average annual earnings (including wages and salaries plus "other labor income," and measured in thousands of dollars) is related to unemployment and last year's profits. This relationship reflects two facts. First and probably more important, annual earnings are heavily influenced by overtime pay which varies inversely with the level of unemployment. Secondly, pressure of union demands varies directly with profits and inversely with the level of unemployment. The undifferenced level of profits is used since the *existence* of profits acts as a target for wage demands.

Private Wage Bill:

$$\Delta W = \Delta(wE) = w_{-1} \Delta E + E_{-1} \Delta w \quad (15)$$

By definition the wage bill is the product of average earnings and employment. To keep the model linear, this nonlinear relationship is replaced by the linear approximation shown.

Depreciation:

$$\Delta Dep = .0456 \, \Delta G^* + .763 \quad (16)$$

Property Income:

$$\Delta P = \Delta G^* - \Delta W - \Delta Dep - \Delta T_{fe} - \Delta T_{cd} - \Delta T_{bp} \quad (17)$$
$$- \Delta T_{ss} - \Delta T_{os} - \Delta SI_r$$

Property income (ΔP) is a residual from the GNP after deducting wage costs, depreciation (ΔDep), employer contributions for social insurance (ΔSI_r), and indirect business taxes: federal excises (ΔT_{fe}), customs duties (ΔT_{cd}), business property (ΔT_{bp}), state sales (ΔT_{ss}), and other state taxes on business (ΔT_{os}).

Corporate Profits:

$$\Delta P^* = .902(\Delta P - \Delta P_f) - 1.027 \quad (18)$$

This relates profits (ΔP^*) to total property income net of farm income (ΔP_f). There is, of course, no strong theoretical basis for the particular distribution of corporate business found in the U.S. economy. This equation is an empirical representation of the distribution of property income under existing institutional arrangements.

Dividends:

$$\Delta Div = .229 \, \Delta(P^* - T_{fc} - T_{sc}) \quad (19)$$
$$(.064)$$
$$+ .0198(P^* - T_{fc} - T_{sc} - Div)_{-1} - .0191$$
$$(.052)$$

Current dividends (ΔDiv) depend on current profits after federal (T_{fc}) and state (T_{sc}) corporate profits taxes, and on last year's level of undistributed profits.

Disposable Income:

$$\Delta Y = \Delta W + \Delta W_G + (\Delta P - \Delta P^*) + \Delta Div + \Delta i_G + \Delta X_u + \Delta X_f + \Delta X_s$$
$$+ \Delta X_{GI} - \Delta T_{fy} - \Delta T_{sy} - \Delta T_{eg} - \Delta T_{op} - \Delta SI_e + \Delta T_{ref} \quad (20)$$

Diposable income is the sum of wages, including government wages (W_G), noncorporate property income ($\Delta P - \Delta P^*$), dividends, government interest payments (i_G), plus transfers, less personal taxes; federal (ΔT_{fy}) and state (ΔT_{sy}) income, estate and gift (ΔT_{eg}), other personal taxes (ΔT_{op}) and personal contributions for social insurance ΔSI_e, all net of tax refunds ΔT_{ref}.

C. Taxes and Government Transfers

1. Federal Taxes

Federal Corporate Profits Tax:

$$\Delta T_{fc} = .500 \, \Delta P^* \quad (21)$$

Federal Personal Income Tax Receipts:

$$\Delta T_{fy} = .111(\Delta W + \Delta W_G) + .150(\Delta P - \Delta P^* + \Delta i_G) + .195 \, \Delta Div \quad (22)$$

This equation relates income tax receipts in the form of withholding, quarterly payments on estimated tax, and final tax payment to the several income components. The coefficients reflect both variation in income shares by tax bracket and the effect of the dividend tax credit.

Federal Personal Income Tax Liability:

$$\Delta T^*_{fy} = .100(\Delta W + \Delta W_G) + .114(\Delta P - \Delta P^* + \Delta i_G) + .154 \, \Delta Div \quad (23)$$

Tax receipts commonly exceed liability. The difference (ΔT_{ref}) appears as a tax refund the following year.

Federal Excise Taxes:

$$\Delta T_{fe} = .099 \, \Delta A + .011 \, \Delta D + .003 \, \Delta ND + .010 \, \Delta G^* + .015 \, \Delta Y \quad (24)$$

Customs Duties:

$$\Delta T_{cd} = .083 \, \Delta R + .012 \quad (25)$$

2. State and Local Taxes

State Corporate Income Taxes:

$$\Delta T_{sc} = .019 \, \Delta P^* \quad (26)$$

State and Local Sales Taxes:

$$\Delta T_{ss} = .033(\Delta A + \Delta D + \Delta ND + \Delta S) \quad (27)$$

State and Local Personal Income Taxes:

$$\Delta T_{sy} = .010(\Delta W + \Delta W_G + \Delta P - \Delta P^* + \Delta Div + \Delta i_G) \quad (28)$$

3. Social Insurance Programs

Private Employer Contributions for Social Insurance:

$$\Delta SI_r = .149 \, \Delta E \quad (29)$$

Personal Contributions for Social Insurance:

$$\Delta SI_c = .129(\Delta E + \Delta E_G) + .050(\Delta P - \Delta P^*) \quad (30)$$

Covered Unemployment:

$$\Delta U_c = .675 \, \Delta U - .140(\Delta LF - \Delta LF_{-1}) \quad (31)$$

The relationship of unemployment covered by compensation programs (ΔU_c) to total unemployment varies with the rate of increase in the labor force. When the labor force is growing rapidly, new entrants, not yet covered, make up a larger proportion of total unemployment.

Unemployment Compensation:

$$\Delta X_u = 1.77 \, \Delta U_c + .101 \tag{32}$$

III. THE MODEL AS A FORECASTING INSTRUMENT

A. The Forecast of 1962

The unknowns of the model are the 32 variables like automobile demand, disposable income, private GNP, etc. that stand on the left side of the equations. The knowns are variables like government purchases from private firms, labor force, household liquid assets, etc. that appear only on the right side of the equations, and whose values must be projected or assigned before the unknowns can be forecast.

The forecast of 1962, calculated and presented in November 1961, employed the projected values shown in table 1. The most important single item was the $16.9 billion increase in consumer holdings of liquid assets. A few of the other key items were: a $6.9 billion projected increase in government purchases from private firms; an increase of .6 million in government employment; increase in government wage payments of $1.5 billion; and a $1 billion rise in military orders. Note that investment in plant and equipment is projected directly on the basis of the McGraw-Hill survey rather than from equation (05). All monetary values are in 1954 dollars.

When the projections of table 1 were inserted in the equations, the solution gave the outlook for 1962 shown in table 2. The first two columns contain a detailed comparison of the forecast of 1961 with the preliminary actual values. The middle column contains the solutions obtained from the equations. These are in first differences and are expressed as increases over 1961. When the forecast increase is added to the preliminary actual level for 1961 the result is the forecast level of 1962 shown in the fourth column. In the last column this forecast has been translated into approximate 1962 prices.[3]

The forecast entails substantial increases in consumption expenditure, especially for automobiles. The forecast level of $18.8 billion for this sector constitutes a record level of automobile sales, exceeding the $17.9 billion reached in 1955. This large increase derives primarily from the high level of consumer liquidity and the small addition to stocks of cars during 1961.

---

[3] To convert the values from 1954 to 1962 prices they were multiplied by deflators obtained by raising 1961 deflators 1.5 percent across the board. The result serves to put the forecast in proper perspective, but should not be thought of as part of the forecast itself.

TABLE 1
Projections Underlying Forecast of 1962

Equation

(01) $A_{-1} = 14.3 \quad \Delta L_{-1} = 16.9 \quad X_f = \Delta X_s = 0$
(02) $D_{-1} = 27.3 \quad \Delta L_{-1} = 16.9$
(03) $\Delta ND_{-1} = 1.2 \quad \Delta L_{-1} = 16.9$
(04) $\Delta S_{-1} = 3.4 \quad \Delta L_{-1} = 16.9$
(05) $\Delta PE = 1.3^a$
(06) $\Delta Aaa = +.02 \quad \Delta \left(\dfrac{FHA + VA}{2}\right) = -.06^b \quad HS_{-1} = 93.1$
(07) $\Delta HS_{-1} = 3.2 \quad \Delta C = 0$
(08) $\Delta PD = .7^a \quad \Delta M_{+1} = 1.0 \quad ID_{-1} = 0.0$
(09) $IND_{-1} = 1.7$
(10) —
(11) $\Delta F = 0 \quad \Delta PE = 1.3^a \quad \Delta g = 6.9$
(12) —
(13) $\Delta LF = 1.2 \quad \Delta E_0 = .2 \quad \Delta E_G = .6$
(14) $P^*_{-1} = 39.6$
(15) $w_{-1} = 4.38 \quad E_{-1} = 46.9$
(16) —
(17) $\Delta T_{bp} = .730 \quad \Delta T_{os} = .087$
(18) $\Delta P_f = 0$
(19) —
(20) $\Delta X_f = \Delta X_s = \Delta X_{GI} = 0 \quad \Delta W_G = 1.5 \quad \Delta i_G = .1 \quad \Delta T_{op} = .35 \quad \Delta T_{ey} = .08$
   $\Delta T_{ref} = 0$
(21) —
(22) $\Delta W_G = 1.5 \quad \Delta i_G = .1$
(23) $\Delta W_G = 1.5 \quad \Delta i_G = .1$
(24) —
(25) —
(26) —
(27) —
(28) $\Delta W_G = 1.5 \quad \Delta i_G = .1$
(29) —
(30) $\Delta E_G = .6$
(31) $\Delta LF = 1.2 \quad \Delta LF_{-1} = 1.0$
(32) —
(Addendum) Δ Imputed Services $= 1.5$

[a] Based on McGraw-Hill survey showing 4 percent increase in plant and equipment expenditure.
[b] FHA ceiling rates projected at their present level throughout 1962. The projected decline reflects the fact that they were above this level in early 1961.

Aside from the consumer sector the main stimulus to the economy derives from projected increases in government outlays, associated with the trend of state and local expenditures and federal defense expenditure. In preparing the forecast no allowance was made for the possible effect of a steel strike during 1962. Inventory accumulation in anticipation of interruption of steel supplies will probably accelerate inventory accumulation in the first half of the year and depress it in the second half. There is no indication that this will alter the overall level for the year.

11. Forecasting and Analysis with an Econometric Model

TABLE 2
Review of 1961 and Outlook for 1962
(monetary figures, except column 5, are billions of 1954 dollars)

	1961 Forecast	1961 Actual[p]	Forecast Increase	Forecast 1962 (1954 prices)	Forecast 1962 (1962 prices)
Gross National Product	450.1	446.8	27.5[a]	474.3	559.9
Consumption Expenditures					
Automobiles and Parts	14.6	14.3	4.5	18.8	21.2
Other Durables	25.1	24.8	1.9	26.7	28.7
Nondurables	144.7	142.7	5.3	148.0	163.6
Services	119.9	119.6	5.5[a]	125.1	147.9
Private Gross Capital Expenditure					
Plant and Equipment	39.0	37.3	1.3	38.6	48.1
Residential Construction	19.9	17.7	0.1	17.8	21.4
Inventory Investment					
Durables	} 2.4	0.0	2.6	2.6	2.8
Nondurables		1.7	0.4	2.1	2.3
Imports	24.8	22.2	1.9	24.1	24.8
Exports	24.6	26.4	....	26.4	28.7
Government Expenditure on Goods and Services	84.7	84.5	7.8	92.3	120.0
Corporate Profits	40.3	39.6	5.1	44.7	52.5
Dividends	12.4	12.3	0.7	13.0	15.3
Civilian Labor Force[b]					
(millions of persons)	71.3	71.6	0.9	72.5	
Private Wage and Salary Workers		46.9	1.7	48.6	
Govt. Employees (Civilian)	67.0	8.8	0.3	9.1	
Self-employed		11.0	0.2	11.2	
Unemployed[b]					
Number (millions)	4.3	4.9	−1.3	3.6	
Percent of Civilian Labor Force	6.0	6.8	....	5.0	

[p] Preliminary.
[a] Includes imputed services.
[b] Annual average.

The forecast increase in production is adequate to absorb more than the growth of the labor force, and the outlook concludes by showing a reduction of 1.3 million in unemployment, reducing the average for the year to 3.6 million or 5 percent of the civilian labor force.

B. Review of Past Forecasts

The Research Seminar in Quantitative Economics has been making annual forecasts since 1953, each a matter of record published in advance of the year forecast. The econometric model has been revised and improved several times over this period (the version presented here was first used for the 1962 forecast), but the review of past forecasting performance in table 3 will illustrate the general reliability of the method.[4] Each forecast is shown as it was presented, and compared with the

---
[4] The review of the 1961 forecast, compared with the actual outcome, is provided in table 2.

TABLE 3
Review of Past Forecasts

	1953[a] Forecast	1953[a] Actual	1954[a] Forecast	1954[a] Actual	1955[a] Forecast	1955[a] Actual	1956[a] Forecast	1956[a] Actual	1957[b] Forecast	1957[b] Actual
Gross National Product	177.4	178.6	174.8	173.9	176.4	188.5	191.6	191.2	337.0	335.2
Consumption Expenditure	114.4	115.9	117.3	116.7	118.6	125.1	127.4	128.5	226.2	226.1
Private Gross Capital Formation	24.2	24.9	22.7	23.6	25.2	25.9	28.7	26.3	47.2	44.4
Employee Compensation	80.4[f]	79.8[f]	82.3[f]	83.0[f]	81.2[f]	89.5[f]	107.1	104.3	196.5	196.3

	1958[c] Forecast	1958[c] Actual	1959[d] Forecast	1959[d] Actual	1960[e] Forecast	1960[e] Actual
Gross National Product	432.7	432.5	456.7	475.7	432.0	439.2
Consumption Expenditure	282.1	287.3	295.4	310.7	287.1	296.8
Automobiles	. . . .	. . . .	. . . .	. . . .	16.7	15.6
Other Durables	. . . .	. . . .	. . . .	. . . .	25.2	25.2
Nondurables	. . . .	. . . .	. . . .	. . . .	138.9	141.9
Services	. . . .	. . . .	. . . .	. . . .	106.3	113.7
Private Gross Capital Expenditure	61.9	53.7	61.2	70.4	62.4	60.5
Plant and Equipment	. . . .	. . . .	44.0	43.0	40.5	39.3
Residual Construction	. . . .	. . . .	17.8	21.6	19.7	18.0
Inventory	. . . .	. . . .	-.6	5.8	2.2	3.2
Government Purchase of Goods and Services	88.8	90.5	100.1	94.6	83.7	80.3
Net Exports					-1.3	1.6
Employee Compensation	254.3	251.8	261.0	273.4	236.3	257.1
Corporate Profits	39.5	36.5	47.7	45.8	42.7	38.7
Dividends	. . . .	. . . .	. . . .	. . . .	12.2	12.2
Civilian Employment	66.4	66.5	66.0	65.6	65.5[g]	66.7[h]
Unemployment	4.8	4.7	3.4	3.8	4.4[g]	3.9[h]

[a] 1939 prices [c] 1957 prices [e] 1954 prices [g] excludes Alaska and Hawaii
[b] 1947 prices [d] 1958 prices [f] private sector only [h] includes Alaska and Hawaii

actual outcome.[5] Note that from 1953 to 1956 the figures are given in 1939 dollars; thereafter the price level employed was changed almost every year. The increasing elaboration of the model is evident in the table.

As plotted in figure 1, the general accuracy of these forecasts speaks for itself. The direction of movement was correctly forecast each year, and the levels were generally well predicted. The recession of 1954 was forecast with considerable precision. The recovery of 1955 was likewise

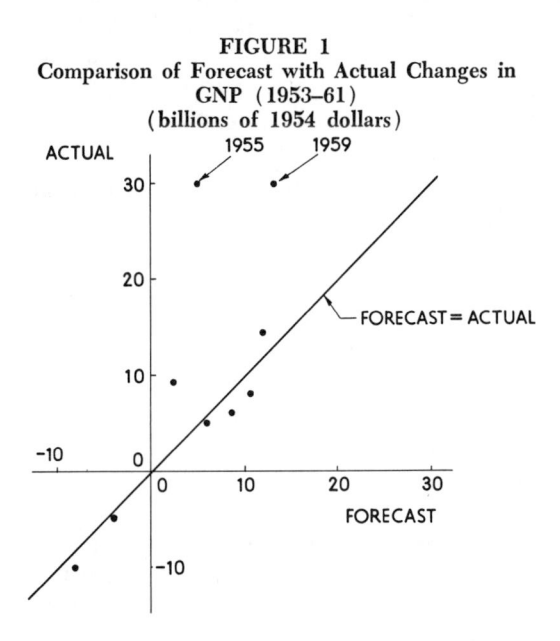

FIGURE 1
Comparison of Forecast with Actual Changes in GNP (1953–61)
(billions of 1954 dollars)

forecast, but the magnitude of the boom that developed was grossly underestimated. The fact that the error of the 1955 forecast is concentrated in the consumer sector lends support to the idea that this was a consumer-generated movement. The recession of 1958 was well predicted. The recovery of 1959 was somewhat underestimated.

In many respects the forecast of 1960 was the most interesting of all. Made in November 1959 at the height of business optimism, and amidst general anticipation of the "soaring 'sixties," its pessimistic outlook for 1960 was greeted with almost complete skepticism, but it proved to be more exact than any other forecast placed on record in advance.

---
[5] Since data revisions occur frequently, there is some question as to what figures should be taken as "actual." Since we want the "actual" figures as close as possible in definition and economic context to the data on which the forecast was based, they are taken from the issue of the *Survey of Current Business* appearing in the February following the forecast year. E. G. the "actual" GNP for 1954 is the value for 1954 published February 1955.

C. Short-Run Policy Multipliers

Simplification of the model is carried out as illustrated in part I. Inspection shows that in equation (05), plant and equipment expenditure (ΔPE) depends only on "known" values: last year's profits after taxes, and the stock of plant and equipment available at the beginning of the year. Similarly in equations (06) and (07), housing starts (ΔHS) and expenditure for nonfarm residential construction (ΔH) depend only on credit availability, construction costs, last year's starts, and the stock of houses at the beginning of the year. To make a forecast, therefore, we use the knowns to estimate ΔPE, ΔHS, and ΔH via equations (05), (06), and (07), and then use these values, together with the other knowns, to solve the remaining equations. The inverse of the model is shown in table 4. This is merely an enlarged version of the little table shown earlier for the illustrative model of part I, and is used in the same way. For example, if the projected values of table 1 are inserted in column P of table 4, multiplied by the weights in the automobile column and summed, the result is 4.5, the forecast increase in automobile demand shown in table 2.[6] Short-run multipliers for any policy variable are readily calculated as before by inserting 1 for the variable everywhere it appears in column P and then (ignoring all terms that do not contain the variable in question) extending a forecast using the columns of table 4.

For example, to find the multiplier on government purchases from private firms, set $\Delta g = +1$ everywhere it appears in column P. The term Δg is found in only one place: in row (11) it is multiplied by 1. To find the effect of $\Delta g = \$1$ on, say, private GNP, we multiply the weight in row (11) of the GNP column by 1:

$$\Delta G^* = 1 \times 1.304 = 1.304$$

That is to say, the short-run multiplier on government purchases is about 1.3. Similarly, the effect on, say, automobile demand is given by

$$\Delta A = 1 \times .092 = .092$$

i.e. the short-run "automobile demand multiplier" on government purchases from the private sector is .092.

In working out a policy multiplier, care must be taken to include changes in *all* exogenous variables affected by the policy action. For

---

[6] To save space some of the less interesting columns of the matrix have been omitted from table 4. Moreover the tax and transfer equations have been consolidated to show only totals for federal taxes, state and local taxes, and social insurance contributions. If values of any omitted variable are required, they can be calculated from the others. For example, to calculate the federal corporate profits tax yield, use the inverse to calculate ΔP^* and substitute this value in equation (21).

11. Forecasting and Analysis with an Econometric Model

TABLE 4
Inverse Matrix

Equation No.	ΔA	ΔD	ΔND	ΔS	ΔID	ΔIND	ΔR	ΔG^*	ΔE
01	1.113	.089	.113	.046	.350	.048	.100	1.660	.113
02	.117	1.092	.118	.048	.351	.050	.101	1.676	.114
03	.130	.103	1.130	.053	.068	.483	.112	1.854	.126
04	.091	.072	.091	1.037	.047	.039	.078	1.298	.088
08	.092	.073	.093	.037	1.048	.040	.078	1.304	.089
09	.092	.073	.093	.037	.048	1.040	.078	1.304	.089
10	−.095	−.076	−.097	−.040	−.050	−.041	.921	−1.318	−.089
11	.092	.073	.093	.037	.048	.042	.078	1.304	.089
12	.884	.623	.793	.321	.439	.339	.192	3.205	1.218
13	−.118	.091	.116	.047	−.008	.049	.010	.167	.011
14	8.621	8.030	10.220	4.133	4.845	4.364	2.283	37.929	2.579
15	.184	.171	.218	.088	.103	.093	.049	.809	.055
16	−.040	−.037	−.047	−.019	−.022	−.020	−.012	−.175	−.012
17	.040	.037	.047	.019	.022	.020	.012	.175	.012
18	−.179	−.166	−.212	−.086	−.100	−.090	−.047	−.786	−.053
19	.202	.188	.240	.097	.114	.102	.054	.890	.061
20	.254	.237	.302	.122	.143	.129	.067	1.119	.076
21	−.046	−.043	−.055	−.022	−.026	−.024	−.012	−.204	−.014
22	−.254	−.237	−.302	−.122	−.143	−.129	−.067	−1.119	−.076
24	−.040	−.037	−.047	−.019	−.022	−.020	−.012	−.175	−.012
25	−.040	−.037	−.047	−.019	−.022	−.020	−.012	−.175	−.012
26	−.046	−.043	−.055	−.022	−.026	−.024	−.012	−.204	−.014
27	−.040	−.037	−.047	−.019	−.022	−.020	−.012	−.175	−.012
28	−.254	−.237	−.302	−.122	−.143	−.129	−.067	−1.119	−.076
29	−.040	−.037	−.047	−.019	−.022	−.020	−.012	−.175	−.012
30	−.254	−.237	−.302	−.122	−.143	−.129	−.067	−1.119	−.076
31	.101	.391	.498	.201	.143	.213	.088	1.461	.099
32	.058	.221	.281	.114	.081	.120	.050	.825	.056

Projections

01	$4.710 - .495A_{-1} + .260\Delta L_{-1} - .177\Delta X_f - .177\Delta X_s$
02	$.262 - .0694D_{-1} + .0784\Delta L_{-1}$
03	$-.149 + .205\Delta ND_{-1} + .143\Delta L_{-1}$
04	$.363 + .530\Delta S_{-1} + .0381\Delta L_{-1}$
08	$0 + .591\Delta PD + .305\Delta M_{+1} - .669 ID_{-1}$
09	$0 - 1.121 IND_{-1}$
10	$.369$
11	$0 + \Delta F + \Delta PE + \Delta H + \Delta g$
12	0
13	$0 + \Delta LF - \Delta E_0 - \Delta E_G$
14	$-.0743 + .00436 P^*_{-1}$
15	0
16	$.763$
17	$0 - \Delta T_{bp} - \Delta T_{os}$

TABLE 4
(*continued*)

Equation No.	ΔW	ΔP^*	ΔDw	$\Delta(P - P^*)$	Federal Tax Receipts	State and Local Tax Receipts	Social Ins. Contr.	ΔX_u	ΔY
01	.609	.694	.076	.076	.585	.066	.035	−.135	.506
02	.615	.780	.085	.084	.545	.068	.036	−.136	.525
03	.680	.875	.096	.096	.600	.072	.040	−.151	.583
04	.476	.606	.066	.066	.414	.060	.028	−.105	.407
08	.478	.638	.070	.069	.432	.028	.028	−.106	.414
09	.478	.638	.070	.069	.432	.028	.028	−.106	.414
10	−.483	−.719	−.079	−.078	−.546	−.030	−.029	.107	−.431
11	.478	.638	.074	.069	.458	.030	.030	−.106	.438
12	6.568	−3.586	−.395	−.390	−1.002	.076	.319	−1.455	3.539
13	−.952	.997	.109	.109	.430	.016	.009	1.181	.516
14	60.808	−25.478	−2.806	−2.767	−4.726	1.091	.579	−3.082	45.619
15	1.297	−.543	−.059	−.060	−.101	.023	.012	−.066	.973
16	−.064	−.980	−.107	−.107	−.544	−.026	−.009	.014	−.211
17	−.064	.980	.107	.107	.544	.026	.009	−.014	.211
18	−.288	.651	.075	−1.038	.106	−.021	−.067	.064	−.946
19	.326	.395	1.040	.043	.497	.045	.019	−.072	1.070
20	.410	.496	.040	.054	.378	.045	.024	−.091	1.346
21	−.075	−.090	−.238	−.010	.886	−.010	−.004	.017	−.245
22	−.410	−.496	−.040	−.054	.622	−.045	−.024	.091	−1.346
24	−.064	−.980	−.107	−.107	.456	−.026	−.009	.014	−.211
25	−.064	−.980	−.107	−.107	.456	−.026	−.009	.014	−.211
26	−.075	−.090	−.238	−.010	−.114	.990	−.004	.017	−.245
27	−.064	−.980	−.107	−.107	−.544	.974	−.009	.014	−.211
28	−.410	−.497	−.040	−.054	−.378	.955	−.024	.091	−1.346
29	−.064	−.980	−.107	−.107	−.544	−.026	.991	.014	−.211
30	−.410	−.497	−.040	−.054	−.378	−.045	.976	.091	−1.346
31	.535	.661	.072	.072	.486	.059	.031	1.651	2.224
32	.303	.374	.041	.041	.274	.033	.018	.932	1.256

Projections
(*continued*)

18	$-1.027 - .902\Delta P_f$
19	$-.0191 + .0198(P^* - T_{fc} - T_{sc} - Div)_{-1}$
20	$0 + \Delta W_G + \Delta i_G + \Delta X_f + \Delta X_s + \Delta X_{GI} - \Delta T_{op} - \Delta T_{eg} + \Delta T_{ref}$
21	0
22	$0 + .111\Delta W_G + .150\Delta i_G$
24	0
25	.012
26	0
27	0
28	$0 + .010(\Delta W_G + \Delta i_G)$
29	0
30	$0 + .129\Delta E_G$
31	$0 - .140(\Delta LF - \Delta LF_{-1})$
32	.101

example, an increase in government employment involves hiring additional people [ΔE_G in rows (13) and (30)] and paying them wages [ΔW_G in rows (20), (22), and (28)]. At an average annual wage of $5000, an addition of $1 billion to the government wage bill will hire .2 million additional employees. To find the multipliers on government wages, therefore, we set $\Delta E_G = .2$. This gives $-.2$ in row (13) and .0258 in row (30) of column P. We also set $\Delta W_G = \$1$ to get 1 in row (20), .111 in (22) and .010 in row (28) of column P. The impact of additional government employment on private GNP is then found by extending these figures by the weights in the corresponding rows of the GNP column:

$$\Delta G^* = -.2 \times .167 + 1 \times 1.119 - .111 \times 1.119 - .010 \times 1.119 \\ -.0258 \times 1.119 \\ = .692$$

To find the effect of the action on total GNP, we must add in the additional value added by government (i.e. government wages and salaries). Thus:

$$\text{Total GNP} = .692 + 1 = 1.692$$

We also recall that government tax policy can be expressed by shifts in the equations themselves. As shown in part I, these shift multipliers are equal to the weights found in the row of the inverse matrix that corresponds to the equation being shifted. Thus we see from the -1.119 in row (22) of the GNP column that a $1 billion shift in the federal personal tax function will reduce private GNP by $1.1 billion, etc. Note again [row (22) of the federal tax column] that an upward shift of $1 billion in the federal income tax *schedule* increases federal·tax *yield* by only $622 million due to the decline in personal income and expenditure associated with the rise in taxes.

Some multiplier effects of a selection of government actions are given in table 5. As before, once the multipliers are worked out they can be combined in any desired proportions. Thus an increase in government purchases of $2 billion coupled with additional government wages of $.5 billion and an upward shift of the personal tax schedule of $1.3 billion would produce a total change in GNP of $(2 \times 1.304) + (.5 \times 1.692) + (1.3 \times -1.119) = \$2$ billion. The same program would raise total employment by .211 million, and add $.67 billion to the federal deficit.

D. A Digression on Deficit Financing

An interesting and important conclusion to be drawn from table 5 is that the impact of a government action cannot be measured by merely the existence, or even the size of a surplus or deficit. In the first place

TABLE 5
Selected Multipliers

Multiplicand	GNP Private	GNP Total	Employment Private	Employment Total	Tax Receipts Federal	Tax Receipts State and Local	Social Insurance Contributions	Social Insurance Transfers	Government Surplus or Deficit (−) Federal	Government Surplus or Deficit (−) State and Local	Government Surplus or Deficit (−) Social Insurance	Government Surplus or Deficit (−) Total
Plant and Equipment[a]	1.690	1.690	.115	.115	.586	.058	.038	−.137	.586	.058	.175	.819
Federal Purchases from Firms	1.304	1.304	.089	.089	.458	.030	.030	−.106	−.542	.030	.136	−.376
Federal Employment[b]	.692	1.692	.063	.263	.209	.016	.044	−.314	−.791	.016	.358	−.417
Federal Personal Income Tax Shift	−1.119	−1.119	−.076	−.076	.622	−.045	−.024	.091	.622	−.045	−.115	.462

[a] Additional expenditure of $1 billion of which half is spent for producers' durable equipment.
[b] Additional expenditure of $1 billion in government wages to hire .2 million workers.

it makes a great deal of difference whose deficit is under discussion, and it is not always clear whether deficit "multipliers" are supposed to be applied to the federal deficit or to the consolidated government sector. In what follows we confine ourselves to the latter. In the second place, surpluses and deficits result from courses of action; they are the difference between certain expenditures and receipts. While it is elementary that expenditures promote and taxes retard economic activity, the net result depends not only on the amounts of expenditures and tax yields, but also on the kinds, and we cannot speak unqualifiedly of a deficit multiplier.

Although this point can be made from purely theoretical considerations, the econometric model shows the substantial order of magnitudes involved. We see from table 5, for example, that a $1 billion consolidated deficit will result from either $1 ÷ .376 = $2.66 billion of federal government purchases or, say a cut of $1 ÷ 462 = $2.16 billion in the federal income tax schedule. Yet the former action raises total GNP by 1.304 × 2.66 = $3.47 billion, while the latter generates an increase of only 1.119 × $2.16 = $2.42 billion.

This result can be generalized. According to the multipliers in the last column of table 5, the consolidated balance (surplus or deficit) is given by

$$\Delta b = -.376 \, \Delta g + .462 \, \Delta a$$

where Δb is the change in the balance and Δa is the shift in the federal income tax schedule. A wide range of combinations of expenditures and taxes will produce the same budgetary balance. In fact, if we set Δb at some fixed value, say $\Delta b = 2$, then

$$2 = -.376 \, \Delta g + .462 \, \Delta a$$

is the equation of an "isobalance" locus. That is, every combination of expenditures and taxation that satisfies this equation produces a $2 billion increase in consolidated surplus. Three isobalance lines—corresponding to a $1 billion surplus, a balanced budget and a $1 billion deficit—are plotted as solid lines in figure 2.

By the same token, the increase in total GNP is given by:

$$\Delta GNP = 1.304 \, \Delta g - 1.119 \, \Delta a,$$

and if we assign, say $\Delta GNP = 5$, then

$$5 = 1.304 \, \Delta g - 1.119 \, \Delta a$$

is the equation of an "iso-GNP" locus. Three of these are plotted as broken lines in figure 2.

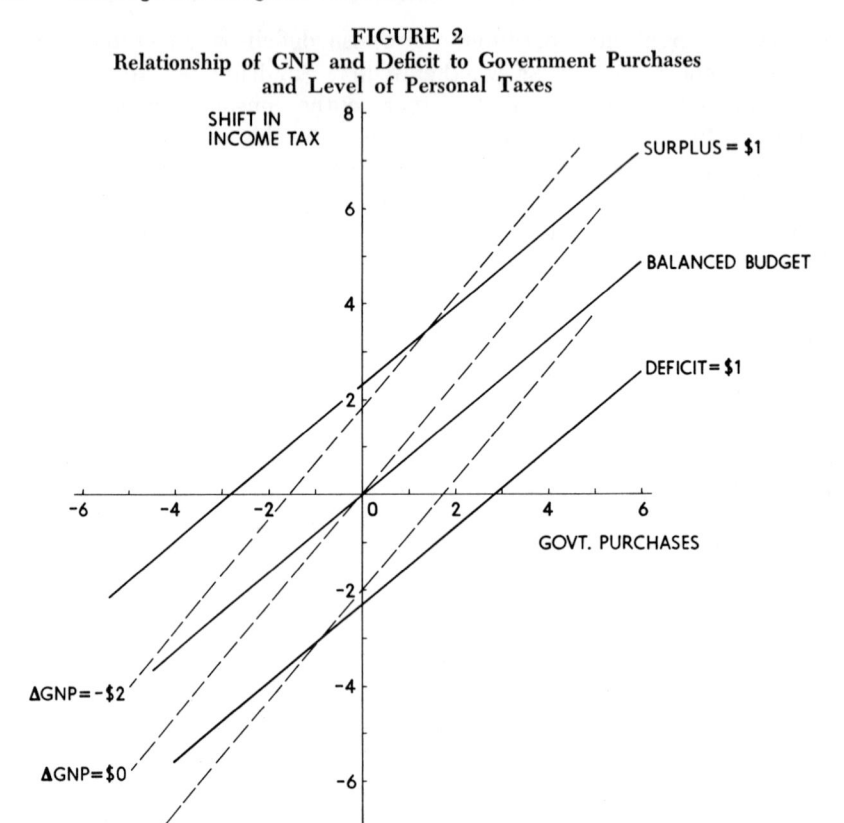

FIGURE 2
Relationship of GNP and Deficit to Government Purchases and Level of Personal Taxes

Inspection of the figure immediately shows that any specified increase in GNP can be attained in association with a wide range of balances and that any deficit or surplus may be associated with a wide range of impacts on GNP. In fact, a government program can simultaneously generate a substantial deficit and a sharp deflation, or a substantial surplus and general expansion. Since transfers, corporate profits taxes, defense orders, and government employment will have still other isobalance and iso-GNP lines, this merely scratches the surface of the possibilities.

E. Dynamic Responses and Long-Run Multipliers

As shown in part I, dynamic responses are studied by iteration. Among the initial impacts of any program, we must find the effects on automobile demand, inventory accumulation, plant and equipment, and other variables whose values reenter the system with a lag. These form a set of additional knowns for the next year. Using these values, in turn, gives rise to another set, etc. Repeating this operation enables us to follow the implications of a given program over as long a period as desired. It appears, however, that the dynamic elements stabilize by the end of the fifth year, and the system can be treated as in equilibrium after five iterations.

A complete study of the dynamic behavior of each variable in response to each possible policy action cannot be presented here, but table 6

TABLE 6
Dynamic Responses to a Permanent Increase of $1 Billion
in Government Expenditure
(tabulated figures are deviations from initial levels)

	Year				
	1	2	3	4	5
Gross National Product[a]	1.304	1.619	1.582	1.545	1.335
Automobiles and Parts	.092	.088	.050	.042	.014
Other Durables	.073	.104	.113	.117	.104
Nondurables	.093	.159	.193	.215	.213
Services	.037	.075	.104	.126	.134
Plant and Equipment	0.	.186	.173	.133	.082
Inventory					
Durable Goods	.048	.079	.017	−.010	−.031
Nondurable Goods	.040	.023	.012	.008	−.002
Net Foreign Investment	−.078	−.101	−.103	−.103	−.098
Government Purchases	1.	1.	1.	1.	1.

[a] Detail may not add to total because of rounding.

shows the response of the GNP and its components to a permanent increase of $1 billion in government expenditure. The tabulated figures are the values of the variables measured as deviations from their levels as of year 0 before the shift in expenditure policy.

In response to increased government expenditure, the GNP rises by $1.3 billion the first year and under the stimulation of the dynamic factors climbs to a maximum of $1.6 billion over its initial level. It declines thereafter under the back-pressure of accumulating stocks. The behavior of the individual components is in keeping with their respective natures. Automobile demand rises immediately to its maximum and declines slowly as the stock of cars on the road accumulates. Consumer expenditure for durables rises sharply and levels off, while outlays on nondurable goods and services continue to rise throughout the period, although at declining rates.

Investment in plant and equipment spurts in response to the immediate improvement in the corporate profits and tapers off as the new plant becomes available. Inventory accumulation occurs at a high rate, but durable inventory overshoots and the rate of accumulation is forced somewhat below the year 0 level.

IV. CONCLUSION

To approximate the behavior of a complex economy by a set of 32 linear approximations is a heroic simplification. Yet experience has shown the statistical model to be a useful and flexible device for economic forecasting. Moreover, while the system of equations is small in relation to the vast structure of pure theory, it is considerably more elaborate than other devices that can be brought to bear on a practical level. Indeed, if an econometric model is nothing else, it is a highly sophisticated method of observing the past operation of the economy and systematizing the information obtained.

Yet, once the technical work of constructing the model is completed, a competent economist needs little more than a knowledge of elementary algebra to understand its nature, or to apply it to a wide range of analytical problems. Properly used, the model provides quantitative estimates of economic responses to specified changes in conditions. It goes without saying that the accuracy of these estimates is below the level that might be inferred from the precision of their statement in the text. But they show the proper order of magnitude involved and fall well within the practical tolerances required for effective policy evaluation.

12. Consumer Attitudes, Buying Plans, and Purchases of Durable Goods: A Principal Components, Time-Series Approach[*]

F. GERARD ADAMS

For more than ten years, the University of Michigan Survey Research Center has gathered data on consumer attitudes and buying plans in its periodic sample surveys. According to the SRC, "Information on consumer sentiment and expectations is collected because they exert a great influence on demand for durable goods and housing and thereby on economic trends in general." But tests of the relationship between attitudes, intentions, and consumer behavior have produced conflicting results and have caused doubts as to the usefulness of the attitude variables for purposes of forecasting.

The attitudes and buying plans data reflect various aspects of consumer sentiment. It is not clear to what extent these are separate attitudinal dimensions, and which of these, if any, have a useful role in forecasting. Analyses of the predictive power of attitudes and buying plans in cross-section reinterview data have tended to discredit the relevance of attitudes, but not of buying plans. Klein and Lansing, Tobin, and others have found that after predicting on the "objective variables," the effects of the attitudinal variables individually (and combined into an index) are not statistically significant in the cross section. On the other hand, intentions to purchase do add significantly to the explanation of realized purchases.

Aggregate time series give the opposite result. While the earliest time series studies of aggregate data by the Consultant Committee on Consumer Survey Statistics, Okun, and Mueller were inconclusive, more recently the Mueller studies and other calculations by the Survey Research

---

[*] *Review of Economics and Statistics*, vol. 46, no. 4, (November 1964), pp. 347–55.

Center have consistently shown that in aggregate time series, attitudes make a significant contribution to explaining fluctuations in aggregate durables purchases, while buying intentions do not make a statistically significant net contribution to the forecast. Proponents of the attitudes data have argued that the ultimate test of their usefulness is their performance as an aid to prediction in aggregate time series. The case for or against the predictive value of consumer attitudes and intentions data is still open.

This paper, part of a larger effort to reexamine the role of subjective data in predicting consumers' expenditures on durable goods, is focused on the behavior of the aggregate time series. The paper is addressed to the following questions:

1) To what extent and in what regard do aggregate data on various consumer attitudes and intentions measure separate aspects of consumer sentiment?
2) Do the various attitude and intentions variables make a significant net contribution to predicting consumer durable expenditures?

INFORMATIONAL CONTENT OF SRC ATTITUDES AND INTENTIONS DATA

Conceptually, it would be possible to pose an infinite variety of attitude probing questions. It is not clear, however, to what extent the responses would provide information on separate aspects of consumer attitudes and intentions and what these would be. The nature of the separately identifiable attitudinal dimensions may throw light on the role of attitude variables in forecasting.

In this section we examine the informational content of a limited yet varied selection of attitude questions posed by the Survey Research Center.[1] The questions, which match the components of the SRC attitudes index, were (our abbreviation for each attitude is in parentheses before the question):

(PF_1) We are interested in how people are getting along financially these days. Would you say that you and your family *are better off* or worse off financially *than you were a year ago?*

---
[1] In fairness to the Survey Research Center, it should be noted that the various dimensions of attitudes were originally selected on the basis of an elaborate body of theory concerning the role of psychological variables in consumer decision making. This theory perceives the totality of each consumer's attitudes as a whole, to which each attitude makes a contribution. But the attitudinal variables may not operate additively, their influences may differ at different times and among different consumers, and the effects of the different attitudinal dimensions are not separable. Thus, Katona would not focus on the nature or role of particular attitude variables, as we are doing, but would be concerned with an evaluation of the overall effect of all attitudes in the form of an index of consumer attitudes which, in frequent instances, will include even the intentions variables.

(PF_2) Now looking ahead—do you think that *a year from now* you people *will be better off* financially or worse off or just about the same as now?

(BC_1) Now turning to business conditions in the country as a whole—do you think that *during the next twelve months* or so *we'll have good times financially*, or bad times, or what?

(BC_2) Looking ahead, which would you say is more likely—that in the country as a whole *we'll have continuous good times during the next five years or so*, or that we will have periods of widespread unemployment or depression, or what?

(MC_1) Now about things people buy for their house—I mean furniture, house furnishings, refrigerator, stove, TV, and things like that. Do you think now is a *good* or bad time *to buy such large household items?*

(MC_2) Now speaking of prices in general, I mean the prices of the things you buy—do you think they will go up in the next year or so, or go down, or stay where they are now?" Would you say that these (. . . rising prices; falling prices; unchanged prices . . .) *would be to the good*, or to the bad, or what?

(BP_H) Do you expect to buy or build a house for your own use during the next twelve months?

(BP_C) Do you people expect to buy a car during the next twelve months or so? Does anyone else in the family expect to buy a car during the next twelve months?

These questions measure different attitudinal characteristics, if indeed, they measure attitudes at all. PF_1 is addressed to a question of fact, or to the respondent's perception of fact (whether the respondent feels financially better off this year than last). The question is phrased broadly so as to cover various aspects of the respondent's financial status. As a measure of attitudes, the question has some validity whether the response corresponds to the respondent's real situation or not. PF_2, BC_1, and BC_2 are expectational; the first about personal conditions and therefore reflecting personal developments known to be in prospect (as well as, more broadly, expectations), the latter two about business conditions in general. MC_1 is attitudinal about current conditions, although the response "good time to buy" may be motivated by a variety of considerations. MC_2 is an attitudinal question about price expectations, but it is not clear whether a "good" response (i.e., that price trends "are to the good") should be positively or negatively related to current purchases. In fact, we are not even sure what price trends are "good" or "bad."[2]

---

[2] In recent surveys, the attitudinal measure of price expectations has been based directly on the consumer's expressed feeling (to the good/bad) about price trends. Before 1957, the series were tied together on the assumption that small price increases (modest inflation) were "to the bad" but that anticipated price stability, decline, or rapid increases would be "to the good."

The buying plan variables involve an issue of fact (whether or not the consumer intends to make a purchase). They evoke a response which reflects the objective variables of the consumer's economic status (income, stock of durables, etc.) and the impact of attitudes as well. Whether intentions variables contain elements of information which have not already been reflected in objective and attitudinal data has raised some controversy. Katona argues that, in view of the indefiniteness of consumer planning, ". . . consumer buying intentions are attitudes held at a given time. . . . The two are theoretically and practically so closely related that their separation is not justified." The Consultant Committee and Okun and Tobin have focused attention on buying plans as distinct from attitudes. Thus, buying intentions may be considered another dimension of attitudes, as reflections of objective factors and attitudes, or as separate variables serving as discriminants (though not wholly effective ones) between purchasers and nonpurchasers among people with identical objective and attitudinal positions.

The Data

The aggregative measures of attitudes used in this study are based on data obtained by the Survey Research Center in its "Interim Surveys" and in some of its "Surveys of Consumer Finances," over a period from 1952 to 1962. Altogether, 24 surveys are included. They were spaced at varying intervals and vary in size from 1,000 to 3,000 observations. Attitudinal indexes were obtained by assigning values as follows:

Attitudes	Buying Plans	
Favorable response	Will buy	+1
Uncertain or so-so response	Probably will buy	0
Unfavorable response	Will not buy	−1

These values for each of the individual responses were aggregated, and the aggregates were used in index form.

Components of Attitude and Intentions Variables

Since the various attitudinal variables measure different, yet interrelated aspects of the consumer's outlook and buying plans, we raise in this section the question of the interrelationships between them and of the separate, that is, orthogonal components which they reflect.

The attitudinal and buying plans variables are arranged in table 1 in the order of the magnitude of the adjusted correlation coefficients between them.

TABLE 1
Simple Correlation Between Attitudinal and Buying Plans Variables

Simple Correlation Coefficients	Attitude Variables	Buying Plans Variables
Positive		
>0.8	$BC_1 \times BC_2$	
0.7–0.8	$PF_1 \times BC_1, PF_1 \times BC_2$	
0.6–0.7	$PF_2 \times BC_1, PF_2 \times MC_1, BC_1 \times MC_1$	$MC_1 \times BP_H$
0.5–0.6	$PF_1 \times PF_2, PF_2 \times BC_2$	$BC_1 \times BP_H$
0.4–0.5		$BC_1 \times BP_C$
<0.4[a]	$PF_1 \times MC_1, BC_2 \times MC_1$	$PF_1 \times BP_C, PF_2 \times BP_C, BC_2 \times BP_C$ $MC_2 \times BP_C, PF_1 \times BP_H, PF_2 \times BP_H$ $BC_2 \times BP_H, BP_C \times BP_H$
Negative		
>−0.4[a]	$BC_2 \times MC_2, PF_1 \times MC_2$	
−0.4–−0.5	$PF_2 \times MC_2, BC_1 \times MC_2$	$MC_2 \times BP_H$
−0.7–−0.8	$MC_1 \times MC_2$	

[a] Not significant at the .05 level.

As one would anticipate, there are close relationships between the subvariables of the three broad attitude categories, i.e., BC_1 is closely related to BC_2, MC_1 to MC_2 (though negatively),[3] and PF_1 to PF_2. Other important intercorrelations are between the business outlook variables and personal financial status and expectations (PF_1 and PF_2) and between business outlook variables and good time to buy (MC_1). This pattern of relationships suggests the presence in the diverse attitudinal variables of a common element which reflects consumers' views toward business conditions, personal financial status, and "good (or bad) time to buy."

With regard to the buying plans, the significant correlations with BC_1 and MC_1 suggest an informational overlap. On the other hand, correlations with other attitudinal variables are less pronounced, and the buying plans appear to contribute their own informational content or to reflect other nonattitudinal variables.

In order to distinguish the separate elements of variation among the six attitudinal and two buying plans series, analysis of principal components was applied. This analysis is a method of summarizing the separate informational elements contained in a number of related variables. The principal components can be described as the linear combinations of the original variables which have the properties that:

---

[3] The negative relationships between MC_1 and MC_2 and between MC_2 and the other variables appear to result from the coding of the responses to the question about price expectations.

1. They have maximum variance, i.e., the first principal component is the one with the highest variance and the others are obtained in order of their variance. This means that each accounts for as much as possible of the variance of the standardized original variates and that the sum of its squared correlations with the standardized original variates is at a maximum.[4]
2. They are orthogonal—their covariances equal zero.
3. The weights applied to the original values have unit sum of squares.

The variances of the principal components turn out to be the characteristic roots of the variance-covariance matrix of the original variables and the weights are the corresponding characteristic vectors. There are as many real nonnegative roots as there are variables. The principal components may be interpreted as weighted indexes of the original variates, each of which puts maximum emphasis on a separate informational component of the data. This is another way of saying that each principal component implies measurement from a new set of axes so arranged as to maximize the variance of the observations along one axis and minimize it along the others.

One obtains the variance of each principal component, the share of the total variance of the original (normalized) variables which it explains, and the weights. The latter are at the same time the correlations between the PC's and the original variables and permit an evaluation of the informational content of each component. The principal components table (table 2) summarizes this information.

The first principal component alone accounts for 52 percent, and jointly,[5] the first four components account for 92 percent of the summed variance of the eight variables. The first component is most closely related to BC_1 and matches 90 percent of the variance of the BC_1 variable. The considerable intercorrelation between the variables noted above is reflected in the fact that principal component 1 is also fairly highly correlated with other attitudinal variables.[6] Principal component 2 reflects most importantly the separate variation of MC_2 with which it is positively correlated. The third and fourth principal components relate most closely to the separate variation of the buying plans variables. However, they also show significant relationships to some of the attitude variables, although not with BC_1. It appears that the buying plans vari-

---

[4] M. A. Girschick, "Principal Components," *Journal of the American Statistical Association* (September 1936), 519–28.

[5] Since the PC's are orthogonal their variances may simply be added. Similarly, the sums of the r_{ij}^2's may be taken across each row, and account for all the variance of the respective attitude variable.

[6] The explanation of the principal components is sometimes problematical since they may have significant relationships with more than one of the underlying variables.

TABLE 2
Principal Components of Attitudes and Buying Plans
(aggregate time series data 1952–1962)

	Principal Components					
	PC_1	PC_2	PC_3	PC_4	PC_5	*Others*[a]
Percent of Total Variance Explained	*52.4*	*15.8*	*12.9*	*10.7*	*6.0*	*2.2*
Variable	\multicolumn{6}{c}{Correlation of Principal Component with Attitude and Intentions Variables}
PF_1	.834	−.491	.234	.068	.097	
PF_2	.723	.181	.006	−.489	.415	
BC_1	.949	−.038	.079	−.052	−.149	
BC_2	.793	−.025	.415	−.213	−.402	
MC_1	.675	.536	−.400	−.190	−.006	
MC_2	−.589	.678	.401	−.192	−.140	
BP_C	.452	.400	.495	.571	.252	
BP_H	.662	.279	−.485	.411	−.170	

$r_{ij(.05)} = 0.388$.
[a] No significant correlations.

ables contain informational aspects which, while not separate from attitudes, do not correspond simply to the most important principal components of the latter. The fifth component relates significantly only to PF_2. The remaining three principal components account for 2 percent of the variance and do not have significant correlations with any attitudes. One may conclude that the principal components may be described as follows:

Component 1—a measure of the short-term business outlook. This component also reflects other related measures of attitudes to economic conditions.

Component 2—a reflection of the separate variation of price expectations (MC_2).

Components 3 and 4—summarize aspects of the variation of the buying plans variables.

Component 5—accounts for some separate variation of personal financial expectations (PF_2).

Other components—account for scattered random movements.

The importance of the component related to short-term expectations about business conditions is particularly noteworthy. This factor accounts, to a large extent, for the effectiveness of attitudes as predictors of expenditures on durables. The role of business expectations may explain the paradoxical results of past tests of the predictive effectiveness of the attitudes in cross section and time series. Since business conditions are external to the consumer, the business outlook may be viewed as a factor which is substantially common to all individuals appearing in a cross section at a particular time. Each consumer's perception of business conditions, or at least his response to a question about them may, of course, differ. But changes in the aggregate will reflect the acquisition of common external information on business prospects. While the business outlook variable shows up clearly in the movements of aggregative time series, it may not be apparent in a single cross section where its impact may have been largely in changing the mean level of the whole distribution.

ATTITUDE AND BUYING PLANS VARIABLES AS PREDICTORS OF EXPENDITURES ON DURABLES

In this section, we will consider the role of attitudes as independent variables in a simple forecasting model for consumers' durable goods purchases. The questions to be considered are whether aggregative measures of consumers' attitudes (all attitudes or some of them) help to predict aggregative durable purchases and, if they do so, whether they make a significant net addition to a prediction based on "objective" variables and/or expressed purchasing plans. The attitudinal variables will be introduced first in unweighted index form corresponding to the SRC Attitudes Index. Then, the effect of individual attitudes will be considered.

The analysis has been based throughout on a simple regression model as follows:

Dependent variable at quarter $t + 1$ (in real terms per capita) $= a_0 + a_1$ Income at quarter t (real disposable personal income per capita) $+ a_2$ Attitudes at quarter t $+ a_1$ Purchasing plans at quarter t.

The dependent variables considered were:

D —expenditures on consumer durable goods, per capita, in billions of 1954 dollars, seasonally adjusted.
D_{NA}—consumer expenditures on durable goods other than automobiles and parts per capita, in billions of 1954 dollars, seasonally adjusted.
D_A —consumer expenditures on automobiles and parts per capita, in billions of 1954 dollars, seasonally adjusted.

12. Consumer Attitudes, Buying Plans, and Purchases of Durable Goods 191

Time, t, is the quarter during which the attitude survey was carried out.

The lags in these equations were intended to be most favorable for showing up the effect of buying plans (which are firmer the shorter the lag) and least favorable for attitudes whose separate effect is more likely to show up over a longer period. Alternative forecasting periods are discussed briefly below. Concurrent income could have been used in place of lagged income. This would show up the pure forecasting effect of attitudes and buying plans. The use of lagged income was, however, more consistent with the broader aims of the present project. In practice, it makes very little difference whether concurrent or lagged income is used.

Predictive Effectiveness of the SRC Attitude Index

The SRC has tested its Index of Consumer Attitudes for some years and has obtained good results for its predictive power in aggregative time series data. The regression equations summarized in table 3 elaborate on the SRC tests. As indicated, the data on expenditures (D, D_{NA}, and D_A) and income (Y) are on a per capita basis. In these equations, B is an unweighted average of buying plans for houses and cars. The I_6 variable corresponds to the attitudes part of the SRC index. For each dependent variable, equations were estimated consecutively on income, on income and attitudes, on income and buying plans, and on income, attitudes and buying plans. Values were included only for those quarters in which surveys were taken and in the respective quarters following as called for in the equations.

These calculations give results which are broadly in line with other such tests based on aggregate time series data.[7] There is a significant relationship between attitudes and expenditures in every case. Purchase plans also show a significant effect, but only when the attitude variable is not included in the equation. In the same equation, attitudes completely swamp the effect of buying plans and the latter make no further net contribution. This would suggest that the predictive effect of the buying plans corresponds to their overlap with the attitudes and that their orthogonal aspects do not contribute to the forecast.

In the case of total consumers' durable expenditures (D), income (Y) accounts for a small part of the variation of expenditures; the attitudes index makes a large and statistically significant contribution. An equation which combines as independent variables Y, I_6, and B has an adjusted coefficient of determination no higher than if B is left out.

---

[7] No attempt to consider the effectiveness of the data from the point of view of forecasting turning points has been made, there being no continuous attitude time series.

TABLE 3
Regression Equations for Consumers'
Durable Expenditures on the Attitude Index
and Buying Plans

Equation Number	Dependent Variable	= a_0	+ $a_1 Y_t$	+ $a_2 I_{6t}$	+ $a_1 B_t$	$\bar{R}^2$
1.....	D_{t+1}	69.918	0.089 (.037)			0.175
2.....	D_{t+1}	−170.653	0.113 (.026)	2.097 (.424)		0.609
3.....	D_{t+1}	44.432	0.066 (.033)		0.672 (.240)	0.377
4.....	D_{t+1}	−147.516	0.102 (.028)	1.820 (.510)	0.228 (.227)	0.609
5.....	D_{NAt+1}	− 16.379	0.070 (.011)			0.627
6.....	D_{NAt+1}	− 58.356	0.074 (.011)	0.366 (.174)		0.679
7.....	D_{NAt+1}	− 22.873	0.064 (.011)		0.171 (.077)	0.686
8.....	D_{NAt+1}	− 46.505	0.068 (.011)	0.224 (.204)	0.117 (.091)	0.689
9.....	D_{At+1}	154.554	−0.037 (.040)			−0.007
10.....	D_{At+1}	−143.929	0.011 (.027)	2.261. (.443)		0.526
11.....	D_{At+1}	88.060	−0.039 (.035)		0.723 (.254)	0.222
12.....	D_{At+1}	145.054	−0.068 (.043)		0.650[a] (.291)	0.125
13.....	D_{At+1}	−119.223	−0.001 (.029)	1.966 (.527)	0.243 (.236)	0.527
14.....	D_{At+1}	− 49.976	0.040 (.038)	1.901 (.541)	0.299[a] (.262)	0.486

[a] Buying plans for cars only, seasonally adjusted. Tests for the seasonality of the attitude any buying plans showed a significant seasonal variation only in BP_o and PF_2. Adjustment for seasonality does not make a large difference in prediction.

Durable expenditures other than for automobiles and parts (D_{NA}) are explained to a much larger extent by income, but attitudes make a significant net contribution. In this case, purchase plans have about the same effect as attitudes and overlap them. This is not surprising since the purchase plans variable employed here refers to plans to buy houses and cars, neither one of which is a part of D_{NA}. Thus B here is, in effect, another measure of consumer attitudes as reflected in their plans to purchase houses and cars and this may account for the result obtained.[8]

---

[8] Data for buying plans for furniture and major household appliances are available on an annual basis for eight years. Regressions including such a variable yield results consistent with our other calculations. In the following equations, D_{NA} is per capita

12. Consumer Attitudes, Buying Plans, and Purchases of Durable Goods

In the case of automotive purchases, income is not a significant variable but again attitudes make a large net explanatory contribution. Buying plans in general, and for cars separately, have a significant effect, but it is relatively small and it drops out when the attitude and buying plans variables are used together.[9]

The results obtained correspond to the findings of the Mueller and SRC studies of the aggregate time series. Some alternative formulations were tried and are summarized here.

1. Other studies of these figures have obtained higher $\bar{R}^2$'s in some similar equations. Calculations have shown that this can be accounted for by (a) the fact that our variables are all on a per capita basis so that we lose the common movement in the series due to population growth, and (b) that no interpolations were made when survey values were not available, these periods being simply omitted in our analysis.

2. The use of concurrent income, Y_{t+1}, rather than Y_t raises very slightly the explanatory power of the equations but makes no other difference.

3. Prediction over a two-quarter period, i.e., the use of $\dfrac{D_{t+1} + D_{t+2}}{2}$ instead of D_{t+1}, is practically the same as prediction for one quarter and in some instances a little improved. This improvement corresponds to the greater stability of the relationships over a two-quarter period which has occasionally been noted. Prediction over a four-quarter period is less effective in terms of the $\bar{R}^2$'s obtained. Moreover, the effect of attitudes is no longer significant in the nonautomotive part of durable expenditures.

4. Experiments with other independent variables (in addition to income and attitudes) for predicting $D_{A_{t+1}}$ (where the $\bar{R}^2$'s obtained are

---

expenditures on nonautomotive durables and B_D is buying plans for furniture and major household appliances.

$$\frac{D_{NA_{t+1}} + D_{NA_{t+2}}}{2} = 61.466 + 0.072\ Y_t + 0.462\ I_{6t} \qquad \bar{R}^2 = .643$$
$$\phantom{\frac{D_{NA_{t+1}} + D_{NA_{t+2}}}{2} = 61.466 +} (.020) \qquad (.257)$$

$$\frac{D_{NA_{t+1}} + D_{NA_{t+2}}}{2} = 23.880 + 0.068\ Y_t + 1.102\ B_{Dt} \qquad \bar{R}^2 = .558$$
$$\phantom{\frac{D_{NA_{t+1}} + D_{NA_{t+2}}}{2} = 23.880 +} (.020) \qquad (.795)$$

$$\frac{D_{NA_{t+1}} + D_{NA_{t+2}}}{2} = 75.175 + 0.073\ Y_t + 0.386\ I_{6t}$$
$$\phantom{\frac{D_{NA_{t+1}} + D_{NA_{t+2}}}{2} = 75.175 +} (.020) \qquad (.276)$$
$$+\ 0.688\ B_D \qquad \bar{R}^2 = .629$$
$$(.767)$$

While the regression coefficients are not statistically significant for either I_6 or B_D, the equation incorporating I_6 has greater explanatory power, and the addition of the buying plans variable makes no net contribution to the adjusted coefficient of determination.

[9] Strangely enough, it seems to make little difference whether B_C or B_H or B are used here, nor whether B_C, which has a significant seasonal variation, is seasonally adjusted.

relatively low) were carried out. When $D_{A_{t+1}}$ is defined, as it is here, in per capita real terms, additional independent variables such as:

credit conditions (dummy variable);
price of automobiles;
automobile sales in year $t - 6$ quarters to $t - 2$ quarters;
automobile sales in year $t - 10$ quarters to $t - 6$ quarters;

do not have significant coefficients and do not improve $\bar{R}^2$.

Effects of Separate Attitudinal Variables

The separate effects of the six attitudinal variables are examined on the basis of the same simple regression scheme used above. The equations obtained are summarized in table 4.

The values of the adjusted coefficients of determination may be compared conveniently with those obtained from equations on Y and I_6, which are 0.609, 0.679, and 0.526 for D_{t+1}, $D_{NA_{t+1}}$, and $D_{A_{t+1}}$, respectively. The MC_1 and BC_1 variables are the most effective variables in all cases. Other attitudinal variables are much less powerful predictors though still statistically significant in many instances. The effectiveness of MC_1 (which exceeds that of BC_1 in the case of all durables and in the nonautomotive case), should particularly be noted. Presumably, MC_1 which is after all a catchall for the consumer's own evaluation of the "time to buy," combines elements of attitudes in such a way as to maximize its ability to forecast in these cases.

The effect of the various attitudes is not the same as among predicting nonautomotive and automotive and total durable expenditures. With regard to nonautomotive durables, the individual attitude variables have greater explanatory power than the attitudes index, I_6. It appears that MC_1, BC_1, and BC_2 (the broad economic outlook variables) relate to purchasing. The MC_2 variable also has a significant effect but opposite from the expectation implied by the SRC's scaling. Personal financial status and expectations, PF_1 and PF_2,[10] do not register anything more than is already taken into account by the income variables.

With regard to automotive purchases (D_A and a large part of D), all attitudes except MC_2 (price expectations) have significant coefficients. The effect of MC_1 and BC_1 is as above. It is less clear why the BC_2 variable is less relevant here. In turn, the PF_1 variable has a somewhat smaller yet still important effect. This may reflect the fact that since automobiles represent a large expenditure per unit, their purchases are perhaps more closely tied to specific improvements in individuals' financial conditions than other durables purchases. The PF_1 variable measures past change in income or financial status, whereas the Y variable mea-

---

[10] Seasonal adjustment of the PF_2 variable somewhat improves $\bar{R}^2$, but the coefficient of the seasonally adjusted variable is not statistically significant with D_{NA}.

12. Consumer Attitudes, Buying Plans, and Purchases of Durable Goods 195

TABLE 4
Regression Equations for Consumers' Durable Expenditures on Attitude Variables

Equation Number	Dependent Variable	= a_0	+ $a_1 Y_t$	+ $a_2\ Attitude_t$	$\bar{R}^2$
\multicolumn{6}{l}{Personal Financial$_1$ (Better off than a year ago?)}
15......	D_{t+1}	−64.456	0.079 (.029)	1.606 PF_{1t} (.412)	0.510
16......	$D_{NA t+1}$	−35.283	0.068 (.011)	0.226 PF_{1t} (.158)	0.644
17......	$D_{A t+1}$	−31.600	−0.026 (.030)	1.758 PF_{1t} (.429)	0.406
\multicolumn{6}{l}{Personal Financial$_2$ (Expect to be better off?)}
18......	D_{t+1}	−36.025	0.034 (.041)	2.006 PF_{2t} (.837)	0.327
19......	$D_{NA t+1}$	−33.598	0.061 (.014)	0.326 PF_{2t} (.278)	0.633
20......	$D_{A t+1}$	−53.523	−0.075 (.043)	1.277 PF_{2t} (.882)	0.163
\multicolumn{6}{l}{Business Conditions$_1$ (Business conditions over the next year?)}
21......	D_{t+1}	61.742	0.038 (.030)	1.074 BC_{1t} (.242)	0.564
22......	$D_{NA t+1}$	−18.282	0.058 (.011)	0.250 BC_{1t} (.087)	0.722
23......	$D_{A t+1}$	106.825	−0.069 (.032)	1.136 BC_{1t} (.258)	0.445
\multicolumn{6}{l}{Business Conditions$_2$ (Business conditions over the next five years?)}
24......	D_{t+1}	20.244	0.077 (.032)	0.817 BC_{2t} (.282)	0.390
25......	$D_{NA t+1}$	−30.831	0.066 (0.10)	0.238 BC_{2t} (.087)	0.715
26......	$D_{A t+1}$	65.119	−0.027 (.035)	0.828 BC_{2t} (.305)	0.202
\multicolumn{6}{l}{Market Conditions$_1$ (Good time to buy?)}
27......	D_{t+1}	219.184	−0.065 (.041)	1.221 MC_{1t} (.255)	0.596
28......	$D_{NA t+1}$	28.905	0.023 (.013)	0.370 MC_{1t} (.078)	0.817
29......	$D_{A t+1}$	266.763	−0.171 (.046)	1.237 MC_{1t} (.284)	0.439
\multicolumn{6}{l}{Market Conditions$_2$ (Price expectations to the good?)}
30......	D_{t+1}	130.025	0.060 (.084)	−0.099 MC_{2t} (.259)	0.139
31......	$D_{NA t+1}$	−88.360	0.020 (.022)	−0.173 MC_{2t} (.069)	0.703
32......	$D_{A t+1}$	133.949	−0.024 (.090)	−0.031 MC_{2t} (.276)	0.092

sures level of income. The failure of price expectations (MC_2) to have an effect either positive or negative, in this case is surprising. It should be noted, however, that the variable deals with general price expectations, not the price of automobiles, and that it has a time path quite distinct from the economic outlook variables.

These results point to the importance of consumer expectations about business conditions in forecasting durable expenditures. Since these expectations are also part of the PF_1 and MC_1 variables (the high correlation between PF_1, MC_1 and the first principal component), the latter will also serve as effective predictors. The significant but much less important predictive power of the other attitudes suggests the need to investigate their net contributions to the forecast and find the ideal combination of attitudinal variables for forecasting.[11]

CONCLUSIONS

This paper has been concerned with the nature and predictive effectiveness of attitudes and buying plans as aggregate time-series data. The analysis leads to the following principal conclusions:

While the attitude data reflect diverse attitudinal dimensions, there is considerable informational overlap among them. Consumer expectations about the short-term business outlook are the most important component of the time-series variation of attitudes. This attitudinal dimension can be expected to show up better in time series than in cross section, a factor which may explain the inconsistent results of past time-series and cross-section tests.

Regression analysis of the attitudes and of buying plans as predictors of consumer durable expenditures show that attitudes make a significant contribution to forecasting durable expenditures. Buying plans do not improve the correlation once the income and attitudes are present in the equation, so that in time series the orthogonal components associated with buying plans appear to have no forecasting value.

These results support the case for attitudes as a key consumer anticipations variable and as a means of forecasting. But a predictive relationship need not be structural and the ties between the attitudinal outlook and consumer expenditures on durables bear further examination. Nevertheless, a reassessment of the relative usefulness of attitudes and buying plans data is called for.

[11] Our investigation of these questions suggests that the unweighted SRC index of six consumer attitudes is a good, though not ideal, combination of attitudinal variables.

part FOUR
Costs

INTRODUCTION

The literature on empirical cost studies has become increasingly technical. Severe data and econometric problems have forced investigators into ever more sophisticated methods, and armed their critics with ever more powerful weapons. J. Johnston's article surveys the issues as well as the evidence. His penetrating analysis succeeds in quieting some of the fuss, and his results are worth knowing.

Still, not everyone is satisfied that the more serious statistical problems have been solved. Some cost investigators have therefore turned from the classical methods of statistical estimation to other approaches. Leading examples are provided by the papers of John Haldi and David Whitcomb, who apply the so-called "engineering rule," and George Stigler, who applies the "survivor" principle to the investigation of scale economies. Perhaps more experience with these approaches will confirm their usefulness; perhaps not. In any case they illustrate well the fact that one need not estimate cost functions in order to obtain important information about some of their properties.

The article by M. C. Meimaroglou is analytical rather than empirical in content. It extends standard break-even analysis to what many of us think is the more realistic case of nonconstant marginal costs and revenues. It is a useful bridge between the **U**-shaped curves of the economist and the straight lines of the accountant.

William Henry and James Segraves view costs as a long-range planning problem and use the broiler industry for purposes of discussing economies of scale. Theirs is a pragmatic approach, illustrating how the tools and techniques of managerial economics have numerous applications in the area of cost determination.

13. Statistical Cost Functions: A Reappraisal*
J. JOHNSTON

Statistical cost functions attempt to determine the nature of the intra-firm relationship between costs and output from statistical analyses of accounting data. The two major findings suggested by research in this field are (1) that short-run total costs are linearly related to output, so that marginal costs are substantially constant over a wide range of output; and (2) that long-run average cost tends to decline with increases in the scale of output, quickly at first and then more slowly, but with little or no indication of the expected rise at high output levels. A variety of criticisms has been directed at these findings. The purpose of this paper is to pass nine of these major criticisms in review, and it will be suggested that they fall into three groups. Firstly, there are some which do not stand up to serious scrutiny; secondly, there are certain arguments which are superficially plausible, but which can be shown to be incomplete and misleading; thirdly, there are those whose validity remains more or less intact after scrutiny.

The first six criticisms relate to the short-run cost function, and the last three to the long-run function.

1. Firstly, it has been suggested that the statistical methods employed impart a bias toward linearity. Ruggles, for example, argues that quite pronounced curvature in MC and AC will give very little curvature in the total cost function. He produces two diagrams of the same overall size, one showing average and marginal curves and the other the corresponding total cost curve. The former show marked curvature, while the latter is practically linear. Ruggles' concern is with analyses which attempt to establish the nature of the cost-output relation solely by graphical considerations, and for such attempts the criticism is valid. It does not apply, however, to statistical analyses embodying numerical tests of hypotheses. Manipulation of the vertical scale on a diagram cannot then tell us anything about the existence of a linear

---
*The Review of Economics and Statistics, vol. 40, no. 4 (November 1958), pp. 339–50.

bias. This can only be established by a consideration of the method of statistical inference employed. Actually, if the cost data were as shown by Ruggles, the statistical analysis would yield a cubic total cost function, for he postulates *exact functional* relationships.

The real problem in the context, however, as Ruggles recognizes, is that the cost function, like most economic relations, is stochastic. It is then true that statistical analysis cannot prove that a certain cost relationship is the true one: statistical analysis provides a procedure for the rejection of a hypothesis, if the probability of a particular relationship having generated the sample observations is less than some fairly small preselected value; and several different hypotheses may well be not inconsistent with the observations. Three important points to note, however, are (a) that in the majority of cases where statistical tests have been applied, the hypothesis of a linear total cost function has not been rejected, (b) that most often no statistically significant improvement on the linear hypothesis is achieved by the inclusion of second- or higher-degree terms in output, and (c) that supplementary tests, such as the examination of incremental costs ratios, usually confirm the linear hypothesis.

2. A second source of linearity bias in the statistical analyses is alleged to be the correction of the observed cost data for factor price changes. The theory of cost curves traces out the implications of various hypotheses about the production function on the assumption either that factor prices are constant and independent of the purchases of a firm or that they are dependent upon the firm's purchases. Actual cost observations frequently come from successive time periods during which factor prices may have changed substantially in response to influences other than the firm's purchases. Two common methods of correcting for these factor price changes are deflation of the actual cost figures by a factor price index number or the recalculation of the cost figures by applying some selected set of factor prices to the actual factor inputs of each period.

It has been argued by Caleb A. Smith that, where the proportions in which factors are applied can be varied in response to changes in their relative factor prices, this second method of correction will lead to an overstatement of the costs of every period except the period to which the selected factor prices relate. Smith noted that the ratio of labor to nonlabor factor prices had ranged from 65 percent to 100 percent in the years covered by the U.S. Steel study, but he was unable to surmise how the shape of the cost curve might have been affected. In the hands of Staehle, this valid point of Smith's is cited as one reason why one must expect a bias toward linearity in statistical cost functions. It can be shown that Staehle's conclusion has no general validity and

13. Statistical Cost Functions: A Reappraisal

that, in fact, in the case postulated by orthodox theory a likely result is an *increase* in the curvilinearity displayed by the cost-output data. A thorough analysis is required, and it seems desirable to examine the problems involved in both types of cost correction.

The analysis has to be carried out for specific types of production function. Suppose that there are two variable factors of production, A and B, the amounts employed in period t being a_t and b_t. Let the production function be

$$x_t = K a_t^\alpha b_t^\beta \tag{1}$$

where x_t is output in period t, and K, α, and β are the parameters of the production function. Let $p_t^{(a)}$ and $p_t^{(b)}$ denote the prices of the two factors in period t, and we make the orthodox assumption that, as these factor prices change, the proportion in which A and B are combined is varied to minimize costs for any given output. The familiar marginal productivity condition enables us to express b_t in terms of a_t and the factor prices:

$$b_t = a_t \frac{\beta}{\alpha} \cdot \frac{p_t^{(a)}}{p_t^{(b)}}.$$

Substituting for b_t in (1) gives x_t as a function of a_t, and taking the inverse gives

$$a_t = x_t^{\frac{1}{\alpha+\beta}} K^{-\frac{1}{\alpha+\beta}} \left[\frac{\beta}{\alpha} \cdot \frac{p_t^{(a)}}{p_t^{(b)}} \right]^{-\frac{\beta}{\alpha+\beta}}.$$

Total cost in period t is, by definition,

$$\Pi_t = a_t p_t^{(a)} + b_t p_t^{(b)}.$$

Substituting successively the expressions obtained for b_t and a_t gives,

$$\Pi_t = C x_t^{\frac{1}{\alpha+\beta}} [p_t^{(a)}]^{\frac{\alpha}{\alpha+\beta}} [p_t^{(b)}]^{\frac{\beta}{\alpha+\beta}} \tag{2}$$

where

$$C = K^{\frac{-1}{\alpha+\beta}} \left[\frac{\beta}{\alpha} \right]^{\frac{-\beta}{\alpha+\beta}} \left[1 + \frac{\beta}{\alpha} \right]. \tag{3}$$

We see from (2) that total cost in period t is a function of output x_t, the parameters of the production function, and the prices of the factors in period t. If we assume that factor prices are constant per period, say at levels $p_0^{(a)}$ and $p_0^{(b)}$, then the cost function is

$$\Pi_t = C x_t^{\frac{1}{\alpha+\beta}} [p_0^{(a)}]^{\frac{\alpha}{\alpha+\beta}} [p_0^{(b)}]^{\frac{\beta}{\alpha+\beta}}. \tag{4}$$

The price terms in (4) may now be merged with the constant C to give a new constant C', and we have the cost function

$$\Pi_t = C' x_t^{\frac{1}{\alpha+\beta}}$$

which corresponds to the production function (1). The assumption of a different set of constant factor prices would give the same *form* of total cost function, but with a different constant in place of C'.

If the parameters of the production function are constant from period to period, but factor prices vary, then actual costs are given by (2). Suppose we are interested in the cost function (4). Then it is obvious from a comparison of the two expressions that there does exist, in this case, a price index number whose application to the recorded costs would give the Π_t of (4) *exactly*. The required price index number is a weighted geometric mean of price relatives, namely,

$$P_t = \left[\frac{p_t^{(a)}}{p_0^{(a)}}\right]^{\frac{\alpha}{\alpha+\beta}} \left[\frac{p_t^{(b)}}{p_0^{(b)}}\right]^{\frac{\beta}{\alpha+\beta}}. \qquad (5)$$

The application of this result in practice would require knowledge that the production function was of logarithmic form and an estimate of the relative importance of the α, β parameters. Three questions therefore remain for examination.

(a) If an index number of the form (5) is used, but incorrect weights are attached to the price relatives, what bias will be introduced into the "corrected" cost figures? In particular, will there be any bias toward linearity, when $\alpha + \beta \neq 1$?

(b) What bias would spring from the second type of cost correction with this form of production function?

(c) Do simple forms of index numbers exist which would *exactly* correct observed cost figures for other types of production function?

We shall examine each of these questions in turn.

Suppose we use a price index number of the form.

$$P_t = \left[\frac{p_t^{(a)}}{p_0^{(a)}}\right]^{w_1} \left[\frac{p_t^{(b)}}{p_0^{(b)}}\right]^{w_2} \qquad (6)$$

where $w_1 + w_2 = 1$. Corrected costs Π_t', are then given by

$$\Pi_t' = C x_t^{\frac{1}{\alpha+\beta}} [p_t^{(a)}]^{\frac{\alpha}{\alpha+\beta} - w_1} [p_t^{(b)}]^{\frac{\beta}{\alpha+\beta} - w_2} [p_0^{(a)}]^{w_1} [p_0^{(b)}]^{w_2} \qquad (7)$$

where C is as given in (3) above. The relative bias in the corrected cost figures may then be defined as $(\Pi_t' - \Pi_t)/\Pi_t$ where Π_t is given by (4). The exponents of $p_t^{(a)}$ and $p_t^{(b)}$ in (7) are necessarily equal numerically but opposite in sign. Taking the exponent of $p_t^{(a)}$ as the positive one we may write

$$\frac{\alpha}{\alpha+\beta} - w_1 = w_2 - \frac{\beta}{\alpha+\beta} = \gamma \qquad \gamma \geq 0. \tag{8}$$

Using (4), (7), and (8) the relative bias may be found as

$$\text{Relative bias} = \left[\frac{p_t^{(a)}}{p_0^{(a)}} \cdot \frac{p_0^{(b)}}{p_t^{(b)}}\right]^\gamma - 1. \tag{9}$$

Defining $p_t^{(a)} = c_{1t} p_0^{(a)}$ and $p_t^{(b)} = c_{2t} p_0^{(b)}$, we have

$$\text{Relative bias} = \left[\frac{c_{1t}}{c_{2t}}\right]^\gamma - 1 \qquad \begin{array}{c} \gamma \geq 0 \\ c_{1t} > 0 \\ c_{2t} > 0. \end{array} \tag{10}$$

Thus the relative bias in period t, for this type of production function, depends upon the *ratio* of the proportionate changes in the factor prices and upon the errors in the weights used in the index number. The extent of this bias for two selected values of γ is shown in table 1.

TABLE 1
Relative Bias
(percent)

c_{1t}/c_{2t}	$\gamma = 0.1$	$\gamma = 0.2$
0.2	−14.9	−27.5
0.5	− 6.7	−13.1
1.0	0	0
2.0	7.2	14.9
3.0	11.6	24.6
4.0	14.9	31.9
5.0	17.4	38.0

It is seen that this bias may be positive or negative. It is zero, no matter what the error in weighting the factor price index number, when the two factor prices have changed in the same proportion. For a given error in weighting, the bias increases numerically the further the ratio of the proportionate change in the two factor prices departs from unity. As the error in weighting increases, so does the absolute value of the bias for all (c_{1t}/c_{2t}) values. When $\gamma = 0.1$ the relative bias will lie in the range ± 7 percent, provided (c_{1t}/c_{2t}) lies between 0.5 and 2.0: for the same range of (c_{1t}/c_{2t}) the bias will be within ± 15 percent when $\gamma = 0.2$. A value of 0.1 for γ implies a fairly large proportionate error in the estimation of the weights. For example, if $\alpha = 0.6$, $\beta = 0.4$ and we take $w_1 = w_2 = 0.5$, then $\gamma = 0.1$ which represents a 17 percent underestimate of $\alpha/(\alpha+\beta)$ and a 25 percent overestimate of $\beta/(\alpha+\beta)$.

While the extent of the bias may be fairly great, it is clear that there is no a priori reason why it should produce a tendency toward linearity in statistical cost functions. Where $(\alpha + \beta) < 1$, the true cost function will be convex to the x-axis, and a bias toward linearity would require a *negative* correlation between (c_{1t}/c_{2t}) and x_t. If $(\alpha + \beta) > 1$ a linearity bias would require a *positive* correlation between (c_{1t}/c_{2t}) and x_t. There is no obvious a priori reason why one or the other correlation should exist, nor why, if the negative correlation exists, it should more likely be associated with the case $(\alpha + \beta) < 1$ than with the opposite case, nor why, if a positive correlation exists, it should more likely be associated with the case $(\alpha + \beta) > 1$. Notice that, if $(\alpha + \beta) = 1$, the true cost function is linear, and the existence of either correlation between (c_{1t}/c_{2t}) and x_t would give a bias toward *curvilinearity*.

Turning next to the Smith-Staehle problem we examine for this same production function (1) the bias introduced by the recalculation of the cost figures using $p_0^{(a)}$ and $p_0^{(b)}$ as weights to be applied to the actual inputs a_t and b_t. Since the cost minimization condition gives $b_t = a_t \frac{\beta}{\alpha} \cdot \frac{p_t^{(a)}}{p_t^{(b)}}$, corrected costs are then

$$\Pi_t' = a_t \left[p_0^{(a)} + \frac{\beta}{\alpha} \frac{p_t^{(a)}}{p_t^{(b)}} p_0^{(b)} \right]. \tag{11}$$

The true costs in which we are interested are still given by (4), and in this case the relative bias is now found to be

$$\frac{\Pi_t' - \Pi_t}{\Pi_t} = \frac{\left[1 + \frac{\beta}{\alpha} \cdot \frac{c_{1t}}{c_{2t}} \right]}{\left[1 + \frac{\beta}{\alpha} \right]} \left[\frac{c_{2t}}{c_{1t}} \right]^{\frac{\beta}{\alpha+\beta}} - 1. \tag{12}$$

Illustrations of this bias are given in table 2.

TABLE 2
Relative Bias
(percent)

c_{1t}/c_{2t}	$\frac{\beta}{\alpha} = \frac{1}{2}$	$\frac{\beta}{\alpha} = 1$	$\frac{\beta}{\alpha} = 2$
0.25	19.1	25.0	26.0
0.50	5.0	6.0	5.9
0.75	0.9	0.9	0.9
1	0	0	0
2	5.8	6.1	5.0
3	15.5	15.5	12.1
4	26.0	25.0	19.1
5	36.5	34.2	25.4

The bias is everywhere positive or zero, as expected. Again, if we consider a range of c_{1t}/c_{2t} between 0.5 and 2.0 the bias is less than 7 percent. The nonnegative nature of the bias gives a different result from the previous case. Now a positive *or* a negative correlation between c_{1t}/c_{2t} and x_t will lead to an overstatement of the true costs at *both* low and high output levels. Thus if the true cost function is convex from below, as the orthodox theory assumes, the effect of these chance correlations is to *increase* the degree of curvature: while if the true cost function is linear, the effect is to impart a bias toward curvilinearity. Thus Staehle's position is exactly reversed: a bias depends upon the existence of one or other chance correlation, but the bias is one toward *curvilinearity* not linearity. A linear bias could only exist if the observed output levels were confined to a range where the true cost function was concave from below.

Finally, it may be noted that for other simple types of production function no simple form of index number may exist which will transform observed costs exactly into true costs. This is true, for example, of the production function:

$$x = 2Hab - Aa^2 - Bb^2$$

where H, A, and B are constants such that $H^2 > AB$. The bias resulting from any particular method of correction may be evaluated above with similar results.

The magnitude of the biases revealed by tables 1 and 2 is perhaps surprising. However, they are in general likely to increase the spread of the cost output points in the Π_t direction without imparting any systematic bias toward or away from linearity. They will, unfortunately, augment the stochastical element inherent in costs and thus reduce the discriminating power of a given number of observations below that ideally obtainable, but a systematic bias is dependent upon particular chance correlations between price changes and output levels, and even then the bias may easily be toward curvilinearity rather than the reverse.

It should be emphasized that the whole of this section assumes that the proportions in which the factors are combined are changeable in the short run and are in fact changed in response to variations in relative factor prices. The possible seriousness of the bias has to be carefully assessed in individual cases according to the amount of variation in relative prices in the period under study and the possibilities of factor substitution in the production process.

3. A third source of linear bias in the statistical cost function is alleged to lie in the necessity of working with the time period for which the accounting data have been drawn up. A distinction is drawn between this time period and the unit time period of economic theory, in which the proportions between factors and the rate of output are assumed

to be unchanged. It is then suggested that if the accounting time period consists of several unit time periods, and "if the output is not spread evenly over each unit period, the use of the average rate of output during the [accounting] period assumes a linear cost function and by this assumption biases the statistically determined cost function toward linearity, since the midpoint of a secant connecting any two points on a curve whose second derivative does not change sign lies closer to a straight line connecting the end points of the curve than does the corresponding point of the curve itself."[1] This point is superficially plausible, but the argument is incomplete and, as we shall see, misleading.

Suppose we make an orthodox assumption that the total cost function in the unit time period of economic theory is

$$\pi_i = \alpha + \beta x_i + \gamma x_i^2 + \epsilon_i \qquad \gamma > 0 \tag{13}$$

where π_i denotes the total cost associated with an output rate x_i and ϵ_i denotes the disturbance term. If one had a sample of N pairs of observations on (π_i, x_i) one might compute the least-squares estimate c of γ. A test of the hypothesis $\gamma = 0$ could then be made by computing

$$\text{var}(c) = \frac{\sigma_\epsilon^2}{N s_{x^2}^2 (1 - r^2)} \tag{14}$$

and referring the ratio $c / \sqrt{\text{var}(c)}$ to the normal distribution, where σ_ε^2 is the variance of the disturbance term, $s_{x^2}^2$ is the variance of the x^2 values in the sample, and r is the sample correlation coefficient between x and x^2.

Now suppose that the accounting period consists of n unit time periods, and that the accounting data are in the form of total costs (Π) and total output (X). From (13) we then have

$$\Pi = \sum_{i=1}^{n} \pi_i = n\alpha + \beta \sum_{i=1}^{n} x_i + \gamma \sum_{i=1}^{n} x_i^2 + \sum_{i=1}^{n} \epsilon_i$$

which may be written

$$\Pi = n\alpha + \beta X + \gamma X^2 - 2\gamma \sum_{i<j} x_i x_j + \sum_{i=1}^{n} \epsilon_i \tag{15}$$

where

$$X = \sum_{i=1}^{n} x_i.$$

Since $\sum_{i<j} x_i x_j$ is necessarily positive, it is clear that total costs from the

---
[1] Hans Staehle, "The Measurement of Statistical Cost Functions: An Appraisal of Some Recent Contributions," in *Readings in Price Theory* (Chicago, 1952), p. 274.

accounting records will be less than the figure that would be obtained by substituting total output (X) into the function

$$\Pi = n\alpha + \beta X + \gamma X^2 \qquad (16)$$

obtained from (13) by stepping up the fixed cost from α to $n\alpha$ to give the appropriate figure for the accounting period. Consequently, the curvature shown by the accounting data will be *less* than that of the short-run cost function (13). In fact, ignoring the disturbance term, the limits within which the accounting data must lie are given by (16) and

$$\Pi = \dot{n}\alpha + \beta X + \left(\frac{\gamma}{n}\right) X^2. \qquad (17)$$

These curves are shown in chart 1. The relationship (16) shows what total costs in the accounting period would be if the whole of the output were produced in a single unit time period, output in each of the other $(n-1)$ unit periods being zero; while (17) shows what costs would be if the total output of the accounting period were spread equally over the n unit periods.

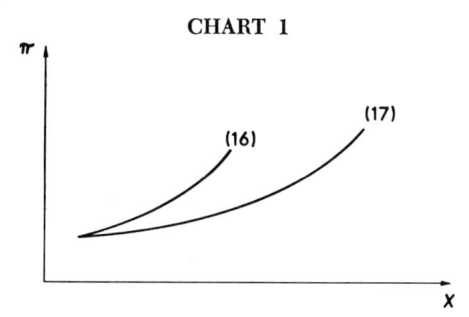

CHART 1

It is thus clear that the curvature displayed by the accounting data will be less than that of the ideal, but unobtainable, unit period data. This fact alone is not sufficient to establish a linear bias. The crucial question is the power of accounting data to detect this reduced curvature compared with the power of comparable unit period data to detect the curvature of the unit period curve.

To tackle this question, let us assume that

$$2 \sum_{i<j} x_i x_j = \delta X^2 \qquad 0 < \delta < 1. \qquad (18)$$

This implies that the downward pull of the term $2\gamma \sum_{i<j} x_i x_j$ in (15) on

costs moves proportionately to the square of total output. Using (18) we can rewrite (15) as

$$\Pi = n\alpha + \beta X + \gamma(1 - \delta)X^2 + \sum_{i=1}^{n} \epsilon_i. \tag{19}$$

From N pairs of observations on Π and X one might make a least-squares estimate, c', of the parameter $\gamma(1 - \delta)$ in (19).

To test the hypothesis $\gamma(1 - \delta) = 0$ one would set up a critical region defined by

$$c' > k \cdot se(c')$$

where k is a constant determined by the level of significance of the test and $se(c')$ is the standard deviation of the sampling distribution of c'. If one works with unit period data, the corresponding critical region for the test of the hypothesis, $\gamma = 0$, is defined by

$$c > k \cdot se(c)$$

where c is the least squares estimate of γ in (13). The probability of obtaining a sample value of c in its critical region is

$$P_1 = \int_{k \cdot se(c)}^{\gamma} f(c) \, dc + 0.5 \tag{20}$$

and the probability of obtaining a sample value of c' in its critical region is

$$P_2 = \int_{k \cdot se(c)}^{\gamma(1-\delta)} f(c') \, dc' + 0.5 \tag{21}$$

where $f(c)$ and $f(c')$ denote the sampling distributions of c and c' which, on the assumption of a normal disturbance term, are normal about γ and $\gamma(1 - \delta)$ respectively. The values of P_1 and P_2 depend upon u_1 and u_2 defined as follows:

$$u_1 = \frac{\gamma - k \cdot se(c)}{se(c)} = \frac{\gamma}{se(c)} - k$$

$$u_2 = \frac{\gamma(1 - \delta)}{se(c')} - k. \tag{22}$$

Since k is constant for any given significance level, the u's depend on t_1 and t_2, defined as

$$t_1 = \frac{\gamma}{se(c)} \qquad t_2 = \frac{\gamma(1 - \delta)}{se(c')}. \tag{23}$$

From (14) above it can be seen that the ratio t_1 is given by

$$t_1 = \frac{\gamma \sqrt{N} \cdot s_x^2 \sqrt{(1 - r^2)}}{\sigma_\epsilon}. \tag{24}$$

Referring to (19), the variance of c' is given by

$$\text{var}(c') = \frac{\sigma_{\Sigma\epsilon_i}^2}{N s^2_{x^2}(1-\rho^2)} \qquad (25)$$

where ρ denotes the correlation coefficient between X and X^2, and s^2_X is the variance of the X^2 values in the sample. If we assume the ϵ_i to be independent over time and to have constant variance, then $\sigma_{\Sigma\epsilon_i}^2 = n\sigma_\epsilon^2$. Next, in order to compare the power of accounting and unit period observations, we must make some assumption about the spread or dispersion of the output observations in each hypothetical sample. We shall start with the assumption that the coefficient of variation is the same in each case. This would be the case if

$$X = nx. \qquad (26)$$

For example, if the unit period were a month, the accounting period a year, and we had, say, four annual output observations of 132, 96, 120, 120, then assumption (26) means that we wish to contrast the power of these observations with that of the "corresponding" monthly observations 11, 8, 10, 10. Notice that assumption (26) does *not* mean that the rate of output must be evenly spread over the n unit periods constituting any given accounting period. For example, the annual output of 132 units could be made up of varying monthly outputs, provided only that they summed to 132 and also satisfied the condition $2\sum_{i<j} x_i x_j = \delta X^2$.

From (26) we then have

$$s^2_{X^2} = n^4 s^2_{x^2} \text{ and } \rho = r.$$

Thus the ratio t_2 may be written

$$t_2 = \frac{\gamma(1-\delta)n^{3/2}\sqrt{N} \cdot s_x^2 \sqrt{(1-r^2)}}{\sigma_\epsilon}. \qquad (27)$$

Comparing (27) and (24) we see that

$$\frac{t_2}{t_1} = n^{3/2}(1-\delta). \qquad (28)$$

Thus if the condition

$$n^{3/2}(1-\delta) > 1 \qquad (29)$$

holds the accounting data will have a greater power of detecting curvature, for (29) implies $u_2 > u_1$ and hence $P_2 > P_1$. Referring to the definition of δ in (18) above, it can be shown that the largest value which

δ can assume is $(n-1)/n$. This occurs when $x_1 = x_2 = \cdots = x_n = X/n$, so that

$$2\sum_{i<j} x_i x_j = \left[\frac{X^2}{n^2}\right] n(n-1).$$

Thus the smallest possible value of $(1-\delta)$ is $1/n$, and in this case condition (29) becomes

$$\sqrt{n} > 1$$

which is necessarily satisfied by all positive integers greater than unity.

The conclusion therefore is that, on the assumptions made, the power of accounting observations to detect curvilinearity in the cost function is greater than the power of comparable observations on unit periods, even though the effect of the merging of unit periods is to show a curvature less than that of the "true" short-run cost function.

There are two comments to be made on this conclusion. Firstly, it depends upon assumption (18), that $2\sum_{i<j} x_i x_j = \delta X^2$. This assumption implies that, in the absence of stochastic elements, the accounting data would lie on a smooth curve somewhere between the two curves depicted in chart 1. If this assumption is not exactly fulfilled, then the variance of the disturbance term in (19) will be greater than $n\sigma_\epsilon^2$. This will reduce the value of t_2/t_1 below that shown in (28). If, for example, the variance of the disturbance in (19) were doubled, the value of t_2/t_1 would now be $n^{3/2}(1-\delta)/\sqrt{2}$. Even if δ takes on its maximum value this t_2/t_1 ratio will still exceed unity for all $n \geq 3$. The second assumption was that the coefficient of variation was the same for the hypothetical samples of accounting and unit period data. This might not be the case. Suppose, to take an extreme assumption, that successive unit outputs (x_i) were distributed normally and at random about mean value (μ) with standard deviation σ. The accounting outputs (X) will then be distributed normally and randomly about mean value $(n\mu)$ with standard deviation $\sqrt{n} \cdot \sigma$. It can be shown that in this case the t_2/t_1 ratio becomes

$$\frac{t_2}{t_1} = \frac{(1-\delta)\sqrt{n} \cdot \sqrt{(2\sigma^4 + n^2\mu^4)}}{[2\sigma^4 + \mu^4]} \qquad (30)$$

If μ is at all large in relation to σ this ratio is approximately $n^{3/2}(1-\delta)$, which is exactly the value obtained in (28) above. If, on the other hand, we set the ratio of the two square-root terms at unity, a value which it must in fact exceed, the t_2/t_1 ratio can still exceed unity for appropriate values of δ and n. For example if $\delta = \frac{1}{2}$, $t_2/t_1 > 1$ provided $n > 4$. Thus even in the case of random outputs it is still quite possible for the accounting data to have greater power of detecting curvature than do the unit data.

4. A fourth objection to the statistical findings of constant marginal cost in the short run is that the observed facts of market behavior contradict these findings: ". . . . if marginal costs were constant over a wide range of output and then rose steeply for each firm, the output of the competitive industry would vary in the short run chiefly through variations in the number of plants in operation and hardly at all through variations in the rate of output of plants that stay in operation. But this is the opposite of the facts."[2]

But Stigler, in looking at the facts, is not testing the single hypothesis of constant MC: he is testing a composite three-part hypothesis, namely that perfect competition prevails, so that entrepreneurs determine output solely by the principle of securing equality of price and MC, secondly that MC is constant up to high output levels for each firm, and thirdly that the level of constant MC varies between firms. Lack of agreement between observation and expectation could be due to the failure of some or all of the parts of the hypothesis. Disagreement could, for example, be consistent with the truth of the second part, while the first part was false. Even if one agreed that Stigler's method provided a valid test of the hypothesis of constant MC, it would still be necessary to present data on a number of plants and average plant output for each industry for which linear cost functions have been derived. Stigler's data relate only to coal mining and cotton spinning. They cannot serve as a general refutation of constant MC, unless one makes the assumption that perfect competition exists everywhere.

5. A fifth and major criticism centers around the defects of depreciation figures. "Since studies of cost-output relations have relied on financial accounting data which typically utilize straight-line methods of 'depreciation,' there is introduced into the cost function an important element of linearity which is solely attributable to the accounting techniques. An 'economically correct' allocation might yield significantly different results."[3] The authors of the National Bureau volume seem to favor the method of successive valuation for the determination of the economically correct fixed cost, but they admit that in practice a really correct estimate is impossible. It is, however, clear that for any time period less than the life of the equipment, the accountant's allocable fixed cost will not necessarily coincide with the unknown figure that would be yielded by the method of successive valuation.

This discrepancy only introduces a linear bias into the statistical cost function if use depreciation is in fact nonlinearly related to output. If use depreciation is zero, then the level at which fixed costs are estimated for the period will not affect the statistical estimation of marginal cost either with respect to its shape or position. If a wear and tear

---

[2] G. J. Stigler, *The Theory of Price* (rev. ed., New York, 1952), p. 167.
[3] *Cost Behavior and Price Policy* (National Bureau of Economic Research, New York, 1943), p. 76.

element enters into depreciation, then the straight-line procedure would understate total costs in periods of high output and overstate them in periods of low output. The error thus introduced depends upon the nature of use depreciation. If, for example, use depreciation is linearly related to output, then the marginal cost estimate from accounting data will be consistently too low, but the accounting data will give an essentially correct picture of the *shape* of the true marginal cost function. If, finally, use depreciation rises sharply at very high output levels, the accounting data based on straight-line depreciation will contain a serious linear bias at the top end of the output scale.

It would seem that no one is yet in a position to generalize about the relative importance of these three hypotheses about use depreciation. A series of cooperative studies by economists and accountants would be extremely helpful. We can, however, in this context disagree with the Institute of Chartered Accountants in England and Wales, who still recommend the straight-line principle, and commend the following suggestion of the American cost accountants: "A compromise between straight line and production methods is obviously called for. This consists of recognizing a fixed minimum charge for depreciation which is present at all levels of activity from zero to 100 percent. Superimposed on this is a variable charge based on service output or working hours."[4]

6. Criticism has been justly directed against statistical studies of multiple product firms, where an output index has been constructed to measure changes in the level of a diversified output range. Such an index is usually constructed by weighting quantity relatives with estimates of the average direct costs for each product. As Staehle says, "This process seems highly objectionable, though it is difficult to see what other solution could be suggested. It indeed amounts to determining output by costs, i.e., to introducing a spurious dependence where measurement of an independent relationship is really wanted."

The fault here is not all the statistician's. In studying the relationship between total costs and an output index, he is trying to force reality into the straitjacket of the single, homogeneous product firm of economic theory, for little progress has as yet been made with the theory of the multiple product firm. The real world preponderance of multiple product as against single-product firms is probably the inverse of the space their respective analyses occupy in economic theory. The theorist, in this context, is like a zoologist, whose task is to study the octopus. He reacts to the complexity of the beast by defining an octopus with only a single tentacle and proceeding to study that hypothetical creature very thoroughly, but unfortunately the real octopus with many tentacles may behave very differently from an imaginary octopus with only one.

---

[4] *Cost Accountants' Handbook*, ed. T. Lang (New York, 1945), p. 1221. © Copyright 1945, The Ronald Press Company, New York.

A possibly useful approach to the study of the multiple product firm is to investigate what cost-output relationships hold for each product separately and to see whether there are any interrelationships between such cost functions. It is also possible to use an output index to provide a test of the linearity and independence of the individual product cost functions. If the weights employed are the estimated average variable costs, then the output index indicates what total variable costs would be if all the individual functions were linear and independent. Correlation with the actual total variable costs should then give a linear regression with intercept not significantly different from zero and slope not significantly different from unity.

7. A very sweeping criticism of the use of cross-section, contemporaneous accounting data to study the long-run cost function has been made by Friedman. He argues that such data "for different firms or plants gave little if any information on so-called economies of scale." There are two strands to this argument. Firstly, he considers a competitive industry with no specialized factors of production. The average cost curve would then be the same for all firms and independent of the output of the industry, so that we would expect all cross-section observations to show the same scale of output and the same average cost. Observed differences in the size of firms could only be due to "mistakes" or historical changes in the optimum size of firm. Even then such mistakes should be appropriately valued by a perfect capital market, or written off by internal accounting procedures, so that average cost should still be the same for all firms. When this model is extended to allow for specialized factors of production it is seen that firms may be of different sizes in order to give "appropriate scope" to the specialized resource controlled by the firm, but the capital market and the accountants, when doing their job properly, should still show the same average cost for each firm.

It is perfectly true that in a perfectly competitive world, observed variations in average cost would merely tell us something about the imperfections of the capital market and the accounting profession. But such a world is, by definition, incompatible with the existence of economies of scale, and we would not need to engage in a study of the nature and extent of such economies.

The second strand in Friedman's argument is that costs should be defined as identical with total receipts. In a less than perfectly competitive world, average costs in this sense could then differ between firms, and such differences would reflect not only any possible economies of scale but also variations in the prices charged by large and small firms. The theory of cost curves assumes that in costs we include only those payments necessary to secure the factor services required for the output in question. If costs in this sense are, say, lower in large firms so that higher profits and rents per unit of output accrue in the large firms, it seems both misleading and illogical to redefine costs to include all rents and profits.

Most cross-section studies have not used the Friedman cost concept, but have relied on accounting data, which typically include depreciation and maintenance charges but not profits. Ignoring variations in the original cost of capital equipment due to different price levels at the time of purchase, such accounting data provide an index number type of comparison of the total flow of service inputs (both capital and labor) in the various firms. Relating each input figure to the corresponding output thus provides a rough test of the existence of economies of scale.

8. A more general difficulty with the use of cross-section data is the variability of conditions between firms of different size at any given period of time. Variations are possible and likely in the age, type, and cost of equipment. Variations will be present also in the quality of the executives. In fact, even a slight acquaintance with the work of industrial consultants emphasizes the tremendous variations existing in the technical and economic efficiency of different firms. If all firms were on the boundaries of the appropriate production surfaces, as assumed by the economic theorist, the consulting firms would go out of existence through bankruptcy.

These factors make for variations about the cost-scale line. It would be a very unlikely event if the chance correlation of such factors with scale gave the declining cost-scale line found in the large majority of cross-section studies.

One possible difficulty of interpretation of the **L**-shaped pattern of average costs arises. Is it real evidence of the existence of economies of scale, or does it mean instead that it is the efficient firms which grow big? There are three points to be made here. Firstly, some of the cross-section studies relate to public utilities, such as electricity and gas supply, where the total production required within a defined area is largely dependent on the density of commercial, industrial, and domestic consumers in that area. The existence of local authority or private enterprise monopolies has resulted usually in a single undertaking per area, the size of the plant being geared to the total demand. In such cases the large plants did not emerge from a competitive struggle between a number of small firms, but they nonetheless show substantially lower costs than the smaller undertakings. Such size advantages were the justification for the granting of local monopolies. Secondly, it does not necessarily follow that a small firm with low costs will retain such low costs when it expands. Efficient production on a medium or large scale often requires that the whole plant be designed and constructed *ab initio* for that scale of production. Thirdly, there are many well known and plausible reasons to expect a decline in costs with increasing scale, and while the interpretation of statistical correlations in economics is hazardous, they must in general be viewed in the light of all the other information that one has about the problem in hand. In this case there seems to be impressive agreement between the statistical results and theoretical expectation, with the one qualification that the statistical results do not show with any certainty or regularity the anticipated preponderance of diseconomies with the highest scale levels observed.

9. A final criticism made of cross-section studies is labelled the regression fallacy. I shall give two examples.

a. "Suppose a firm produces a product the demand for which has a known two-year cycle, so that it plans to produce 100 units in year one, 200 in year two, 100 in year three, etc. Suppose, also, that the best way to do this is by an arrangement that involves identical outlays for hired factors in each year (no 'variable' costs). If outlays are regarded as total costs, average cost per unit will obviously be twice as large when output is 100 as when it is 200. If, instead of years one and two, we substitute firms one and two, a cross-section study would show sharply declining average costs. When firms are classified by actual output, essentially this kind of bias arises. The firms with the largest output are unlikely to be producing at an unusually low level: on the average, they are clearly likely to be producing at an unusually high level, and conversely for those which have the lowest output."[5]

b. "Suppose that three firms on average (over, say, a decade) produce 100 units each per year at an average cost of $10. In any one year, because of weather, catastrophe, illness or death of a salesman, regional differences in business, etc. ('chance fluctuations'), the firms will have sales (outputs) above or below the decade average of 100. Suppose firm A sells only 80 units in a given year, firm B, 100 units, and firm C, 120 units. Suppose further that for each firm costs include (1) $500 of fixed costs plus (2) $5 of variable costs per unit of output. Tabulating the results:

Firm	Output	Average cost
A	80	$11.25
B	100	10.00
C	120	9.17

This fall in average cost with output would seem to show that there are definite economies of large scale production, and yet actually the result is due only to the facts that all costs are not variable in the short run and that output is subject to chance fluctuations."[6]

Stigler's argument would only be a valid criticism of cross-section cost studies if *all* the firms in a given study had the same capacity.

---

[5] *Cost Behavior and Price Policy*, pp. 236–37.
[6] G. J. Stigler, *The Theory of Price* (rev. ed., New York, 1952), p. 167.

In this author's empirical work on cross-section data, this was certainly not the case, nor am I aware of any study where such an error was made. In a study of electricity generation, data were obtained for plants with installed capacities ranging from 10,000 kw. to 345,000 kw.: it was also possible to incorporate plant size as well as output into the statistical analysis and to compute a series of short-run cost curves corresponding to different plant sizes, so that a direct picture of long-run costs was obtained from the pattern of the short-run curves. A similar series of short-run curves for different sizes of firm was presented in a study of road passenger transport, where the annual passenger mile figures for different firms ranged from 1 million to 47 million. In a study of building societies in the United Kingdom, a wide range of societies was included with annual gross incomes ranging from £4,000 to over £650,000, while a similar study of insurance companies embraced companies with annual premium incomes ranging from £50,000 to £50,000,000.

The essential point in Friedman's argument lies in his proposition that the firms with the largest output "are clearly likely to be producing at an unusually high level, and conversely for those which have the lowest output." No empirical evidence is advanced in support of this proposition, while Joel Dean in a study of long-run costs in a chain of shoe stores advances the contrary proposition. Although Friedman makes no attempt to justify his proposition in the context quoted, it is an obvious twin brother to the assumption underlying his recent theory of the consumption function, and it may perhaps be paraphrased as follows. Each firm will have a normal level of output, to which its capacity will have been geared, and there will be some distribution of normal outputs for the firms in an industry. Actual output for any firm in a given period may well be greater or less than its normal output due to transient factors of a random nature. If the normal and transient components of output are independent, and if we classify firms by actual output in a given period, then firms with an observed output above the industry mean will have a *positive* average transient component, while firms below the industry mean will have a *negative* average transient component.

It remains to be seen whether this proposition is true in general or only in special cases, and whether it is sufficiently important *quantitatively* to cast serious doubt on the results of cross-section cost studies. Suppose we denote normal output by x_1, and assume that x_1 has a normal distribution with mean μ and standard deviation σ. Let transient output (x_2) also be normally and independently distributed about zero mean with unit standard deviation. Denoting actual output by

$$y = x_1 + x_2$$

we must then study the conditional distribution of x_2, given y, and in particular find the mean value of x_2 for any given y. On the assumption of independence between x_1 and x_2 it may be shown that

$$f(x_2|y) = \frac{1}{\sigma \sqrt{(\sigma^2 + 1)} \sqrt{2\pi}} \epsilon^{-\frac{1}{2\sigma^2/(\sigma^2+1)} \left[x_2 - \frac{y-\mu}{\sqrt{(\sigma^2+1)}} \right]^2}$$

so that

$$E(x_2|y) = \frac{y - \mu}{\sqrt{(\sigma^2 + 1)}}.$$

Thus if the observed output (y) exceeds the mean output of all firms in the industry (μ), the average transient component for these firms will be positive; and this average, moreover, increases in proportion to the excess of y over μ. And similarly the average transient component will be negative for all firms with an observed output below the industry average. Although we have assumed a normal distribution for x_1 and x_2, substantially the same conclusion emerges for any uni-modal distribution for x_1 combined with, say, a symmetrical distribution for x_2.

A special case where the above conclusion does *not* hold is where x_1 has a rectangular distribution. Suppose, for example, that the distributions of x_1 and x_2 are as given in table 3:

TABLE 3

x_1	$P(x_1)$	x_2	$P(x_2)$
8	0.2	−1	0.3
9	0.2	0	0.4
10	0.2	1	0.3
11	0.2		
12	0.2		

Then y will range over the values 7 to 13, and the means of the conditional distributions of x_2 are shown in table 4.

TABLE 4

y	7	8	9	10	11	12	13
$E(x_2|y)$	−1	−½	0	0	0	½	1

In this case there is no bias over the central range of values, but merely a twist in each tail. This result might have practical importance in the present context if the distribution of firms by normal output was uniform, or declined only slightly, over a substantial output range.

The second point is the possible distortion caused by this factor, if it exists, in the cross-section studies. We notice that Friedman has also abolished all variable costs from his example, but they must be retained in any realistic analysis. If the short-run cost curve had the orthodox **U**-shape, and if constant returns to scale prevailed, then Friedman's hypothesis would lead us to expect the cross-section studies to show a **U**-shaped long-run average cost curve. If, however, average variable costs were constant over observed output ranges in all firms, then the conjunction of Friedman's hypothesis and an actual situation of constant returns to scale would cause the cross-section study to show *declining* long-run average costs. In theory, constant returns might prevail everywhere and the transient component of output might be of sufficiently great importance to account for the substantial decline in long-run costs found in most cross-section studies. The problem can be dealt with by the incorporation of plant size as a variable in the statistical analysis, by classification of firms on the basis of plant size, or by an analysis which attempts to determine the relative importance of the transient output component. It seems to me unwarranted to set aside the results of the many existing cross-section studies solely because of a possible downward bias, whose relative importance has yet to be determined.

The statistical findings of constant MC in the short run are subject to the criticisms discussed in (1) to (6) above. The most serious relates to the accounting treatment of the "cost" of capital equipment and the difficulty of ascertaining the user cost of capital assets. MC may rise at extremely high output rates; but over substantial ranges of output, in cases where divisibility or segmentation of capital equipment is possible, it is probably constant. As Stigler has emphasized in an important article, the traditional **U**-shaped MC curve rests on the assumption that the capital equipment is indivisible, but completely adaptable in form to varying quantities of the cooperating factors. The empirical results suggest that divisible equipment possessing varying degrees of adaptability to cooperating factors is probably more typical of modern industrial processes. The empirical results on long-run costs seem to me to confirm the widespread existence of economies of scale: the evidence on diseconomies is much less certain for, while there is in some studies a suggestion of an upturn at the top end of the size scale, it is usually small in magnitude and well within the range of variation displayed by the data.

14. Economies of Scale in Industrial Plants[*]

JOHN HALDI and DAVID WHITCOMB

This paper presents evidence derived from engineering data on economies of scale in manufacturing and processing plants. The evidence presented here relates solely to production cost. Costs associated with factors such as marketing, general overhead, transportation, dispersal of market, and raw materials are excluded from this study. The chief purpose underlying this research was to provide some empirical justification for investigations into the nature and extent of investment barriers created by economies of scale in less developed countries. In light of this purpose, certain dynamic phenomena (such as learning curves) that have a scale effect will also be discussed briefly.

Our main conclusion is that in many basic industries, such as petroleum refining, primary metals, and electric power, economies of scale are found up to very large plant sizes (often the largest built or contemplated). These economies occur mostly in the initial investment cost and in operating labor cost, with no significant economies observed in raw material cost. Scale economies can also result from learning curve effects, spreading of setup costs, and certain stochastic processes associated with inventories. With some reservations, we feel that these general results based on data from Western countries can also be applied to less developed countries, where limited demand and the resulting inability to realize potential economies of scale can present a barrier to investment.

Evidence that there are economies of scale in plant production cost is not inconsistent with the observation that in the United States most industries have at least several plants, often differing in size. This is explained both by historical development and by the other elements of total cost which we have excluded. Average transportation cost rises with the output of a single plant, since average distance to market rises, *ceteris paribus*. Furthermore, product differentiation may place an ulti-

---

[*] *The Journal of Political Economy*, vol. 75, no. 4, (August 1967), pp. 373–85. © Copyright 1967, by The University of Chicago Press.

mate demand constraint on expansion, with market diseconomies appearing as that constraint is approached.

I. ECONOMIES OF SCALE IN STATIC COST CURVES

The traditional long-run envelope cost curve assumes that all considerations like technology and price structure are fixed. Although the envelope curve is easily defined, its actual shape is difficult to determine even under the best conditions because it reflects only a small portion of the cost schedules of many plants of different sizes.

A. Sources and Scope of the Data

In determining short-run cost curves for entire plants, one can use either engineering studies or historical accounting data. We prefer engineering studies.

Data from Accounting Records. It is difficult to obtain actual data on the construction and operating costs of industrial plants because these data are usually closely held. If actual cost records were available, we still could not necessarily derive reliable estimates of economies of scale. Even with complete historical cost data on any particular industry, one would have a major problem identifying cost changes due to differences in scale from those cost changes caused by other variables. Observed cost variation between two plants in an industry can result not only from differences in size but also from (1) unstable demand, so that existing capacity is used differently; (2) nonhomogeneous output; (3) age differences, with the newer plant embodying technological improvements unrelated to scale and unavailable to the older plant; (4) different locations, with the cost of preparing the construction site having little relationship to scale; and (5) other factors, such as different technology induced by differences in relative factor prices.

Besides the statistical identification problems inherent in the use of historical cost records, Milton Friedman has noted that another serious conceptual problem may also arise with accounting data. If a firm has made a mistake and is either larger or smaller than the optimal size, the loss from that mistake will have become capitalized either by accounting practice or by changes in the ownership of the firm. Thus there is good reason to expect that accounting data may not yield reliable estimates of scale economies. In fact, in a perfect capital market, an estimating process based on market valuation of equity would always yield constant returns.

Engineering Studies. Engineers' cost estimates are especially useful to a study on economies of scale because they embody assumptions consistent with those underlying the envelope curve. That is, an engineering study generally varies capacity while keeping constant relative factor prices, supply conditions, product homogeneity, location, and so forth. Engineering studies do admit changes in technique but only within the limits of the technology available at a given time and optimal for each plant size. Such adjustments are, of course, not only admissible but are assumed in the construction of the envelope curve.

Engineering studies can, on the other hand, be rather unreliable. Sometimes engineers forecast cost rather accurately, and sometimes they err considerably. But it is the slope and not the height of the envelope curve that reflects economies of scale. Because those unforeseen factors that cause engineering estimates to err can shift the entire curve without seriously affecting the slope, engineering studies may successfully reflect the extent of economies of scale even when they are wrong about the absolute level of costs. Sometimes the usefulness of engineering studies is also limited by the fact that they estimate costs for only a few plant sizes in a relatively narrow capacity range. The range of sizes covered can often be much smaller than an economist would like. Fortunately, though, our data generally covered a wide range of sizes.

The bulk of our evidence on economies of scale as revealed through static cost curves is derived from the engineering literature. The information is mostly from the 1950s and 1960s and comes entirely from North American and European sources. The data are limited chiefly to manufacturing plants in certain industries, and omitted are other components to total "system" cost, such as transportation and selling costs. We have thus adopted a sort of input-output approach to analyze manufacturing value added as a separate, distinguishable sector of the economy. To isolate technological economies of scale in the manufacturing portion of total product cost, we have assumed that (1) all labor and raw material inputs are available in unlimited quantities at constant prices, and (2) cost estimates for larger plants do not reflect demand conditions for output which might limit plant size. Under these assumptions, production costs do not reflect any increasing or decreasing returns in other sectors of the economy; for example, any quantity discounts, or diseconomies in the gathering together of inputs or dispersion of outputs are assumed to be reflected in the production functions of other sectors. To make inferences about total system cost one must, of course, aggregate over all relevant sectors.

To isolate better the various sources of scale economies within a single plant, we collected data on (1) the cost of individual units of industrial equipment, (2) the initial investment in plant and equipment, and (3) operating costs (namely, labor, raw materials, and utilities). These three groups of data are discussed below.

B. Cost of Basic Industrial Equipment

Equipment cost constitutes a major portion of the total investment in new plants. In this section we therefore present data on scale economies in numerous items of basic industrial equipment, along with a brief rationale for these observed economies. An outstanding virtue of equipment cost data is the almost total lack of problems caused by nonhomogeneous product mixes, construction specially designed for expansion to avoid future bottlenecks, and so forth, which are so troublesome when dealing with complete plant data.

Technological Scale Economies. For many items of equipment and machinery, an increase in capacity and output does not require a proportionate increase in material and labor. This arises from two phenomena: (1) indivisibilities of machinery and individual workers, which have been discussed at length in the literature; and (2) a family of geometric relationships which relate the material required for the building of equipment to the equipment's capacity. The amount of material required for containers (tanks, furnaces, kettles, pipes, and so on) depends principally on the surface area, whereas capacity depends on the volume inclosed. Thus for a pipe of a given length, for example, circumference will be the chief determinant of material requirements, whereas capacity depends on the cross-sectional area of the pipe.

We can express all these geometric relationships by a generalized exponential function of the form

$$C = aX^b, \qquad (1)$$

where C represents cost, X output capacity, and a is a constant; the exponent b may be called the "scale coefficient." A value of $b < 1$ implies increasing returns to scale, $b = 1$ shows constant returns, and $b > 1$ implies decreasing returns. Geometric relationships apply to many basic industrial processes. An exponential function therefore provides an appropriate basis for fitting a least-squares line to cost-capacity data, and all data reported on in this paper have been fitted to equation (1).

Empirical Results. Table 1 summarizes estimates of the scale coefficient for a large assortment of common industrial equipment. In most instances, the exponential or linear log function fits the data well throughout the observed range of capacities.

Most of the underlying cost-size observations came from catalogues of industrial equipment. The bulk of these raw data was collected by industrial cost estimators and published in engineering journals. A small amount of raw data was collected by the present authors, and in several instances we had to estimate the scale coefficient from the data given by other authors. Most of the equipment items are used in the chemical

TABLE 1
Summary Distribution of Economies of Scale
in Basic Industrial Equipment

Value of the Scale Coefficient, b*	Installed Plant Equipment† No. of Estimates of b (1)	Percentage (2)	Other Equipment‡ No. of Estimates of b (3)	Percentage (4)	Total No. of Estimates of b (5)	Percentage (6)
Under .30	22	3.3	5	20.0	27	3.9
.30– .39	44	6.6	3	12.0	47	6.8
.40– .49	96	14.5	6	24.0	102	14.9
.50– .59	143	21.6	0	0	143	20.8
.60– .69	142	21.5	5	20.0	147	21.4
.70– .79	90	13.7	2	8.0	92	13.4
.80– .89	60	9.0	0	0	60	8.7
.90– .99	29	4.4	1	4.0	30	4.4
1.00–1.09	18	2.7	2	8.0	20	2.9
Over 1.10	18	2.7	1	4.0	19	2.8
Totals	662	100.0	25	100.0	687	100.0

* Estimate of b in $C = aX^b$.
† Much of the equipment in this column directly embodies the technological relationships discussed in the text. Included here are containers, pipes, reaction vessels, kilns, and so forth.
‡ This category includes equipment like construction and mining machinery.
Source: Table 4 of an Appendix available from the authors upon request.

and other process industries; the choice of items was probably dictated by the various interests of the cost analysts. Frequently an estimated installation cost was added to the basic equipment price. In these particular observations, the basic equipment price is not subject to estimation error, but the installation cost is. The articles from which these estimates are taken generally do not give enough information to permit us to apply standard statistical tests. To allow for sampling error, therefore, let us arbitrarily classify scale coefficients where b is between 0.90 and 1.10 as not significantly different from 1.0. With this adjustment, out of a total of 687 scale coefficients, 618 (90.0 percent) show increasing returns, and 50 (7.3 percent) show constant returns. Only 19 (2.8 percent) observed scale coefficients reflect decreasing returns, which is not surprising. We should expect to observe few values of b greater than 1.0 because, when decreasing returns set in, large units usually are not built, and prices for these sizes are simply not available. Instead, multiple units are used (multiple pot lines in alumina reduction plants, for example).

Possible Bias. The scale coefficients summarized in table 1 were derived from quoted market prices. If all sizes of a particular type of equipment were sold in perfectly competitive markets, prices would everywhere reflect true social cost. However, entry is generally easier for manufacturers of small equipment items, so there are usually more producers of an item of small equipment, and both the market and the profit rate for small items of equipment are at least as competitive as the market and the profit rate for large equipment. Hence our estimated scale coefficients may slightly overestimate social costs for the larger units, thereby understating the "real" economies of scale.

For broad long-range planning, it would be desirable to know something about attainable social cost as well as actual cost under existing conditions. To evaluate our data under such a requirement, we would have to know the extent to which potential economies of scale are realized in the manufacture of various sizes of equipment. Unfortunately, available information did not allow us to make quantitative estimates of potential cost reduction from unexploited economies of scale. But we note that as a rule many small units of equipment are manufactured for each large unit produced. For example, many more small electric motor are made than large ones. Thus, manufacturers of smaller equipment probably come closer to achieving maximum potential economies of scale (and reflecting them in equipment prices) than do manufacturers of larger equipment. Hence, any unexploited economies of scale in equipment manufacturing probably lie more with larger equipment, with resulting understatement of the potential scale economies in manufacturing and processing plant investment.

C. Construction Cost of Plants and Process Areas

Inferences from Equipment Cost Data. Although table 1 shows increasing returns for most equipment, it does not immediately follow that the investment cost of entire plants will exhibit a similar pattern. Nevertheless, the data encourage such an inference, and its basis is examined briefly here.

Engineers can design larger plants by (1) expanding all equipment uniformly, (2) breaking design bottlenecks, (3) changing technique, or (4) using multiple units. The first three methods generally lead to some economies of scale in total construction cost.

1. *Expand All Equipment Uniformly.* Let the installed cost of equipment be given by

$$C_i = a_i X_i^{b_i}, \qquad (2)$$

where the terms are defined as in equation (1). Then total equipment cost, C^*, is equal to the sum of the equipment cost,

$$C^* = \Sigma a_i X_i^{b_i}. \qquad (3)$$

If all b_i are less than one, cost will not increase proportionately with capacity.

2. *Break Bottlenecks.* When bottlenecks are caused by indivisibilities in the size of some equipment, parts of the plant may possess unutilized capacity. In this case, we need enlarge only certain critical areas to increase total capacity. When it is possible to expand design capacity by breaking bottlenecks, any scale economy in the equipment of processes expanded will result in even larger economies for the whole plant. Even if the expanded units exhibit diseconomies, the total plant may still achieve increasing returns until all major bottlenecks have been overcome. The economic literature frequently describes this situation as one in which economies of scale exist up to "the point of the least common denominator."

3. *Change Technique.* When engineers change technique, they intend to accomplish the same end result by a different method (for example, pure capital substitution or capital-labor substitution). Since engineers can always duplicate smaller units of equipment and smaller plants, they will use different techniques in large plants only when these techniques are more economical. Thus when different techniques are observed in the design of larger plants they will generally reflect economies of scale.

4. *Use Multiple Units.* Multiple units are normally used when equipment scale economies have been exhausted. Barring economies in peripheral equipment, expansion by this method alone should not be expected to give further plant economies of scale.

We know of no method for directly estimating scale economies in plant investment cost by aggregating equipment data. However, this discussion of how engineers design larger plants helps show the relevance of the equipment cost data to our basic purpose: exploring the nature and extent of plant economies of scale. Cost-capacity figures for equipment are not subject to statistical confounding problems, and the scale coefficients are usually derived from actual price quotations rather than from engineers' estimates. For these reasons they tend to be the most accurate data available, and they considerably increase our confidence in the scale coefficients given in table 2 for the investment cost of entire plants.

Data on Actual Plant Costs. The engineering studies presented here usually represent a set of hypothetical plants, each producing the same product with the same technology available (although optimum technique may vary), and differing only in size. A few of the estimates are not for hypothetical plants but come instead from carefully selected historical data on actual plants. Table 2 summarizes estimates of the scale coefficient for 221 long-run cost curves. All estimates of plant cost and many of the scale coefficients were calculated by cost engineers and were reported in the journal articles given in the bibliography to the Appendix noted above. When only cost-capacity figures were available, scale coefficients were computed by the present authors. As with

TABLE 2
Summary Distribution of Economies of Scale in Plant Investment Costs*
(number of estimates of scale coefficient b in $C = aX^b$)

Industry	Under .40 (1)	.40-.49 (2)	.50-.59 (3)	.60-.69 (4)	.70-.79 (5)	.80-.89 (6)	.90-.99 (7)	1.00-1.09 (8)	1.10 and Up (9)	Totals (10)
Cement	...	...	...	1	1	...	...	1	...	3
Chemicals, excluding petroleum:										
Fertilizer	...	...	...	2	3	...	...	1	1	6
Gases	4	3	6	9	15	4	1	1	2	45
Industrial chemicals	...	2	3	10	11	9	6	1	...	42
Plastics	...	...	...	1	...	...	2	...	...	3
Rubber	...	...	...	2	1	2	1	1	2	8
Miscellaneous chemicals	3	...	...	2	1	...	1	1	...	8
Desalination	...	...	...	...	4	1	...	...	...	6
Electric power	...	1	7	1	2	2	2	...	...	15
Petroleum refining and by-products	...	5	6	15	15	13	2	...	1	57
Aluminum	...	...	...	2	3	3	4	1	2	15
Pulp and paper	...	...	...	...	2	2	1	...	1	6
Shipping	...	...	...	...	1	...	...	...	...	1
Miscellaneous	2	1	...	...	2	1	...	...	...	6
Totals	9	12	22	45	61	37	20	6	9	221
Percentage	4.1	5.4	10.0	20.4	27.6	16.7	9.0	2.7	4.1	100.0

*Number of individual plant studies classified by industry and by extent of scale economies.
Source: Table 6 of an Appendix available from the authors upon request.

the equipment data, redundant estimates were eliminated. Building, equipment, and installation labor make up the investment costs. Site preparation costs are sometimes included, but always on the basis of a "standard site." Interest on funds expended before the plant begins operating is not included. For these reasons, economies of scale may be overstated slightly, since larger plants may have longer gestation periods.

Virtually all of the plants reported on here produce fairly homogeneous standardized products (where nonhomogeneous products are made, a standard product mix was used for all sizes). However, the "industries" in table 2 are not strictly homogeneous (we found a number of different scale coefficients for each industry), and industrywide generalizations are limited. For the aluminum industry, where larger plants use multiple production units (pot lines), the scale coefficients are high, with seven of fifteen estimates at or above the 0.90 level (approximately constant returns). This result coincides with the a priori reasoning given above. Among various types of plants in the industry—bauxite alumina, ingots, and extrusions—there seemed to be no uniformly consistent pattern. Another standardized product is sulfuric acid, but it is made by several processes. Table 2 contains eleven scale factors for sulfuric acid, and, despite the variety of processes, all scale coefficients fall within a narrower range than that exhibited by many other products with multiple estimates. This was also true for acetylene and hydrogen, but not for oxygen (all classed under "gases").

Sample size and goodness-of-fit information were often unavailable for many of the original estimates because they were presented in summary form. However, the size range covered was usually available. The ratio of the largest to the smallest capacity varies from 1.33 to 1,500, but most ratios fall between 4 and 20. Because we know so little about most of the original estimates and what errors they may embody, we were not able to apply standard tests of statistical significance to the estimated scale coefficients. In the absence of better confidence limits, we again arbitrarily classify estimates of b between 0.90 and 1.10 as not significantly different from 1.0. By this criterion, 186 of 221 estimates of the scale coefficient show increasing returns, 26 show constant returns, and only 9 show decreasing returns. The median scale coefficient is 0.73. On this basis, we conclude that economies of scale in production cost are significant and widespread for the types of plants surveyed here.

D. Operating Cost

We defined operating cost as in-plant production cost less taxes and payments to capital (including depreciation). We relied exclusively on engineering estimates of operating cost. As with equipment and plant investment costs, we eliminated nonindependent estimates. Multiple estimates appear in the same "industry" because industries are not homogeneous and because there are often several processes for making the same product. The results, given in table 3, show clearly that many plants exhibit substantial economies of scale in total operating costs.

In an independent study, Isard and Schooler derived 35 estimates of scale coefficients for operating labor cost in the petrochemical industry. These are shown in column (4) of table 3. They differ considerably from our 17 labor scale coefficients for several industries, shown in column (3) of table 3. Their scale coefficients were mostly smaller than the ten we were able to obtain for the petrochemical industry. Possible explanations may be that (a) the petrochemical industry is not very homogeneous, and the types of plants surveyed vary from one study to the other; or (b) most of our observations are for process units—plants within a petrochemical complex—whereas their estimates were for complete plants.

TABLE 3
Summary Distribution of Economies of Scale in Plant Operating Costs

Value of the Scale Coefficient, b*	Total Operating Cost		Labor Cost Only			
	No. of Estimates (1)	Percentage (2)	Our Results: No. of Estimates (3)	Isard and Schooler† No. of Estimates (4)	Total No. of Estimates (5)	Percentage (6)
Under .40	4	12.5	8	29	37	71.2
.40– .49	1	3.1	1	4	5	9.6
.50– .59	5	15.6	6	2	8	15.4
.60– .69	3	9.4	1	0	1	1.9
.70– .79	10	31.3	1	0	1	1.9
.80– .89	9	28.1	0	0	0	0
.90– .99	0	0	0	0	0	0
1.00–1.09	0	0	0	0	0	0
1.10 and up	0	0	0	0	0	0
Totals	32	100.0	17	35	52	100.0

* Estimates of b in $C = aX^b$.
† W. Isard and E. W. Schooler (1955).
Source: Table 7 of an Appendix available from the authors upon request.

Many of the studies summarized in table 3 did not break operating labor into individual components; for example, operating labor, supervision, raw material, and so on. Cost data that were available are summarized in table 7 of the Appendix, and following is a brief summary of what these data show.

1. Raw Materials. There appear to be no great scale economies attainable in the consumption of primary raw materials.

2. Utilities. Unit costs for utilities sometimes decline slightly with size increases because larger furnaces, motors, and other such equipment units perform more efficiently than smaller ones.

3. **Labor.** What data we could obtain showed that large economies of scale in labor costs are possible for process-type plants. Labor's chief function in process plants is to watch gauges, adjust valves, and perform maintenance tasks. Consequently, large increases in capacity often require few extra workers.

4. **Supervision and Management.** The data indicate substantial economies of scale in supervisory and management costs, about on the order of economies of scale for operating labor. We found no direct evidence for the familiar proposition that diseconomies of scale arise through exhaustion of managerial capability as plant scale increases. This source of diseconomies is usually thought to operate indirectly, however, and most estimates would not be expected to measure it.

5. **Maintenance.** The evidence in table 7 of the Appendix indicates substantial economies of scale in maintenance costs. These arise from several sources: (*a*) Some repair and janitorial costs have a geometric cost-capacity relationship similar to construction costs; (*b*) there are indivisibilities in some labor costs for equipment repair; and (*c*) costs of spare parts inventories often exhibit stochastic scale economies (discussed in section II).

E. Manufacturing and Processing Cost: Conclusions

Determining the optimum plant size for a particular supply-demand situation requires more information than is outlined here. However, the data obtained in this study support the opinion of engineers who feel that unit processing and manufacturing costs decline as plants increase in size, up to very large plant sizes. More specifically:

1. We can generally expect initial investment cost (and, therefore, the amortization portion of total cost) in most types of plants and equipment to exhibit economies of scale up to the largest plants observed in industrial countries. In the more capital-intensive industries, savings in capital cost are an important source of scale economies.

2. In process plants, operating expenses for labor, supervision, and maintenance also show significant economies of scale.

3. Consumption of utility services shows slight economies of scale, and consumption of raw materials generally shows none.

II. DYNAMIC AND STOCHASTIC SOURCES OF INCREASING RETURNS

The envelope curve shows only how cost varies with changes in plant size and the average rate of output. Larger firms may also derive cost advantages from certain dynamic and stochastic processes. Like the more traditional economies of scale, these also give rise to some of the external economies so widely discussed in the development literature.

Manufacturing Progress Functions and Setup Costs. Within limits, workers become more efficient as they repeat the same task. For this reason, the length of production run can be an important factor in scale economies. Manufacturing progress functions, frequently called "labor learning curves," introduce the length of production run as an explicit variable and depict growth in worker efficiency with repetition.

Cost reduction from learning curves has consequences similar to those of other scale economies. Firms with the largest share of a given market can, in the absence of diseconomies elsewhere, achieve longer production runs than smaller firms. Verdoorn in assessing the importance of this source of increasing returns, estimates that between the United States and Europe, differences in production run length may affect costs more than differences in plant sizes. This source of cost reduction is probably somewhat more important in assembly-line or job-order type plants than in continuous-process plants like oil refineries.

Longer production runs can cause other and even more obvious economies. Job-order shops must frequently incur a substantial setup cost for each production run; the more units to which these costs can be allocated, the smaller will be the setup cost per unit. Further, longer production runs often make it possible to reduce cost significantly by automating production and substituting capital for labor. As with other economies of scale, market size determines whether the potential economies from long production runs are in fact realizable.

Stochastic Increasing Returns. The traditional theory of the firm does not consider ordinary day-to-day uncertainty from random variations in a firm's operations. But in many commonplace situations, random variations may be a factor in reducing costs in large plants. We might call the cause of such reductions "stochastic economies of scale." There are many stochastic models that cover differing sets of circumstances and that reflect prevailing cost-size relationships. Although describing such a model in detail is beyond the scope of this discussion, we can outline the principle behind it.

Plants always keep spare parts on hand to take care of possible machinery breakdowns. Let one such part be a "widget," and assume X widgets are in regular operation throughout the plant. Assume further that one widget failure is independent of other such failures. By constructing a model that embodies (1) the probability function describing widget failures, (2) the time necessary to replenish the inventory of widgets, (3) the cost of downtime, and other pertinent factors, we can determine the optimum inventory of spare widgets. If the number of widgets in regular operation increases as the plant grows (through duplication of machinery), the optimum inventory of spares per unit of capacity will decrease. This is because the variance of the number of expected breakdowns does not increase proportionately to increases in the number of widgets used (due to the law of large numbers).

In conclusion, we point out that a great deal of additional empirical research needs to be done in order to develop a broader base of understanding about economies of scale. We need to know more about economies in transportation relative to volume carried and diseconomies relative to length of haul; about economies in marketing, finance, and administration of multiplant firms; and about the effect of technological change on efficient scale.

15. The Economies of Scale*

GEORGE J. STIGLER

The theory of the economies of scale is the theory of the relationship between the scale of use of a properly chosen combination of all productive services and the rate of output of the enterprise. In its broadest formulation this theory is a crucial element of the economic theory of social organization, for it underlies every question of market organization and the role (and locus) of governmental control over economic life. Let one ask himself how an economy would be organized if every economic activity were prohibitively inefficient upon alternately a small scale and a large scale, and the answer will convince him that here lies a basic element of the theory of economic organization.

The theory has limped along for a century, collecting large pieces of good reasoning and small chunks of empirical evidence but never achieving scientific prosperity. A large cause of its poverty is that the central concept of the theory—the firm of optimum size—has eluded confident measurement. We have been dangerously close to denying Lincoln, for all economists have been ignorant of the optimum size of firm in almost every industry all of the time, and this ignorance has been an insurmountable barrier between us and the understanding of the forces which govern optimum size. It is almost as if one were trying to measure the nutritive values of goods without knowing whether the consumers who ate them continued to live.

The central thesis of this paper is that the determination of the optimum size is not difficult if one formalizes the logic that sensible men have always employed to judge efficient size. This technique, which I am old-fashioned enough to call the survivor technique, reveals the optimum size in terms of private costs—that is, in terms of the environment in which the enterprise finds itself. After discussing the technique, we turn to the question of how the forces governing optimum size may be isolated.

*The *Journal of Law and Economics*, vol. 1 (October 1958), pp. 54–71.

I. THE SURVIVOR PRINCIPLE

The optimum size (or range of sizes) of enterprises in an industry is now ascertained empirically by one of three methods. The first is that of direct comparison of actual costs of firms of different sizes; the second is the comparison of rates of return on investment; and the third is the calculation of probable costs of enterprises of different sizes in the light of technological information. All three methods are practically objectionable in demanding data which are usually unobtainable and seldom up to date. But this cannot be the root of their difficulties, for there is up-to-date information on many economic concepts which are complex and even basically incapable of precise measurement (such as income). The plain fact is that we have not demanded the data because we have been unable to specify what we wanted.

The comparisons of both actual costs and rates of return are strongly influenced by the valuations which are put on productive services, so that an enterprise which over- or undervalues important productive services, will under- or overstate its efficiency. Historical cost valuations of resources, which are most commonly available, are in principle irrelevant under changed conditions. Valuations based upon expected earnings yield no information on the efficiency of an enterprise—in the limiting case where all resources are so valued, all firms would be of equal efficiency judged by either average costs or rates of return. The ascertainment on any scale of the maximum value of each resource in alternative uses is a task which only the unsophisticated would assume and only the omniscient would discharge. The host of valuation problems are accentuated by the variable role of the capital markets in effecting revaluations and the variable attitudes of the accountants toward the revaluations.

The technological studies of costs of different sizes of plant encounter equally formidable obstacles. These studies are compounded of some fairly precise (although not necessarily very relevant) technical information and some crude guesses on nontechnological aspects such as marketing costs, transportation rate changes, labor relations, etc.—that is, much of the problem is solved only in the unhappy sense of being delegated to a technologist. Even ideal results, moreover, do not tell us the optimum size of firm in industry A in 1958, but rather the optimum size of new plants in the industry, on the assumption that the industry starts *de novo* or that only a small increment of investment is being made.

The survivor technique avoids both the problems of valuation of resources and the hypothetical nature of the technological studies. Its fundamental postulate is that the competition of different sizes of firms sifts out the more efficient enterprises. In the words of Mill, who long ago proposed the technique:

Whether or not the advantages obtained by operating on a large scale preponderate in any particular case over the more watchful attention, and greater regard to minor gains and losses usually found in small establishments, can be ascertained, in a state of free competition, by an unfailing test. . . . Wherever there are large and small establishments in the same business, that one of the two which in existing circumstances carries on the production at the greater advantage will be able to undersell the other.[1]

Mill was wrong only in suggesting that the technique was inapplicable under oligopoly, for even under oligopoly the drive of maximum profits will lead to the disappearance of relatively inefficient sizes of firms.

The survivor technique proceeds to solve the problem of determining the optimum firm size as follows: Classify the firms in an industry by size, and calculate the share of industry output coming from each class over time. If the share of a given class falls, it is relatively inefficient, and in general is more inefficient the more rapidly the share falls.

An efficient size of firm, on this argument, is one that meets any and all problems the entrepreneur actually faces: strained labor relations, rapid innovation, government regulation, unstable foreign markets, and what not. This is, of course, the decisive meaning of efficiency from the viewpoint of the enterprise. Of course, social efficiency may be a very different thing: the most efficient firm size may arise from possession of monopoly power, undesirable labor practices, discriminatory legislation, etc. The survivor technique is not directly applicable to the determination of the socially optimum size of enterprise, and we do not enter into this question. The socially optimum firm is fundamentally an ethical concept, and we question neither its importance nor its elusiveness.

Not only is the survivor technique more direct and simpler than the alternative techniques for the determination of the optimum size of firm, it is also more authoritative. Suppose that the cost, rate of return, and technological studies all find that in a given industry the optimum size of firm is one which produces 500 to 600 units per day, and that costs per unit are much higher if one goes far outside this range. Suppose also that most of the firms in the industry are three times as large, and that those firms which are in the 500 to 600 unit class are rapidly failing or growing to a larger size. Would we believe that the optimum size was 500 to 600 units? Clearly not: an optimum size that cannot survive in rivalry with other sizes is a contradiction, and some error, we would all say, has been made in the traditional studies. Implicitly

---

[1] *Principles of Political Economy* (Ashley ed.), p. 134. Marshall states the same argument in Darwinian language: "For as a general rule the law of substitution—which is nothing more than a special and limited application of the law of survival of the fittest—tends to make one method of industrial organization supplant another when it offers a direct and immediate service at a lower price." *Principles of Economics*, p. 597 (8th ed., 1920).

all judgments on economies of scale have always been based directly upon, or at least verified by recourse to, the experience of survivorship.

This is not to say that the findings of the survivor technique are unequivocal. Entrepreneurs may make mistakes in their choice of firm size, and we must seek to eliminate the effects of such errors either by invoking large numbers of firms so errors tend to cancel or by utilizing time periods such that errors are revealed and corrected. Or the optimum size may be changing because of changes in factor prices or technology, so that perhaps the optimum size rises in one period and falls in another. This problem too calls for a close examination of the time periods which should be employed. We face these problems in our statistical work below.

We must also recognize that a single optimum size of firm will exist in an industry only if all firms have (access to) identical resources. Since various firms employ different kinds or qualities of resources, there will tend to develop a frequency distribution of optimum firm sizes. The survivor technique may allow us to estimate this distribution; in the application below we restrict ourselves to the range of optimum sizes.

The measure of the optimum size is only a first step toward the construction of a theory of economies of scale with substantive content, but it is the indispensable first step. We turn in later sections of this paper to the examination of the methods by which hypotheses concerning the determinants of optimum size may be tested.

II. ILLUSTRATIVE SURVIVORSHIP MEASURES

The survivor principle is very general in scope and very flexible in application, and these advantages can best be brought out by making concrete applications of the principle to individual industries. These applications will also serve to display a number of problems of data and interpretation which are encountered in the use of the survivor technique. We begin with the American steel industry.

In order that survivorship of firms of a given size be evidence of comparative efficiency, these firms must compete with firms of other sizes—all of the firms must sell in a common market. We have therefore restricted the analysis to firms making steel ingots by open-hearth or Bessemer processes. Size has perforce been measured by capacity, for production is not reported by individual companies, and capacity is expressed as a percentage of the industry total to eliminate the influence of the secular growth of industry and company size. The geographical extent of the market is especially difficult to determine in steel, for the shifting geographical pattern of consumption has created a linkage between the various regional markets. We treat the market as national, which exaggerates its extent, but probably does less violence to the facts than a sharp regional classification of firms. The basic data are given in table 1.

TABLE 1
Distribution of Output of Steel Ingot Capacity by Relative Size of Company

Company Size (percent of industry total)	1930	1938	1951
1. Percent of Industry Capacity			
Under 0.5	7.16	6.11	4.65
0.5 to 1	5.94	5.08	5.37
1 to 2.5	13.17	8.30	9.07
2.5 to 5	10.64	16.59	22.21
5 to 10	11.18	14.03	8.12
10 to 25	13.24	13.99	16.10
25 and over	38.67	35.91	34.50
2. Number of Companies			
Under 0.5	39	29	22
0.5 to 1	9	7	7
1 to 2.5	9	6	6
2.5 to 5	3	4	5
5 to 10	2	2	1
10 to 25	1	1	1
25 and over	1	1	1

Sources: *Directory of Iron and Steel Works of the United States and Canada*, 1930, 1938; *Iron Age*, January 3, 1952.

Over two decades covered by table 1 (and, for that matter, over the last half century) there has been a persistent and fairly rapid decline in the share of the industry's capacity in firms with less than half a percent of the total, so that we may infer that this size of firm is subject to substantial diseconomies of scale.[2] The firms with 0.5 to 2.5 percent of industry capacity showed a moderate decline, and hence were subject to smaller diseconomies of scale. The one firm with more than one fourth of industry capacity declined moderately, so it too had diseconomies of scale. The intervening sizes, from 2.5 to 25 percent of industry capacity, grew or held their share so they constituted the range of optimum size.

The more rapid the rate at which a firm loses its share of the industry's output (or, here, capacity), the higher is its private cost of production relative to the cost of production of firms of the most efficient size. This interpretation should not be reversed, however, to infer that the size class whose share is growing more rapidly is more efficient than

---

[2] In 1930 the firm with 0.5 percent of the industry capacity had a capacity of 364,000 net tons; in 1951, 485,000 net tons. Of course, we could have employed absolute firm size classes, but they are less appropriate to many uses.

other classes whose shares are growing more slowly; the difference can merely represent differences in the quantities of various qualities of resources. In the light of these considerations we translate the data of table 1 into a long-run average cost curve for the production of steel ingots and display this curve in figure 1. Over a wide range of outputs there is no evidence of net economies or diseconomies of scale.

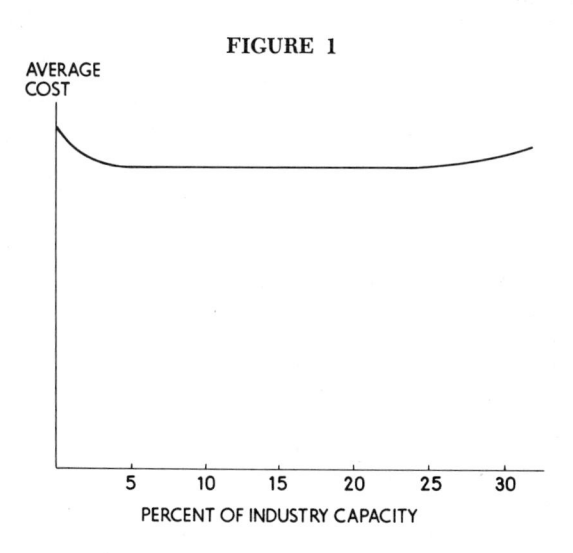

FIGURE 1

AVERAGE COST vs PERCENT OF INDUSTRY CAPACITY (5, 10, 15, 20, 25, 30)

Although the survivor test yields an estimate of the shape of the long-run cost curve, it does not allow an estimate of how much higher than the minimum are the costs of the firm sizes whose shares of industry output are declining. Costs are higher the more rapid the rate at which the firm size loses its share of industry output, but the rate at which a firm size loses a share of industry output will also vary with numerous other factors. This rate of loss of output will be larger, the less durable and specialized the productive resources of the firm, for then exit from the industry is easier. The rate of loss will also be larger, the more nearly perfect the capital and labor markets, so that resources can be obtained to grow quickly to more efficient size. The rate of loss will be smaller, given the degree of inefficiency, the more profitable the industry is, for then the rate of return of all sizes of firms is larger relative to other industries.

By a simple extension of this argument, we may also estimate the most efficient size of *plant* in the steel ingot industry during the same period (table 2). We again find that the smallest plants have a tendency to decline relative to the industry, and indeed this is implied by the company data. There is no systematic tendency toward decline in shares

TABLE 2
Distribution of Output of Steel Ingot Capacity

Plant Size (percent of industry total)	1930	1938	1951
1. Percent of Industry Capacity			
Under 0.25	3.74	3.81	3.25
0.25 to 0.5	6.39	5.81	7.20
0.5 to 0.75	6.39	4.18	3.82
0.75 to 1	9.42	12.29	10.93
1 to 1.75	21.78	15.56	20.67
1.75 to 2.5	13.13	16.73	17.01
2.5 to 3.75	23.49	17.18	8.10
3.75 to 5	8.82	12.07	12.46
5 to 10	6.82	12.37	16.56
2. Number of Plants			
Under 0.25	40	29	23
0.25 to 0.5	20	16	18
0.5 to 0.75	11	7	6
0.75 to 1	11	14	12
1 to 1.75	18	13	15
1.75 to 2.5	6	8	8
2.5 to 3.75	8	6	3
3.75 to 5	2	3	3
5 to 10	1	2	3

Source: Same as Table 1.

held by plants between 0.75 percent and 10 percent of the industry size. We may therefore infer that the tendency of very small plants and companies to decline relative to the industry is due to the diseconomy of a small plant, and the tendency of the largest company (U.S. Steel) to decline has been due to diseconomies of multiplant operation beyond a certain scale.

An equally important and interesting industry, passenger automobiles, uncovers different problems. Here we can use production data instead of capacity, and have no compunctions in treating the market as national in scope. The basic data for the individual firms are given in table 3.

A striking feature of the automobile industry is the small number of firms, and this poses a statistical problem we have glossed over in our discussion of steel: what confidence can be attached to changes in the share of industry output coming from a firm size when that size contains very few firms? For the automobile industry (unlike steel) we possess annual data, and can therefore take into account the steadiness of direction or magnitude of changes in shares of various firm sizes, and to this extent increase our confidence in the estimates. We may also extend the period which is surveyed, although at the risk of combining periods with different sizes of optimum firms. Aside from recourse to related data (the survivorship pattern of the industry in other

TABLE 3
Percentages of Passenger Automobiles Produced in United States
by Various Companies 1936–41 and 1946–55

Year	General Motors	Chrys-ler	Ford	Hudson	Nash	Kaiser	Willys Over-land	Packard	Stude-baker	Other
1936	42.9	23.6	22.6	3.3	1.5	...	0.7	2.2	2.4	0.8
1937	40.9	24.2	22.6	2.7	2.2	...	2.0	2.8	2.1	0.5
1938	43.9	23.8	22.3	2.5	1.6	...	0.8	2.5	2.3	0.3
1939	43.0	22.7	21.8	2.8	2.3	...	0.9	2.6	3.7	0.3
1940	45.9	25.1	19.0	2.3	1.7	...	0.7	2.1	3.1	0.1
1941	48.3	23.3	18.3	2.1	2.1	...	0.8	1.8	3.2	0.1
1946	38.4	25.0	21.2	4.2	4.6	0.6	0.3	1.9	3.6	0.2
1947	40.4	21.7	21.3	2.8	3.2	4.1	0.9	1.6	3.5	0.5
1948	40.1	21.2	19.1	3.6	3.1	4.6	0.8	2.5	4.2	0.7
1949	43.0	21.9	21.0	2.8	2.8	1.2	0.6	2.0	4.5	0.2
1950	45.7	18.0	23.3	2.1	2.8	2.2	0.6	1.1	4.0	0.1
1951	42.2	23.1	21.8	1.8	3.0	1.9	0.5	1.4	4.2	0.1
1952	41.5	22.0	23.2	1.8	3.5	1.7	1.1	1.4	3.7	...
1953	45.7	20.3	25.2	1.2	2.2	1.0		1.3	3.0	...
1954	52.2	13.1	30.6	1.7		0.3		0.5	1.6	...
1955	50.2	17.2	28.2	2.0		0.1			2.3	...

Source: Hard's Automotive Yearbook 1951, 1955, 1956.

countries, for example), there is no other method of reducing the uncertainty of findings for small number industries.

The survivorship record in automobiles (summarized in Table 4) is more complicated than that for steel. In the immediate prewar years there was already a tendency for the largest company to produce a rising share and for the 2.5 to 5 percent class to produce a sharply declining share; the smallest and next to largest sizes showed no clear tendency. In a longer span of time, however, the smallest companies reveal a fairly consistently declining share. In the immediate postwar period, the 2.5 to 5 percent size class was strongly favored by the larger companies' need to practice price control in a sensitive political atmosphere, and the same phenomenon reappeared less strongly in the first two years after the outbreak of Korean hostilities. From this record we would infer that there have been diseconomies of large size, at least for the largest size of firm, in inflationary periods with private or public price control, but substantial economies of large scale at other times. The long-run average cost curve is saucer shaped in inflationary times, but shows no tendency to rise at the largest outputs in other times.

TABLE 4
Percentage of Passenger Automobiles Produced by Companies of Various Sizes

	Company Size (as percent of industry)				Number of Companies	
Year	Over 35 Percent	10-35 Percent	2.5-5 Percent	Under 2.5 Percent	2.5-5 Percent	Under 2.5 Percent
1936	42.9	46.2	3.3	7.6	1	5*
1937	40.9	46.8	5.5	6.8	2	4*
1938	43.9	46.1	5.0	5.0	2	4*
1939	43.0	44.4	9.1	3.5	3	4*
1940	45.9	44.1	3.1	6.9	1	6*
1941	48.4	41.6	3.2	6.8	1	5
1946	38.4	46.2	12.4	3.0	3	4
1947	40.4	43.0	13.6	3.0	4	3
1948	40.1	40.3	18.0	1.5	5	2
1949	43.0	42.9	10.0	4.0	3	4
1950	45.7	41.3	6.8	6.1	2	5
1951	42.2	44.9	7.2	5.7	2	5
1952	41.5	45.2	7.2	6.1	2	5
1953	45.6	45.5	3.0	5.8	1	4
1954	52.2	43.7	0	4.1	0	4
1955	50.2	45.4	0	4.4	0	3

Source: Table 3.
* Or more.

The automobile example suggests the method by which we determine whether changing technology, factor prices, or consumer demands lead to a change in the optimum firm size. We infer an underlying stability in the optimum size in those periods in which the survivorship trends are stable. Indeed it is hard to conceive of an alternative test; one can judge the economic importance, in contrast to technological originality, of an innovation only by the impact it has upon the size distribution of firms.

Before we leave these applications of the survivorship technique we should indicate its flexibility in dealing with other problems which seem inappropriate to our particular examples. For example, a Marshallian may object that firms must begin small and grow to optimum size through time, so that the size structure of the industry in a given period will reflect this historical life pattern as well as the optimum size influences. In an industry such as retail trade this interpretation would be quite plausible. It can be met by studying the survivor experience of firm sizes in the light of the age or rate of growth of the firms. Again, one may argue that firms of different sizes have different comparative advantages at different stages of the business cycle. Such a hypothesis could be dealt with by comparing average survivorship patterns in given cycle stages with those calculated for full cycles.

Let us now turn to the methods by which one may test hypotheses on the determinants of optimum size.

III. INTER-INDUSTRY ANALYSES OF THE DETERMINANTS OF OPTIMUM SIZE

Once the optimum firm size has been ascertained for a variety of industries, the relationship between size and other variables can be explored. This is, in fact, the customary procedure for economists to employ, and the present investigation differs, aside from the method of determining optimum size, only in being more systematic than most such investigations. For example, numerous economists have asserted that advertising is a force making for large firms, and they usually illustrate this relationship by the cigarette industry. Will the relationship still hold when it is tested against a list of industries which has not been chosen to illustrate it? This is essentially the type of inquiry we make here.

Although the survivor method makes lesser demands of data than other methods to determine optimum firm size, it has equally exacting requirements of information on any other variable whose influence is to be studied. In the subsequent investigation of some 48 ("three-digit") manufacturing industries, whose optimum firm size is calculated from data in *Statistics of Income,* we have therefore been compelled to exclude some variables for lack of data and to measure others in a most imperfect manner. The industries we study, and the measures we contrive, are given in table 5; we describe their derivation below.

TABLE 5
Basic Data on Forty-eight Manufacturing Industries

Industry	Optimum Company Size (in thousand dollars of total assets) (1948–51)	Optimum Range Class Limits (in thousand dollars) From	Optimum Range Class Limits (in thousand dollars) To	Average Establishment Size (in thousand dollars of value added) (1947)	Number of Chemists and Engineers per 100 Employed (1950)	Advertising Expenditure as Percent of Gross Sales (1950)
Motor vehicles, incl. bodies and truck trailers	$827,828	$100,000	$open	$ 3,715	1.5879	0.4395
Petroleum refining	765,716	100,000	open	3,420	6.9171	0.4562
Blast furnaces, steel works, and rolling mills	525,485	100,000	open	8,310	2.0956	0.1321
Dairy products	446,483	100,000	open	110	0.7865	1.5221
Distilled, rectified, and blended liquors	248,424	100,000	open	2,090	0.9041	1.3674
Pulp, paper, and paperboard	203,794	100,000	open	1,645	1.4927	0.3357
Paints, varnishes, lacquers, etc.	175,404	100,000	open	394	6.0431	1.3539
Railroad equipment, incl. locomotives and streetcars	150,217	100,000	open	3,407	2.7171	0.3611
Tires and tubes	141,600	10,000	open	11,406	2.0974*	0.9453
Grain mill products ex. cereals preparations	128,363	100,000	open	210	1.0344	1.2492
Drugs and medicines	123,662	100,000	open	552	6.2599	8.3858
Smelting, refining, rolling, drawing, and alloying of nonferrous metals	100,398	10,000	open	1,658	2.9845†	0.4088
Office and store machines	65,914	10,000	open	1,411	2.5860	1.5812
Bakery products	58,960	50,000	100,000	192	0.2359	2.1335
Yarn and thread	44,375	10,000	open	687	0.4461	0.3238
Carpets and other floor coverings	37,337	10,000	100,000	1,119	1.2391	1.7295
Broadwoven fabrics (wool)	31,265	10,000	open	1,211	0.4461	0.3400
Watches, clocks, and clock work operated devices	31,025	10,000	50,000	705	1.2027	5.3238
Cement	29,554	10,000	100,000	1,600	2.1277‡	0.2726
Malt liquors and malt	28,922	10,000	open	1,750	0.9041	4.7962
Agricultural machinery and tractors	28,291	1,000	open	684	2.1816	0.8956
Structural clay products	24,001	10,000	100,000	253	1.6292	0.4552
Newspapers	23,428	10,000	100,000	168	0.1348§	0.1948
Knit goods	17,918	10,000	100,000	273	0.1244	0.8522
Confectionery	13,524	5,000	50,000	335	0.5950	2.6281
Commercial printing including lithographing	11,939	5,000	50,000	97	0.1348§	0.6474
Furniture—household, office, public building, and professional	11,378	5,000	50,000	209	0.3990‖	0.9152

* Rubber products.
† Primary nonferrous.
‡ Cement, and concrete, gypsum, and plaster products.

TABLE 5 (*continued*)

Industry	Optimum Company Size (in thousand dollars of total assets) (1948–51)	Optimum Range Class Limits (in thousand dollars) From	To	Average Establishment Size (in thousand dollars of value added) (1947)	Number of Chemists and Engineers per 100 Employed (1950)	Advertising Expenditure as Percent of Gross Sales (1950)
Men's clothing.	$ 10,077	$ 5,000	$ 50,000	$ 247	0.0456#	0.8795
Dyeing and finishing textiles, excl. knit goods.	9,625	5,000	50,000	545	1.1223	0.3472
Canning fruit, vegetables, and seafood.	6,536	1,000	open	240	0.9144	1.8462
Broadwoven fabrics (cotton).	5,847	50	open	2,595	0.4461**	0.2822
Footwear, exc. rubber.	4,359	1,000	100,000	524	0.1474	1.1619
Paperbags, and paperboard containers and boxes.	4,127	1,000	100,000	428	0.6939	0.1854
Cigars.	3,753	250	50,000	174	0.2274††	2.3188
Meat products.	2,665	500	100,000	322	0.5983	0.4264
Nonferrous foundries.	2,365	500	50,000	172	2.9845†	0.2793
Fur goods.	1,966	1,000	5,000	55	0.0456#	0.4119
Partitions, shelving, lockers, etc.	1,545	500	50,000	121	0.3990‖	0.8678
Narrow fabrics and other small wares.	1,382	500	5,000	226	0.4461**	0.3212
Wines.	1,304	500	5,000	227	0.9041‡‡	3.5854
Women's clothing.	1,304	500	50,000	150	0.0456#	0.9150
Books.	1,137	50	50,000	399	0.1348§	2.8796
Periodicals.	1,117	250	10,000	307	0.1348§	0.5245
Leather—tanning, curring, and finishing.	764	0	10,000	720	0.8140	0.1813
Concrete, gypsum, and plaster products.	762	250	10,000	53	2.1277†	0.6855
Window and door screens, shades, and venetian blinds.	667	100	10,000	110	0.3990‖	1.0581
Nonalcoholic beverages.	546	100	50,000	75	0.9041‡‡	4.0740
Millinery.	468	250	5,000	108	0.0456#	0.4438

§ Printing, publishing, and allied industries
‖ Furniture and fixtures.
†† Tobacco manufactures.
‡‡ Beverage industries.
# Apparel and accessories.
** Yarn, thread, and fabric mills.

1. *Size of Firm.* The optimum size of firm in each industry is determined by comparing the percentage of the industry's assets possessed by firms in each asset class in 1948 and 1951.[3] Those classes in which the share of the industry's assets was stable or rising were identified, and the average assets of the firms within these sizes was calculated. The range of optimum sizes is also given in Table 5. An industry was excluded if it had a very large noncorporate sector (for which we could not measure firm size) or gave strong evidence of heterogeneity by having two widely separated optimum sizes (as, for example, in "aircraft and parts").

2. *Advertising Expenditures.* We have already remarked that extensive advertising is often mentioned as an explanation for the growth of large firms, especially in consumer goods industries such as cigarettes, liquor, and cosmetics. The argument supporting this view can take one of three directions. First, national advertising may be viewed as more efficient than local advertising, in terms of sales per dollar of advertising at a given price. Second, long-continued advertising may have a cumulative impact. Finally, and closely related to the preceding point, the joint advertising of a series of related products may be more efficient than advertising them individually. We measure the variable by the ratio of advertising expenditures to sales, both taken from *Statistics of Income*.

3. *Technology and Research.* A host of explanations of firm size are related to technological characteristics and research. Complicated production processes may require large companies, or at least large plants. The economies of research are held to be substantial; the outcome of individual projects is uncertain, so small programs are more risky; a balanced research team may be fairly large; and much capital may be required to bring a new process to a commercial stage and to wait for a return upon the outlay.

At present there is no direct measure available for either the importance of research or the intricacy of technology. We use an index, chemists and engineers as a ratio to all employees, that may reflect both influences, but probably very imperfectly. When it becomes possible to make a division of these personnel between research and routine operation, a division which would be very valuable for other purposes also, the interpretation of an index of technical personnel will be less ambiguous.

4. *Plant Size.* Plant size normally sets a minimum to company size, and therefore exerts an obvious influence on the differences among indus-

---

[3] These particular dates were dictated by the data; there were large changes in industry classification in 1948, and no minor industry data were tabulated for 1952. A better, but more laborious, determination of optimum size could have been made if the data for intervening years were utilized.

tries in company size. We are compelled to resort to a measure of plant size—value added per establishment in 1947—which is not directly comparable to company size because the 1947 Census of Manufacturers did not report corporate establishments at the requisite level of detail.

Preliminary analysis revealed that there is no significant relationship between firm size and advertising expenditures, so this variable was omitted from the statistical calculations. The average ratio of advertising expenditures to sales was 1.97 percent in consumer goods industries and 0.57 percent in producer goods industries, but in neither group was there a significant relationship between the ratio and firm size.[4]

A regression analysis confirms the impression one gets from table 5 that the other variables we examine are positively related to optimum firm size:

$$X_1 = -5.092 + 34.6\ X_2 + 42.7\ X_3,$$
$$(10.8) \quad\quad (12.2)$$

where

X_1 is firm size, in millions of dollars of assets,
X_2 is plant size, in millions of dollars of value added,
X_3 is engineers and chemists per 100 employees.

The standard errors of the regression coefficients are given below the coefficients.

An examination of table 5 suggests that the correlation would be higher if the data were somewhat more precise. The size of plant is unduly low in motor vehicles, because of the inclusion of suppliers of parts. Moreover the plant sizes have not been estimated by the survivor technique. Technological personnel are exaggerated in nonferrous foundries because we are compelled to use the ratio for a broader class, and the same is true of concrete products. The relatively small size of company in footwear, as compared to plant size, is at least partially due to the fact that the machinery was usually leased, and hence not included in assets. Industries which are "out of line" have not been omitted, however, for similar considerations may have caused other industries to be "in line." Yet the general impression is that the correlation would rise substantially with improved measurements of the variables.

The range of optimum sizes is generally wide, although the width is exaggerated, and our measurements impaired, because the largest asset class (over $100 million) embraces numerous firms of very different sizes—growth and inflation are outmoding the size classes used in *Statistics of Income*. In ten industries only this largest size has had a rising share of industry assets, and in another nine industries it is included in the range of sizes with rising shares. When the upper limit of optimum

---

[4] The respective rank correlation coefficients were −.187 and −.059.

sizes is known, the range of optimum sizes is typically three or four times the average size of the firms in these sizes.

The results of this exploratory inter-industry study are at least suggestive—not only in their specific content but also in pointing out a line of attack on the economies of scale that escapes that confession of failure, the case method. The chief qualifications that attach to the findings are due to the imperfections of the data: the industry categories are rather wide; and the measure of technical personnel is seriously ambiguous. At least one finding—a wide range of optimum firm sizes in each industry—is so general as to deserve to be taken as the standard model in the theory of production.

IV. INTRAINDUSTRY ANALYSIS OF THE DETERMINANTS OF OPTIMUM SIZE

One may also examine the varying fates of individual firms within an industry in the search for explanations of optimum size. If, for example, firms moving to optimum size were vertically integrated and those moving to or remaining in nonoptimum size were not so integrated, we could infer that vertical integration was a requisite of the optimum firm in the industry. This approach has the advantage over the inter-industry approach of not requiring the assumption that a determinant such as advertising or integration works similarly in all industries.

The intraindustry analysis, however, has a heavy disadvantage; it can be applied only to those variables for which we can obtain information on each firm and in industries with numerous firms hardly any interesting variables survive this requirement. Because we could examine so few influences, and because the results were so consistently negative, we shall be very brief in describing our results in the industry—petroleum refining—in which this approach was tried.

The basic survivor experience for companies and plants in petroleum refining is given in tables 6 and 7, for the postwar period 1947–1954. In each case only operating plants are included, and asphalt plants and companies are excluded. Capacities are measured in terms of crude oil; as in the case of steel plants, actual outputs cannot be obtained for all companies.

There is a family resemblance between the data for petroleum and steel companies: in each case there has been a substantial reduction in the share of the largest company. In the petroleum refining industry, the size range from 0.5 percent to 10 percent has contained all the size classes which have stable or rising shares of industry capacity.

The plant survivor data suggest that the disappearance of the smaller companies has been due to the relative inefficiency of the smaller plants,

TABLE 6
Distribution of Petroleum Refining Capacity
by Relative Size of Company

Company Size (percent of industry capacity)	1947	1950	1954
1. Percent of Industry Capacity			
Under 0.1	5.30	4.57	3.89
0.1 to 0.2	4.86	3.57	3.00
0.2 to 0.3	2.67	2.16	2.74
0.3 to 0.4	2.95	2.92	1.65
0.4 to 0.5	2.20	0	.89
0.5 to 0.75	3.04	4.66	5.05
0.75 to 1.00	.94	0	1.58
1.0 to 2.5	11.70	12.17	10.53
2.5 to 5	9.57	16.70	14.26
5 to 10	45.11	42.15	45.69
10 to 15	11.65	11.06	10.72
2. Number of Companies			
Under 0.1	130	108	92
0.1 to 0.2	34	24	22
0.2 to 0.3	11	9	11
0.3 to 0.4	8	8	5
0.4 to 0.5	5	0	2
0.5 to 0.75	5	8	8
0.75 to 1.00	1	0	2
1.0 to 2.5	6	7	6
2.5 to 5.0	3	5	5
5.0 to 10.0	7	6	7
10.0 to 15.0	1	1	1
Total	211	176	161

Source: Bureau of Mines, Petroleum Refineries, including Cracking Plants in the United States, January 1, 1947, January 1, 1950, January 1, 1954, Information Circulars 7455 (March 1948), 7578 (August 1950), and 7963 (July 1954).

for all plant size classes with less than 0.5 percent of the industry's capacity have also declined substantially. The sizes between 0.5 percent and 2.5 percent of industry capacity have all grown relatively, and the top plant size has declined moderately, so that the growth of company sizes beyond 2.5 percent of industry capacity has presumably been due to the economies of multiple plant operation.

It has been claimed that backward integration into crude oil pipelines was necessary to successful operation of a petroleum refinery. We tabulate some of the material bearing on this hypothesis in table 8. There does not appear to be any large difference between the changes in market shares of firms with and without pipelines. Since all firms with more than 0.75 percent of industry refining capacity have some pipelines, a comparison (not reproduced here) was made between changes in their market shares and crude pipeline mileage per 1,000 barrels of daily refining capacity. There was no relationship between the two variables.

TABLE 7
Distribution of Petroleum Refining Capacity by Relative Size of Plant

Plant Size	1947	1950	1954
1. Percent of Industry Capacity			
Under 0.1	8.22	7.39	6.06
0.1 to 0.2	9.06	7.60	7.13
0.2 to 0.3	6.86	4.95	3.95
0.3 to 0.4	5.45	4.99	7.28
0.4 to 0.5	4.53	6.56	4.06
0.5 to 0.75	9.95	10.47	11.82
0.75 to 1.0	5.35	7.07	8.33
1.0 to 1.5	12.11	10.36	13.38
1.5 to 2.5	17.39	23.64	22.45
2.5 to 4.0	21.08	16.96	15.54
2. Number of Plants			
Under 0.1	184	158	138
0.1 to 0.2	64	53	51
0.2 to 0.3	27	19	16
0.3 to 0.4	15	14	21
0.4 to 0.5	10	15	9
0.5 to 0.75	17	16	19
0.75 to 1.0	6	8	10
1.0 to 1.5	10	8	11
1.5 to 2.5	9	12	12
2.5 to 4.0	7	5	5
Total	349	308	292

Source: Same as table 6.

TABLE 8
Industry Shares of Petroleum Refining Companies with and without Crude Pipelines in 1950

Company Size (average of 1947, 1950, and 1954 percentage of industry capacity)	Companies with Pipelines Number 1950	Companies with Pipelines Share 1947	Companies with Pipelines Share 1954	Companies without Pipelines Number 1950	Companies without Pipelines Share 1947	Companies without Pipelines Share 1954
Under 0.1	25	1.40	1.12	60	2.87	2.18
0.1 to 0.2	17	2.19	2.50	5	0.77	0.77
0.2 to 0.3	6	1.48	1.63	2	0.34	0.50
0.3 to 0.4	5	1.90	1.63	0	....	....
0.4 to 0.5	1	0.40	0.55	2	0.54	1.22
0.5 to 0.75	7	3.59	4.72	1	0.38	0.61
0.75 to 1.0	0	....	....	0	....	....
1.0 to 2.5	7	11.54	13.10	0	....	....
2.5 to 5.0	4	11.11	11.69	0	....	....
5.0 to 10.0	7	45.11	45.69	0	....	....
10.0 to 15.0	1	11.65	10.72	0	....	....
Not in existence all years	16	2.30	0.05	79	2.43	1.33
Total	96	92.67	93.40	149	7.33	6.60

Source: *International Petroleum Register.*

The intraindustry analysis has its chief role, one may conjecture, in providing a systematic framework for the analysis of the data commonly employed in industry studies. A complete analysis of the plausible determinants of firm size requires such extensive information on the individual firms in the industry as to make this an unattractive method of attack on the general theory.

V. CONCLUSION

The survivor technique for determining the range of optimum sizes of a firm seems well adapted to lift the theory of economies of scale to a higher level of substantive content. Although it is prey to the usual frustrations of inadequate information, the determination of optimum sizes avoids the enormously difficult problem of valuing resources properly that is encountered by alternative methods.

Perhaps the most striking finding in our exploratory studies is that there is customarily a fairly wide range of optimum sizes—the long-run marginal and average cost curves of the firm are customarily horizontal over a long range of sizes. This finding could be corroborated, I suspect, by a related investigation: if there were a unique optimum size in an industry, increases in demand would normally be met primarily by near proportional increases in the number of firms, but it appears that much of the increase is usually met by expansion of the existing firms.

The survivor method can be used to test the numerous hypotheses on the factors determining the size of firm which abound in the literature. Our exploratory study suggests that advertising expenditures have no general tendency to lead to large firms, and another experiment (which is not reported above) indicates that fixed capital-sales ratio are also unrelated to the size of firms. The size of plant proves to be an important variable, as is to be expected, and the survivor method should be employed to determine the factors governing plant size. A rather ambiguous variable, the relative share of engineers and chemists in the labor force, also proves to be fairly important, and further data and work is necessary to disentangle research and routine technical operations. The determination of optimum size permits the investigator to examine any possible determinants which his imagination nominates and his data illuminate.

16. Break-Even Analysis with Stepwise Varying Marginal Costs and Revenues*

M. C. MEIMAROGLOU

Cost and profit behavior in relation to volume of activity constitutes a major topic for both economic analysis and business practice—a subject which becomes more and more important in today's industrial economies as a result of the reduced flexibility of production costs which follows the impact of technological progress and automation on cost structures.

To deal with the subject, management employs data representing total costs, revenues, and profits. Its approach to the problem, based on flexible budgeting, sampling of costs, and empirical projections of costs and revenues, is summarized in the break-even chart, in which the total cost and total revenue functions in their relation to activity level are plotted in the form of straight lines, and the vertical distance between the two lines represents the corresponding profit (or loss).

SPECIAL ASSUMPTIONS OF STANDARD BREAK-EVEN ANALYSIS

The chief difference between the method of approach employed by management and that of the economist centers about the special assumptions implicit in the representation of the total cost and revenue functions in the entrepreneur's break-even chart.

The straight-line form of the total cost and revenue functions which is used in standard break-even analysis corresponds to an indefinitely decreasing average cost per unit (with marginal cost as lower limit), a constant average revenue per unit, and an indefinitely increasing average profit per unit (with marginal profit as upper limit). Thus, if taken literally, the chart would seem to tell the entrepreneur that it would pay him to increase his volume of activity indefinitely and without limit. But, of course, this only means that the break-even chart, *in its present form*, though a most valuable tool in determining the break-

---

* Budgeting, vol. 13, no. 2 (November 1964), pp. 1–7.

16. Break-Even Analysis: Stepwise Varying Marginal Costs and Revenues

even point of operation or in representing the pattern of variation of total costs, revenue, and profits *within a certain range* of activity levels, is inadequate to describe what happens *beyond* that range, i.e., to provide a complete picture which can be useful in guiding entrepreneurial policy. In particular, it cannot help the entrepreneur in determining an optimal scale of operations because it is preloaded by the linearity of his cost and revenue functions to tell him that larger outputs are *always* more profitable, even though this is rarely, if ever, true in practice.

This bias of the break-even chart is often reflected in the entrepreneur's notion of the objective of his business activity. The theory of the firm usually assumes that the entrepreneur seeks to maximize profit. However, the majority of business men recognize more consciously the objective of "greater sales volume" which, besides being a generally accepted measure of success, constitutes for them a simpler and more palpable substitute for the "profit maximization" objective in their everyday decisions. Moreover, they sometimes appear to confuse maximum sales with maximum profit, thus assuming tacitly that the activity level which yields the one, necessarily will also provide the other. This can sometimes prove highly misleading.

A linear cost function also assumes away any possibility of rising marginal costs. But in practice production costs will sometimes increase beyond some scale of output and marketing costs will almost certainly do so. It is essential for a businessman to know at which point of the scale of activity marginal costs begin to rise, and to what extent. Such information would be most useful for control of costs with varying levels of activity and for the determination of prices and outputs.[1]

It is evident from the preceding discussion that the break-even chart requires some refinements to permit a more realistic representation of the variation of total costs, revenues, and profits, reflecting increases in marginal costs and decreases in marginal revenues. The methods required to effect such refinements will now be described.

Cost Variation and Break-Even Analysis

Whenever normal capacity is exceeded, marginal costs per unit are bound gradually to increase. The most common among the reasons for such increases are:

---

[1] It may also be useful as a guide to a discriminatory pricing policy. In Europe many firms seeking to expand their foreign business sell on the export market at prices lower than those which are charged locally. They also sometimes offer reduced prices when participating in governmental or other important bids. In such cases, an intimate knowledge of marginal cost changes when production exceeds the normal level of activity, is a most useful guide for determining the lowest prices at which exports can profitably be provided.

1. In the case of production costs:
   — payments for overtime or work on Sundays and holidays,
   — night shift bonuses,
   — bonuses for increased production,
   — increasing wear and tear of machinery due to more intensive operation,
   — bottlenecks in the flow of the production process arising for the same reason,
   — increased repair costs to avoid loss of operating time when breakdowns occur,
   — electricity consumption for night operation, etc.
2. In the case of financing costs:
   — possibly higher interest rates and financing charges for obtaining additional working capital, and
3. In the case of marketing costs:
   — increasing advertising outlays, salesmen's bonuses and distribution costs to market the additional volume of production.

Marginal costs per unit may also rise to an appreciable extent *well below* normal activity in the case of utilization of machinery of different types and efficiency, destined for producing the same articles. This is common in industrial enterprises in the course of gradual modernization of their plant machinery: for instance, if part of the total productive capacity consists of modern, automatic, machinery with low running costs, it is natural that the new machinery will be utilized in preference to the old until the lower-cost part of total productive capacity is absorbed, and thus variable (i.e. marginal) costs per unit will rise when production shifts to the utilization of the old machinery. This may represent a substantial difference in costs, which should not be ignored, as it could even affect the calculation of the break-even point.

The engineers and accountants of a manufacturing enterprise should have all the technical and financial data necessary to provide management with a fairly reasonable estimate of most of the cost increases described above, except in the case of costs related to marketing, wear and tear of machinery, repair bills and effects of bottlenecks which, however, call for some amount of guesswork even at lower levels of activity. The difficulty in presenting a cost function incorporating these increases does not lie primarily in the absence of data for their estimation, but in the *length of the period* covered by the estimate.

Break-even charts are usually drawn up to cover a whole year of operation. During such a long period, important changes in the rate of production may occur, due to seasonal or other reasons, which are bound to vitiate any more refined picture of the total cost function. For instance, it may be estimated that a 5 percent increase over normal capacity would result in a 6 percent increase in the marginal cost per unit; but if such increase in production, instead of being evenly distributed throughout the year, took place in one month, this would mean a 60 percent increase over the normal capacity corresponding to one month of operation, and might result in a 20 percent increase in the cost per unit of the additional quantity. Increases in marginal costs are also bound to occur even when production remains within the limits of the annual normal capacity if variations in the rate of operation take place during the year, entailing production beyond normal capacity in certain months. Under such circumstances, any attempt at refinement of the break-even chart would appear useless and unrealistic.

The above difficulty would be obviated if the break-even chart were drawn up for a shorter period, in which the rate of operation would be reasonably uniform. A period of one month would be proper from that point of view, and would, moreover, present the advantage that in enterprises maintaining a cost accounting system, expenses are usually appropriated by month and therefore can be distinguished to pertain to a particular month.

It is suggested, therefore, that a break-even chart in a more refined form, reflecting major changes in marginal costs per unit, can be prepared for a *monthly* period, within the limits of approximation tolerated in break-even analysis. Given a reasonable degree of stability in production factor prices and operating conditions, the use of such a chart may be extended over all the months of the same year, and serve as a projection of varying monthly costs in the case of seasonally fluctuating activity.

To represent the total cost function in such a monthly chart, essentially the same methods can be used as in the construction of its annual equivalent. However it is necessary to determine the following:

1. The points on the scale of activity where marginal costs are expected to rise. This can be done by estimation from existing technical and financial data, and the number of such points will depend on the degree of refinement sought;
2. The total costs must also be estimated at each of the points of changing marginal cost. This can be accomplished by direct evaluation and the remainder of the cost function can be obtained by assuming a straight-line pattern of variation between each two consecutive cost variation points.

This procedure is illustrated in figure 1 on page 254.

Nonlinear Revenue Functions

As regards the total revenue function, its representation in straight-line form assumes that sale prices will remain the same whatever the level of production. However, in reality prices are subject to variation

FIGURE 1
DIRECT EVALUATION

TOTAL COST

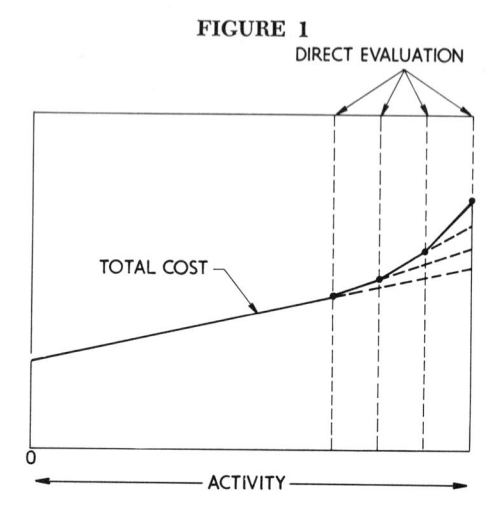

ACTIVITY

related to the volume of activity, which arises either from discriminatory pricing or increasing saturation of the market as the level of production of some commodity increases.

In the case of overall price reduction as a result of increasing market saturation, the revenue function takes the form of consecutive segments of alternative straight lines through the origin corresponding to the levels of activity considered, as shown in figure 2.

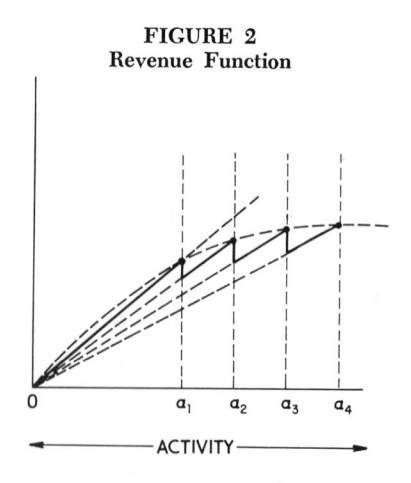

FIGURE 2
Revenue Function

a_1 a_2 a_3 a_4

ACTIVITY

Discriminatory pricing, on the contrary, entails marginal revenue decreases by segments of the scale of activity, on the assumption that the firm will satisfy the needs of its various categories of customers in an order of priority according to price. In this case it would not

16. Break-Even Analysis: Stepwise Varying Marginal Costs and Revenues

be difficult to determine the point or points of the scale of monthly activity beyond which marginal revenue per unit decreases, and the revenue function would take the form represented in figure 3.

FIGURE 3
Revenue Function

The Revised Break-Even Chart

On the basis of the preceding observation, it is suggested that the monthly break-even chart may assume the appearance of figure 4.

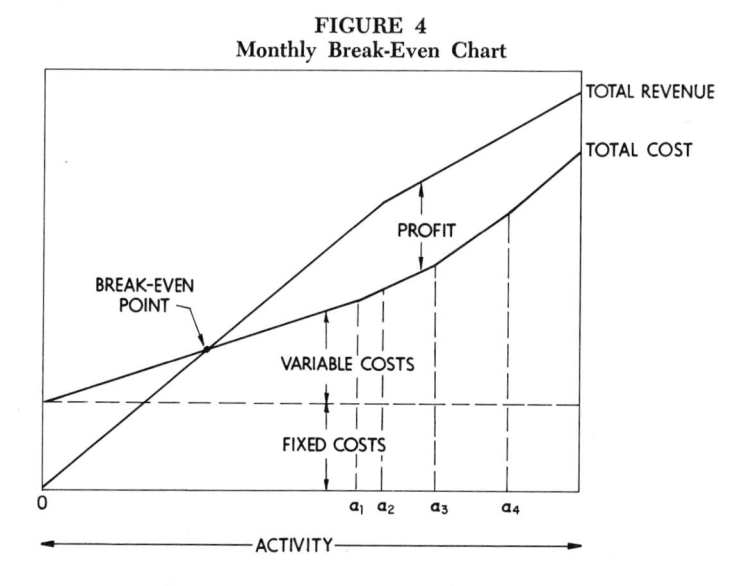

FIGURE 4
Monthly Break-Even Chart

In the above figure it is assumed that marginal cost per unit increases stepwise at point a_1, a_3, and a_4 of the scale of activity and that marginal revenue decreases in the same fashion at point a_2, as a result of discriminatory pricing.[2]

The concept of stepwise variation of marginal unit costs and revenues seems to be more conform with reality than the continuous variations assumed by economic theory. Besides the fact that most of the cost increases mentioned above actually occur in a stepwise manner, there are instances where activity can only vary stepwise, allowing of no possibility of small continuous changes of marginal unit costs. Similarly, discriminatory pricing fully justifies the assumption of stepwise decrease of marginal revenue per unit. But full application of this concept, by taking into account all possible points of variation, may nevertheless complicate excessively both the relevant calculations and the form of presentation of the break-even chart. The number of points of variation should therefore in practice be limited to the most important changes of activity envisaged.

Determination of the Point of Maximum Profit

The activity level which yields the highest attainable level of company profit can be found by direct examination of a piecewise linear break-even chart. It is, of course, the point where the vertical distance between the total revenue and total cost curves is greatest. However some further geometric points can be illuminating here.

It will be observed in figures 5 and 6 that maximum profit is obtained

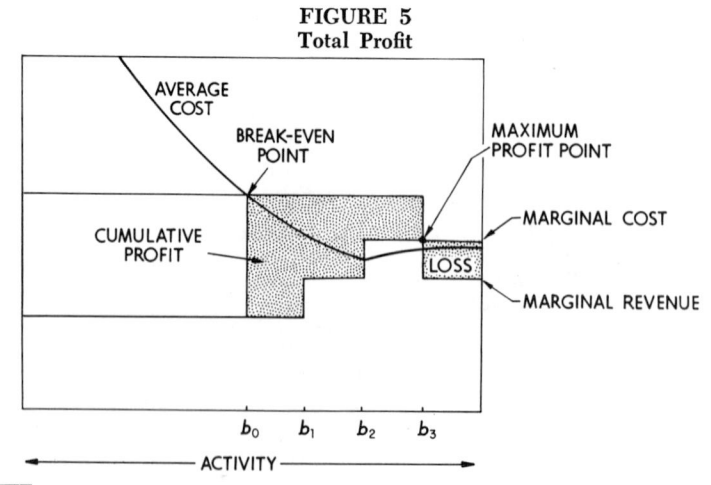

FIGURE 5
Total Profit

---

[2] It should be noted, however, that if total sales are taken as our measure of activity level, the total revenue function would be a straight (45°) line, through the origin and the decrease in the marginal revenue per unit would be reflected in a steeper upward movement of the total cost function, steeper than that shown in the figure, because of this case one would calculate marginal cost per dollar of sales.

16. Break-Even Analysis: Stepwise Varying Marginal Costs and Revenues   257

FIGURE 6
Total Profit

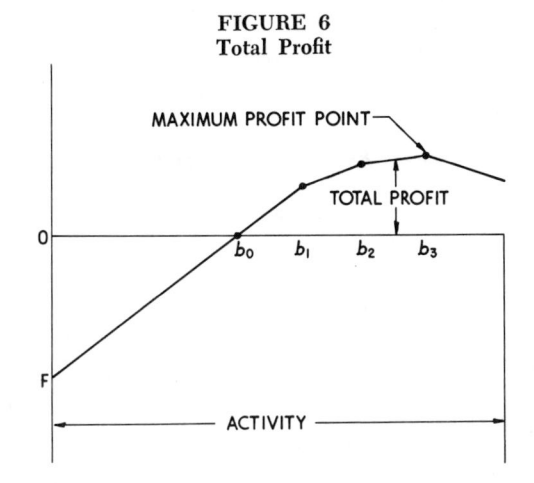

at point b_3 of the scale of activity, i.e. at the point at which marginal profit becomes a negative number. The cumulative profits realized from the break-even point to point b_3 are represented by the first shaded area in figure 5. Any additional activity beyond point b_3 results in losses represented by the second shaded area in the figure, which should be subtracted from the profits already accumulated to arrive at the net total profit realized.

Determination of the Break-Even Point

Should marginal cost increase at a point of the scale of activity below the break-even point of operation, as illustrated in figure 7 on page 258, the break-even point may be calculated as follows:
Let:

F = total fixed costs
m_1 = marginal cost per unit corresponding to activity level from 0 to point a_1
m_2 = marginal cost per unit corresponding to activity level from point a_1 to point a_2
r = revenue per unit corresponding to activity level from 0 to point a_2,
x = break-even point, expressed in units and located between points a_1 and a_2.

Then we have the following equality:

$$x.r = F + a_1.m_1 + (x - a_1)m_2$$

in which

$$x = F - \frac{a_1(m_2 - m_1)}{r - m_2}$$

Determination of the Lowest Average Cost Point

Another interesting feature of the concept of stepwise varying marginal cost and revenue is that it simplifies the determination of the point of lowest average unit cost.[3]

As is known from economic theory, the lowest average cost per unit is obtained at the point of intersection of the marginal cost curve with the average cost curve. On the basis of the assumption that marginal cost increases stepwise, it can be proved that such an intersection can only occur at a point of variation of marginal cost, and *not* anywhere between two such points. Thus in looking for the lowest average cost point it suffices to compute average cost only at the points where marginal cost changes.

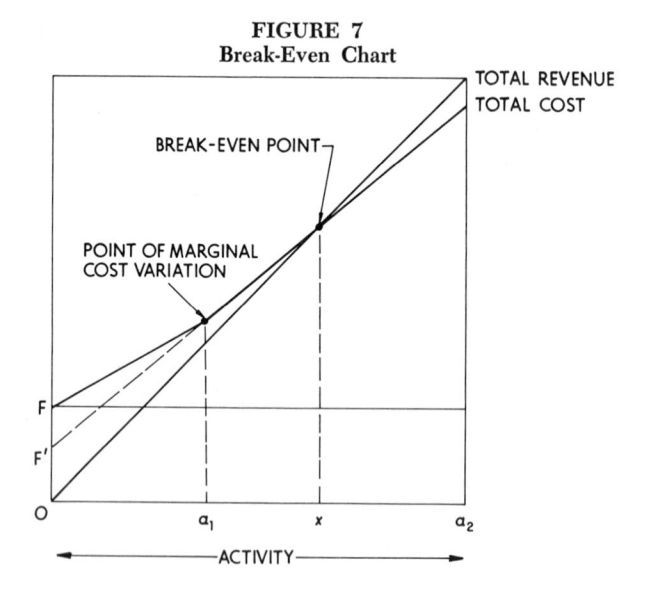

FIGURE 7
Break-Even Chart

The proof of the preceding theorem is given in the appendix, and it is illustrated in figures 8 and 9. In figure 8 we see that so long as marginal cost continues below average cost, the latter will continue to fall and so will not have reached its minimum point. On the other hand, in figure 9 the lowest point on the average unit cost curve

---

[3] In the mulitproduct firms the term "unit cost" should be taken to mean the cost per unit of activity, according to whatever measure of activity is chosen.

16. Break-Even Analysis: Stepwise Varying Marginal Costs and Revenues

FIGURE 8
Cost Per Unit

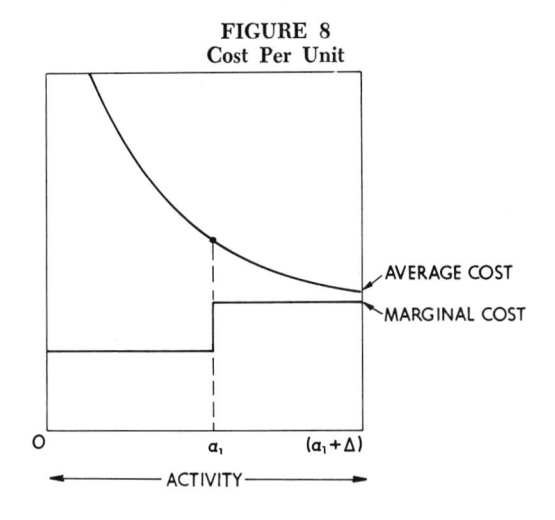

AVERAGE COST
MARGINAL COST

a_1 $(a_1 + \Delta)$
ACTIVITY

FIGURE 9
Cost Per Unit

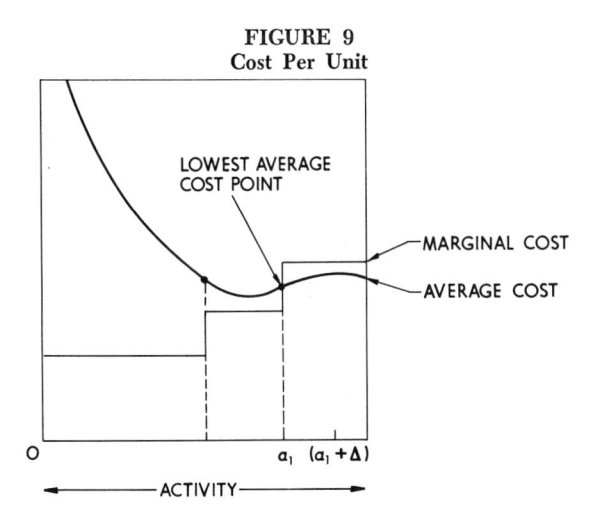

LOWEST AVERAGE COST POINT
MARGINAL COST
AVERAGE COST

a_1 $(a_1 + \Delta)$
ACTIVITY

occurs at activity level a_1. This is a point where marginal cost varies, and here the marginal and average cost curves intersect. It will also be observed from either figure 8 or 9 that in any range of activity level within which marginal cost is constant the average cost curve approaches the marginal cost asymptotically and hence the two curves cannot intersect. This, then, is the source of the great economy of calculation in the piecewise linear breakeven chart. *Significant points such as the point of minimum average cost can only occur at activity levels such as a_1 where marginal costs change, and so only such points need be taken into account in decision calculations.*

Form of the Average Cost Curve

For reasons similar to those which were just discussed, after each point of marginal cost change beyond the lowest average cost point, the average cost curve will be asympotic from below to the corresponding new step representing marginal cost, in the manner illustrated in figure 10 below. Thus, with stepwise varying cost the average cost curve will be somewhat—but not essentially—different in form from the **U**-shaped curve assumed by economic theory. This is in contrast with the implication of the linear total cost curve of standard break-even analysis, which, as we have seen, forces us to assume that average costs decline indefinitely, the larger the level of activity.

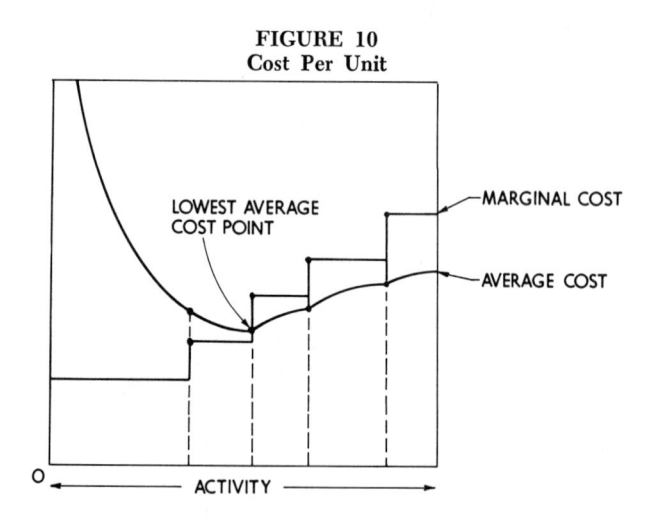

FIGURE 10
Cost Per Unit

Conclusion

The determination of the relationship of costs and profits to the volume of activity presents many problems, differing from one branch of industry to another according to the peculiarities of each. It is not contended that the concept of stepwise varying cost and revenue can be applied to all cases with the same measure of facility.

However it is almost always likely to be well worth the effort involved in undertaking to go beyond the standard break-even procedure. The crude linearity assumption of the standard chart enables management to see quickly and easily the minimal level of activity necessary to avoid loss. But it cannot be used with any degree of confidence to determine other activity levels which may be of such significance for the welfare of the company. Only with a break-even chart which takes into

16. Break-Even Analysis: Stepwise Varying Marginal Costs and Revenues

account variations in production and marketing costs and in total revenues resulting from different sales levels can one find:

a)   The point of minimum unit cost,

b)   The total profits corresponding to different activity levels beyond the break-even point (so that the activity level necessary to achieve any given profit goal can be determined with confidence),

c)   The activity level which yields maximum profits to the company.

The last of these is, of course, of particular importance to management. It will be recalled that the linearity of standard break-even charts forces upon us the absurd conclusion that there is no such profit maximizing activity level—that increased output of whatever magnitude will always contribute more to company profit! Only with recognition of the nonlinearity which is to be found in reality do we avoid this unacceptable implication, and only then can our analysis help us to determine how maximum profits can be obtained.

All of this can be accomplished without excessive complexity of calculation, with the aid of a break-even chart which is piecewise linear. In practice, the costs and revenues corresponding to many types of activities will, indeed, vary in a piecewise linear manner, i.e., prices or costs will only change at certain discrete activity levels. But even where this is not precisely true, piecewise linearity can provide a reasonable and workable approximation for the full curvature of a true cost and revenue functions, one which will enable management to make its decisions more effectively and with greater confidence.

Appendix: The Simple Mathematics of Piecewise Linear Break-Even Analysis

The assumption that marginal cost and marginal revenue vary stepwise permits calculation of the total cost, revenue or profit corresponding to any point of the scale of activity respectively as functions of consecutive marginal costs, marginal revenues, or both.

Let:

F = Total fixed costs

a_0 = the zero activity level

$a_1, a_2, \ldots a_n$ = activity levels where either marginal cost or marginal revenue, or both, vary.

$m_1, m_2, \ldots m_n$ = marginal cost, and

$r_1, r_2, \ldots r_n$ = marginal revenue, corresponding to activity levels from $a_0 - a_1, a_1 - a_2, \ldots a_{n-1} - a_n$ respectively.

Then total cost, C, corresponding to any point a_n of the scale of activity, may be expressed as:

$$C = F + (a_1 - a_0)m_1 + (a_2 - a_1)m_2 + \cdots + (a_n - a_{n-1})m_n$$

or:

$$C = F + \sum_{i=1}^{n} (a_i - a_{i-1})m_i,$$

the corresponding total revenue, R, may be expressed as:

$$R = (a_1 - a_0)r_1 + (a_2 - a_1)r_2 + \cdots + (a_n - a_{n-1})r_n$$

or:

$$R = \sum_{i=1}^{n} (a_i - a_{i-1})r_i,$$

and total profit, P, as:

$$P = (a_1 - a_0)(r_1 - m_1) + (a_2 - a_1)(r_2 - m_2) + \cdots \\ + (a_n - a_{n-1})(r_n - m_n) - F$$

or:

$$P = \sum_{i=1}^{n} (a_i - a_{i-1})(r_i - m_i) - F.$$

Total profit may also be expressed as a function of consecutive marginal costs and marginal revenues beyond the break-even point. Let:

b_0 = break-even point
$b_1, b_2, \ldots, b_n$ = activity levels, beyond the break-even point, where either marginal revenue, or both, vary
$m_{b1}, m_{b2} \ldots m_{bn}$ = marginal cost, and
$r_{b1}, r_{b2} \ldots r_{bn}$ = marginal revenue, corresponding to activity levels from $b_0 - b_1, b_1 - b_2, \ldots, b_{n-1} - b_n$ respectively,

Then total profit corresponding to any point b_n of the scale of activity may be expressed as:

$$P = (b_1 - b_0)(r_{b1} - m_{b1}) + (b_2 - b_1)(r_{b2} - m_{b2}) + \cdots \\ + (b_n - b_{n-1})(r_{bn} - m_{bn})$$

or:

$$P = \sum_{i=1}^{n} (b_i - b_{i-1})(r_{bi} - m_{bi}).$$

We may now prove the following theorem: Given a piecewise linear total cost function, if marginal and average cost are unequal at some point of variation of marginal cost, then average and marginal cost will continue to be unequal so long as there is no further change in marginal cost. Moreover, the average cost curve will approach the mar-

16. Break-Even Analysis: Stepwise Varying Marginal Costs and Revenues

ginal cost curve asymptotically throughout this range of activity levels in which marginal cost remains constant. To prove this, let:

$(a_i + \Delta)$ = some level of activity at which marginal cost does not change,
a_i = the largest activity level below $(a_i + \Delta)$ at which marginal cost changes,
K = total cost at activity level a_i
T = total cost at activity level $(a_i + \Delta)$
c = average cost at point $(a_i + \Delta)$, and
m = marginal cost at point $(a_i + \Delta)$.

Then we have the following equality:

$$T = K + m\Delta$$

or:

$$c = \frac{K + m\Delta}{a_i + \Delta}$$

Moreover, assume marginal cost is not equal to average cost at output a_i, then:

$$\frac{K}{a_i} = m + D, \text{ where } D \neq 0$$

Substituting into the previous equation for K, we have:

$$c = \frac{ma_i + Da_i + m\Delta}{a_i + \Delta}$$

or:

$$c = m + \frac{Da_i}{a_i + \Delta} = m$$

Of course, if marginal and average cost happen to be equal at a_1, D will be equal to zero, and marginal and average cost will continue to be equal through $(a_1 + \Delta)$, i.e. until the next step in the marginal cost function.

Moreover, if at a_1 average cost is above marginal cost, so that $D \} O$, the same will be true at $(a_1 + \Delta)$ and as the value of $(a_1 + \Delta)$ increases average cost will approach marginal cost asymptotically from above, as shown in figure 8. The reverse will be true if at a_1 average cost is below marginal cost, as shown in figure 9.

These results are also evident on geometric grounds.

17. Economic Aspects of Broiler Production Density*

WILLIAM R. HENRY and JAMES A. SEAGRAVES

This paper explores a long-range planning problem of the broiler industry. Broiler-processing costs decrease as plant size is increased, but costs of producing and delivering live birds go up as larger numbers are required at a central location. If a supply area is enlarged, longer hauls between broiler farms and the central location are necessary; if production density is increased in an existing supply area, labor costs for broiler growing may increase. What combination of central processing volume and surrounding production density will yield lowest total unit costs for processed broilers and thus put a supply area as a whole in the best possible competitive position?

The following procedure is used: First, relationships of selected transportation cost items to average one-way lengths of haul between farms and off-farm facilities are estimated; the items considered are chick delivery, feed delivery, visits by fieldmen, live-haul loading, live-haul trucking, and losses of marketable weight during the live haul. Second, the above transportation costs are added to processing costs for various combinations of production density and processing volume, and least-cost combinations are derived. Third, substitution between additional outlays for transportation and higher payments for broiler-growing labor are examined, and trade practices that encourage development of optimum volume-density combinations are outlined. Finally, implications of scale-density relationships for the competitive positions of regions are pointed out, and a potential limitation upon maximum geographic production density is noted.

RELATIONSHIPS OF TRANSPORTATION COSTS TO AVERAGE LENGTHS OF HAUL—MANY TRANSPORTATION COSTS ARE LINEAR FUNCTIONS OF AVERAGE LENGTHS OF HAULS

Most of the transportation costs affected by production density are associated with trips from off-farm facilities to farms and back. Loads

*Journal of Farm Economics, vol. 42, no. 1 (Feb. 1960), pp. 1–17.

are carried one way and inter-farm travel is negligible. In such hauling, the unit cost of providing a particular service is composed of handling (loading and unloading), over-the-road travel (fuel and other regular servicing, wear depreciation and repair, and wages of traveling employees), and overhead (taxes, insurance, interest, storage, licenses, etc.).

If commercial volumes are involved, unit handling cost is a constant. Unit over-the-road cost varies directly with the average distance each unit must be hauled. Unit overhead cost depends upon the size of truck fleet required to handle a given volume; as average length of haul is increased, discrete additions must be made to the fleet.[1] If a constant over-the-road speed is maintained, additions to the fleet come at regular intervals as average length of haul is increased.

From the above considerations, the unit cost of providing a particular hauling service is approximately a linear function, with a positive constant term, of the average length of haul. The service of providing visits by fieldmen does not quite fit the pattern described above, but cost of this service is approximately a linear function of average length of haul to broiler farms.

AN ASSUMED CIRCULAR SUPPLY AREA IS CONVENIENT FOR BUDGETING TO ESTIMATE TRANSPORTATION COST FUNCTIONS

Unit transportation costs as functions of average lengths of haul are valid regardless of shapes of supply areas, distribution of production, or specific locations of off-farm facilities. Also, where commercial volumes are involved, economics of size in the transportation services of interest may be disregarded. These two considerations allow an important simplification in estimating the cost functions. Any commercial level of output can be assumed for any hypothetical supply area, and the cost functions can then be estimated by budgeting associated activities as average length of haul is varied by changing production density.

The hypothetical supply area used by the authors is isolated and circular; it has all off-farm facilities of interest located at the center, and farm production of broilers is evenly distributed throughout the circle. The authors also assume a steady output rate within each of two seasons and near perfect coordination of all production and marketing activities.

Budgeting to minimize affected costs requires time and space factors for travel within the area. These factors can be easily determined because of the following geometric properties of the assumed supply area:

---

[1] Variations from constant rates of production may also increase the size of truck fleet required to handle a given annual volume.

(1) The relationship among average length of haul, annual volume, and geographic production density is

$$A = \frac{2}{3}\sqrt{\frac{V}{\pi D}}$$

where A is the average length of haul in air miles, V is the annual volume in number of birds, and D is geographic density in birds per square mile per year.[2]

(2) The air distance between adjacent farms is the square root of the land area per broiler farm. This property is helpful in estimating costs of providing visits by fieldmen.

Estimates of production and marketing costs affected by changes in average length of haul are listed in table 1. Cost levels are budgeted at 10-mile intervals for average lengths of haul varying from 10 to 70 miles. When costs of the separate items are summed across to get total cost for a particular average length of haul, there is an implicit assumption that hatchery, feed supply, live-hauling, and processing firms share a common central location. The costs presented in Table 1 are based on 1959 North Carolina data which are detailed in the notes to the table.

COMBINATIONS OF TRANSPORTATION AND PROCESSING COSTS

The transportation costs of table 1 could be combined with processing costs under many different assumptions about the locations of other off-farm facilities relative to the processing plant. In this paper, costs are combined under the assumption that all off-farm facilities doing business with a particular processing plant are located at or near this plant. Combined costs apply to the output of a single plant and are not affected if the other off-farm facilities of interest also service other plants.

---

[2] Air distance of average length of haul is related to radius of the hypothetical supply area, R, such that $A = 2/3\ R$. Volume of business in the supply area is related to production density and area, such that

$$V = D\pi R^2 \text{ and } R = \sqrt{\frac{V}{\pi D}}$$

In empirical studies, air distance should be converted to road distance. In the vicinity of Robbins, North Carolina, the average road distance is $1.703 + 1.16A$, where A is air distance in miles. The above equation is a regression estimate based upon a 10 percent sample of all broiler farms in this supply area in June 1957.

TABLE 1
Costs of Feed Delivery, Live Haul, Weight Losses, Chick Delivery, and Fieldmen as Functions of Average Length of Haul to Broiler Farm

Average Length of Haul	1 Feed Delivery	2 Live Haul: Truck	3 Live Haul: Labor	4 Live Haul: Weight Losses	5 Chick Delivery	6 Field-men	7 Total of Six Items	8 Cost of Added 10 Miles
Miles			Dollars per Hundredweight Live Broilers					
10	.1064	.0713	.1749	.0176	.0121	.1134	.4957	—
20	.1485	.0897	.1927	.0352	.0157	.1170	.5988	.1031
30	.1984	.1169	.2105	.0528	.0193	.1205	.7184	.1196
40	.2507	.1353	.2283	.0704	.0229	.1241	.8317	.1133
50	.3005	.1625	.2461	.0880	.0265	.1496	.9732	.1415
60	.3528	.1897	.2639	.1056	.0340	.1531	1.0991	.1259
70	.4026	.2081	.2817	.1232	.0376	.1567	1.2099	.1108

Notes on basis of estimates and sources of data

The assumed operations are designed to supply live birds to a single-shift processing plant operated during early morning hours for 250 days annually, 8 hours per day. In 77 summer days the plant processes 4,290 birds per hour. During the remaining 173 work days the plant processes 4,526 birds per hour. During the year the firm handles 8,533,000 birds. A 48-hour week is assumed in chick and feed delivery. Truck overhead costs are based on minimum integral numbers required to do the work within the available time; cost estimates are conventional except that depreciation of transportation equipment is considered to be a function of mileage rather than time. Feed efficiency of 2.5 pounds to 1 pound of live weight and average live weight of 3.25 pounds are assumed.

Costs are based upon steady operation at designed capacity of the processing plant and near-perfect coordination of all activities of the integrated firm. Absolute levels of costs do not represent costs prevailing in the Southeast because the constant term is underestimated. However, the estimated increases in transportation costs with increases in average lengths of hauls should be in line with actual experiences of firms in the Southeast.

The following assumptions underlie the specific cost estimates:

Col. 1. Costs are based on 7-ton auger-unloading bulk feed trucks. Number of trucks required for the assumed firm ranges from 4 at the 10-mile average length of haul to 12 at the 70-mile average length of haul. (J. A. Seagraves, *Bulk Feed Handling Reduces Labor Costs*. A. E. Info. Ser. 68, Dept. of Agr. Econ., N. C. State Coll., November 1958).

Col. 2. Overhead costs are $2,410 per truck per year and variable costs are $0.1165 per mile (not including wages of driver). Overhead costs are based on minimum integral number of trucks required for summer hauling. Trucks are used for two loads per shift when this is possible. The number of trucks required for the assumed firm ranges from 6 at the 10-mile average length of haul to 9 at the 70-mile average length of haul. Ten truckloads of 264 coops each are hauled on each of 77 days in summer, and 8 truckloads of 304 coops each are hauled on each of 173 days for the remainder of the year. Average speed of live-haul trucks is 30 miles per hour. Costs do not include office overhead, communication costs, or salary income to the manager of the trucking firm.

Col. 3. Fourteen birds are hauled in each coop except for 77 summer days when 13 are put in each coop. Birds can be caught and loaded at the rate of 20 coops per man-hour with on-truck cooping and bulk weighing. (W. R. Henry, *On-Truck Crating Reduces Broiler Hauling Costs*, A. E. Info. Ser. 63, Dept. of Agr. Econ., N. C. State Coll., 1958) Truck drivers are assumed to help with loading. Wage rates of $1.00 per hour for loading crew and $1.25 per hour for driver are assumed, and a crew foreman is paid $350 per month. The crew is paid while traveling to and from broiler farms. Crew travel is in 8-passenger station wagons owned by crew members who are paid 8 cents per mile. Average travel rate for crew is 30 miles per hour.

Col. 4. The cost of decreases in chilled eviscerated weight is approximately equal to the value of the pounds of live weight lost at the market price per pound for live birds. Costs are based on live price of 16 cents per pound and live weight losses at the rate of 0.34 percent per hour. Only "over-the-road" costs of weight losses are included. These costs are additions to the lowest weight-loss cost attainable with length of haul near zero. (W. R. Henry and Robert Raunikar, *Weight Losses of Broilers During the Live Haul*, A. E. Info. Ser. 69, Dept. of Agr. Econ., N. C. State Coll., December 1958).

Col. 5. Overhead costs are $1.062 per hatchery truck per year and variable costs are $0.1153 per mile (including wages of driver at $1.50 per hour). Overhead costs are based on 2 trucks for 60- and 70-mile average hauls and 1 truck for shorter hauls. Truck capacity is 25,000 chicks; average load is 20,000 chicks. Loading and unloading are assumed to take 2 hours per load.

Col. 6. Fieldman costs are based on 196 farms evenly distributed in the supply area, weekly visits and record maintenance requiring 1 hour per farm, and average travel speed of 40 miles per hour. Automobiles are provided by fieldman and they receive 5 cents per mile for travel. Costs are based on 5 fieldmen for 10- to 40-mile average hauls and 6 fieldmen for 50- to 70-mile hauls. Fieldman are paid salaries of $500 per month.

"EFFECTIVE" PRODUCTION DENSITY MEASURES DENSITY FROM THE POINT OF VIEW OF A PARTICULAR FIRM

This paper deals with production density in terms of its effect upon unit costs for the outputs of particular firms. Any particular firm may have to share business in the surrounding trade area with competitors offering the same services. Thus, the "effective" production density from the point of view of a particular firm may be much smaller than the geographic production density of its supply area.

The authors propose to define effective production density by reference to the assumed supply area used in estimating transportation cost functions. Suppose the average length of haul and the volume of business are known for a particular firm. There is some hypothetical production density for the reference area that would result in the same average length of haul for the same volume of business. This hypothetical density is the effective density in the trade area of the firm in question. Specifically,

$$D' = \frac{4V}{9\pi A^2}$$

where D' is effective density in birds per square mile per year, A is the average length of haul in air miles, and V is the annual volume of business in number of birds.

Effective production density, as defined above, has three desirable characteristics. First, the two dimensions of average length of haul and volume of business are readily measurable. Second, average length of haul is also an axis for the transportation cost functions of interest. Finally, effective production density can be used for inter-firm and inter-area comparisons without specifying shapes of supply areas, specific locations of off-farm facilities, distributions of production, or trade shareing in supply areas.[3]

OPTIMUM SIZES OF PROCESSING PLANTS ARE RELATED TO EFFECTIVE PRODUCTION DENSITIES OF THEIR SUPPLY AREAS

Several studies have shown that unit processing costs fall as plant size is increased if plants of various sizes are steadily operated at their designed rates of output. For this paper, cost of processing in model plants of various sizes in New England are adjusted to correspond with

---

[3] Average length of haul is often used by businessmen in the broiler industry for interfirm and inter-area comparisons of production density. Effective density is a better index for such comparisons than average length of haul used alone.

Southern conditions. A curve is drawn through the adjusted costs to smooth a discontinuity at the 1,200-bird-per-hour capacity and to allow interpolation of estimated costs. The resulting relationship of adjusted costs to plant size is shown in table 2.

TABLE 2
Estimated Costs of Processing Broilers in Plants of Various Sizes, Based on 1959 Southern Conditions

Plant Size, Birds per Hour	600	1,200	1,800	2,400	3,600	4,800	7,200	9,600
Processing costs, dollars per 100 live pounds	3.69	3.41	3.21	3.10	2.90	2.79	2.67	2.62

Since transportation costs are combined here under the assumption that other off-farm facilities are located at or near the processing plant, the transportation costs are taken from the "total" column of Table 1 and are approximated as a linear function passing through the costs at the 10-mile and 70-mile length of haul. This function is

$$C = \$0.3769 + \$0.0119M$$

where C is cost per 100 pounds of live weight, and M is the average length of haul in miles of road distance.

Processing costs per unit for plants of various sizes are depicted by the middle curve of figure 1. Transportation costs per unit for an area with an effective density of 500 birds per square mile are shown by the lower curve, and the corresponding average lengths of haul are posted at intervals along this curve. The processing cost curve and the transportation cost curve are simply added together to obtain the upper "total" curve. Total cost per unit reaches its lowest point at a plant capacity of 4,800 birds per hour.

Total processing and transportation costs for six levels of effective density are shown in figure 2. In computing each curve, effective production density is held constant at a selected level and average length of haul is increased as plant size is increased. The air distance to road distance relationship of the Piedmont broiler area of North Carolina is used in computing transportation costs.[4]

---
[4] The methods used to construct the planning curves of figure 2 could be used with other sets of factor costs for other regions, with alternative assumptions about operating practices, and with economies of scale of integrated hatchery and feed mill incorporated.

FIGURE 1
Selected Transport Costs, Processing Costs and Combined Costs, for Effective Production Density of 500 Birds per Square Mile per Year, Average Lengths of Haul, in Miles, Posted along Transport Cost Curve

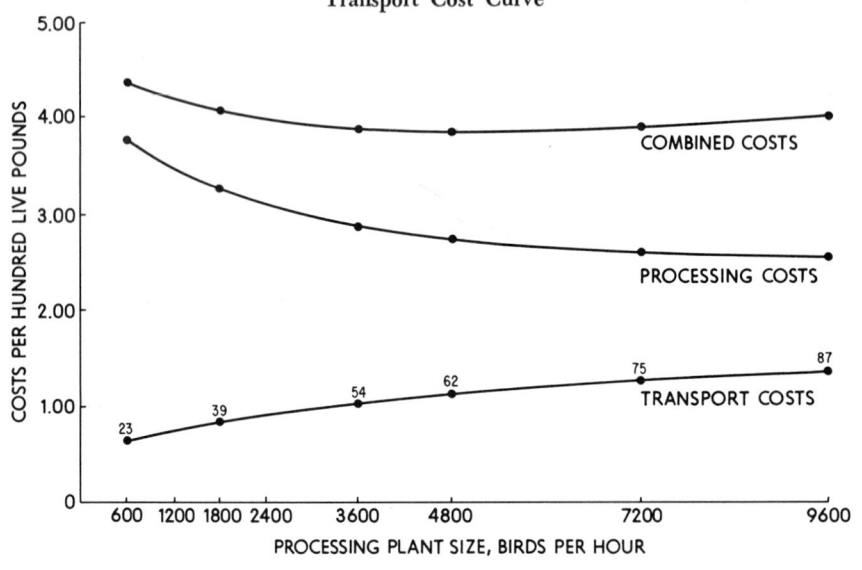

FIGURE 2
Relationship of Processing Plant Size to Combined Costs of Transportation and Processing for Different Effective Production Densities

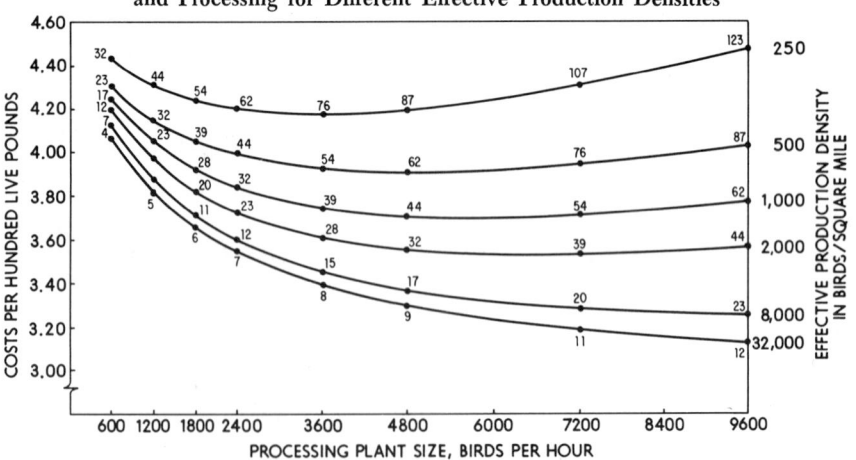

Relatively shallow planning curves of Figure 2 mean that, with constant effective density, there is little difference in total unit costs for a wide range of processing plant sizes. For example, with effective density at 250 birds per square mile lowest total unit costs are $4.18 for a

TABLE 3
Totals of Processing and Transportation Costs for Commonly Located Broiler Production and Marketing Facilities in Supply Areas Having Various Production Densities

Effective Production Density in Birds per Square Mile per Year	\multicolumn{8}{c}{Design Capacity, Birds per Hour, 2,000 Hours Annually}
	600	1,200	1,800	2,400	3,600	4,800	7,200	9,600
	\multicolumn{8}{c}{(dollars per hundred live pounds)}
250	4.45	4.32	4.23	4.22	**4.18**	4.21	4.32	4.46
500	4.35	4.17	4.05	4.01	3.92	**3.91**	3.95	4.04
1,000	4.27	4.06	3.92	3.86	3.74	3.70	**3.69**	3.74
2,000	4.21	3.99	3.83	3.75	3.61	3.55	**3.51**	3.53
4,000	4.18	3.93	3.76	3.68	3.50	3.44	**3.38**	**3.38**
8,000	4.15	3.90	3.72	3.62	3.45	3.37	3.29	**3.27**
16,000	4.13	3.87	3.69	3.59	3.41	3.31	3.22	**3.20**
32,000	4.12	3.85	3.66	3.56	3.38	3.28	3.18	**3.14**

3,600-bird-per-hour plant, while the range from 1,800 to 4,800 birds per hour does not have total unit costs in excess of $4.23. Selected coordinates of planning curves for supply areas having various production densities are listed in table 3. Boldface type identifies costs for plants of optimum size. In each case, plant sizes can be increased or decreased from optimum with little effect upon total unit costs.

SUBSTITUTION BETWEEN ADDED OUTLAYS FOR TRANSPORTATION AND HIGHER PAYMENTS FOR BROILER GROWING

If production density is increased, internal economies of larger processing plants can be combined with external economies of greater production density to yield substantial reductions in total processing and transportation costs figure 3 shows interrelationships of optimum plant size, effective production density, and total costs. Coordinates of the curve in figure 3 are the least-cost combinations from table 3. Minimum total unit costs decrease from $4.18 at an effective density of 250 birds per square mile per year to $3.20 at an effective density of 16,000 birds per square mile per year. This 98-cent saving per hundred live pounds is due to economies of size in processing (28 cents) and reduced transportation costs (70 cents).

The curve in figure 3 is based on an assumption that production density can be increased without raising production cost. While this assumption may be realistic in the long run for some supply areas, higher payments for broiler growing would be necessary in many others to get increased density.

FIGURE 3
Combined Economies of Scale and Production Density. Processing Plant Capacities, in Birds per Hour, Posted along Curve

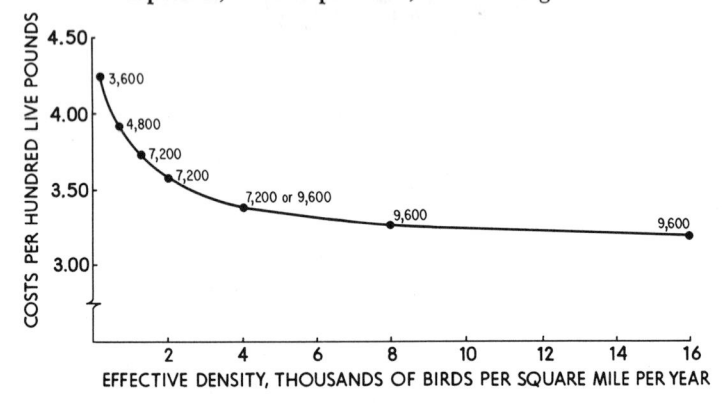

OPTIMUM PRODUCTION DENSITY DEPENDS UPON THE SUPPLY CURVE FOR BROILER-GROWING LABOR

Costs of obtaining increased production density are mainly increases in labor returns to broiler growers to bid labor away from alternative employments. Payments to growers who own their housing and equipment must, over the long run, cover the costs of these inputs, but these costs are not dependent upon location of these facilities (except for increases in site values near urban centers, which are not important in the context of this paper). Other inputs used in broiler growing (chicks, feed, brooding fuel, health aids, etc.) are provided from off-farm sources. Their supply prices at the center of operations do not depend upon locations of growers. Therefore, if there is a rise in unit production cost as production density is increased, it is derived from the supply curve for labor for broiler growing.[5]

If a given volume is to be produced in a particular supply area, the optimum production density of this area depends upon its least-cost combination of transportation costs that decrease and labor costs that increase as production density is increased. Optimum combinations of this type cannot be determined without precise information about supply

---

[5] Three other factors that might set limits to production density were considered: (1) In the short run, capital for construction of new broiler housing may be limiting, but broiler businessmen who are interested in maximizing profits over the long run can overcome this limitation; (2) Increased likelihood of disease spreading from house to house in broiler areas could discourage increases in production density, but contagion-reducing practices that should be used even when production is widely scattered would eliminate this limitation; (3) A possible reduction in value of broiler litter for crop fertilization as broiler growing becomes more centralized was discussed in the original version of this paper.

curves for broiler-growing labor. However, information that may be useful in making adjustments toward optimum density can be developed.

Suppose annual volume of production is to be increased by a processing plant and the firms supply live birds to it. Which is the better strategy—an expansion of the supply area with density constant or an increase in production density with average length of haul constants? The increase in production density will be preferred if savings in transportation cost, by avoiding increased length of haul, is greater than the increase in grower labor returns that will produce the necessary increase in production density. Otherwise, enlarging the supply area will be preferred.

Assume a circular supply area, centrally located facilities, and evenly distributed production. Transportation costs increase $0.0119 per hundred live pounds for every mile added to average length of haul. Labor inputs for broiler growing are about one-half minute per 3.25 pound bird, or 0.2566 hours per hundred live pounds. A saving of one mile in the average length of haul would cover the cost of a wage increase of $0.0119/0.2566, or $0.0464 per hour.

Now, note two characteristics that apply exactly to the assumed broiler supply area and approximately to typical operating conditions: (a) if average length of haul is held constant, any percentage increase in volume must be accompanied by an equal percentage increase in production density; (b) any increase in average length of haul resulting from holding density constant as volume increases is determined by the percentage increase in volume and the average length of haul before the increase.[6]

Based upon the conditions of the two paragraphs above, figure 4 shows equally costly increases in hourly grower labor returns and increases in average lengths of haul when annual volume is to be increased by various percentages with various initial values for average lengths of haul.

---

[6] Starting with

$$D' = \frac{4V}{9\pi A^2}$$

as defined above, to increase V to bV while D' remains constant, A^2 must be increased to bA^2; i.e., A must be increased to $A\sqrt{b}$, or by an amount $\Delta A = A(\sqrt{b} - 1)$. If road mileage, R, were proportional to air mileage, A, then R would increase by the corresponding amount $R = R(\sqrt{b} - 1)$. Where R is a linear function of A containing a constant term, however, this relationship is only approximate. In our case, $R = 1.703 + 1.16A$; i.e. $(R - 1.703) = 1.16A$. The corrected increase in road mileage is therefore

$$\Delta R = (R - 1.703)(\sqrt{b} - 1)$$

Therefore the increase in road mileage, ΔR, is a linear function of the original mileage, R, with a small negative constant term.

FIGURE 4
Comparisons of Increases in Hourly Grower Wages with Equally Costly Alternative Increases in Average Length of Haul When Broiler Servicing and Processing Volume Is to Be Increased by Various Percentages

EQUALLY COSTLY ADDED AMOUNTS:

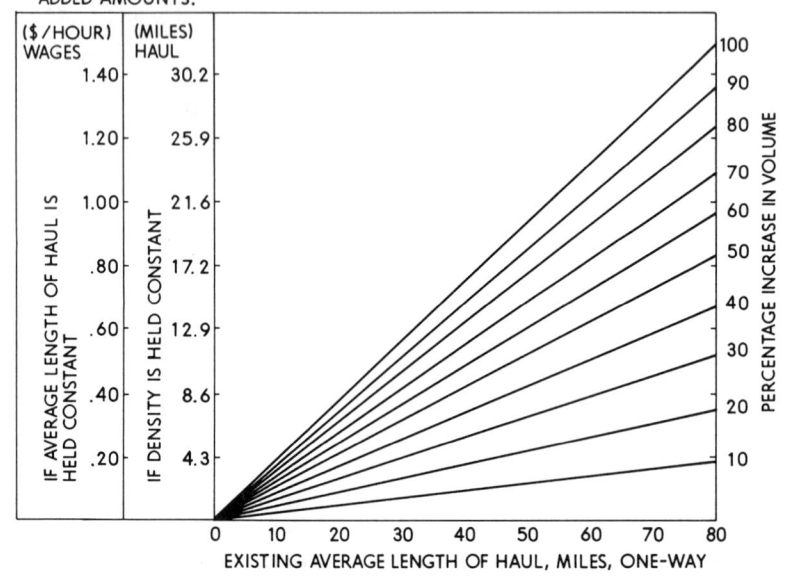

(graph with axes:
- Left: ($/HOUR) WAGES IF AVERAGE LENGTH OF HAUL IS HELD CONSTANT: 1.40, 1.20, 1.00, .80, .60, .40, .20
- Left: (MILES) HAUL IF DENSITY IS HELD CONSTANT: 30.2, 25.9, 21.6, 17.2, 12.9, 8.6, 4.3
- Bottom: EXISTING AVERAGE LENGTH OF HAUL, MILES, ONE-WAY: 0, 10, 20, 30, 40, 50, 60, 70, 80
- Right: PERCENTAGE INCREASE IN VOLUME: 10, 20, 30, 40, 50, 60, 70, 80, 90, 100)

In order to use figure 4, choose one of the slanting lines corresponding to the percentage increase in volume—for example, a 100 percent increase. Next, draw a vertical line from the present average length of haul to an intersection with the slanting line—for example, from the 50-mile length of haul. Project a horizontal line from the intersection to the scales on the left margin and read the two values found there—in the example, 20.7 and $0.96. Hourly grower labor returns could be increased by as much as $0.96 without exceeding the alternative increase in unit transportation cost as average length of haul is increased by 20.7 miles. If the required 100 percent increase in production density can be achieved with a smaller increase in hourly grower labor return, it is the better choice of the two alternatives. In many cases, increases in density would be more profitable than increases in sizes of supply areas.

Even if no increase in volume is anticipated, a broiler production and marketing organization may be able to reduce total costs by increasing production density near the operating center. Average length of haul is reduced approximately in proportion to the square root of the increase in geographic density of production coming to the plant. If production density is doubled, average length of haul is reduced to approximately

$\sqrt{1/2}$, or 0.707, times its former length. With density quadrupled, average length of haul is approximately $\sqrt{1/4}$, or 0.5, times its former length.

TRADE PRACTICES MAY NEED CHANGING IF BROILER AREAS ARE TO TAKE ADVANTAGE OF ECONOMIES OF DENSITY

An integrated production and marketing organization stands to capture all savings resulting from decreased average length of haul. If such an organization grows broilers in its own housing with hired labor, it can locate broiler housing and equipment close to the operating center. No institutional factors restrict exploitation of economies of density.

However, an obstacle may exist where an integrated broiler producing and processing firm offers typical contracts for broiler growing in grower-owned housing. An ordinary "incentive" contract provides no greater incentive to nearby than to distant growers. Such a firm might find it highly profitable to establish contracts with mileage differentials that would partially reflect out-haul and in-haul costs associated with mileage. The average level of payment for broiler growing might be kept unchanged. Over time, the mileage differentials might be adjusted to give nearby growers the full amounts of savings in transportation costs. Gradual adjustment of the mileage differential would provide time for nearby growers to increase their capacities and for remote growers to depreciate buildings and equipment. As the effective density of the supply area increased, the integrated firm would benefit because the average cost per pound to obtain the desired volume would be gradually lowered. Such a mileage differential should be built into contracts in such a way that other variable payment provisions, such as incentives for efficient feed conversion, would not be affected.[7]

Obstacles are more difficult to overcome where hatchery, feed supply, broiler growing, live-haul, and processing firms are related by contracts, informal agreements, or open market trading. Each firm stands to gain to some extent if production density is increased, but none can capture all the gains. In any event, these gains come about only if nearby growers are given incentives to increase production. In this type of producing and marketing organization, consideration should be given to the following arrangements: (1) use by the hatchery of mileage charges in pricing baby chicks; (2) use by haulers of mileage charges in rates for live hauling; (3) use by feed dealers of mileage differential contracts with growers; (4) payments by processors for live birds on a delivered and plant-weight basis. Such arrangements would accumulate savings from nearby growing in returns to feed dealers. The feed dealers could then

---

[7] Differentials based on zoning might be more practical than differentials based on mileage. They would lead to similar ultimate results: Increased production density, shorter hauls, and lower total production costs.

reflect these savings in contracts with growers. Over time, the supply areas would become more compact, hourly grower-labor returns would increase, and total costs per pound of processed broilers would decrease.

COMPARISON OF REGIONAL OPPORTUNITIES TO REDUCE COSTS BY INCREASING EFFECTIVE DENSITIES

Geographic production densities vary widely when specialized broiler-producing regions are compared. Areas with greatest geographic densities are generally believed to have resulting competitive advantages. However, it is effective production densities affecting unit costs building up at particular processing plants, not geographic production densities of regions, that should be compared.

EFFECTIVE PRODUCTION DENSITIES ARE NOT CLOSELY CORRELATED WITH GEOGRAPHIC DENSITIES

The authors queried selected broiler processors by mail during April 1959. Each processor was asked to provide his weekly rate of processing, in number of broilers, and the average length of live hauls in the week prior to receipt of the questionnaire. From this information the effective production density in the supply area of each plant was estimated. Results of the survey are shown in table 4.

TABLE 4
Estimates of Effective Broiler Production Densities in the Supply Areas of Processing Plants, April 1959, and a Comparison with Geographic Densities for Estimated 1958 Production

Region	Number of Plants Providing Data	Average Length of Live Haul, Mean for Region (Miles)	Effective Density Birds/Sq. Mile/Yr. Range	Effective Density Birds/Sq. Mile/Yr. Mean[a]	Geographic Density Birds/Sq. Mile/Yr.[b]
Maine	4	27.5	2,143–5,270	3,695	3,971
Delmarva	5	23.5	2,380–6,120	4,515	51,874
Central North Carolina	12	47.2	151–8,143	1,382	11,994
North Georgia	4	28.8	1,719–4,619	2,984	38,565
N.W. Arkansas	5	28.0	491–8,360	4,141	22,568

[a] The weighted average for those plants providing data.
[b] Based on estimated 1958 production and the following counties and square miles for each region: Maine: Kennebec, Knox, Penobscot, Somerset, Waldo, 9,317 sq. miles.
Delmarva: Kent and Susex in Deleware, Caroline, Talbot, Wicomico, Somerset and Worcester in Maryland, 3,335 sq. miles.
Central North Carolina: Chatham, Moore, Montgomery, Randolph, 2,668 sq. miles.
North Georgia: Banks, Barrow, Cherokee, Cobb, Dawson, Forsyth, Fulton, Gilmer, Habersham, Hart, Hall, Jackson, Lumpkin, Stephens, White, Aiken (S.C.), 4,823 sq. miles.
N. W. Arkansas: Benton, Carroll, Madison, Washington, McDonald (Mo.), 3,855 sq. miles.

The long hauls of the North Carolina Piedmont stand in sharp contrast to those of the other four regions. Average total cost of live hauling (truck, labor, and weight losses) is estimated to be about one eighth cent per pound higher in Central North Carolina than in the other regions. For this comparison, labor wages, truck costs, and broiler prices are standardized at North Carolina levels.

In the four regions having greater production densities than North Carolina, effective densities range from 3,000 to 4,500 birds per square mile per year. Compared among themselves, none of the four regions appears to have a significant competitive advantage in effective density. It may be noted that there are wide variations in effective densities within these regions, and that all could have substantial reductions in transportation costs if effective density were increased to levels approaching 16,000 birds per square mile per year. Efforts to increase effective densities are expected to be accelerated in all regions as the potential gains are appraised by individual firms.

Geographic densities, birds per square mile per year, are listed in the final column of table 4. Effective density refers to the density for each processing firm while geographic density is based on the combined production of all firms in the area. Geographic densities also would be larger than effective densities if the road pattern and the broiler growing did not cover the entire geographic area. One of the main conclusions of this paper is that the effective production density for each firm is a more useful concept than geographic density in applied studies of this type. Effective density is also very simple to calculate and it requires only knowledge of the volume and average length of haul for each firm.

If the use of the broiler litter by-product is limited to fertilization of nearby cropland then the amount of cropland eventually could become a limiting factor on production density. This possibility was considered in the original version of this paper. Potential density was calculated using the assumption that the litter from 1,000 broilers would profitably be used on no more than one acre of nearby cropland each year. Potential densities were compared with geographic densities for 11 broiler-producing regions. Geographic density in 1954 was less than half of this potential density in North Georgia, less than one fourth for Delmarva, but, generally speaking, the results indicated that broiler litter was being used on only about one eighth of the available cropland.

CONCLUSIONS

Economic aspects of broiler production density were investigated by generating costs for assumed operations of varying size and areas of varying production density. Input-output coefficients and factor prices are fairly typical of conditions in the southeastern United States. The conclusions of this investigation are as follows:

1. Costs of transporting feed, chicks, and production supervisors to broiler farms and hauling live birds to processing plants are estimated to increase at a rate of 1.19 cents per 100 pounds of live broilers for each mile added to average length of haul. Substantial reductions in total costs may be possible if production density is increased and the average length of haul for a given scale of operations is reduced.

2. The optimum sizes for processing plants are related to production densities of supply areas. However, combined transportation and processing costs are not much changed when plant sizes are varied from the optimum (table 3).

3. Although labor costs for broiler growing may increase with production density, the advantages of greater concentration of broiler growing are sufficiently large that progressive firms can be expected to encourage greater concentration in the future. Present pricing schemes are a hindrance to this concentration under most arrangements involving contract growing.

4. Effective production density, based on the volume of production for each firm and its average length of haul, is a useful conceptual device when one wants to include transportation costs in either budgeting or survey studies of economics of size.

Further investigations are needed to evaluate potential economies of centralized broiler growing in factory-type operations. Possibilities for improved techniques of feed and bird transport and for uses of broiler litter other than in crop fertilization might be given special attention. In addition, careful studies of economies of scale in chick hatching and feed milling are needed.

part FIVE
Pricing

INTRODUCTION

The relative places of demand and cost in the pricing decisions of firms of the real world—as opposed, presumably, to those of theory—was once a lively topic of debate in the economic journals. The participants arranged themselves mainly into two camps, the "marginalists" and the "full costers," the latter denying virtually any role to demand and some of the former coming dangerously close to denying any role to costs. Not so much is heard about the question nowadays, partly because interest in it has run its course (economics being no less prey to fashion than most disciplines), but mostly because we are coming to realize that the marginalists were talking primarily about *determinants* and the full costers mainly about *mechanics*. But each new generation of students begins with a clean slate, and must be convinced of the practical importance of demand.

The classic article by George Stigler is concerned not with the empirics but with the theory of demand and pricing in a particular situation. It remains as controversial as it is entertaining.

The articles by Robert Lanzillotti and Warren Haynes are concerned with the practical aspects of pricing, and present rather contrasting points of view. Interestingly, the contrast goes in the direction opposite to that which might be expected. Lanzillotti, who studies large firms with, one supposes, sophisticated marketing and operations research departments, finds little attention being paid to demand; Haynes, who studies small businesses, finds rather a lot.

The article by Martin Howe is concerned more with conceptual matters, though with adequate attention paid to empirical findings. The article complements those of Lanzillotti and Haynes. With a nice twist of the usual practice, it raises interesting questions about the *practical* utility of the full-cost schemes. It serves as a useful antidote to the naive views of pricing which students are likely to get in some of their other courses.

Joel Dean's classic article treats the separate issue of transfer pricing. It is the standard introduction to this subject and directs attention to the main principles of rational pricing policy in any context. This subject is as disturbing as it is important, for Dean states that to be economically effective autonomous divisions of most large companies *must* establish transfer prices. Most existing transfer price systems are inadequate and huge quantities of time and patience are required to install competitive transfer prices. Yet, once a "good" system is obtained executives should be prepared to meet certain objections which critics always raise.

Jack Hirshleifer provides an analysis of difficulties in transfer pricing that Dean did not consider (chiefly, imperfectly competitive external markets). Hirshleifer recognizes that autonomous divisions are, in effect, internal profit centers for the firm, but each top executive group of each profit center wants to maximize the position, however defined, of *its* division to the exclusion, if necessary, of overall corporate profits. Hirshleifer's theoretical analysis establishes a mode of pricing that leads autonomous profit centers to make pricing decisions which result in the largest aggregate profit for the firm as a whole, even when external markets are not perfectly competitive, so long as there is no strong interdependence between the centers.

18. The Kinky Oligopoly Demand Curve and Rigid Prices*

GEORGE J. STIGLER

Just before World War II, the theory was advanced that there exists a kink in the demand curve for the product of an oligopolist and that this kink goes far to explain observed price rigidities in oligopolistic industries. The theory has rapidly gained wide acceptance: many economists give it some place in their theoretical system, and some economists make it *the* theory of oligopoly price.

The theory is an ingenious rationalization of the price rigidities that were reported in many statistical studies of prices during the thirties, and no doubt this explains its popularity. But no one, so far as I know, has examined in detail either the pure theory of the kinky demand curve or the degree of correspondence between the price patterns implied by the theory and the observed price patterns in oligopolistic industries. These two tasks will be undertaken in part I and part II, respectively, of this paper.

I. THE FORMAL THEORY

1. The Received Theory

The theory of the kinky demand curve was advanced independently and almost simultaneously by R. L. Hall and C. J. Hitch in England and Paul M. Sweezy in America. The latter's version will be summarized first.

The Sweezy Version. The market situation contemplated by Sweezy is one in which rivals will quickly match price reductions but only hesitantly and incompletely (if at all) follow price increases. This pattern of expected behavior produces a kink at the existing price ($= p_0$ in figure 1) in the demand curve for the product of an oligopolist,[1] and the cor-

---

* *Journal of Political Economy*, vol. 55, no. 5 (October 1947) pp. 432–49. © Copyright 1947, The University of Chicago Press.

[1] The demand curve for the product of an oligopolist can be defined only if the reactions of rivals to price changes are known. The upper branch of the demand curve in Figure 1 represents the quantities that consumers will buy from

FIGURE 1

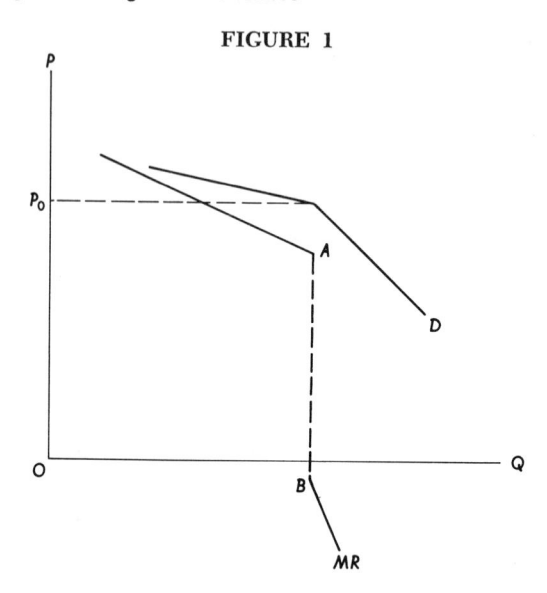

responding marginal revenue curve will possess a discontinuity the length of which is proportional to the difference between the slopes of the upper and lower segments of the demand curve at the kink. Sweezy assumes that "the marginal cost curve passes between the two parts of the marginal revenue curve," so that fluctuations in marginal cost are not likely to affect output and price.

He considers also two other possibilities. An oligopolist may believe that secret price cuts will remain secret, in which case the demand curve becomes elastic throughout and the kink disappears. Or the oligopolist may be a price leader, so that price increases will be followed and the kink again disappears.

Sweezy assumes that shifts in demand will not affect the price at which the kink occurs and argues that the results of increases and decreases of demand are asymmetrical:

1. An increase of demand will make the demand curve less elastic in its upper branch, since rivals are operating closer to capacity,[2] and

---

one oligopolist at various prices if rival producers set a price of p_0; the lower branch represents the quantities that consumers will buy if the rivals charge identical prices. This demand curve is objective in the sense that it is consistent with the facts of the market if rivals behave in the specified manner. Sweezy appears to view it as subjective because it is based upon beliefs concerning rivals' price reactions which may have to be revised (although no occasions for revision of beliefs are treated in his article).

[2] Sweezy, Paul M. "Demand under Conditions of Oligopoly," *Journal of Political Economy*, vol. 47 (August 1939), p. 571. Presumably the rivals' higher rates of production lead them to follow the price increase (although this reaction causes trouble), or, if they maintain prices the buyers are rationed.

more elastic in the lower branch because rivals "are less worried about losses in [of?] business." If marginal costs are also shifting upward as demand increases, "an increase in demand is more likely to lead to a price increase than to a price cut."

2. A decrease in demand will have the converse effects—increased elasticity of the upper branch and decreased elasticity of the lower branch—so the discontinuity of marginal revenue will be increased and the oligopolists will be "more anxious than ever" to hold to the existing price.

Except where price leaders exist or secret price concessions are possible, therefore, oligopoly price may rise in good times and will not be reduced in bad times.

The Oxford Version. Hall and Hitch conclude, after reporting interviews with some 38 entrepreneurs on price policy, that businessmen seek prices that cover average cost, regardless of marginal revenue and marginal cost (which they seldom know). This "full-cost" principle is apparently the result of tacit or open collusion, consideration of long-run demand and costs, moral conviction of fairness, and uncertainty of effects of price increases and decreases. The particular results of the interviews need not be discussed here.

The entrepreneur therefore sets a price that covers average cost (including "profits") at the expected or some conventional output (see figure 2). Increases or decreases of demand will usually shift the kink

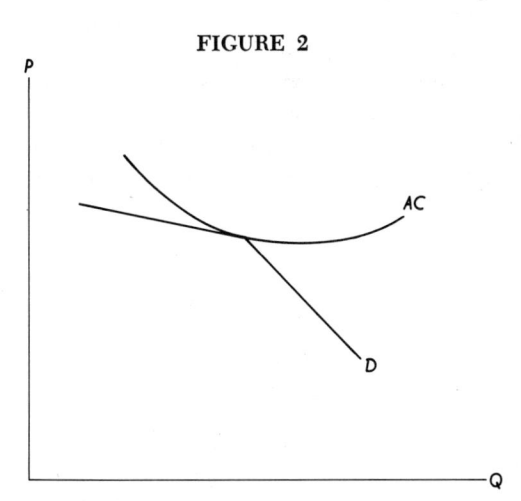

FIGURE 2

to the right or left and leave price unchanged, but there are two exceptions to this rule:

1. If the demand decreases greatly and remains small for some time, the price is likely to be cut in the hope of maintaining output. The

chief explanation for this price cut is that one rival becomes panicky and his irrational behavior forces the others to cut prices.

2. If the average cost curves of all firms shift by similar amounts, due perhaps to changes in factor prices or technology, this is "likely to lead to a revaluation of the 'full cost' price." However, ". . . . there will be no tendency for [prices] to fall or rise more than the wage and raw material costs."

The full-cost principle would suggest also that prices will vary inversely with output, i.e., that high prices are necessary to cover the high average costs of small outputs. This price pattern is not followed, apparently, because the oligopolists (1) place a value on price stability, (2) are influenced by the kink, and (3) wish to keep plant running as full as possible, giving rise to a general feeling in favor of price concessions.

Comparison of the Versions. The Sweezy version is a consistent application of the kinky demand curve to price determination, without conflicting principles to modify its workings. The Oxford version embraces also the "full-cost" principle (and apparently also the "large-output" principle), although the possibilities of conflict between the two are manifold. Hall and Hitch resolve some of the conflicts by abandoning the kink (e.g., when prices follow production costs) and some by abandoning the "full-cost" principle (e.g., when entrepreneurs do not raise prices in depression). They take no account of the difficulties raised by differences among the average costs of various oligopolists or of many other troublesome features of the "full-cost" principle. Their thesis that the kink follows changes in wage rates and material prices implies a degree of collusion—or at least such beautiful rapport—among the oligopolists that it is hard to see why a kink should appear at all (see below). Their fluid version can explain any pattern of prices, and therefore forecast none, and accordingly I shall henceforth devote primary attention to the Sweezy version.

2. Elaboration of the Theory

The discussions of the kinky demand curve have been rather laconic. Certain implications of the theory must be elaborated in order to derive specific price patterns for the subsequent empirical tests.

The Length of the Discontinuity in Marginal Revenue. The length of the discontinuity in marginal revenue is proportional to the difference between the slopes of the demand curve on the two sides of the kink. The longer this discontinuity, the greater the fluctuations in marginal cost (and in demand, if the kink stays at the same price) that are compatible with price stability and therefore the greater the probability of rigid prices in any interval of time. Some of the factors that affect the length of this discontinuity are:

a) *The number of rivals (of a given degree of closeness, measured by the cross-elasticity of demand).* We should expect that a price increase is more likely to be followed if there are few rivals than if there are many, because the rivals will realize that the temporary gains from holding down their prices will soon be erased. If this is so, the discontinuity will be short (in time) or nonexistent when there are few rivals. The larger the number of rivals, the less likely are they to follow one oligopolist's price increases; on the other hand, the less likely are they also to match his price reduction, at least immediately. It seems probable, therefore, that the discontinuity is longest with an immediate number of rivals, say, five to ten.

b) *The relative size of rivals (of a given degree of closeness).* When one firm (or an inner clique) is dominant in size, it will presumably be the price leader. When this firm increases its price, rivals are likely to follow (for individually they can sell as much as they wish at the ruling price); when the firm cuts prices the rivals must follow. Hence the dominant firm will have no kink in its demand curve. The smaller firms cannot raise their prices above the leader's unless he is rationing buyers but can shade prices without being followed immediately or perhaps at all. Again there will be no kink.

c) *The differences among the rivals' products.* The discontinuity will be longer, the more homogeneous the products, because customers will shift more rapidly to the low-price firm.

d) *The extent of collusion.* Should explicit collusion replace the standoffish attitude visualized by the theory, the kink will vanish; there is no kink in a monopolist's demand curve.

Other factors affecting the length of the discontinuity in marginal revenue could be mentioned, for example, the number of buyers. But these factors do not lend themselves to the type of empirical tests that will be employed in part II and will not be discussed.

The Workings of the Kink. In order to study the workings of the kinky demand curve, let us consider two producers (of equal size) of similar, but not identical, commodities. The initial demand and marginal revenue curves of duopolist A are given in figure 3; they are denoted by the subscript 1. Assume now that the aggregate demand for the two commodities increases so that A's demand curve shifts to D_2, but marginal costs do not change. Then A will increase his price to p_2. What will duopolist B do?

If B's costs and demand are similar to A's, the former will simultaneously raise his price to p_2. But then D_2 must be redrawn above p_0 because this branch was drawn on the assumption that the rival's price was

FIGURE 3

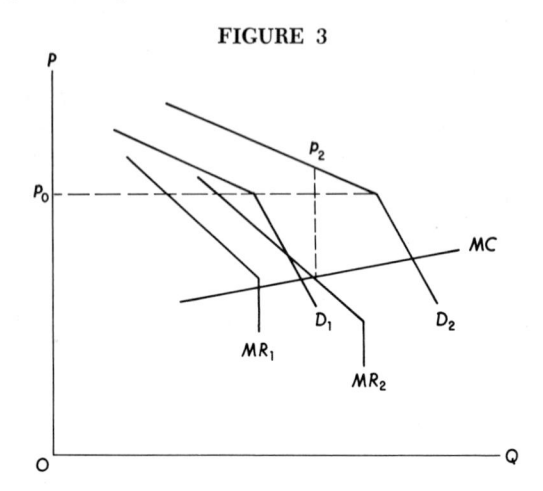

p_0. The situation becomes classical duopoly—with the usual wide range of possible patterns of behavior. It would be foolish to put a new kink in D_2 (as redrawn) at the level p_2. Experience has shown that the rival will follow a price increase, and businessmen will learn from this experience that there is no kink.

On the other hand, B may still find it profitable to stay at price p_0. But then his demand curve must shift to the right, for it was drawn on the assumption that A set a price of p_0 or less. If this demand shift leads B to set a new price, then A's demand curve must be redrawn. Again the existence of the kink is contradicted by experience.

The theory of the kinky demand curve explains why prices that have been stable should continue to be stable despite certain changes in demand or costs. But the theory does not explain why prices that have once changed should settle down, again acquire stability, and gradually produce a new kink. One possible explanation might be that a period of stability of demand and costs has created a tradition of stable prices, so that, when demand or cost conditions change materially, the kink has emerged to preserve price stability.

Other Kinks and Discontinuities. For present purposes it is not necessary to discuss additional implications of the theory of kinky demand curves, but two are of sufficient interest to deserve brief mention.

The pattern of oligopolistic behavior underlying the kinky demand curve will also produce a discontinuous marginal cost curve. If one firm reduces its wage rate, for example, other firms will not follow, but these other firms will match wage increases. At the output corresponding to this input kink, there will be a discontinuity in marginal cost. A good part of the appeal of the kinky demand curve theory is that it is easy to draw demand and cost curves that lead to price stability. This appeal is definitely weakened if the marginal cost curve is also discontinuous, as the reader can readily verify.

The same general line of reasoning leads to kinks in the curves of other variables of policy—advertising, quality changes, etc. Indeed, the logic of the theory requires only that there be one variable—output—against which the discontinuities in the other variables may be displayed.

3. Alternative Theories of Price Stability

Explanations of price stability are not common or prominent in the neoclassical price theory of Marshall's era. (Part II of this paper contains some evidence that bears on the question whether this is a cause for commendation or condemnation.) Of course it would be a grotesque caricature to describe this theory as requiring a change of price in response to every quiver of the demand or the cost curve. Three factors making for price stability were generally incorporated (without emphasis) into the neoclassical theory.

Long-Run Considerations. In the long run the demand curve is usually more elastic because buyers can make changes in technology, commitments, and habits that permit use of substitutes and because new rivals will be attracted at certain prices. Therefore an exorbitant current price may lose more (discounted) revenue in the future than it adds in the present. This type of consideration argues against raising prices greatly in short-run periods of inelastic demand but does not imply price rigidity.

Administrative Weaknesses in Collusion. When a group of producers arrives at a mutually agreeable or tolerable price by collusion, this price will have a strong tendency to persist. When some of the firms will be injured by a price change (which must often occur when their costs, market areas, and product structures differ), they will naturally oppose change. When all will gain from a price change, they will usually wish different amounts of change. Opening the question of prices may therefore lead to a pitched battle, and one can seldom be sure that things will stay in hand. Frequent resort to this area of political-economic determination must be avoided, so changes are postponed as long as possible. If they are postponed long enough, the need for them will pass.

Cost of Price Changes. The nature of the product and market may be such that small or frequent price changes cost more than they yield. There are costs of informing buyers of price changes: new lists, advertising, etc. If long-term contracts contain provisions that the buyer will receive any price reductions during the life of the contract, the short-run marginal revenue from a price reduction may be small or negative. Even when there are no contracts, price reductions may incur the ill will of early buyers of a "style" good.

4. A Comparison of the Implications of the Theories of Price Stability

There is no reason why the kinky demand curve cannot be joined with the other explanations of price stability. But there is also no purpose in adding it to the neoclassical theory unless it explains price behavior in areas where the other explanation is silent or contradicts the implications of the neoclassical theory in areas where both apply. For the empirical tests in Part II, the following differences between the implications of the kinky demand curve and the neoclassical theory will be used:

a) The kinky demand curve theory is silent on monopolies, for the essential feature of retaliation by rivals is absent. Should monopoly prices be rigid, the forces that explain this rigidity (say cost of price changes) may suffice to explain an equal amount of price rigidity under oligopoly. Unless the factors making for monopoly price rigidity do not operate under oligopoly, we can dispense with the kink unless greater rigidity is found in the oligopolistic industries.

b) The discontinuity in marginal revenue will disappear, and with it the reason for price rigidity, if formerly independent firms enter into collusion. The neoclassical theory emphasizes the administrative weaknesses in collusion, on the other hand, and this argues for greater price rigidity.

c) Prices will be relatively flexible with very few and with many firms in the industry, and relatively rigid with a moderate number of firms (say, five to ten), according to the kink theory. The neoclassical theories of oligopoly are neither outspoken nor unanimous on this question, but there is a general suggestion that price flexibility increases continuously with the number of firms.

d) When there is a dominant firm or set of firms (acting together) in the role of price leader, prices should be more flexible than if there is no price leader, on the kink theory. The neoclassical theory is silent on this point.

e) Given the number and size configuration of firms, prices should be more flexible the more heterogeneous the products, under the kinky demand curve theory. The neoclassical theory has no such implication.

II. EMPIRICAL TESTS OF THE THEORY

One may submit to empirical tests either the assumption of entrepreneurial behavior underlying the theory of the kinky demand curve or the implications of the kink for price behavior. The former alternative requires an analysis of the sequence of price changes made by oligopolists in an industry; the latter alternative can be developed by a comparison of observed price rigidity with that prophesied by the theory.

1. The Validity of the Assumption

If price increases of one firm are not followed by rivals, but price reductions are followed, the oligopolists have a basis in experience for believing that there is a kink in their demand curves. If price reductions are not followed by rivals, or price increases are as closely followed, no such objective basis for a kink exists.

The cigarette industry (with three large firms) offers a good example of the type of experience that would create a belief in the existence of a kink. On September 28, 1918, the American Tobacco Company raised the list price of Lucky Strikes from $6.00 to $7.50 per thousand, but the rivals continued to charge the lower price. The sales of Lucky Strikes fell 31 percent from September to November, when the price was reduced to $6.00, and continued to decline for several months. The later price history in this industry, however, is not such as to create a belief in the existence of a kink:

April 20, 1928: Reynolds (Camels) announced a reduction from $6.40 to $6 per thousand, effective April 21. American Tobacco followed on April 21 and Liggett and Myers on April 23.
October 4, 1929: Reynolds announced an increase to $6.40, effective October 5, and both rivals followed on that day.
June 23, 1931: Reynolds announced an increase to $6.85, effective June 24, and both rivals followed that day.
January 1, 1933: American Tobacco reduced its price to $6, effective January 3, and both rivals followed that day.
February 11, 1933: American Tobacco reduced its price to $5.50, and both rivals followed the same day.
January 9, 1934: Reynolds increased its price to $6.10, and both rivals followed the same day.[3]

These price changes, incidentally, were relatively larger than they appear: the manufacturer's net was smaller by a three-dollar tax and trade discounts.

The more complicated pattern of price changes for automobiles is illustrated for two leading firms in figure 4. The prices of the two firms changed at different dates and by different amounts, and price increases were more nearly simultaneous than price reductions. Price experience in this field should not lead a firm to believe that price reduc-

---

[3] Federal Trade Commission, *Agricultural Income Inquiry* (Washington, D. C., 1937), I, 448.

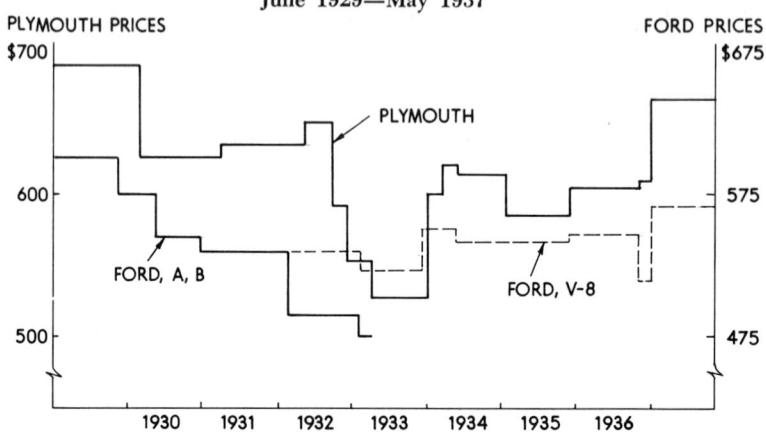

FIGURE 4
Factory Prices of Plymouth and Ford Four-Door Sedans, June 1929—May 1937

Source: Federal Trade Commission, *Report on Motor Vehicle Industry* (76th Cong., 1st sess., House Doc. 468 [Washington, D.C., 1940], pp. 894–95, 895.

tions will be matched immediately or wholly nor that in a period of business recovery rivals will fail to increase prices.

Six anthracite companies produced 62.5 percent of the aggregate output in 1930, and eight companies usually produce 70 to 80 percent of aggregate output. The prices of seven companies, for each size of coal, are listed (in very large type) every week in the *Coal and Coal Trade Journal*. These prices are identical and they almost invariably change n the same day. There is no evidence of a kink: prices change often in a marked, but by no means rigid, seasonal pattern.

Some direct evidence argues against the existence of a kink in the demand curve for steel produced by United States Steel: Bethelehem, for example, has faithfully followed the price increases. But the important evidence is indirect: there is no evidence of price rigidity within this industry. The official price lists and trade-journal quotations have been honored almost exclusively in the breach, and the transactions take place at prices that appear to be fairly sensitive to demand conditions. It is debatable whether the steel industry, with its price leader, should have rigid prices on the kinky demand curve theory, and it is also debatable whether the price leader often leads the industry in lowering prices.

Three firms produce most of the dynamite used in mining, quarrying, and construction in the United States. The wholesale prices for 40 percent ammonium dynamite, per 50-pound bag, moved as follows during the thirties:

18. The Kinky Oligopoly Demand Curve and Rigid Prices 291

February 27, 1933: All firms reduced the price from $12.25 to $10.50.
March 12, 1934: Du Pont and Hercules reduced the price to $10; Atlas followed 17 days later.
January 14, 1935: All firms increased the price to $10.50.
May 7, 1936: Du Pont and Hercules reduced the price to $9.50; Atlas followed the next day.
May 8, 1937: Du Pont and Atlas increased the price to $10.50; Hercules followed 3 days later.[4]

Again there is no empirical basis for believing the kink exists.

Socony-Vacuum and Atlantic Refining are two important sellers of gasoline in the Boston area. Aside from three periods in 1934 and 1935 when Socony-Vacuum's price was less than Atlantic's the prices of the two firms changed as shown in the accompanying list in the period 1929–37.

Simultaneous price changes	40
Increases	22
Opposite	1
Decreases	17
Delay in following price increases	12
Days	
1	9
2	1
3	1
4	1
Delay in following price decreases	10
Days	
1	1
2	3
3	1
10	1
21	1
23	1
28	1
47	1

It appears, then, that price increases are more nearly simultaneous than price decreases—the opposite of the kinky demand curve assumption.[5]

The most striking case of contradiction of the assumption of the theory, however, is provided by potash. On June 1, 1934, the American Potash and Chemical Corporation issued a price list that carried about

---

[4] I am indebted to Mr. Edward W. Proctor of Brown University for the information in this paragraph, which was secured by correspondence with Du Pont, Atlas Powder, and Hercules Powder. The three companies have headquarters in Wilmington; the latter two were created in 1912 by an antitrust action.

[5] I am indebted to Mr. Melvin D. Sargent of Brown University for the information on gasoline prices. The price quotations are from *Oil Price Handbook,* 1929–37 (Cleveland: National Petroleum News, 1938).

26 percent reductions from the prices in the previous year. The other firms failed to follow. On June 26 the lower prices were withdrawn, and the company lamented: "It was expected that other potash producers would likewise announce their prices in accordance with long prevailing custom. No such announcements have been forthcoming. Under the circumstances this company is compelled to withdraw the schedule of prices and terms referred to."

In these seven industries there is little historical basis for a firm to believe that price increases will not be matched by rivals and that price decreases will be matched. This indicates only that not every oligopoly has reason to believe that it has a kinky demand curve, and most adherents of the theory would readily concede this. On the other hand, here are seven industries in which the existence of the kinky demand curve is questionable—a list that is longer by seven than the list of industries for which a prima facie case has been made for the existence of the kink.

2. The Validity of the Implications

The kinky demand curve would prove to be an incorrect or unimportant construction if oligopoly prices were as flexible as monopoly and/or competitive prices. It is not possible to make a direct test for price rigidity, in part, because the prices at which the products of oligopolists sell are not generally known. For the purpose of such a test we need transaction prices; instead, we have quoted prices on a temporal basis, and they are deficient in two respects.

The first deficiency is notorious: Nominal price quotations may be stable although the prices at which sales are taking place fluctuate often and widely. The disparity may be due to a failure to take account of quality, "extras," freight, guaranties, discounts, etc.; or the price collector may be deceived merely to strengthen morale within the industry. The various studies of steel prices, already referred to, contain striking examples of this disparity, and others can be cited. We cannot infer that all nominally rigid prices are really flexible, but there is also very little evidence that they are really rigid.

The second deficiency is that published prices are on a temporal basis. If nine-tenths of annual sales occur at fluctuating prices within a month (as is true of some types of tobacco), and the remainder at a fixed price during the rest of the year, the nominal price rigidity for eleven months is trivial. With each price we ought to have the corresponding quantities sold: for a study of price rigidity, "April" would better be the fourth one-twelfth of the year's sales than the fourth month of the year.

Despite these shortcomings, a comparison of the implications of the kinky demand curve for price behavior with observable behavior (even if observable only in bulletins of the Bureau of Labor Statistics) has some value. If the theory cannot explain the pattern of rigidity of quoted prices among industries, there is no presumption that it would explain the pattern of transaction price rigidity among industries.

Our tests are made by comparing observed price rigidity in a group of industries with the relative rigidities forecast by the theory for industries with these market structures. We choose the period, June 1929, through May 1937, which embraces both a complete business cycle and the periods used in most empirical studies of price rigidity. We require three types of information:

1. *A list of oligopolistic industries.* The two basic criteria are (a) a fairly precise knowledge of the industry structure, and (b) continuous price and output series. The industries are described briefly in the Appendix.

2. *Some measure of expected price changes in the absence of restrictions on price changes.* Shifts in demand are of primary (although far from exclusive) importance, and we measure them roughly by the coefficient of variation of production (or some related series) in 1929, 1931, 1933, 1935, and 1937.

3. *A measure of price rigidity.* The basic test used is frequency of change in the monthly price quotations; for the theory under examination implies that there will be *no* changes—not merely that the price changes will be small. This test is supplemented by the coefficient of variation of monthly prices for two reasons. First, the price series have technical features that lead to more numerous price changes than actually occur. They are often averages of weekly quotations, and hence show two changes in the monthly averages when a price change occurs within a month. They are often averages of prices of several firms, and if each firm makes one price change the average can display as many changes as there are firms. Second, it can be argued that the kink is an exaggeration—that actually there is a sharp bend in the demand curve of the firm so that small price changes are what the theory prophesies. But frequent small price changes would still be improbable because of the cost of making price changes.

The basic data that are used in the tests are summarized in table 1. It will be observed that the two tests of price rigidity differ substantially: the coefficient of rank correlation between number of price changes and coefficient of variation of prices is $+.69$ for the nineteen oligopolies listed in Table 1.

Monopolies versus Oligopolies. The monopolies listed in table 1 are unsurpassed for price rigidity, despite the fact that their outputs varied more than those of most oligopolistic industries. This finding, which could be supported by more cases, suggests the possibility that

TABLE 1
Measures of Market Structure for 21 Products and of Their Price Flexibility and Output Variability, June 1929–May 1937

	Number of Firms in Industry	Price Leader	Price Flexibility — Number of Price Changes	Price Flexibility — Coefficient of Variation	Coefficient of Variation of Output
Oligopolies:					
Bananas	2	Yes	46	16	17
Boric acid	3	No	7	17	16
Cans	4	Yes	6	5	27
Cement	12	No	14	11	41
Copper	4	No	63	37	43
Gasoline*	11	No	84	22	16
Grain-binder	2	Yes	5	3	63
Linoleum	2	No?	12	9	30
Newsprint	9	No	6	16	16
Plaster	3	Yes	4	5	29
Plate Glass	2	No	8	13	34
Plows	6	No	25	6	50
Rayon	8	No	26	30	34
Soap	3	No	9	12	7
Starch	4	Yes	20	12	13
Sulphur	2	Yes	0	0	24
Tires	8	No	36	9	16
Tractors	4	Yes	6	6	76
Window glass	3	No	20	21	24
Monopolies:					
Aluminum	1	....	2	6	47
Nickel	1	....	0	0	35

* In Pennsylvania and Delaware.

the forces that make for price rigidity in monopolies are sufficiently strong to account for the lesser rigidity in oligopolies. One might argue that special factors are at work in monopoly, but the only two that come to mind are fear of governmental attention or action and the conservatism that comes with size. The former, however, is even more effective against oligopolies because of the importance of conspiracy in the antitrust laws, and the latter is presumably also a function of absolute size. It should be added that the neoclassical theory does not provide a satisfactory explanation for this extraordinary rigidity of monopoly prices.

According to the kink theory, there will be no kink when the oligopolists enter into explicit collusion; and hence prices would be expected to become more flexible. All empirical evidence contradicts this implication. Of our industries, at least two had periods of collusion. There was a combination of rayon producers to fix prices between October 21, 1931, and May 23, 1932: There were no price changes during this period, none in the preceding period of equal length, and four in the subsequent period of equal length. There are only two periods of protracted rigidity in the price series for copper: the first occurs under Copper Exporters (a Webb-Pomerene cartel), the second under N.R.A.

A number of examples are also provided by other industries. On August 30, 1932, the six important growers and canners of pineapple entered a ten-year agreement to restrict output and market through the Pineapple Producers Cooperative Association. In the 39 months preceding this date there were 17 price changes in canned pineapples; in the subsequent 57 months, 8 changes. Prices of typewriters were very rigid during a period when the four important producers were charged with colluding.

If the disappearance of the kink through collusion has a tendency to increase price flexibility, this tendency is completely submerged by the opposite effects of administrative limitations on cartel price policy.

The Number of Firms. The number of firms that enters into the formation of price policy is difficult to determine; a completely satisfactory determination would require knowledge of cross-elasticities of demand, the entrepreneur's knowledge and objectives, and similar data. As an unsatisfactory substitute for this information, we have been guided by two criteria: that sufficient firms be included to account for two thirds to three fourths of the output of the product and that the largest firm omitted from the count sell less than a tenth of the amount sold by the largest firm in the industry. Although these rules are arbitrary, they focus attention on relevant variables: if we do not include enough firms to account for a predominant share of output, the firms will not be able to control prices (attenuated oligopoly); and if we exclude firms large relative to those that are included, we may be omitting firms that are in the oligopolistic relationship. The precise number of firms, even by these arbitrary criteria, is in doubt in more than half the industries listed in table 1, but it was thought better to give a single number than a range that invites mechanical averaging to secure a single number.

Our expectation, on the kink theory, is that a very few rivals will have relatively flexible prices because the impossibility of maintaining a price lower than a rival's will be evident. On the other hand, with many rivals the fear that price cuts will be matched is reduced, and again the kink disappears. We do not test this latter implication because it is identical with that of the neoclassical theory.

If the data in table 1 are summarized by number of firms, we find a definite tendency for price flexibility to increase with the number of firms in the industry (table 2). The coefficient of rank correlation between number of firms and number of price changes is $+.41$, that between number of firms and coefficient of variation of prices is $+.31$. There is virtually no relationship between fluctuations of output and number of firms, nor is the strength or direction of relationship between number of firms and price flexibility affected if industries with price leaders are segregated. Thus there is a weak tendency for a greater number of firms to be associated with a greater frequency and amplitude of price changes, the contrary of the implications of the kinky demand curve.

TABLE 2

Number of Firms in Industry	Number of Industries in Sample	Price Flexibility — Number of Price Changes	Coefficient of Variation	Average of Coefficients of Variation of Outputs
2	5	14.2	8.2	33.6
3, 4	8	16.8	14.4	29.4
6, 8	3	29.0	15.0	33.3
9, 11, 12	3	34.7	16.3	24.3

Price Leadership. The term, "price leadership," is used in two very different senses in economic literature. In the one sense it refers to a dominant firm that sets the price, allows the minor firms to sell what they wish at this price (subject perhaps to nonprice competition), and supplies the remainder of the quantity demanded. In the other sense, price leadership refers to the existence of a firm that conventionally first announces price changes that are usually followed by the remainder of the industry, even though this firm may not occupy a dominant position. For example, International Paper was for a long period the price leader in newsprint although it produced less than one seventh of the output, and it was succeeded in this role by Great Northern, a smaller firm. This latter type of price leadership has been illuminatingly described by S. A. Swensrud of Standard Oil of Ohio:

> In any territory all suppliers are watching the same things. They watch the statistical position of the industry as a whole, that is, production of crude oil and gasoline, sales of petroleum products, and stocks of crude oil and gasoline. . . . They watch the ambitions of competitors to increase their share of the business in the territory. They gage their ambitions by reports of salesmen on price concessions to commercial customers, by observations of the amount of business done by trackside operators and sellers of unbranded and locally

18. The Kinky Oligopoly Demand Curve and Rigid Prices   297

branded gasoline, by the reports of salesmen as to competitive offers being made to dealers, and by reports of salesmen as to the extent of secret price cuts, discounts, and the like being offered by retailers. All these facts are constantly before local managers and central organizations.

Now suppose that secret price cutting by dealers in some particular area breaks out into the open in the form of a cut in the posted price because some dealer becomes disgusted with the uncertainty as to how much business he is losing to competitors granting secret discounts. As the openly admitted price reduction operates, the local officers of all suppliers are assailed with demands from dealers, relayed and in some instances emphasized by salesmen, for a reduction in the tank-wagon price. . . . The local manager of the leading marketer of course faces more demands than any other manager. He attempts to gage the permanence of the retail cut. Frequently local managers elect to make no change in the tank-wagon price. Ordinarily this decision springs from the conclusion that the local price war will soon run its course because it is not supported by weakness in basic markets. On other occasions the local manager concludes that the causes of the retail price cutting rest primarily on the availability of sufficient low-price gasoline so that the condition may be considered deep seated, and he therefore authorizes or recommends a local reduction in the tank-wagon price. . . . Thus the particular local territory becomes a subnormal territory, that is, one in which prices are out of line with those generally prevailing in the marketing area.

The major sales executives of all companies watch carefully the number and size of subnormal markets. . . . If the number of local price cuts increases, if the number and amount of secret concessions to commercial consumers increase, if the secret unpublicized concessions to dealers increase, it becomes more and more difficult to maintain the higher prices. . . . Finally, some company, usually the largest marketer in the territory, recognizes that the subnormal price has become the normal price and announces a general price reduction throughout the territory. . . .

In summary, therefore, the so-called price leadership in the petroleum industry boils down to the fact that some company in each territory most of the time bears the onus of formally recognizing current conditions. . . . In short, unless the so-called price leader accurately interprets basic conditions and local conditions, it soon will not be the leading marketer. Price leadership does not mean that the price leader can set prices to get the maximum profit and force other marketers to conform.[6]

The difference between these two types of price leadership from the viewpoint of the theory of kinky demand curves is basic. The dominant firm has no kink in its demand curve because rivals have no reason for charging a lower price: they are permitted to sell as much as they wish at the leader's price. The second type of leader, the barometric firm, commands adherence of rivals to his price only because, and to the extent that, his price reflects market conditions with tolerable

---

[6] W. S. Farish and J. H. Pew, *Review and Criticism . . . . of Monograph No. 39* ("T.N.E.C. Monographs," No. 39A [Washington, D.C., 1941]), pp. 47–49.

promptness. The widespread development of barometric firms is therefore explicitly a device to insure that there will be no kink, or that the kink will not prevent readjustment of price to important changes in cost or demand conditions.

Only the price leadership exercised by dominant firms, therefore, is relevant in testing the implication of the kinky demand curve theory that there will be no kink when there is price leadership. Accordingly, we classify as industries with price leaders only those in which there is a relatively large firm, producing, say, 40 percent of the output of the industry at a minimum, and more if the second largest firm is large (because otherwise the situation approaches classical duopoly). On this basis there are seven leaders among our nineteen industries (see table 1), and they are compared with the remaining twelve industries in table 3. Except for the number of price changes of two-firm industries (where bananas dominates the result), the prices of industries with price leaders are less flexible than those of industries without price leaders, despite the larger fluctuations of output of the former group. This is contrary to Sweezy's conjecture and is in keeping with the price rigidity found in monopolistic industries.

TABLE 3

	Industries with Leader	Industries without Leader
Two-firm industries:		
Number in sample	3	2
Average number of price changes	17	10
Average coefficient of variation of prices	6.3	11.0
Average coefficient of variation of outputs	34.7	32.0
Three- and four-firm industries:		
Number in sample	4	4
Average number of price changes	9	24.8
Average coefficient of variation of prices	7.0	21.8
Average coefficient of variation of outputs	36.2	22.5

Goodness of Substitutes. It is almost inherent in the methods of quotation of price statistics that most of the commodities examined in this article are nearly homogeneous. If products are rather heterogeneous, the significance of an average price becomes doubtful and the B.L.S. does not report it. Of our nineteen industries, only six have products whose prices appear to differ significantly and persistently among firms: soap, tractors, grain-binders, plows, tires, and linoleum. Their prices appear to change less often and less widely, on average, than those of homogeneous products as shown in table 4. It should be noted that we might, with some justification, have designated our monopolies (aluminum and nickel) as oligopolies with differentiated products.

TABLE 4

	Homogeneous Products	Heterogeneous Products
Number of products	13	6
Average number of price changes	23.4	15.5
Average coefficient of variation of prices	15.8	7.5
Average coefficient of variation of outputs	25.7	40.3

3. Conclusion

The empirical evidence reveals neither price experiences that would lead oligopolists to believe in the existence of a kink nor the pattern of changes of price quotations that the theory leads us to expect. The industries included in these tests are not very numerous, but they are sufficiently varied and important to suggest that similar adverse results would be secured from a larger sample.

But is this adverse conclusion really surprising? The kink is a barrier to changes in prices that will increase profits, and business is the collection of devices for circumventing barriers to profits. That this barrier should thwart businessmen—especially when it is wholly of their own fabrication—is unbelievable. There are many ways in which it can be circumvented. We have had occasion to notice the development of price leadership of the barometric variety as one device, and the old-fashioned solution of collusion is not always overlooked. In addition there is the whole range of tactical maneuvers that Neumann and Morgenstern's theory of games has uncovered. In the multidimensional real world there are many ways to teach a lesson, especially when the pupil is eager to learn.

19. Pricing Objectives in Large Companies*

ROBERT F. LANZILLOTTI

The sharpened interest in administered prices and inflation has focused attention once again on the inadequate state of knowledge of the price-making process. In particular, more empirical information is needed with respect to (a) the motivational hypothesis of the firm, i.e., the specific objectives upon which business firms base pricing decisions, and (b) the mechanics of price formulation. This article is addressed to the first problem; it will present some data on pricing objectives of the firm which have been developed in the course of a general study of pricing policies and practices of large industrial corporations.

I. SCOPE OF PRESENT STUDY

The procedure followed involved the postprandial variety of research. Lengthy interviews were undertaken with officials of twenty companies over periods ranging up to about one week in most cases.[1] A second set of interviews was undertaken several years later to fill in gaps in the data and to ascertain if any changes had been made in price policy since the original interviews. Pricing obviously being a sensitive area, some officials did not care to discuss their policies except in general terms, but these persons paved the way to individuals who were more willing and, in some cases, more aware of the practices employed and reasons for them.

The questions were designed to elicit information concerning: (1) whether any formal or informal commercial goals had been adopted by the corporation; (2) the procedures employed for implementing and

---

* *The American Economic Review*, vol. 48, no. 5 (December 1958), pp. 921-40.

[1] The companies were selected from among the largest corporations on the basis of the willingness of management to cooperate by permitting extensive interviews with top company officials: Aluminum Company of America, American Can, A & P Tea Company, du Pont, General Electric, General Foods, General Motors, Goodyear, Gulf, International Harvester, Johns-Manville, Kennecott Copper, Kroger, National Steel, Sears, Standard of Indiana, Standard Oil Company of New Jersey (ESSO), Swift, Union Carbide, and U.S. Steel.

evaluating the goal; (3) the techniques of price determination (i.e., the mechanics of pricing); and (4) the functions of pricing executives (individuals, committees, special divisions, etc.)—including extent of authority on price matters, kinds of materials utilized by them in setting prices, and relative weights given to various price-influencing factors. The portion of the information presented in this paper concerns, for each of the twenty companies, the principal and collateral objectives which are regarded as guiding pricing decisions.

The twenty corporations have one feature in common each of them is among the 200 largest industrial corporations, and over one half fall within the 100 largest industrials, in terms of assets. But they differ in a wide variety of ways from each other. Some, like Johns-Manville, U.S. Steel, International Harvester, and Union Carbide, dominate a whole industry and are price leaders. At the other extreme, there are companies like Swift and A & P which face so many competitors of various sizes and abilities that in spite of their absolute size they are very far from being able to make decisions for the market, and do not think of competition in terms of actions of one or a few competitors. The other companies fall between these extremes.

II. COMPANY GOALS: RATIONALIZATIONS OF PRICING METHODS

It is important to recognize at the outset that a company statement of policy is not necessarily an accurate representation of what that policy is.[2] Also, company rationalizations of pricing do not always represent the first step in planning price policy, and not all pricing of a given company is determined by the general company objective.

In a few cases officials insisted that there was little latitude in selecting a policy. However, for the most part, the prominence of each of the corporations in their respective industries makes most of them masters, to a significant degree, of their fates; hence, they are able to adjust pricing to the company's general goal.

Table 1 presents a summary of the principal and collateral pricing goals of the twenty companies as determined from interviews with their respective officials. The most typical pricing objectives cited were: (1) pricing to achieve a target return on investment; (2) stabilization of price and margin; (3) pricing to realize a target market share; and (4) pricing to meet or prevent competition. In most of the companies, one of the goals predominates, but as the listing of collateral objectives

---

[2] The following analysis is based upon the author's interpretations of views expressed orally by officials of the corporations concerned. Of course, neither the companies nor the author wish these views to be interpreted as necessarily the official views of the companies.

indicates, price making by any one firm was not always ruled by a single policy objective.[3]

III. PRICING TO ACHIEVE A TARGET RETURN ON INVESTMENT

Target return on investment was perhaps the most frequently mentioned of pricing goals.[4] About one half of the companies explicitly indicated that their pricing policies were based mainly upon the objective of realizing a particular rate of return on investment, in a given year, over the long haul, or both; but in most cases the target was regarded as a long-run objective. The average of the targets mentioned was 14 percent (after taxes); only one was below 10 percent; and the highest was 20 percent.

Under this pricing system both costs and profit goals are based not upon the volume level which is necessarily expected over a short period, but rather on standard volume; and the margins added to standard costs are designed to produce the target profit rate on investment, assuming standard volume to be the long-run average rate of plant utilization. In effect, the procedure is designed to prevent cyclical or shorter-run changes in volume or product-mix from unduly affecting price, with the expectation that the averaging of fluctuations in cost and demand over the business cycle will produce a particular rate of return on investment.

[3] To illustrate, in U.S. Steel out of a variety of divergent views mentioned, three rationales can be distinguished. (1) The first is the "ideal" price, i.e., pricing that is believed to be "just, fair, and economic," with reference to a general target of about 8 percent after taxes on stockholders' investment plus long-term debt. This strand is colored by the management's concept of the corporation as the industry leader vested with the responsibilities and subject to the inhibitions of a public utility. In fact, one official said he was "unable to understand or properly describe the Corporation's pricing policy except as something like the approach of the public utilities." (2) The second rationale centers on the difference between the "ideal" system and what officials regard as the "practical exigencies of steel price-making," i.e., limitations imposed upon price policy "by followers who are disloyal and prices of competitive products that get out of hand." (3) A third policy objective is essentially a target market share and is embodied in the motto: "to obtain as a minimum that share of all markets for the products sold, product by product, and territory by territory, to which the corporation's capacity in relation to the industry as the whole entitles it, and to accomplish this participation ratio through the exercise of judgment so as to insure the maximum continuing return on investment to the Corporation."

[4] Target-return pricing is defined as the building up of a price structure designed to provide such a return on capital employed for specific products, product groups, and divisions, as to yield a predetermined corporate average return. In most cases managements referred to stockholders' equity (net worth) plus long-term debt. Usually a standard cost system is used as a means of allocating fixed cost to various product divisions, with the standards premised on an assumed rate of production, typically about 70 percent to 80 percent of capacity, and an assumed product-mix as "normal."

Firms that were conscious of shooting for a particular target return on investment in their price policies were those that sold products in a market or markets more or less protected and in which the companies were leaders in their respective industries. In Alcoa, du Pont, Esso, General Electric, General Motors, International Harvester, Johns-Manville, Union Carbide, and U.S. Steel, the pricing of many products was hinged to this particular objective, and with the expectation of being able to reach the target return. Target-return pricing was usually tied in with a long-run view of prices, especially on new products where an "orderly" stepping down ("cascading") of prices was followed by du Pont, Union Carbide, and Alcoa.

A distinction should be made, however, between those companies that use target return on investment as a rigid and primary guide to pricing and those to whom it is more useful as a benchmark in an area where prices otherwise might be subject to wide and dangerous variations.[5]

Columns 4 and 5 of Table 1 show the average and range of the profit rates realized by the 20 companies over the 1947–1955 period. It will be noted that the target figures are *less* than the actual returns: for the nine-year period, the target-return companies earned on the average slightly more to substantially more than their indicated profit objective (International Harvester being the only exception). Also, there is a rather wide range in the profit rates for each company.

The actual profit rates may be higher than the targets for several possible reasons: (a) the targets may only be nominal or minimal goals; (b) the generally prosperous nature of the period in question in which company operations exceeded "Normal" or average percentage of capacity upon which costs and prices were determined; and (c) some of the companies have found that pricing on an historical-cost basis using the

---

[5] To illustrate, the use of rate-of-return pricing by U.S. Steel (likened by its officials to a public utility's "fair return"), apparently has not always been consistently followed. Under market pressure, U.S. Steel has at times had to accept much less than this return; when desperate for business, as in 1938, its competitors offered substantial concessions below published prices on almost every type of business. A very different situation shows up in the discussions of the target return by officials of General Motors. Instead of vainly attempting to realize its target in good years and bad, General Motors takes a long-run view and has sufficient assurance of its retention of a minimum market share to accept a diminished profit rate in years when diminished output bears a heavy unallocated overhead. Du Pont seems to assume its ability to realize a target return, especially in connection with new products. The same could be said for Union Carbide, the other chemical producer in the sample. International Harvester, although as vulnerable as U.S. Steel to wide swings in volume of business, appeared to be less worried by competitors' ability to jeopardize its prices based on long-run normal cost and return. Harvester was not able to maintain its prices during the great depression, and there is no evidence that such reductions as it made correspond merely to changes in direct cost. But in spite of frank admission by Harvester's management that the company was faced by tough competition, company officials appeared to be much more independent in their pricing policy than U.S. Steel.

TABLE 1
Pricing Goals of Twenty Large Industrial Corporations

Company	Principal Pricing Goal	Collateral Pricing Goals	Rate of Return on Investment (After Taxes) 1947-1955[a] Avg.	Range	Average Market Share[b]
Alcoa	20 percent on investment (before taxes); higher on new products [about 10 percent effective rate after taxes]	(a) "Promotive" policy on new products (b) Price stabilization	13.8	7.8-18.7	Pig & ingot, 37 percent; sheet, 46 percent; other fabrications, 62 percent[c]
American Can	Maintenance of market share	(a) "Meeting" competition (using cost of substitute product to determine price) (b) Price stabilization	11.6	9.6-14.7	Approx. 55 percent of all types of cans[d]
A & P	Increasing market share	"General promotive" (low-margin policy)	13.0	9.7-18.8	n.a.
du Pont	Target return on investment—no specific figure given	(a) Charging what traffic will bear over long run (b) Maximum return for new products—"life cycle" pricing	25.9	19.6-34.1	n.a.
Esso (Standard Oil of N.J.)	"Fair-return" target—no specific figure given	(a) Maintaining market share (b) Price stabilization	16.0	12.0-18.9	n.a.
General Electric	20 percent on investment (after taxes); 7 percent on sales (after taxes)	(a) Promotive policy on new products (b) Price stabilization on nationally advertised products	21.4	18.4-26.6	—[e]

Company	Goal		Rate of return (%)	Range	Notes
General Foods	33⅓ percent gross margin: ("⅓ to make, ⅓ to sell, and ⅓ for profit"); expectation of realizing target only on new products	(a) Full line of food products and novelties (b) Maintaining market share	12.2	8.9–15.7	n.a.
General Motors	20 percent on investment (after taxes)	Maintaining market share	26.0	19.9–37.0	50 percent of passenger automobiles[f]
Goodyear	"Meeting competitors"	(a) Maintain "position" (b) Price stabilization	13.3	9.2–16.1	n.a.
Gulf	Follow price of most important marketer in each area	(a) Maintain market share (b) Price stabilization	12.6	10.7–16.7	n.a.
International Harvester	10 percent on investment (after taxes)	Market share: ceiling of "less than a dominant share of any market"	8.9	4.9–11.9	Farm tractors, 28–30 percent; combines, cornpickers, tractor plows, cultivators, mowers, 20–30 percent; cotton pickers, 65 percent; light & light-heavy trucks, 5–18 percent; medium-heavy to heavy-heavy, 12–30 percent
Johns-Manville	Return on investment greater than last 15-year average (about 15 percent after taxes); higher target for new products	(a) Market share not greater than 20% (b) Stabilization of prices	14.9	10.7–19.6	n.a.
Kennecott	Stabilization of prices		16.0	9.3–20.9	n.a.

[a] Federal Trade Commission, *Rates of Return (After Taxes) for Identical Companies in Selected Manufacturing Industries, 1940, 1947–55*, Washington [1957], pp. 28–30, except for the following companies whose rates were computed by the author using the methods outlined in the Commission Report: A & P, General Foods, Gulf, International Harvester, Kroger, National Steel, Sears Roebuck, and Swift.

[b] As of 1955, unless otherwise indicated. Source of data is company mentioned unless noted otherwise.

[c] *U.S. v. Alcoa et al.*, "Stipulation Concerning Extension of Tables III–X," dated May 31, 1956, U.S. District Court for the Southern District of New York.

[d] As of 1939, U.S. Department of Justice, *Western Steel Plants and the Tin Plate Industry*, 79th Cong., 1st Sess., Doc. No. 95, p. L 1.

[e] The company states that on the average it aims at not more than 22 to 25 percent of any given market. Percentages for individual markets or products were not made available, but it is estimated that in some markets, e.g., electrical turbines, General Electric has 60 percent of the total market. Cf. Standard and Poor's, *Industry Surveys*, "Electrical-Electronic-Basic Analysis," Aug. 9, 1956, p. E 21.

[f] Federal Trade Commission, *Industrial Concentration and Product Diversification in the 1000 Largest Manufacturing Companies: 1950*, Washington, January 1957, p. 113.

TABLE 1
(*Continued*)

Company	Principal Pricing Goal	Collateral Pricing Goals	Rate of Return on Investment (After Taxes) 1947–1955[a] Avg.	Range	Average Market Share[b]
Kroger	Maintaining market share	Target return of 20 percent on investment before taxes[g]	12.1	9.7–16.1	n.a.
National Steel	Matching the market–price follower	Increase market share	12.1	7.0–17.4	5 percent
Sears Roebuck	Increasing market share (8–10 percent regarded as satisfactory share)	(a) Realization of traditional return on investment of 10–15 percent (after taxes) (b) General promotive (low margin) policy	5.4	1.6–10.7	5–10 percent average (twice as large a share in hard goods v. soft goods)
Standard Oil (Indiana)	Maintain market share	(a) Stabilize prices (b) Target-return on investment (none specified)	10.4	7.9–14.4	n.a.
Swift	Maintenance of market share in livestock buying and meat packing		6.9	3.9–11.1	Approximately 10 percent nationally[h]

	Target return on investment[i]				
Union Carbide	8 percent on investment (after taxes)	Promotive policy on new products; "life cycle" pricing on chemicals generally	19.2	13.5–24.3	—[j]
U.S. Steel		(a) Target market share of 30 percent (b) Stable price (c) Stable margin	10.3	7.6–14.8	Ingots and steel, 30 percent; blast furnaces, 34 percent; finished hot-rolled products, 35 percent; other steel mill products, 37 percent[k]

[g] Target return on investment evidently characterizes company policy as much as target market share. In making investment decisions the company is quoted as follows: "The Kroger Co. normally expected a return on investment of at least 20 percent before taxes." See McNair, Burnham, and Hersum, *Cases in Retail Management*, New York 1957, pp. 205 ff.

[h] This represents the average share of total industry shipments of the four largest firms in 1954. *Cf. Concentration in American Industry*, Report of Subcommittee on the Judiciary, U.S. Senate, 85th Cong., 1st Sess., Washington 1957, p. 315.

[i] In discussions with management officials various profit-return figures were mentioned, with considerable variation among divisions of the company. No official profit target percentage was given, but the author estimates the *average* profit objective for the corporation to be approximately 35 percent before taxes, or an effective rate after taxes of about 18 percent.

[j] Chemicals account for 30 percent of Carbide's sales, most of which are petrochemicals, a field that the company opened 30 years ago and still dominates; plastics account for 18%—the company sells 40% of the two most important plastics (vinyl and polyethylene); alloys and metals account for 26 percent of sales—top U.S. supplier of ferroalloys (e.g., chrome, silicon, manganese), and the biggest U.S. titanium producer; gases account for 14 percent of sales—estimated to sell 50 percent of oxygen in the U.S.; carbon, electrodes, and batteries account for 12 percent of sales—leading U.S. producer of electrodes, refractory carbon, and flashlights and batteries; and miscellaneous—leading operator of atomic energy plants, a leading producer of uranium, the largest U.S. producer of tungsten, and a major supplier of vanadium. *Cf.* "Union Carbide Enriches the Formula," *Fortune*, February, 1957, pp. 123 ff.; Standard and Poor's, *Industry Surveys*, "Chemicals-Basic Analysis," Dec. 20, 1956, p. C44; and "Annual Report for 1955 of the Union Carbide and Carbon Corporation."

[k] The range of the corporation's capacity as a percentage of total industry capacity varies from 15 percent to 54 percent, as of January 1957. For more detail see *Administered Prices, Hearings Before the Subcommittee on Antitrust and Monopoly of the Senate Committee on the Judiciary*, 85th Cong., 1st Sess., Pt. 2, *Steel*, Washington 1958, pp. 335–36.

company's traditional objective does not provide adequate capital for replacement and expansion at current costs, and accordingly have made allowance for this factor in their pricing formulas. Thus, if actual profit rates were "adjusted" for changes in the price level, the actual profits would more closely approximate the stated targets.

Whichever of the foregoing may be the most plausible explanation of the differences between actual and target profit rates, the findings indicate that a distinction must be made between year-to-year and secular profits objectives. The evidence on actual profit rates, taken in conjunction with the targets mentioned, raises serious questions whether these companies are attempting to "maximize" profits on a year-to-year basis. Moreover, to construe the actual profit rates (as against target rates) as evidence of a long-run maximization policy would require the demonstration that the prices charged were based not upon the targets but on what the firms believed they could get as a maximum. In any event, for this sample of firms and for this time period, there are limitations upon profit maximization as an adequate explanation of the relationships between profit targets and actual profit rates.

It is perhaps significant that there has been an increasing tendency in recent years for the companies in the sample to adopt some form of target-return pricing, either across-the-board or at least for particular products. In a few cases it was found that managements had developed a target-return policy between the time of the first interviews with the company and subsequent interviews several years later. The reasons for this movement toward greater use of a target-return approach are varied, but the major influences seem to have been: (a) an increasing awareness of and concern by managements for profit-capital-investment planning and capital budgeting, especially in the conglomerate company within which there is keen competition for capital funds by many units; (b) the desire for a good common denominator for evaluating the performance of divisions and product groups; (c) the wartime experiences of most of the companies with "cost-plus," "cost plus fixed fee," and other contractual arrangements with the government which focused attention on the return on investment; and (d) the emulation, by competitors and others, of successful large companies which have followed a target-return policy for many years (several companies in the sample mentioned that they had patterned their general target-return policy after that of du Pont or General Motors).

It is not surprising that new products above all are singled out for target-return pricing. Since they have no close rivals, new products are usually expected to produce a predetermined level of profit return on the investment represented.[6] No rigid length of time after the introduc-

---

[6] A good example of the kinds of data utilized in determining which new products will be added or which existing facilities will be expanded is one company's procedure

tion of the product was mentioned in which the target is supposed to be achieved. However, the time horizon is more short range vis-à-vis established products in the sense that the target payout is delineated from the start. Accordingly, pricing may take the form of "skimming" the market by exploiting the inelasticity of demand in different markets (maintaining a selected price as long as actual or potential competition permits), or a "penetration" price policy designed to develop mass markets via relatively low prices, provided a rapid expansion of the market and higher returns may be obtained later. This approach is most typical of du Pont, Union Carbide, Alcoa, International Harvester, and General Foods. The prescribed target for new products is usually higher than on established products, at least initially. But the target approach is not limited to unique products; it is also typical of low-unit-profit high-volume commodities (e.g., steel, aluminum, and chemicals).

Minimum target profit figures also are used by most of the companies as a basis for sloughing off products and in arriving at "make-or-buy" decisions. An exact minimum target figure was rarely mentioned, but good justifications were required of operating divisions or product departments when returns consistently fell below the corporate average. Not infrequently, officers made statements along the following lines: "If the average corporate return were, say, 20 percent and the return on investment for a particular item kept falling below 10 percent, it would be dropped unless (a) a good customer needs it in order to keep a full line, or (b) it is a by-product anyhow, and anything it brings in is really gravy."

A variety of explanations was given by the companies to justify the

---

for capital investment decisions. The request by a division for new funds shows (a) estimated new commitment (new fixed investment, working capital, and noncapital expenditures); (b) estimated total utilized investment (the new investment plus transfer of existing investment); (c) estimated annual operating income (i.e., income before depreciation, amortization, depletion, other income and income taxes); and (d) estimated return on investment income, which is shown both as a ratio to the new commitment and the total utilized investment. No figure was mentioned as a minimum return; normally new products were expected to return better than the corporate average, but expansions of existing facilities have been made on a projected return of no greater than 20 to 25 percent before taxes.

An elaborate check-off list is designed to insure attention to various aspects of projected demand, supply, costs, and competition. Of particular interest are such items as: capacities, captive requirements and future expansion plans of competitors; company's estimated market share before and after expansion; degree of diversity of customers; extent to which success of venture depends upon short- or long-term contracts; the effects of changes in tariff rates on competition from abroad; selling prices used for sales to other units of the company; shape of short-run unit cost curve; comparative cost position of competitors; the degree to which an alternative exists of either making or buying important intermediates; flexibility of proposed facilities for production of other products; the probabilities of obsolescence of the process or products; and the relative position of the company with respect to research and development, technical knowledge, labor supply, patents, and raw materials.

particular size of the profit target used as a guide in pricing decisions. The most frequently mentioned rationalizations included: (a) fair or reasonable return, (b) the traditional industry concept of fair return in relation to risk factors, (c) desire to equal or better the corporation average return over a recent period, (d) what the company felt it could get as a long-run matter, and (e) use of a specific profit target as a means of stabilizing industry prices. At least one of the foregoing, and most frequently the first, was mentioned by the companies interviewed, and in a few cases the entire list was offered as justification for the company profit goal.

This reinforces the observation made earlier that no one single objective or policy rules all price making in any given company. In fact, in many companies a close interrelationship exists among target-return pricing, desire to stabilize prices, and target market share (either a minimum or maximum objective); this is especially true of U.S. Steel, Union Carbide, and Johns-Manville. It would seem, however, that a target-return approach is ordinarily incompatible with a market-share policy; that is, if a company desires to expand its share of the market, it will be inclined to place less emphasis on rigid adherence to a predetermined target.

IV. STABILIZATION OF PRICE AND MARGIN

The drive for stabilized prices by companies like U.S. Steel, Alcoa, International Harvester, Johns-Manville, du Pont, and Union Carbide involves both expectation of proper reward for duty done, i.e., "proper" prices, and a sense of *noblesse oblige*. Having earned what is necessary during poor times to provide an adequate return, they will refrain from upping the price as high as the traffic will bear in prosperity. Likewise, in pricing different items in the product line, there will be an effort (sustained in individual cases by the pricing executive's conscience) to refrain from exploiting any item beyond the limit set by cost plus.

The distinction between target return on investment as a pricing philosophy and cost-plus pricing in the companies surveyed is difficult to define. Some of the companies that clearly employ the target-return-on-investment procedure in pricing new products—the area of most frequent use of target-return pricing—use cost-plus pricing for other products. The difference between the two rationalizations lies in the extent to which the company is willing to push beyond the limits of a pricing method to some average-return philosophy. According to a General Motors executive, the target plays a prominent role in the formulation of the cost-plus method. But in the case of International Harvester, U.S. Steel, A & P, Johns-Manville, Alcoa, or Union Carbide, it seems fair to say that the pricing executive sets the prices of many products on a cost-plus basis (except where competition precludes such action) without questioning the appropriateness of the traditional mark-up.

Cost plus, therefore, may be viewed as one step on the road to return-on-investment as a guide, or precept for price policy. But some firms never go any farther. The standard can be accepted as self-sufficient; just as the target return perhaps needs no modification to make it accord with profit maximization (with all the necessary qualifications). Pricing executives seldom look beyond the particular formula with which they are accustomed to justify their decisions. They differentiate between price policies according to the degree of control they exercise; but not by the gap between the price policy and an ideal of profit maximization. They appear as ready to accept cost plus at a reasonable volume as an ultimate standard for pricing as any other principle.

V. TARGET MARKET SHARE

A maximum or minimum share of the market as a determinant of pricing policy was listed almost as frequently, and seemed to govern policy almost to the same extent as target return on investment. Share of the market was ordinarily thought of in terms of a maximum, bearing witness to the power of the corporations interviewed. Being giants, they were careful to limit themselves; they apparently did not wish to gobble up any market they entered, unless it was one which they had created, like nylon, asbestos pipe, aluminum screen wire, cable products, or some synthetic chemical.

Hence, the target share of the market as a guide to pricing tended to be used for those products in which the firm did not, at the outset, enjoy a patent or innovative monopoly. Du Pont made no mention of shooting for a given share of the cellophane or nylon market, nor did Union Carbide in the Prestone market; Johns-Manville set no limit to its market share in specialized insulation materials; American Can was not thinking in terms of winning against stiff competition a moderate share of the market for vacuum packed cans; nor was Alcoa in the wire and cable market. But a General Electric official spoke at length of the company's policy of not exceeding 50 percent of any given market because it then would become too vulnerable to competition. Johns-Manville officials likewise indicated that product and sales development are geared to attaining a given percentage of the market for a product line. The company endeavors, executives indicated, to maintain the offensive, rather than to be subject to attack because of their large product share. The company felt strongly that 20 percent of competitive markets was the maximum share in which it was interested. This policy ruled in those areas where Johns-Manville was *not* the price leader. It stresses sales, service, and superior quality of its product in order to maintain its prices somewhat above those of its competitors. Apparently the program of reaching no more than a given market share and of moving ahead against competition does not find expression in price reductions.

It is not possible to reach any general conclusions from comparisons of target market-shares and actual share of business realized by the companies mentioning this as a policy for pricing purposes. This is due on the one hand to the unwillingness of the companies to specify in detail particular target-share percentages, and on the other to the lack of sufficiently detailed information for the companies in question, especially for the highly diversified firms. Patently, most of these companies have very significant proportions of national markets.[7]

VI. "MEETING OR MATCHING COMPETITION"

To some of the officials interviewed, the requirement that the product price "meet competition" appeared, at first glance, to preclude the existence of any pricing policy at all. Meeting competition according to their view cannot be regarded as a rationalization of action; it is the action itself.

The rationalization of this policy of meeting competition is far from elaborate; at first blush it is perhaps unnecessary. How can "meeting competition" be dignified as one out of several alternative guides to action? In chemicals, du Pont seems to apply a rule of thumb of adopting the going price in the markets for many standardized products where it never had or else had lost the leadership—e.g., carbon tetrachloride, hydrogen peroxide, disodium phosphate, nitric acid, hydrochloric acid, and various rubber chemicals. Moreover, in the case of many products selling on a freight-equalization basis, prices were not set at a high executive level; the pricing in many cases had not been reviewed for years, having been established beyond the ken of anyone now in the

---

[7] One interesting example of the connection between pricing (livestock bidding), market share, and investment policy is found in Swift. An analysis of livestock buying raises the question whether there is something of an understanding by the major packers of what constitutes their "normal share" of the animals sold in given public stockyards, which was the essence of the Department of Justice's complaint (1948) against Armour, Swift, Cudahy, and Wilson (since dismissed). It would seem that the relative constancy of the proportions of livestock purchased by the principal meat packers is traceable in large part to the short-run fixity of plant capacity, the desire to keep that plant operating at least up to a specific minimum level of utilization (governed partly by labor commitments), and the ever present threat that another packer may secure a larger share of the animals and the market for dressed meats. In view of these considerations, the percentages of animals purchased by the major packers would logically evidence substantial constancy over periods of weeks or months in given markets. But, unless this same approach is carried over into the planning of plant sizes in new locations (or enlargement of established plants), as well as the rate of utilization of these facilities, this would seem to be an insufficient explanation for the long-run stability of shares.

organization. Yet, even here there is perhaps more discretion than the officials are willing or accustomed to admit. In the pricing of neozone, du Pont was forced—though it had introduced the chemical—to change its price policy because of the tactics of competitors, who shifted the basing point. But need the matter have stopped there? Was there not a decision by du Pont to go no further than matching the Akron-based price? In many other cases du Pont undoubtedly could, if it chose, have altered the basing points or other features of the marketing of chemicals of which it produced more than an inconsequential market share.

In many cases the policy of meeting competition appears to be materially influenced by market-share psychology. Esso Standard, while going to great lengths to devise a cost-plus theory, has modified it when and where it seemed necessary or desirable. Standard of Indiana was even more specific in basing its policies on "meeting"—or forestalling—competition. Esso and, to a much lesser extent, Standard of Indiana refrained from publishing or trying to reduce to definiteness the details of the policy. A number of questions related to the companies' rationalizations are basic to understanding the functioning of the policy, for clearly neither company changed prices instantaneously when facing "competition": Did they meet the exact price charged, at the refinery or to the retail dealer? How long did a substandard price have to prevail before it could undermine a cost-plus price? Whose competitive price brought action? How were competitors rated in effectiveness? Answers to these questions are basic to an understanding of the policy. But the oil companies have not divulged the facts that would permit full and consistent treatment of the theory of "meeting competition" as seen by their managements.

It seems also that in some cases the companies are not simply meeting competition—they are preventing it. This appears to have been the purpose of A & P in localizing price cuts to make matters difficult for a competitive store on its opening day, or General Foods in reducing the price of Certo and Sur-Jell in the Northwest where rival pectins were strong. Standard of Indiana, a dominant seller not overfond of price wars, may easily justify meeting competition locally on the basis that the policy offers a permanent threat to potential price cutters.

In other cases, the companies are aware of specific competitive products whose prices must be matched by their own if volume is to be expanded. Union Carbide knew that its synthetic organic chemicals, like the various alcohols, had to meet or undersell the price of the natural products if the investment was ever to be returned. In other cases, where a standardized commodity—e.g., bakery flour, livestock feeds, and frozen fish sold by General Foods, flour by General Mills, or wholesale meat by Swift—is simply marketed at a price over which no firm, or even small group of firms, can have control, then pricing policy ceases to have meaning. The phrase "meeting competition" is either inapplicable or inaccurate, since there is no specific competition to meet—only the market price.

VII. OTHER RATIONALIZATIONS

There are other pegs on which managements hang pricing decisions. In view of American Can's undisputed (at least until 1954) leadership in the metal container industry, and its bargaining power vis-à-vis both its suppliers and customers, it is somewhat surprising that the company should not have set out an explicit pricing goal in terms of return on investment. The management seems to be more concerned with the assurance of funds for innovating research than any particular target return on investment, although the maintenance of its market share through its closing-machine leasing policy indirectly accomplishes the same objective. The company's pricing policy could be construed as "marginal" in the sense that it automatically (via its contracts) transmits to its customers increases or decreases in costs of materials (tin plate) or labor in the can factories. In turn, this adjustability in price seems to have had the effect of stabilizing American Can's margin, the price of its services as the owner of can-closing equipment and engineering services, and, at the same time, the price of cans throughout the canning season.

The companies cited many instances involving the need for resolution of conflicts of interest between integrated and nonintegrated firms and between established giants and newcomers, which displaced the usual bases for their pricing decisions. The Robinson-Patman and Sherman Acts, even when they have not been the basis for actions against the companies, were used as fundamental rationalizations of policy.

VIII. A COMPOSITE VIEW OF PRICING OBJECTIVES

Because it is big the large firm envisages itself as a part of a socially integrated group, with responsibilities for the whole pipeline and production (including full-line offerings) and associated distribution. They see themselves in a continuing relationship not only with their own distributors, but even with dealers and ultimate customers, and with their suppliers—even when the latter lacked, or especially when they lacked, the bargaining power of a larger firm. The market, in effect, is regarded as a creature of the firm, and the firm has the responsibility for preserving these relationships and perpetuating its own position.

The size of these firms also makes them an obvious target for antitrust suits, legislation, Congressional investigation, and similar restraining

19. Pricing Objectives in Large Companies

forces. To a certain extent, size thus entails a vulnerability and generates a sense of *noblesse oblige*. This is reinforced by the disposition of the government and the community generally to look on and appeal to these firms as "pattern setters" for industry generally; and in pricing they are expected to avoid taking full advantage of immediate profit opportunities. This attitude is perhaps most clearly expressed in the *Economic Report of the President* of January 1957, which stated:

Specifically, business and labor leadership have the responsibility to reach agreements on wages and other labor benefits that are fair to the rest of the community as well as to those persons immediately involved. . . . *And business must recognize the broad public interest in price set on their products and services.* (p. 3, italics added.)

From this point, it is an easy step to the position taken by the typical large firm that it is entitled to a "just price" and "fair return" on investment. In the case of some companies, like U.S. Steel, the resolution of conflicts of interest between integrated and nonintegrated firms, between established giants and newcomers, and between the pattern setter and the community generally, has modified company price policy to a point where even the managements have come to refer to it as akin to that of a public utility. This may be a logical development in cases where unpleasant experiences of cutthroat competition—especially in fairly standardized products like steel, copper, gasoline, and aluminum—have generated a disposition by management to avoid price changes except through periodic, thoroughly considered, and well-publicized alterations in recognized base prices. By relating price revisions to changes in direct costs (especially increases in wage costs), the firm avoids the annoyance to itself and its customers (who they claim vastly prefer stable prices) of frequent changes in price structure.

This desire for stabilized pricing, oftentimes described with a blanket adjective as "administered," usually implies that the company or companies set some kind of target to which their price policies conform. The price, according to this view, is under the control of one firm acting as the price leader of a group of firms that make policy for the industry. The contention of the business executives themselves is that an administered price, like the tank-wagon price of gasoline, far from being an independent creation of the price leader, is merely a device for approximating a market equilibrium. According to this view, there are so many possibilities of substitution of one product for another, or an off-brand for a name brand, that the limits of discretion are much narrower than is generally supposed. Administration of prices, officials contend, thus merely avoids the decision to use cutthroat competition—which itself would be another form of administered pricing; it also avoids temporary exploitation of shortages. Refraining from raising prices when a higher price is necessary to equate supply with demand, is also justified by management on the grounds that over the long run higher prices would disturb equilibrium by bringing unneeded capacity into the industry. But it is impossible to accept the conventional justification for leadership. It can masquerade as resulting in a genuine "equilibrium" only if the word is made equivalent to whatever is the decision of the leading firms.

The foregoing data, above all, make it clear that management's approach to pricing is based upon *planned* profits. The company proceeds on the assumption of the need for a certain amount of capital to undertake the investment in plant expansion and new facilities which are envisaged for the long haul in order to maintain and/or improve market position. In some cases, quite in contrast to the thinking of management before the second world war, this desire to hold position and to penetrate wider markets requires that capital investment should be planned with built-in excess capacity (this is best illustrated by the fact that prices are premised on the assumption of operating at a rate of 75 or 80 percent of capacity, which is assumed to be the long-run normal). In deciding upon which products and productive facilities will be added or expanded, the top-level corporation appropriations committee relies upon estimates of returns on utilized investment. The only way in which price policy can be viewed in such companies as these, with their wide variety of products and selling in a large number of different markets, is in terms of profits-investment ratios. This criterion serves as an effective guide for pricing decisions at divisional and departmental levels. If we are to speak of "administered" decisions in the large firm, it is perhaps more accurate to speak of administered *profits* rather than administered *prices*.

IX. CONCLUSIONS

The principal purpose of this paper has been to contribute to our knowledge of the actual process by which prices are formed in industry, with the expectation that the data will help in constructing a more realistic theory of the firm capable of yielding useful predictions of industrial price behavior. The general hypothesis which emerges is that (a) the large company has a fairly well-defined pricing goal that is related to a long-range profit horizon; (b) its management seeks—especially in multiproduct multimarket operations—a simultaneous decision with respect to price, cost, and product characteristics; and (c) its pricing formulas are handy devices for checking the internal consistency of the separate decisions as against the general company objective. Under this hypothesis no single theory of the firm—and certainly no single motivational hypothesis such as profit maximization—is likely to impose an unambiguous course of action for the firm for any given situation; nor will it provide a satisfactory basis for valid and useful predictions of price behavior.

In pursuit of price policies that will yield the maximum satisfaction of the company's community of interests, the findings show that one company will prefer stability, another will seek to expand its market share, or to engage in continuous discovery and preemption of new fields, while others will be content to meet competition, to satisfy a set target, or to aim at combinations and variations of these goals. It seems reasonable to conclude that the pricing policies are in almost every case equivalent to a company policy that represents an order of priorities and choice from among competing objectives rather than policies tested by any simple concept of profits maximization. Managerial specialists down the line are given a framework of requirements that must be met, while managers at the top, of course, are free to and do change these requirements to meet particular situations.

Another relevant aspect of the data for theoretical analysis is the conception of the market held by managements of large corporations. Individual products, markets, and pricing are not considered in isolation; the unit of decision making is the enterprise, and pricing and marketing strategies are viewed in this global context. Because of the tremendously complex joint-cost problems and the lack of knowledge of actual relationships between costs and output or sales, on the one hand, and the joint-revenue aspects of multiproduct companies, on the other, pricing is frequently done for product groups with an eye to the overall profit position of the company. This means that costing of products ends up as a result of price policy rather than the reverse. In view of the various external pressures on the company and the nature of the strategy of the enterprise, however, it is doubtful if prices would bear any closer relationship to actual costs were detailed cost data available to management. The incentive to realize target rates of profits for the long haul better suits the objectives of management-controlled companies than any desire to profiteer or to seek windfall profits.

It might appear that there are conflicts between the objectives of price leaders and price followers, e.g., between such companies as U.S. Steel and National Steel. Actually, however, it is a matter of leaders having fairly well-defined target objectives, whereas price followers evidently do not have independent targets. Their objective, especially where undifferentiated products make up the bulk of the product line, will be determined by the target set by the price leader. If the target is acceptable, the follower is content to hold a market share and will adjust price policy accordingly.

In more general cases, including differentiated product markets as well as undifferentiated, the extent to which companies—with the dimensions and diversification of those under discussion—serve as leaders or followers on individual products or product groups depends upon the profit-importance of a particular product in a given company's line, the nature of the product—whether a producer or a consumer good—and the size and degree of diversification of companies with which there are product overlaps. Moreover, the manner in which interfirm policies will be coordinated will depend upon the above factors as they bear upon particular products, plus the overall objectives of the enterprise as a unit and its general market strategy.

A further implication of the findings for the theory of the firm is the relationship found between price and investment decisions. The information on this aspect is limited, but nevertheless the setting of and attempt to follow specific target returns on investment are manifest at two separate levels of operations: short-run pricing and investment decisions. The investment decision presupposes a price (and usually a market-share) assumption, which, in turn, determines short-run price decisions thereafter. Thus, investment decisions in effect are themselves a form of pricing decision, and over time become an inherent part of price policy.

Finally, the general approach of these large corporations to price policy, and the attendant price behavior, raise some important issues for public policy. Their very size—both absolutely and relatively—permits the managements to select from among various alternative courses of action. This is a fairly clear manifestation of economic or market power. In partial reflection of this power, plus a variety of other reasons related to their size, vulnerability to public criticism, and potential antitrust action, these corporations tend to behave more and more like public utilities, especially the target-return-minded companies. To complicate the issue further, target-return pricing implies a policy of stable or rigid pricing, even though exceptions are found within particular product lines.

A crucial question raised by these facets of policy is: What is the net impact on economic growth and stability? More specifically, do target-return pricing, profits planning, and the attendant price behavior, tend to promote or inhibit stability and growth? Much more adequate empirical data on corporation objectives and detailed study of individual company pricing, profits, and investment planning over the course of economic fluctuations are needed before answers can be given to this question.

20. Pricing Practices in Small Firms[*]

W. WARREN HAYNES

An advance in our knowledge of the price mechanism requires research into the pricing practices of individual firms. Recent studies have extended our knowledge of pricing in large firms, though they leave considerable disagreement about the interpretation of the findings. Pricing in small firms is a relatively neglected subject. This article tries to fill in part of this gap by summarizing the main findings of an extensive study of small business pricing.

The study is based on intensive interviews with the officials of 88 small firms. The firms include 26 retailers, 6 wholesalers, 21 service outlets, 28 manufacturers, 5 garden or landscape nurseries, and 2 combined retail and service firms. The study makes use of an interview and case approach, rather than the structural questionnaire technique. It tries to overcome the tendency to accept the initial responses of company officials as valid by follow-up interviews at later dates and by cross-checks on the responses of different officials. Throughout an attempt is made to uncover the deeper reasons for the pricing decisions, rather than to take at face value all of the rationalizations of practice which are likely to show up in interviews.

Earlier studies suggest the central issues requiring investigation, which include: (1) The extent to which measurements of full cost influence pricing; (2) the extent to which demand considerations, including the policies of competitors, influence pricing; (3) the extent to which the observed pricing processes are consistent with the assumptions and tenets of "marginalism"; (4) the extent to which the objective of the firms is maximum profits or, alternatively, a target return or a mixture of other goals; (5) the flexibility of prices or price formulas with changing conditions over time, an issue closely related to that of marginalism but not synonymous with it; (6) the extent of trial and error in pricing; and (7) the appropriate classification of these firms by market structure, including the influence of market structure.

[*] *The Southern Economic Journal,* vol. 30, no. 4 (April 1964), pp. 315–24.

The procedure in the sections that follow is to start with the simpler issues: ones that can be answered clearly and directly on the basis of the interviews. These include the fairly objective questions about flexibility and the use of full cost. It will then be possible to move on to the more complex and nebulous issues, such as pricing objectives and the relevance of marginalism.

I. FULL-COST PRICING—A VARIETY OF DEFINITIONS

A recent and generally excellent book on managerial economics expresses a widely accepted view that cost-plus pricing (or full-cost pricing) predominates in business.[1] The present study lends no support to this conclusion as far as small business is concerned. In fact, the conclusion is the opposite: full-cost pricing is the exception rather than the rule.

Part of the disagreement on full-cost pricing arises from a general failure to define what it means. At least three different definitions are implicit in the literature, with frequent unannounced shifts from one definition to the next.

(1) An extreme definition restricts full-cost pricing to the addition of a single predetermined markup to full cost for all goods sold. This definition recognizes a variety of measurements of cost, such as the cost accountant's "standard cost" (including unit overhead at some arbitrary percentage of capacity), or recent actual costs, or costs expected in the coming year. In any case the method for determining cost is specified in advance and a predetermined markup is added.

(2) Multi-product firms predominate even in small business; among the 88 firms in our study, 84 produce or sell a variety of products or services. They apply different markups on different segments of their business. A second definition of full-cost pricing recognizes this use of different markups on various sectors of the business. The base for the markup is standard, actual, or estimated cost, and the markups are still predetermined, but the markups vary from sector to sector within the firm. The pricing procedure is mechanical. Some discussions suggest that the markups are based on what is considered "fair" or "reasonable," which may in turn reflect what is customary. Ethical considerations are claimed to compete with profit maximization as an influence on pricing. One of the issues in this article is the extent of such mechanical markups on full costs in small business.

(3) A third definition of full-cost pricing recognizes not only the cross-sectional flexibility of markups just cited but also flexibility over time. Many firms do use full cost as the starting point but vary the markups according to current competitive conditions.

---

[1] Milton H. Spencer and Louis Siegelman, *Managerial Economics* (Homewood, Ill.: Richard D. Irwin, 1959), p. 292.

The question is whether we can still call the procedure full-cost pricing when such flexibilities appear. It is clear that in such cases pricing is no longer mechanical and that it no longer is in such direct opposition to the usual descriptions of economic theory. The literature on pricing appears to have been caught up in an unusual amount of semantic confusion, with the use of the label "full-cost pricing" to cover a wide variety of behavior.

The findings in the present study include at most six cases of the first variety of full-cost pricing (a single markup on full cost). They include a few additional cases of the second variety (in which several sets of markups are applied to cost with little flexibility over time). They include many more cases in the third category, which permits both cross-sectional flexibility and flexibility over time. And they include still other cases which do not fit into the full-cost framework at all. The findings do not lend much support to the view that full-cost pricing prevails.

Full Cost plus a Single Predetermined Markup

Most of the six companies in this category raise some difficult points of interpretation. The best way to proceed is to cite cases from the study.

Three printing companies represent extreme full-cost pricing. Leading firms and trade associations in the printing industry have long attempted to restrict "cutthroat competition" through a wider adoption of full-cost pricing. Many printers have developed strong ethical objections to "chiseling" by those who shade price. But, as we shall see, it does not follow that all printers, or even a majority of them, avoid flexible pricing practices. The three cases cited here are the ones showing the strictest adherence to formula pricing and the greatest reluctance to make exceptions.

The first of these three printing firms operates on a policy of full cost plus 20 percent. Not all of the costs are determined internally; frequently cost information is obtained from nationally published manuals which provide regional cost data, though these are checked against company experience. The company tries to avoid price differentials, except to the extent that large quantities result in lower unit costs. But even in this extreme case of full-cost pricing, there are exceptions. For example, the markup is only 10 percent on envelopes and letterheads. The management claims that it would lose this business at higher prices and that it must maintain such lines as a service to customers. Thus the elasticity of demand does have an influence on the outcome; cost measurements do not tell the entire story.

Another printing firm follows an even more rigid full-cost policy. Paradoxically, demand conditions appear to account for the ability to apply the cost formula rigidly. The firm has a reputation for high quality and dependability, which protects the firm from competition. The management states that, "We are slightly higher in price and could go even higher because of the quality of work," indicating that in management's view the demand is inelastic.

The last printer in this category is such an extreme full-cost advocate that he insists that he would charge more in poor times because of the higher overhead per unit. So far he has not faced the decline in demand that would test his implausible policy. This printer is not, however, a consistent full-cost pricer, for he lowers markups to secure new customers or in submitting competitive bids.

One furniture company appears to be a rigid practitioner of full-cost pricing. Oddly this company sells its product on a bidding basis that would seem to preclude rigid formulas. But "bidding" in this case does not mean competitive bidding. Certain large customers seek a bid from this single furniture firm and will accept the bid if it is within reason. Again demand conditions (the firm has no difficulty in selling capacity production) help account for the rigid policies, though it is not completely clear why the firm does not try to exploit the favorable demand more fully.

Space limitations preclude outlining the other two cases in detail. It is even doubtful that the last case (a flour mill) belongs in this category, for the management sets prices at full cost (material cost, plus labor cost, plus a percentage for overhead, plus a predetermined percent for profit) only if the resultant price is not more than 5 percent above the general market.

In conclusion, "pure" cases of full-cost pricing are hard to find. Most of the firms cited in this section do make exceptions, though mechanical formulas have an influence on their pricing. Evidence of demand influences appears in even these most extreme cost oriented cases.

Full Cost plus Multiple Predetermined Markups

We are now concerned with a special variety of multiple markups on full cost: predetermined markups which are changed only occasionally over time. We are dealing with cross-sectional flexibility with little flexibility over time. Only five firms fit into this category.

One concrete contractor quotes its prices to builders on a straight full-cost basis. This firm is a member of a cartel and full-cost pricing is apparently a device to limit price competition. In fact, on other lines of business (to homeowners, for example), the firm varies price according to conditions of demand and in slack times even goes below full cost on small jobs to keep employees busy.

A machine shop applies different markups on various categories of work. Its manager makes no price reductions to induce sales or reduce inventories in poor times, nor does he take advantage of the semimonopoly position in the locality on bronze and stainless steel. The fact that he uses round number prices (20¢, 25¢, and 30¢ per pound rather than 18¢, 23¢, 27¢, etc.) is not a fundamental departure from his cost-plus policy, though it does result in variable markups.

Three of the automobile repair shop managers claim not to adjust markups to temporary demand shifts or to differences in demand elasticities (a fourth case to be discussed later is a clear case of flexibility in markups carefully adjusted to conditions). These officials refer to national manuals on parts prices that provide predetermined markups; they also obtain standard times from such manuals for charging labor time and overhead. We suspect that further research might reveal a more flexible use of price discrimination than the managers indicated in the interviews. But even if we give the benefit of the doubt to full-cost pricing, we still find that cases of mechanical formula pricing are the exception.

Full Cost plus Variable Markups

At least twenty of the cases fall clearly into the third category. These firms compute full costs but are flexible in adapting the markups on these costs to circumstances. Space permits a discussion of only a few cases.

At one end of a continuum of flexibility is a printing company which would prefer to avoid flexibility but which makes exceptions. This firm computes hourly machine rates based on estimated total labor costs and allocated overhead. It combines these rates with time standards to arrive at the cost of the particular job. Management uses "judgment" in modifying these estimates and also in determining the appropriate markup; this judgment reflects demand conditions, including the current volume of business. This firm recognizes five classes of business, each with a different markup, but does not always adhere to this schedule of markups. The managers of this printing firm resist lowering the markups below those appropriate to the class of business. They believe that reduced prices: (1) depress market prices and reduce industry profits; (2) offend regular customers; (3) may, when used to fill in idle times, result in a bunching of business that slows down the flow of regular price business; and (4) represent an unethical form of competition. But the management is perfectly willing to provide extra services (such as free editorial time) at no cost.

Managers of most of the other firms are less hesitant about varying markups as conditions warrant. In several furniture firms, for example, they recognize the need to vary markups as the market shifts or as a particular line loses popularity. One automobile repair shop owner exhibits great ingenuity in varying markups on cost, giving better deals to classes of customers who seek competitive bids and who watch the estimates carefully. A builder charges a lower markup when business is slow, reflecting the lower "opportunity cost" of his time in slack periods. A chemicals manufacturer tries to charge what "the traffic will bear," taking into account the volumes he can sell at various prices. On old established products he follows the prices of his large competitors rather closely. On new products he charges higher prices reflecting his greater monopoly control.

Further illustrations would merely elaborate on the flexible way in which firms use full-cost data. The evidence does not suggest the mechanical use of formulas but instead considerable judgment in determining what markups should be added to the costs.

II. FULL COSTS AS REFERENCE OR RESISTANCE POINTS

The argument so far is clear: The use of full costs may be mechanical in a minority of small firms but permits considerable flexibility in pricing in the great majority of cases. Past literature on the subject has too readily leaped to the conclusion that the mere use of full costs must mean that pricing is cost oriented. The majority of the cases in this study (and, despite the limitations of the sample, no doubt the majority of small firms in the nation) adjust prices to the changing market environment. Can we conclude from these cases that full costs are irrelevant? Such a position is too extreme. Many (probably most) firms are influenced by their measures of full cost. In some firms full costs act as resistance points below which prices are not permitted to fall.

Again a few cases will illustrate. One dry cleaning and laundry firm was willing to cut price to full cost but refused to accept business below that point. The firm had an opportunity to obtain some additional business from motels in the slow summer months at prices below full cost but above incremental cost. Incremental reasoning indicated to the research worker that the business would add profits, without any undesirable repercussions in the future. But management believed that accepting business below full cost was unsound, though it could give no reasons for this position.

Similarly, a sheet metal and air conditioning contractor lost a large order (one that management agreed on incremental grounds would add to profits), because of a refusal to go below full cost. The management is willing to shade the markup and even lower salaries to get business, but is not willing to extend flexibility below the full cost limit.

The interviews suggest that even when full cost is not a rigid floor, as it is in the two cases just cited, it exerts an influence on pricing.

The fact that firms so frequently refer to full costs, that they claim to price on the basis of those costs even when follow-up interviews suggest other, perhaps more powerful, influences must mean that the cost estimates have an influence on the final outcome.

It should be mentioned that a firm with hundreds of pricing decisions may find reference to full cost a convenience simplification. The manager may use a great deal of analysis or judgment in determining the markup on one class of goods, but once he has made the decision on markup he can apply it mechanically to individual items. Much of the confusion about pricing results from a failure to recognize two steps in pricing: (1) Determination of a schedule of markups with attention to market forces as well as tradition. (2) Application of full-cost formulas to individual items.

The difficulty in much of the literature on pricing is an insistence on a black-or-white dichotomy between firms that use full costs mechanically and those that follow the precepts of marginalism. The majority of small firms undoubtedly fall somewhere between, demonstrating flexibility when the penalties of rigidity are great but finding it "comfortable" to lean back on a simple formula when the pressure is off. Furthermore, even the mechanical use of full costs may not be in conflict with marginalism when it represents a reasonable adaptation to the market structure or to uncertainty.

III. PRICING WITH NO REFERENCE TO FULL COST

Almost half of the companies made no use of full-cost computations at all. While the nature of the sample would warn against taking the exact number of such firms too seriously, there can be no doubt that a wide segment of small business lies completely outside the scope of the full-cost pricing category.

The most important reason for ignoring costs in these firms is that "cost" is sometimes difficult to determine. Five garden and landscaping firms illustrate this point. What is the cost of growing a particular shrub? An answer would require an estimate of the rental on the land, some way of dealing with the uncertainties of the weather and growing conditions, methods for allocating not only the fixed costs but also most of the labor cost (most small nurseries do not keep records of times spent on different products). There is a problem of determining the opportunity cost of funds tied up in plants with different growth rates. Such complications explain the usual nurseryman's skepticism of cost accounting.

How do nurserymen actually price their product? The small sample of firms in this study suggests that they are influenced by pricing in nearby regions, but only in a loose way. They do not make a systematic study of competitive prices but do become concerned if their prices get too far out of line with competition. They give attention to the rate at which items are selling, raising prices (usually once a year) when supplies appear to be short and reducing prices on items no longer in great demand by the public.

Similarly, the owner of a radio and television repair firm pays little attention to costs, either full or incremental, in his pricing. He charges a flat $3.00 per service call (plus transportation) and a flat $6.50 as a "bench charge" (for work done in the shop), with only rare modifications. The owner apparently believes that higher prices would lead to substantial losses of goodwill and volume. He believes that variations in charges according to time would also lead to reductions in goodwill and volume.

Other cases support this picture of managers with only rough conceptions of demands and costs, who as a result price on a trial-and-error basis. Many such firms give their primary quantitative attention to the income statement, which apparently plays a homeostatic role in motivating price changes. If profits are "unsatisfactory" according to some predetermined profit expectations or aspirations, the managers seek price changes that will improve profits. But the accounting data in such firms provide little help in determining which prices should be changed or the direction of price change.

The cases of retailers and wholesalers are consistent with the preceding discussion. As is well known, retailers use wholesale costs rather than full costs as reference points in pricing. Information on such costs is readily available, which suggests that the convenience of data sources is a major influence on pricing. But small retailers usually do not apply single markups. They vary markups according to demand and competitive conditions, with some unsystematic attention to turnover and the relative costs of storing and selling different items. Some retailers are more rigid than others about varying markups over time. One firm in the study never marks down goods, but sometimes "gives a price" on an item that has occupied shelf space too long. More frequently, however, retailers resort to special sales and variations in price to meet changing conditions.

Retailers are heavily influenced by the price suggestions of manufacturers or wholesalers, indicating that they prefer to escape decision making on prices when that is possible. Such practices do not mean that market conditions are ignored but rather that the analysis of those conditions is made by the manufacturers or wholesalers rather than by the individual retailers.

Our limited sample suggests that stores catering to low or medium income customers pay more attention to price policy and are more flexible in pricing. Any fuller discussion of retailers would take us beyond the scope of the present article. The main point here is that the behavior of both retailers and wholesalers clearly contradicts generalizations about the prevalence of full-cost pricing.

IV. SYSTEMATIC SURVEYS AND USES OF TRIAL AND ERROR

Among the firms that ignore full costs are a few that make systematic studies of cost-volume-profit relationships before embarking on price changes. A new bowling alley, for example, selected prices that had succeeded in similar size alleys in other towns of the same size. The owners made a careful study of rates and volumes in other firms and did not make their decision until they completed a thorough study. They selected rates on the high side of the range in the belief that the trend of feasible prices was upward. In view of the thoroughness of their market analysis, it is not surprising that the actual revenues came close to the forecasts.

Some firms use their trial-and-error experiences with past price changes as guides to future pricing. A billboard firm with branches in several towns has learned from experience the point at which the customers rebel against high prices and curtail their advertising. The owners of this firm believe that other billboard firms are unnecessarily cautious in raising prices; they have found that prices above the "going rate" are viable.

Most small firms do not study past experience systematically. But many of them are influenced by the results of past experience, through direct observation of effects of price changes or by noting the results on the income statements. It would be difficult to quantify the influence of trial and error and past experience, for this influence is subtle and gradual. Most managers would assert that they have learned from past experience, but they are understandably inarticulate on the details of the learning process.

V. MARGINALISM IN PRICING

We are now ready to discuss a central issue on pricing. We have rejected the full-cost theory most strongly antithetical to the traditional marginalist theory. But does this means that our firms are careful practitioners of marginalism? The answer depends on one's definition of marginalism.

Machlup's definition of marginalism—one which is widely accepted by economists—is broad enough to encompass most of the behavior found in this study. Machlup quite correctly notes that subjective estimates of cost and revenues, guesses and hunches, and trial and error, are perfectly consistent with marginalism. A business man who follows the precepts of marginalism does not mathematically determine the exact point at which marginal revenue equals marginal cost. He will take into account the long run as well as the immediate effects of his pricing decisions. Marginalism is even consistent with the temporary application of mechanical markups to full costs if the costs of the flexible adaptation to market forces are too large. Thus this study is generally consistent with Machlup's views.

Unless we define marginalism so broadly as to include nonpecuniary considerations as well as profit maximization and to rationalize any attention to full costs as merely a convenient shortcut, we must conclude that some of the evidence is inconsistent with the complete adherence to marginalism. In some of the cases, ethical considerations come into conflict with the attainment of greater profits. In other cases, the reference to full costs seems clearly to interfere with the application of full-scale marginal reasoning. Some managers are confused by overhead allocations in making decisions which appear inconsistent with marginalism.

Several economists have critized Machlup's definition as too broad—almost so broad as to rationalize any kind of behavior. Machlup's views are correct if we are interested in "certain strong tendencies in a representative sector of business." But if we wish to study individual firm decisions we must be interested in the divergencies in behavior as well as in its general tendencies. The findings in this study suggest that most managers do price in the direction indicated by marginalism up to a point, but that they do let full costs and inertia deflect them from a full application of marginal reasoning. Thus the study supports the conclusion that most small business pricing practices are characterized by "partial marginalism."

The use of modern marginalist methods of accounting might be taken as evidence of marginalism in pricing. Such methods are rare in small business. The closest our cases come to this is the use of projected income statements and break-even charts in the billboard and bowling alley firms. In most small firms there is little formal attention to formal breakdowns of fixed and variable costs. No firms in the sample make any quantitative estimates of "marginal revenue" or "elasticity of demand."

The findings are in contrast to Earley's conclusions on large firms. Earley concluded that his special sample of "excellently managed" large firms did use cost breakdowns and marginal accounting in the direction suggested by theory. In our small firms most of the marginalist behavior that exists is instead a result of subjective evaluations based on past experience.

The evidence favorable to the partial or subjective marginalism position is: (1) the approach of some managers by trial and error to prices that lead to higher profits; (2) the widespread practice of varying markups on different demand elasticities; (3) the flexibility of markups over time, with apparent adjustments to changing market conditions; and (4) the probability that imitative pricing and the adherence to suggested prices permit firms to apply prices which outsiders have found consistent with demand conditions. Such evidence does not support a conclusion that marginalism is applied precisely or consistently; it does suggest that a great deal of pricing behavior is working in a marginalist direction.

VI. PROFIT OBJECTIVES

The traditional assumption in economics is that the objective of pricing is profit maximization. Some economists assert that this assumption was never intended as a description of actual behavior but rather as a useful simplification permitting prediction. A somewhat different view in a recent empirical study is that firms establish profit targets and administer their prices to achieve such targets. The extent of profit maximization in actual pricing is still unknown.

Small firm managers do not refer to "target returns" to the extent observers have found in big business. The management of one furniture firm does stress a profit target, but this is expressed as a percentage of *revenue* rather than of *investment*. Most managers who indicate the influence of targets appear to think in terms of absolute income rather than percentages.

On the other hand, many of the managers express views that indicate that profit maximization is not their sole aim. A college-owned retail store which limited profits out of respect to the financial needs of students is hardly representative, since it has special reasons for placing itself in a "public utility" category. But other cases suggest a wide variation in the drive for profits, with some managers expressing a strong sense of responsibility to the community and ethical objections to charging what the market will bear, and other managers demonstrating an intense striving for higher profits. The cynic may rationalize all limitations on short run profit taking as aimed at building up good will that will contribute to long-run profits; but the interviews suggest that many managers are directly influenced by ethical considerations and by their desire to retain a position of respect in their communities. The manager of one gift shop, for example, would certainly have found it difficult to apply the rather subtle techniques of price discrimination found in an auto repair shop. She would have retired from business rather than resort to such practices. The personal ethics and objectives of individuals are influential in pricing, blunting the force of profit maximization.

VII. CONCLUSIONS

Space does not permit a full discussion of all of the findings of this study. For example, it is possible to give only a hint of the conclusions on the influence of market structures on the pricing behavior of these firms. Economic theory indicates that the pricing behavior of firms depends on the structure of competition; policies that would be appropriate in a highly competitive industry would not, for example, be suitable in oligopoly or monopoly. The present study finds considerable evidence of adaptation to the market structure. The findings indicate that oligopoly is rather common in small business. The cases also include examples of local market monopoly and collusion. It is inappropriate to assume that small business necessarily reflects either pure competition or monopolistic competition of the multi-firm variety.

Much of the stress on full cost is an attempt in oligopolistic industries to reduce the risks of price competition. If competitors can agree on similar accounting systems based on full costs, they may achieve flexibility of prices with changing costs without the danger that competitors will not follow. Some of our cases illustrate such a pattern of pricing. It is strange, however, that the printing industry, which seems so clearly *not* to be an oligopoly (over 80 firms in one locality covered by the study), should place so much stress on full costs. The attempt to limit price competition through adoption of common accounting and pricing formulas would appear to be doomed in such an industry in which the rewards of price shading would often exceed any possible dangers of direct price retaliation.

The major conclusion of this study is that partial marginalism prevails in small business. There is little evidence of the rigid adherence to mechanical full-cost pricing indicated by some previous studies, but costs do serve as resistance or reference points. In general, markups are flexible, with variations among products and variations over time. Inertia and the desire to reduce the volume of decision making reduces the frequency of changes in prices.

The fact that small firm pricing behavior falls between the extremes of mechanical full-cost formulas and the exact application of the precepts of marginalism is not surprising. It would be strange if managers consistently ignored opportunities for increased profits afforded by varying margins from product to product and from time to time. But, in view of uncertainties and the obstacles to measurement, it is impossible for these managers to determine the precise point at which marginal revenues equal marginal costs. Some managers are motivated not only by the desire for profits but also by other personal goals, including maintenance of their status in their communities. The result is a complex pattern of considerable inertia, unsystematic experimentation, widespread price discrimination or at least the tailoring of markups to demand, subjective estimates of market conditions, imitation of the pricing behavior of other firms, and the acceptance of the suggested prices of manufacturers, spotted with a few cases of collusion and a few cases of careful market analysis. The theorist of course prefers a simple explanation of behavior to such a description of diversity and variability. It remains to be seen whether simple generalizations based on the assumption of profit maximization and complete certainty at one extreme or based on the assumption of mechanical full-cost formulas at the other extreme can take the place of more eclectic explanations that come closer to the diversity of observed pricing practices.

21. Variations on the Full-Cost Theme*

MARTIN HOWE

INTRODUCTION

It would now seem to be adequately confirmed that the majority of firms, in fixing prices for a coming planning period, add a margin to average cost, invariably average total cost, at least at the first stage.

This average cost is the cost of an historical rate of output, or of forecast output for the period, or of a "normal," i.e., average over several periods, output. Virtually all investigators state that the precise magnitude of the margin is determined by considerations of reasonableness, convention and history, and that the application of a predetermined margin to cost in price fixing is designed (explicitly or implicitly) to yield a certain ratio of profit to sales or cost; the firm's profit objective is visualised in this specific form. But, as is well known, the profit that will in fact result from the "full-cost" pricing procedure is indeterminate. This is because the sales that will result at the costed price are a function of the firm's demand schedule, which is largely unknown and therefore rarely fully taken into account. These sales will (along with changes in stocks) determine the firm's actual costs of production in the period. These may differ from the costs on which the costed price was based, first because of the existence of fixed costs, and second, because of the possibility that marginal costs may not be constant in relation to output. Consequently, the profits that result may diverge from the objective, in terms of a desired profit on sales. Further, they will also diverge, except by pure chance, from the maximum profits that could have been earned in the period.

It is on the basis of the latter divergence that economists have been critical of the full-cost pricing procedure. In many areas of business decision, techniques have been developed in recent years which make possible optimal solutions in situations too complex for the marginal analysis. Most progress has been made in production decision making

---

* *The Manchester School of Economics and Social Studies,* vol. 32, no. 1 (January 1964), pp. 43–57.

with the aid, in particular, of the techniques of mathematical programming.

Unfortunately, most of the techniques are not very helpful in pricing decisions, where the use of "ritualistic" rather than optimising methods continues, therefore, to predominate. It is interesting, however, that alternative "rituals," often considered by business to be superior to the original full-cost pricing procedure, have been developed. These developments reflect merely dissatisfaction with the profit on sales form of specific profit objective and not dissatisfaction with specific profit objectives themselves compared with maximising profit objectives. It is the purpose of this paper to discuss two of the new versions, rate of return pricing and conversion cost pricing, and to show that they are not immune from the usual criticisms of full cost. Before doing so, however, it may be useful to comment briefly on the preference for specific profit objectives.

The use of specific (or target) profit objectives seems to be of relatively recent origin, being particularly associated with the growth of budgeting in business. Whatever the scope and detail of the budgeting, a prerequisite is an objective. Control through budgeting can only be effective if it is fully appreciated to what end the means of control are directed. It is increasingly argued that the basis of budgeting should be planned *profit* rather than planned *sales*, i.e., that the budgeting procedure should begin with a profit objective rather than end up, after the forecasting of sales and of cost, with a residual of profit. More than 95 percent of 424 firms covered in an American survey directed their annual budgets at a specific profit objective. The essence of budgeting is comparison. In a world of uncertainty, the form of the objective is therefore more likely to be a specified target than unspecified maxima. The latter gives no guide to the firms as to the necessity for action, in order to achieve the objective, as the future unfolds.

OBJECTIONS TO THE PROFIT-ON-SALES OBJECTIVE

Those who favour rate of return pricing consider that the ultimate measure of profitability is the ratio of profit to capital employed. They object to the traditional criterion on the grounds that it ignores the capital investment involved in the activity of the firm the profitability of which is being measured. Two firms, or products, may each earn the same profit on sales, but one may utilise a greater capital investment than the other in achieving that profit. The current cost of the investment involved is rarely fully included in the accountant's costs. Thus, accountants have traditionally refused to accept interest on capital as a legitimate cost: interest on capital will usually be excluded either as a "notional" cost or as a "wholly financial charge." Capital costs are therefore restricted to depreciation. Moreover, depreciation charges are generally based on the historical cost of the assets concerned. It is partly because of these limitations that objectives in the form of profit on sales have been replaced in a growing number of firms by rate of return on capital employed objectives. Rate of return objectives are generally made up of several separately planned elements. Interest on capital ("normal profit"), which the accountant does not consider a cost, may be an explicit element in the profit objective, its magnitude varying with the risk attached to the activity concerned. This basic element in the planned rate of return is rarely related precisely to the firm's current cost of capital, but rather to a "reasonable" long run rate of dividend on the equity capital. The common attitude of managements to dividends expresses no obvious relation between dividends and current profits, but treats dividends rather as the residual after the decision as to the volume of internal financing of growth has been taken. Finally, an important element in planned profit is often an appropriation not to finance future growth, but to cover the enhanced replacement cost of fixed assets over a period of rising prices, an appropriation made necessary by the accountant's adherence to the historical cost basis in calculating depreciation charges.

The various elements of planned profit are revealed in firms' statements of their objectives, e.g. "to earn such a profit as will produce a reasonable return on the capital employed in the business having regard to the risks involved. This return must not only adequate reward shareholders in the firm in the form of dividends, but provide a sufficient margin to cover unforeseen events and to allow of future development. The assets of the business must be maintained intact and controlled expansion pursued." Such statements have an unquestionable aura of reasonableness. But there can be little doubt that the objectives are also influenced by what firms think that they will be able to earn in the long run. In particular, careful consideration is likely to be given to the requirement that the objective should not be set so high that new competition is encouraged. Nonetheless, there is unlikely to be any detailed analysis of market factors in arriving at the objective. Thus, the objective is generally intended to refer to a long period covering several normal planning periods and, often, to the several products of a firm. The objective constitutes a long-run, and often broad bench mark, and variations from it are likely to indicate the strength or otherwise of market forces in any shorter period. When the objective has been fixed in the form of a specified return on capital employed, profit margins to be used in price fixing designed to yield the desired return are derived. The manner in which the margins are derived is discussed in the next section of this paper.

Those who favour the conversion cost variant of full-cost pricing argue that profit should be related to the "value added" by the firm, not to total cost, sales or capital employed. Profit, it is argued, is earned not by the mere passage of raw materials through a plant but by the conversion of the raw material into something more valuable. Since conversion costs are fully included in the accountant's costs (in contrast to capital costs) margins can be readily designed with the aim of providing the profit that the price fixer has in mind, in a manner very similar to that used in traditional full cost pricing.

The use of conversion-cost pricing has been reported in cotton spinning, nonferrous metals, aluminum casting and gold and silver refining. However, this method, though frequently *advocated* by businessmen, is certainly far less widely used than rate-of-return pricing. This is one reason why explicit statement of a firm's profit objective in terms of a desired profit on conversion cost is rare. Another reason is the fact that the method is generally used, and advocated, for pricing the various products of a multi-product firm where, for example, the proportion of raw material to total costs differs widely from product to product. In this use, conversion cost pricing may be associated with an overall profit objective formulated in different terms, e.g., a rate of return on capital employed objective, when the method becomes a variation of rate-of-return pricing. This should become clearer in the course of the next section.

DERIVATION OF MARGINS

A planned objective of profit in relation to capital employed cannot be incorporated into product prices planned for the same period if the usual full-cost approach to pricing is employed. The margin added to cost must specifically be related to the capital employed in producing the product. This may be accomplished in broad or in detailed fashion.

Taking the broad method first, suppose that the objective is to earn 15 percent on capital employed and that the capital employed (which may be capital employed at the beginning, at the end, or on average over the period) is estimated to be £1,000,000. A suspicion of circular reasoning may immediately be noted, since the capital employed, particularly the working capital, will be affected by the prices fixed and the sales that result. However, the charge of circular reasoning applies with even greater force to the next step in which *total* costs are estimated before selling prices are decided; either the costs appropriate to a normal, or standard, rate of utilisation of capital and to a normal, or standard, product mix (where more than one product is produced), or, alternatively, the costs appropriate to the forecast rate of utilization and product mix on the basis of *existing* prices, adjusted in respect of any changes that it is considered will *obviously* occur in the coming period, are used. Suppose total costs estimated in one or other of these ways are £1,500,000.[1] If the

[1] Sometimes total factory costs only are estimated, and estimated selling and administration costs therefore included in the profit margin.

profit objective is to be achieved, the margin applied to total cost in pricing is apparently $\frac{150{,}000}{1{,}500{,}000} \times 100$ i.e. 10 percent, apparently giving a sales revenue of £1,650,000. But again there has been circular reasoning; the prices derived in this way with no explicit consideration of demand may not yield the assumed, or forecast, product mix and rate of capacity utilisation which underlay the whole procedure.

It was probably this kind of approach that Heflebower had in mind when he said that "whether a profit is considered as a cost, or as part of a gross margin added to part or all of direct costs, or is specifically included as a net margin above costs, a return on investment is part of the pricing formula." This seems an overstatement. It is true that there are cases where the use of return on investment in pricing is long established, but empirical studies show that businessmen frequently justify their margins as "reasonable" or "conventional" with no explicit reference to a planned return on capital. The appreciation that this return can be improved by accelerating the turnover of capital, *which therefore should be formally taken into account in pricing*, as well as by varying the profit margin, is undoubtedly of recent origin. Certainly of recent origin is the detailed alternative to the broad method. It takes account of the fact that the capital employed in producing each of the various products of a multi-product firm may differ. With this method, a relationship between capital employed and product cost is calculated product by product. Separation of fixed and working capital is generally suggested on the grounds that it is inappropriate that the desired return on total capital employed should conceal, say, an excessive return on the fixed capital and a meagre return on the investment in working capital. Further, it is the cost of working capital which is particularly ignored in conventional product costs.

Taking fixed capital first, the usual procedure is to assign fixed capital to products, to relate the assigned capital to product cost, or to some element of product cost, and hence to apply to cost such a margin as will yield the desired return on capital. The major problem is the allocation of fixed capital which is common to more than one product. Invariably, the approach is the same as that used for the allocation of common (overhead) costs; thus, manufacturing overhead is distributed on various bases to departments of the factory or to cost centers (subdepartments or groups of similar machines or workers). Thus, if the rent of buildings is distributed in proportion to floor space, the fixed capital, buildings, will be distributed likewise; if the costs of a service department, say the canteen, are distributed to production departments or cost centers in proportion to the numbers employed, then the fixed capital employed in that department will be distributed in the same way, and so on. When the fixed capital has been distributed, it can be allocated to units of the various products passing through the various production departments or cost centers, as overhead costs are allocated, by means of some allocation base, which is generally a common input factor such as machine hours, labor hours, labor cost, etc. This may be clarified by using a published example:[2]

If the fixed assets distributed to two machines (cost centers) producing a certain product are £132,000 and £330,000 respectively, if the capacity of the two machines is 2,000 and 1,000 units of product per hour respectively, if sales are estimated at 3,300 M. units per annum, and if the desired return on capital employed is 25 percent then the fixed investment is converted into a factor per M. units of product, thus:

	Total Fixed Assets Employed	Machine Hours Worked per Annum	Fixed Assets Employed per Machine Hour	Product Output per Machine Hour	Fixed Assets Employed
Machine 1	£132,000 ÷	1,650 =	£80 ÷	2,000 =	£40
Machine 2	£330,000 ÷	3,300 =	£100 ÷	1,000 =	£100

The margin to be applied to total cost (or to any element of cost) in order to yield 25 percent on the fixed investment required by this product is therefore £140 × 0.25 = £35. If desired, the margin can be expressed as a percentage of say total cost:

$$\frac{\text{Total Fixed Assets Employed}}{\text{Unit Total Cost}} \times \frac{25}{100} \times 100 = \text{Desired Margin.}$$

A number of points can be made about this procedure:

1. The distribution of common fixed assets to cost centers is inevitably arbitrary. The distribution of assets invested in ancillary and service facilities is likely to be particularly unsatisfactory.

2. The allocation of the distributed fixed assets to units of products is also inevitably arbitrary. Each allocation base will produce a different end result. While the machine-hour base used above may be the most sophisticated, it is no less arbitrary than any other.

3. In important respects, the costs and asset values used in the calculation are likely to fall short of the requirement that future costs only be used in decision making. To take just one example, the value put on the fixed assets is likely to be their written down book value, i.e. historical cost less accumulated depreciation. With changing prices, this is unlikely to reflect real or present values. When prices are rising, this may be recognised in fixing the profit objective, which will be higher,

---
[2] H. O. Edson, "The Application of Return on Investment to Product Pricing," *The Controller,* vol. 27, 1959, p. 464.

therefore, than when prices are stable. But the addition to be included in the objective is likely to be decided unsystematically, and this treatment is therefore less satisfactory than that which values fixed assets at replacement cost and also computes depreciation on this basis.[3]

4. As with any pricing method which begins with unit costs which include an allocated portion of fixed costs, the procedure rests on circular reasoning: in order to carry through the allocation designed to yield the selling prices, a certain volume of sales has to be assumed which will, however, obviously depend upon the prices fixed. Firms cannot fix their sales and their prices independently,[4] the one is partly a function of the other.

Fewer allocation problems are involved in the treatment of working capital.[5] This rests upon: (1) the rate of turnover of the particular element of working capital, and (2) the selection of factors through which cost and investment are to be related (comparable to the machine-hour input factor used above with respect to fixed capital). The first depends upon policy regarding sales terms, minimum stock levels and cash holdings, etc. Continuing the same example:

If for a certain product sales terms are 30 days net, if policy is to maintain 20 days cash requirements at all times and to maintain finished goods stocks on a 3 months turnover basis, and raw materials and work in progress on a 1 month turnover basis, then:

Element of Current Investment	Period	Cost Factor Percent of Yr.	Factor	Ratio of Factor to Total Cost (percent)		Conversion to Annual Investment Factor
Cash	20 days	5.5 ×	Cash cost	90	=	4.95
Debtors	1 month	8.33 ×	Selling price	125	=	10.41
Finished Goods	3 months	25.0 ×	Factory cost	80	=	20.0
Raw Materials and Work in Progress	1 month	8.33 ×	Factory cost	80	=	6.66
Current Investment of Total Cost						42.02

The margin to be applied to total cost in order to yield 25 percent on current investment required by this produce is therefore

$$\frac{42}{100} \times \frac{25}{100} \times \text{Total Cost.}$$

---

[3] There are also tax implications in recouping the enhanced cost of replacement out of profits.

[4] Except in such special circumstances as an excess of demand over supply at present prices, when the firm could decide how much it will produce, and therefore sell, at those prices.

[5] Although allocation is not entirely avoided, e.g. in a multi-product firm, cash will have to be allocated, perhaps in proportion to sales value.

Again, there are a number of points:

1. The procedure consists in relating to total cost those elements of product cost which are linked to the different elements of working capital investment, e.g., factory cost to investment in stocks where the latter are valued at factory cost. The procedure is therefore dependent upon the method of allocating overhead costs that is employed and each method will yield a different estimate of the current investment involved by a product.

2. Circular reasoning is obviously involved. For example, in the treatment of the debtors element, the factor used is selling price, the fixing of which is, however, the object of the whole exercise. Edson remarks that the 25 percent margin applied in his example is a "knowledgeable approximation," so that again, the apparent precision of the method proves illusory. The prices eventually fixed, and the sales that result, will also affect the firm's investment in stocks—particularly finished goods stock—and, of course, total cost.

With conversion cost pricing, where the objective is in terms of a desired profit on conversion cost margins are derived quite simply. Once the desired profit has been decided upon, the indicated margin can be applied immediately. The sum of productive wages and overhead costs is invariably used in practice as an approximation to conversion cost. The following simple example, using the same approximation, contrasts the conversion and full cost methods.

Full-Cost Pricing			*Conversion Cost Pricing*		
Product	A	B	Product	A	B
Unit Cost:			Unit Cost:		
Raw Material	£30	£60	Raw Material	£30	£60
Productive Wages	25	10	Productive Wages	25	10
Overheads	35	20	Overheads	35	20
Total Cost:	90	90	Total Cost:	90	90
Net Profit, say 10 Percent on Total Cost	9	9	Net Profit, say 20 Percent on Conversion Cost	12	6
Selling Price	£99	£99		£102	£96

It is argued that the prices suggested by the conversion method avoid the distortion introduced in full-cost pricing by the inclusion of raw material costs. But since the passage of materials through the plant is not entirely costless, resort is sometimes made to two margins, the profit margin itself, to be applied to conversion cost, and a smaller margin to be applied to raw material cost solely to cover handling costs, cost of capital locked up in materials, etc. However, this margin is not explicitly related to the investment in raw material stocks by taking account of the rate of stock turnover, and, as with full cost, the method overlooks part of the cost of fixed investment by restricting capital costs to depreciation.

Where the profit objective is in terms of a return on capital employed, the margin added to conversion cost must specifically be related to the capital employed in producing the product. Again this may be carried through in broad or in detailed fashion. The procedures will be identical with those of rate of return pricing discussed above except that margins will be applied to conversion cost, not total cost.

It is clear that the criticisms of circular reasoning and arbitrary cost allocations apply also to conversion cost pricing. Both variations of full cost, rate of return and conversion cost pricing, endeavour to fix prices and sales independently.[6] Both ignore demand considerations. There is clearly contained in both a notion of what profit *ought* to be. One businessman argued with the writer that firms should be *guaranteed* a "steady and satisfactory return on capital employed" and another declared that "two products with the same conversion cost *deserve* to earn the same profit." But firms do not have complete control over the several factors that determine the amount of profit earned. These include the preferences of consumers, the degree of competition and the degree of uncertainty faced by the firm. By adding a particular margin to average cost, a firm cannot guarantee that it will thereby earn a certain rate of return on the capital employed or on conversion cost, however the margin is derived. For the price that is fixed will result in some unique volume of sales which may be greater or smaller than that assumed in the pricing calculations: only if (by chance) the assumed volume is in fact achieved will the desired return actually be earned.[7]

If a more than satisfactory return *is* earned, this is an indication that in the long run more resources should flow into the industry, if a less than satisfactory return, that resources should move out. But the profit return can only properly act in this way if prices have been fixed in the optimal fashion. If they have been fixed by a full-cost method which more or less ignores market considerations, the return could perhaps be improved by adjusting prices. Thus, in figure 1 below *AC* is the firm's Average Cost Curve (it does not much matter for this purpose what the shape of the curve is, but the point is more

---

[6] A good example is a pricing formula suggested in a well-known book on management accounting, I. W. Keller, *Management Accounting for Profit Control* (New York, 1956), p. 396:

$$\text{Net Unit Price} = \frac{C + \dfrac{RF}{V}}{1 - RW}$$

where C = total cost, R = percentage return desired on capital employed, F = fixed portion of capital employed, W = variable portion of capital employed, expressed as a percentage of sales volume, V = annual sales volume, in units.

[7] And if factor prices and efficiency etc. turn out as assumed in the cost calculations.

easily made with U-shaped curves). *MC* is the Marginal Cost Curve, *D* the Sales (Demand) Curve and *MR* the Marginal Revenue Curve: all these curves are likely to be imperfectly known to the businessman (therefore they are drawn in broken line). *ON* is the normal rate of output (as used in the accounting) and *RN* therefore the normal cost of production. Adding a margin, say *PR*, to *RN* gives a selling price *PN*. With the (unknown) demand curve in the position *DD*, if price *PN* is maintained, *OM* can in fact be sold, but at that level of output, profit cannot be maximized. Although the price, *PN*, covers average cost, *SM*, the firm would be unwise to produce *OM* units of output. Its price is inappropriate: fixing the optimum price according to the marginal analysis would yield a maximum profit over and above the normal profit included in costs. It should charge *XZ* per unit on *OZ* units. Its profit would be *XY* per unit. This may or may not represent a return equal to the firm's objective. Yet it is the maximum return that the firm can possibly earn, and it is the adequacy of *this* return that a firm needs to consider.

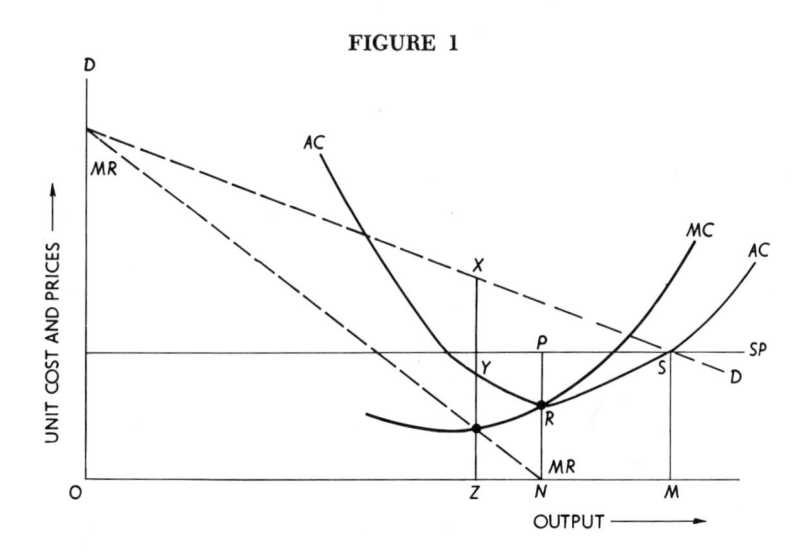

FIGURE 1

CONCLUSION

Recent developments in accounting are of considerable interest to economists. Some of these developments bring accounting much closer to the ideals of economic theory. But in pricing little progress has been made, largely because of the paucity of demand information. Although various new cost approaches to pricing, which may appear both sophisticated and reasonable, have been developed, they pay as little explicit attention to demand as does the original full cost principle. They are therefore equally open to criticism. But it should be pointed out that the prices obtained from these approaches are likely to be considered only desirable or target prices. If short run demand conditions are such that the price arrived at is obviously inappropriate, then it is likely to be adjusted. There cannot be the same objection to the use of cost-based pricing procedures in establishing bench mark prices as in fixing actual, transaction prices. Nevertheless, the one use may well have (perhaps unconscious) influences upon the other; for example, it may lead to a reluctance to reduce price below total cost in any circumstances, or a reluctance to raise prices above the costed level unless, perhaps, some other price has had to be fixed below the target.

22. Decentralization and Intracompany Pricing*

JOEL DEAN

A fist fight determined the intracompany transfer price policy that is in effect today in a major oil company. The issue was the price at which gasoline would be transferred from the company's refinery to its marketing division.

The present heads of the marketing and refining divisions had witnessed, as loyal but appalled lieutenants, the contentious negotiations that culminated in the fight. When these two men came to power, they vowed that their interdivisional bliss would not be marred by any arguments over intracompany pricing as had their predecessors'.

They finally found a way to abolish all disagreements about transfer prices. They simply abolished transfer prices, thereby neatly tossing out the baby with the bath.

This story—now a legend in the company—is probably exaggerated, and other events certainly contributed to the outcome. It does show, however, that the subject of this article is as disturbing as it is important: how and where to set prices for products that are transferred between divisions (or between different stages of processing and distribution) inside the company.

Our industrial system today is made up of many large, multiple-product, multiple-process companies. As these companies have expanded, it has become generally recognized that the best pattern for their managerial organization is one of decentralization, i.e., the setting up of more or less autonomous operating divisions within a company. But as more and more large companies have adopted divisional management, they are finding that splitting up the enterprise and exhorting the divisional managers to go out and set new records for sales or production does not always accomplish the hoped-for profit results.

For an autonomous division to be an economically effective operation it has to follow the same basic rules of behavior as any independent firm competing with other independent firms, and this implies the same

---

Harvard Business Review, vol. 33, no. 4 (July–August 1955), pp. 65–74.

standards of economic performance—profits. But how can it be held to such competitive standards if there is no sound way to price the products transferred to it or from it in dealings with other divisions of the same company? In that question lies the reason for this article.

In the course of the discussion I shall set forth these propositions:

1. Transfer prices are necessary for almost all large companies. Trying to do without them sacrifices so much that it is no solution at all.

2. Intracompany price discrimination is not good business, either for the individual firm or for private enterprise in general.

3. There is need of a new system of transfer prices featuring: (a) profit centers with operational independence, access to sources and markets, separable costs and revenues, and profit intent; and (b) competitive pricing among these centers.

4. Such a system has many advantages. It brings the division manager's interests closer to those of top management, provides a more accurate basis for evaluating his performance, bulwarks his independence, and gives him sound guides in purchasing and marketing decisions.

5. Most present systems for setting transfer prices, by contrast, are inadequate. They employ economically indefensible methods, keep many losses hidden, and have a negative value in the making of management decisions.

6. It takes time and patience to install competitive transfer prices. Top management will find it easier to make the change-over if it follows eight rules drawn from experience. Executives should also be prepared to meet certain objections which critics are likely to raise.

Here are the key terms which will be used in this article:

1. *Transfers* mean movement of product between operating units within the largest policy-making unit, regardless of corporate entities; for example, transfers within the family of companies represented by the Cities Service Oil Company or among the divisions of E. I. du Pont de Nemours & Company.

2. *Product* should be broadly interpreted to include raw materials, components, and intermediate products and services as well as finished products in the ordinary sense of the word.

3. *Transfer price* refers to the net value per unit that records the transaction for the purposes of operating statements.

NEED FOR SOUND PRICING

Why not do the same as the oil company referred to at the start of this article and dispose of the problem altogether by doing without transfer prices?

For most large firms this solution sacrifices too much. Our peace-loving oil company, for example, now has no knowledge of the cost and value of gasoline, heating oil, and other petroleum products at various stages of refining and distribution. Abolition of transfer prices prevents meaningful measurement of the profits of individual operating units, such as refineries, bulk stations, and service stations. It also prevents accurate estimates of the earnings on proposed capital projects. Basic decisions about market penetration, pricing, and capital expenditures are cut adrift from cost or profit moorings. And there is no way to assure that the product will be directed where it will produce the highest dollar return, either as among alternative processes or as among alternative channels and levels of distribution. The river of crude oil suddenly goes underground, disappearing from cost and profit sight, and comes up again at the consumers' doors, millions of processing dollars away.

So abolition is not the right answer. In fact, it is no solution at all. For most large companies the problem remains one of learning how to live with and use some system of internal transfer pricing. Sound transfer prices give division managers both the economic basis and the incentives for correct decisions. They also provide top management with profit and loss information indispensable for evaluation of the results of complex combinations of managerial skills and diverse facilities. Thus correct transfer prices are the basis for attaining the managerial decentralization sought by virtually every large American enterprise today.

One reason this has been such a problem for executives is that no systematic analysis of transfer pricing principles and policies has, so far as I can learn, heretofore been available.

Transfer prices have significance for public policy as well as for private policy. Criticism of vertical integration has focused on pricing of intracompany transfers. It is alleged that discrimination within the company hurts competition. For example, oil refineries are supposed to gain an advantage by charging their marketing affiliates lower prices than their independent customers, and aluminum and copper producers are supposed to benefit similarly in favoring their fabricating affiliates. Actually, shoving the profits around inside the company and into safe corners serves no useful purpose and succeeds only in confusing both operating managers and top management. But the fact that intracompany price discrimination is not the good business that many companies think it is hardly makes public criticism less damaging.

Fortunately, the correct economic solution for the company's managerial problem—transfer prices determined competitively—also solves this public policy problem.

NEW CONCEPT

How can the hodgepodge of intracompany pricing methods that is found in many large companies today be avoided? What is an economically realistic basis for intracompany pricing applied uniformly throughout the whole company? The answer lies in a new system of executive control which has the two intermeshed features of profit centers and competitive transfer prices.

Profit Centers

Before responsibility for profits or losses can be assigned, it is necessary that the management of the particular operation be in fact made primarily responsible for its economic performance. Four characteristics distinguish this type of autonomous unit from service functions.

1. *Operational Independence.* Each profit center must be an independent operating unit, and its manager must have a large measure of control over most if not all operational decisions that affect his profits. This means that he must have considerable discretion in determining the volume of production, methods of operation, product mix, and so forth, subject only to broad policy discretion from top management. The areas of the company where this independence of action cannot exist should properly be considered as service centers. For them, the volume and character of services rendered are to a large extent determined by decisions originating outside their divisions; an example is the public relations department.

2. *Access to Sources and Markets.* The profit-center manager must have control over all decisions relating to sources and markets. He must be genuinely free to buy and sell in alternative markets both outside the company and inside. For example, the manager of the canned meat division of an integrated meat packer must know that it is just as respectable to buy uncured hams outside the company as to buy from the company's own pork division.

Freedom to trade is essential to the new concept because it dissolves alibis. Brother buyer and seller have ample incentive to reach agreement on prices if neither is restricted to a particular source or market. They have almost no incentive, and everybody feels cheated, if these channels are predetermined.

The required access to sources and markets cannot be created by edict; outside sources or markets must either be there or be capable of creation. To illustrate, crank shaft and other major components of an automobile engine require highly specialized machine tools already in the possession of the supplying division. It is impracticable to get a sound figure on what it would cost to supplant the intracompany manufacturing source, since an outside supplier will not make a realistic bid unless the company signifies its willingness to make a long-run commitment sufficient to cover his installation of major facilities. Without this commitment, freedom to trade in such cases is meaningless.

3. Separable Costs and Revenues. A profit center must be able to split off its costs and find an economically realistic price of the end products; otherwise measurement of its profit performance is impossible. This requirement eliminates service-type staff activities from consideration.

4. Management Intent. A distinction between a profit center and a service center can also be drawn in terms of management's intention. Only if the basic goal is profits should the operation be treated as a profit center.

A service activity may contribute as much or more *in fact* to the company's profitability as an operating division, but still not qualify because top management does not and should not judge its performance solely on the basis of profitability. For example, the legal department could be run as a captive law firm and be judged by its performance in producing profits by chasing ambulances inside the company. But despite its ability to meet the requirements of operational independence, access to outside customers and talent, and separable costs and revenues, the legal department should not be made a profit center because individual decisions cannot be controlled by the profit motive.

In surveying operations within the company to determine which should be profit centers, management may want to restudy the fundamental objectives of each operation. The proclivity to view many activities as service center lean-tos for major divisions or the company as a whole should not lead top executives to ignore the advantages of conducting every possible operation as a profit center. Particular care should be taken in marginal cases like this one—

A captive steel mill that produces a substantial part of the requirements of a large manufacturer of equipment turns in a poor profit performance. This is due in part to the fact that it is not judged by profits alone; management's intent is to meet the requirements and specifications of the fabricating divisions at the expense of efficient scheduling and profitable product mix. Under these circumstances, the mill is viewed as a service function. It could, however, be operated as a profit center. While the difficulties of negotiating price premiums for special steels and special scheduling would be great, a price on the mill's unique services to the fabricating divisions would lead to correct allocation and remove the wasteful illusion that these special services are free.

To summarize, the modern integrated, multiple-product firm functions best if it is made into a sort of miniature of the competitive, free-enterprise economic system. The firm should be comprised of independent operating units that act like economic entities, free to trade outside the company as well as inside. Each such entity or profit center will, in seeking to maximize its own profits, do what will also maximize the profits of the entire company, just as individual firms in a private-enterprise society, by seeking their selfish advancement, generate the high productivity and well-being of a competitive economy.

Competitive Pricing

The underlying requisite for profit-center controls is competitive prices negotiated in arm's length bargaining by division managers who are free to go outside the company if unhappy with prices paid by or to brother division managers.

Small differences in the unit price of transferred products can make big differences in the division's profits and executive bonuses. Intracompany pricing must preserve the profit-making autonomy of the division manager so that his selfish interests will be identical with the interests of the company as a whole. This can be accomplished by following three simple principles:

1. Prices of all transfers in and out of a profit center should be determined by negotiation between buyers and sellers.

2. Negotiators should have access to full data on alternative sources and markets and to public and private information about market prices.

3. Buyers and sellers should be completely free to deal outside the company.

The practical benefits of sound transfer pricing for profit-center control are not always obvious. Many companies—especially if they are decentralized—seem to get along fine without it, never knowing what they are missing. This is because decentralization "digs gold with a pickax." In the flush of gratification for this great improvement over old authoritarian ways management may neglect the tools to get the most out of it.

In a big company there is danger that interest in making profits will be diluted as a result of managerial specialization and the separation of operation from ownership. The parochial ambitions of operating managers need to be held in check; performance should be judged in terms of alibi-proof, objectively measured profits. When transfer prices are economically correct and profit centers are properly established, top management can delegate and still have peace of mind, because the division manager's targets and incentives will be so set up that his interests are identical to those of top management.

How to protect the independence of operating divisions against the insidious encroachment of staff advice, the restrictions of policy rules, and the fettering effect of top-level supervision is an ever present problem. The fact that top management finds it necessary to protest so much about the independence of its division managers often shows how limited this independence is in reality. Competitively negotiated transfer prices bulwark the independence of operating divisions by making possible meaningful measurement of economic performance.

The harm that can be done by arbitrary and authoritative pricing of intracompany transfers is hidden. Such prices lead to sins of omission as well as sins of commission. They fail to give definitive indication of the profitability of added volume. They rob management of an economically correct basis for evaluating various profit figures. They provide a distorted and incorrect measure of the economic desirability of different channels of distribution. Bad transfer prices can also misdirect capital investment and cause friction and dissension among executives.

But negotiated competitive transfer prices can prevent these losses. They can make the division's procurement, processing, pricing, and distribution sensitive to market requirements and responsive to competitive alternatives. They provide sound guidance in making purchasing decisions, indicate the extent to which additional processing will be profitable, and direct the flow of products so as to make the greatest net profit for the company. Furthermore, the very process of negotiation avoids arbitrariness and tends to create agreement. This eliminates the cause of much friction and ill feeling.

OTHER PRICING SYSTEMS

What about existing systems of setting transfer prices? How adequate or inadequate are they? Various bases are now in use, such as:

1. *Published market prices.* Example: uncured hams priced to the canning division at prices reported in the *National Provisioner.*

2. *Marginal cost.* Example: electric motors transferred to the refrigerator division at cost of materials plus direct labor.

3. *Full Cost Plus.* Example: gasoline transferred to the transportation division at the refineries' full costs plus a "fair" profit markup.

4. *Sales Minus.* Example: transfers of gasoline from the refinery at the retail price minus an allowance for the marketing department's services in getting it from the refinery to the customer.

5. *Traditional Prices.* Example: the transfer price of financing service, a customary 6 percent.

The choice among the different transfer pricing systems depends both on the kinds of information that are available and on the objectives that the management hopes to accomplish through the system.

If no measurement of the competitive market price exists for the intermediate product, some type of cost basis may have to be used, unless a negotiated price can be based on indirect alternatives of buying and selling units. But choice among cost bases may be narrowed by the kind of cost records used.

In the event that available information does permit a free choice, then what management wishes to accomplish by intracompany pricing should determine the system to be followed. For example, if a company wishes to use intracompany pricing as the primary means for controlling costs and profits, for measuring operational results, and for directing the product flow in the most profitable ways, some sort of market price system is clearly indicated.

Now let us examine the relative advantages and disadvantages of the different systems used today for setting transfer prices, so that we can see how they compare with the competitive pricing method advocated here.

Published Market Prices

Basing intracompany transfers on published statistical reports of market price has much merit. It often approximates the ideal of a competitive transfer pricing system. But practical difficulties arise from three sources:

1. *Conditions may make published statistics an inaccurate statement of the market price for the size, quality, timing, and location of the intracompany transaction.* Market price statistics often have systematic time lags which make them an inaccurate picture of the true market at near turning points. Also, they may represent a different quantity, grade, type of package, or duration from the intracompany transaction.

For example, published prices of intermediate products and services usually pertain to the spot price, whereas the intracompany transfer calls for a long-term contract price, which is usually lower and more stable. Thus, rates for chartered oil tankers, which fluctuate wildly, are not an adequate basis for pricing stable intracompany water transport.

Some of these deficiencies in the published market price can be partly remedied by market-determined price spreads for term contracts as opposed to spot prices, carload lots as opposed to small lots, and bulk as opposed to packaged products. But if these spreads are large, it is likely that they cannot be established objectively in a manner that will be satisfactory to buyer and seller without negotiation.

2. *The market place may not offer a real alternative for the intracompany buyer or seller.* The volume traded on the market may be so small compared with intracompany transactions that an attempt to get supplies there would drive up the price. Or the quality standards of its market plan may be lower than those of the company or fail to meet the peculiarities of design and appeal of the company's own brand, so that price comparisons are futile.

3. *It may be difficult to distinguish between nominal price quotations and real ones.* No matter how honestly and carefully prices are reported,

there are times when a very few strategically placed transactions can make a big difference in the published price. When these published prices affect the divisional manager's promotion and pay, he cannot be expected to be blind to opportunities to "make" the market. Cunning maneuvers of this sort are hardly in the company's interest.

Marginal Cost

Next to negotiated transfer pricing, marginal-cost pricing is most defensible economically. Under this plan transfer prices are based on the additional cost caused by the production of an additional unit of the product. Moderately close approximation to marginal cost can be made by confining costs to those that vary with volume and are traceable—i.e., direct costs. This is the best of the authoritarian pricing schemes for these reasons: (1) it determines cost of underlying processes in terms that are relevant for short-run operating decisions on pricing, promotion, and product policy; (2) the buying division has a guide as to when it is in the company's interest to acquire a product or material from outside sources so long as it knows the short-run marginal cost of producing the product inside the company; and (3) troublesome and contentious problems of assigning overhead costs to joint product operations and changing overhead loadings as a result of variations in operating rates are avoided.

Marginal-cost pricing has, however, several distinct disadvantages:

(1) Divisional profit and loss statements are made meaningless as a measure of economic performance. All contributions to profits are passed along to the final operation, and therefore no profits appear for earlier divisions. This gives the last division, frequently the sales division, a big cushion for maneuvering. No wonder sales divisions like marginal-cost transfer pricing!

(2) Where many divisions handle products in succession, operating management may overlook profitable changes in methods or product flows because the inefficiencies of one division are covered up by the low costs of more efficient divisions that worked on the product in earlier stages.

(3) Commercial abilities that are so desirable in a well-rounded division manager are stunted under marginal-cost transfer pricing. He is isolated from the pitfalls and opportunities of the market and is confined to the role of a service division manager.

Full Cost Plus

Cost-plus pricing sets intracompany prices on the basis of the complete costs of the producing unit plus some allowance for profit. Many variations of the system, both as to the cost base and the add-on, are possible.

The commonest cost base is orthodox accounting costs for the latest period. Normal cost and standard cost are sometimes used. The add-on or profit ranges from a niggardly coverage of overheads to a markup on sales which produces a handsome return on investment. The standard for the amount of profit takes two principal forms: (a) a margin on sales and (b) a rate of return on investment. In practice, partly because of the difficulty of determining profit margins on reasonably similar operations, the margin is usually set arbitrarily.

Bare costs with no add-on were more common in the past than now. They are frequently justified on moral grounds: that it is wrong to take profit out of the hide of a brother division. Today, full cost plus a "reasonable" rate of return on the investment of the selling division appears to be gaining wider acceptance.

Supporters of full cost-plus pricing of transfers claim these conflicting virtues of the system:

(1) That the company is assured of an adequate profit on the entire process if transfer prices at each stage force the addition of a profit.

(2) That no company can make money by selling things to itself and allowing divisions to exploit each other; therefore prices limited to costs plus a fair margin should be used to prevent conflict and promote cooperation.

(3) That cost-plus pricing assures that the economic benefits of integration will be achieved and will be passed on to the company's customers.

(4) That cost-plus pricing makes the producing and supplying units attend to the business of producing cheaply without being diverted by concern about commercial problems of pricing sharply.

None of these virtues, however, minimize the fact that cost-plus pricing is arbitrary and authoritarian. As such, it provides a poor basis for evaluating division performance, it beclouds profits, and it inevitably diverts production into uneconomic channels.

Sales Minus

Basing intracompany transfer prices on what the customers pay has considerable vogue, particularly in organizations which are strongly market oriented. Transfer prices are geared to final selling prices by subtracting allowances that more or less completely provide for the costs and profits of intervening operations. For example, retail price lines of sheets and pillow cases once governed transfer prices for the textile mill subsidiary of a merchandising organization. Similarly, in the case of an integrated wholesale distribution unit, $4 was subtracted from the price paid by the retailer on a certain kind of canned food to get the transfer price from the canning factory to the distribution department. The factory allowed $2 a case for direct costs (transportation, promotion, etc.) and another $2 a case for overhead and profits.

This system has the virtue of being oriented toward the market value of the final product. However, it shifts the full impact of fluctuations in final price to the basic production units of an integrated firm, with the intermediate processing and marketing operations sheltered by an assured margin. In a buyer's market like that recently experienced in textiles, sales-minus pricing for gray goods would come close to what outside textile mills, hungry for business, could be forced to sell at. Under these supply and demand conditions, transfer prices that would approximate competitive market prices and realistically negotiated prices would result from sales-minus pricing. In a seller's market, by contrast, sales-minus pricing will undershoot the market; a division will not be able to get from intracompany transfers what it could get from outsiders or what it could negotiate at arm's length with brother divisions.

Traditional Prices

A weird throwback to medieval times when the concept of "just" price prevailed is occasionally encountered in modern business. The use of traditional prices in transfer pricing belongs in this category. An example is the costing of financial services at 6% in intracompany charges; such a rate has borne no relationship to the market place within the memory of today's executives.

It is hard to see any advantages in this method, beyond the fact that it is as convenient and consistent as most of the concepts of feudalism. But the other methods now in vogue are not much more useful. All have serious shortcomings; none can be relied on to produce profit-oriented decisions by division managers.

INSTALLATION AND OPERATION

We turn now to the more mundane problems of what needs to be done to install and operate competitive transfer pricing.

Comprehensive Study

A practical starting point is a systematic, impartial study of the intracompany pricing methods the company is now using, and the facts that can be marshaled concerning market prices and market price relationships. The next thing to do is to lay the foundation of understanding of the economic and management philosophy, the benefits, and the problems of this new concept of competitively negotiated intracompany dealings.

Managers of profit centers and of service centers need a new orientation—one that is pointed toward the economics of their operation rather than exclusively toward the technology of the operation. When they become managers of profit centers rather than merely managers of factories, they need a new set of ideas, values, and facts, with dimensions broad enough to embrace marketplace choices and competitive return on capital expenditures. All this takes time as well as education. Overnight installation by a presidential decree of the new transfer-price and profit-center policy is not likely to succeed or last.

Gradual Progress

After the research and educational foundation has been laid, a program of gradual installation can be tailored to the company's needs. The following rules should prove helpful:

1. *Widen the coverage gradually.* Start with areas where competitively negotiated pricing is easiest and take on the tougher ones as know-how improves.

2. *Apply first to basic volume.* Start with negotiated prices on the minimum basic quantities needed for planned future production. Negotiate term contracts for the distant future, so that both buyer and seller will have maximum fluidity and alternatives. Then gradually move toward arrangements for the fluctuating sector of volume for which real alternative outside sources get quite restricted. For these negotiations the trading experience and regard for long-term interests gained in previous dealings will help to steady the bargaining by curbing temptations toward exploitation in the short run.

3. *Establish pricing guides through research.* For products and components where the producing division has had no occasion to study market prices and outside trading opportunities, a foundation of knowledge must be laid so that neither brother division will be handicapped by ignorance in negotiating a competitive price. It takes time to dig this information up and to familiarize operating executives with its use.

4. *Set pricing limits temporarily.* These initial limits on the range of prices over which bargaining can take place will become as vestigial as the hip bone of a whale when the system gets into operation. But they provide assurance and prevent undue exploitation of ignorance at the outset. For example, a lower limit on price might be set by an estimate of the marginal cost, and the upper limit might be the commercial price charged outsiders plus 5 percent.

5. *Limit the volume of outside trading initially.* The freedom to trade outside can be temporarily restricted by setting volume limits as, for instance, 75 percent inside the company, 25 percent outside the company. Those who fear that the advantages of integration will be dissipated are reassured by this expedient.

Price Mediator

One executive is needed to (a) pull together the transfer-price and profit-center investigations, (b) organize the conferences and training sessions, and (c) supervise the gradual installation of the new system of economic controls. To ease the transition, both emotionally and economically, this executive also can temporarily undertake to mediate the negotiation of some transfer prices.

Note that the price mediator should not attempt to arbitrate. The experience with price arbitration is almost universally bad. It is expensive and time consuming, and the results do not satisfy either party. Everyone feels cheated, and everyone has an alibi for his profit and volume results. Instead the mediator should aim at securing agreement by keeping the negotiations going, by supplying information, and by exercising business judgment on issues of fact as well as on commercial alternatives. For example, one transfer-price mediator in a meat packing firm reviewed and substantially deflated cost information which was burdened with fictitious charges for packaging and shipping sausage material at successive stages of processing. Up to this time the selling division had been using these costs in good faith for internal decisions as well as in transfer-price bargaining with other divisions. The delusion that these were rock-bottom incremental costs led the selling division to set its refusal price at a level which was above the market. Such a price would have led to idle facilities and would have sacrificed incremental profits if the buying division had been forced to go outside to get the supplies.

One of the functions of the mediator, particularly in the early stages of installation, is to distill the truth from conflicting, misguided, exaggerated, and prejudiced pricing facts which the negotiating parties often bring to a mediation conference. To illustrate again—in negotiating transfer prices for a pharmaceutical firm, the participants faced two major common problems: (a) the outside market was very thin, with a wide spread resulting between highest and lowest prices at which sales were made; and (b) the transactions covered by this range differed from the intracompany transactions in volume, packaging, location, and so on. Quite naturally, each party came to the negotiations with a highly biased sample of market transactions to support its point of view. The triumph of the transfer-price mediator was to demonstrate to both parties that extreme prices, ranging from $.50 a pound to $1.50 a pound, were inapplicable; he managed to narrow the range within which both parties agreed that the real market lay for the transactions in question.

As profit-center managers gain experience in using the competitive pricing system and grow to appreciate its value, the effective mediator will work himself out of a job.

Term Contracts

The period over which the transfer prices are to be negotiated should be at least as long as the planning period required to design and schedule production, or to dig up satisfactory alternative outside sources, whichever time period is longer. For example, the planning and design period for automobiles is so long that in the short run, say over the next quarter, the divisions which make basic engine components have no real alternative market for their product. Similarly, the vehicle divisions could not on short notice dig up alternative outside sources for properly designed engine parts. Many operations are characterized by short-run inflexibility of alternatives especially where design, quality, and packaging must conform to rigid and publicized specifications. A product made to such specifications has passed the point of no return.

In such cases, *short*-run negotiations (less than three or four months for the automobile manufacturer) concerning transfer prices have the hallmark of bilateral monopoly; they are similar to wage-rate negotiations. They generate heat, bad temper, and rarely produce economic transfer prices that are gauged and policed by outside alternatives and freedom to use them.

But over a long period even a branded product like an automobile can properly be subject to transfer prices that have the virtues and characteristics of a free-enterprise system. If long-term specifications contracts are negotiated, the buying unit will generally be able to get outsiders to bid on products made to its requirements, and a producing unit will have a real choice—either to adapt its output to other uses or to again assume the commitments on design, volume, and productive facilities which are tied to the branded product.

Good Businessmen

Successful operation of a profit center under a miniature free-enterprise system within the corporate fold calls for talents and experience often summed up by the tag, "He is a good businessman."

These abilities need to be systematically cultivated because they are not likely to have survived in a big corporate bureaucracy where transfer prices have been authoritarian. Executives of highly centralized companies are likely to have been reared as if they were in one big happy family, in which each child has an assigned set of chores and emphasis is on cooperation and the subordination of individual desires to group interests. Some executives may have forgotten how to make independent decisions. They will need help in taking responsibility for decisions in a profit-center controlled company where anything that affects their profit is their business, where performance is judged by how much profit they can make, and where right, independent opinions quickly improve the executives' profit and loss statements.

ANSWERING OBJECTIONS

Any new system of transfer prices will be criticized, and this one particularly because it removes needed alibis and may blemish careers by exposing executives' inadequacies. In addition, it may appear to be fundamentally opposed to the reason for existence of a large multi-product corporation. Therefore anyone who is considering this new system of intracompany pricing and profit control needs to give some thought to the objections that are likely to be viewed as most telling by those who doubt. The following questions are ones which I have encountered constantly in work in the field.

"Why can't our company get along without transfer prices?" Some companies can. There is no need for management coordination through an apparatus of economic transfer prices and profit achievement measures if all complicated managerial functions can be competently exercised by one small, closely knit group of men. This was found to be true of a regional grocery chain. But very few large companies have such an administrative setup.

In some situations it may be possible to devise mathematical models which can solve empirically all the problems of allocating facilities, materials, and intermediate and finished products without continued exercise of managerial judgment and know-how. In these cases transfer prices are not essential, either. In using the new computers that are here and on the horizon management is handicapped, however, by the shortage of analytical ability and judgment needed to set up models which will adequately reflect fluid and changing alternatives at every stage.

"Why worry, since we already have that kind of transfer price?" Many companies think they have competitive transfer prices, but most of them do not. The consequences of noncompetitive transfer prices are present, but they seem to spring from such other causes as selfishness and lack of team spirit. There are two clear symptoms of noncompetitive pricing which cannot be explained away: (a) a continuous awareness of a conflict between the interest of the operating unit and what appears to its managers to be the interest of the company as a whole, reflected in self-congratulation for putting the company's interest before that of the division; and (b) the prevalence of exhortations not to let transfer prices prevent the company from making money.

"Will the benefits of integration be lost?" Integration which is actually economically justified has such great and clear benefits to both buying and selling divisions that competitive transfer pricing is not a threat. Only integration which does not produce economies—which does not

profit both the buying and the selling division—will be eliminated by virtue of division buyers and sellers going outside the company. This assumes that the division managers are alert to the possible conflict between their short-run and long-run interests, both in maintaining customer relations and in having a stable and sure source of supply.

"Will cooperation be undermined?" Measuring profit-center performance on a competitive economic basis motivates each unit to do what is in its own best profit interst. These interests, if the transfer prices are determined economically and the profit centers properly defined, are identical with the interests of the company. Rivalry to make the best profit showing will certainly encourage shrewd, hard-headed negotiations, but the promotion of mutual economic interests will, as always, stimulate cooperation.

"Does perishability of a product rule out negotiable transfer pricing?" Physical perishability does not create a new kind of problem. Physical perishability causes price sacrifices, and it is this economic perishability alone that matters. Negotiated prices have proved practical for perishable products; indeed, they have been used for them in the market place for thousands of years.

"Will the system work if there is no true market price?" This does not matter. Sometimes the negotiated price will be above the general market average, sometimes below. So long as buyers and sellers are free to know and to choose competitive alternatives, the price will be mutually agreeable and will be determined by supply and demand forces for that particular kind of transaction.

Published data on market prices are likely to be too fragmentary and too unreliable to determine transfer prices; they should be used as a guide only. Sometimes negotiation leads to agreement to use the particular published price as a bench mark. However, this is not because the figure is published but because the negotiating parties agree to its economic validity.

"Will profit centers be shortsighted in their quest for gain?" No system of transfer prices and performance measurement makes judgment unnecessary in appraising the value of hanging on to a customer and in balancing long-run and short-run interests. Shortsightedness is no more likely with good transfer prices than with bad. Profit-center managers have a big stake in their long-run future, and good supervision can clarify this stake and induce a long view when short-run profits conflict.

"Will the sales organization sell too cheaply?" The rather general mistrust of the business acumen of the marketing organization is a peculiarity of the big bureaucracy. From it stem the practices of kidding the sales organization about costs, pushing products down its throat, and rigging transfer prices to make marketing operations look like losers. The result is that atrophy of commercial instincts sometimes associated with sales specialization.

Under the proposed system the sales organization will control factors that determine its profits, will be held responsible for the profits, and will have its profit performance measured. Given this encouragement, there is no reason to expect that salesmen should be any less capable of acting like businessmen than are engineers or accountants.

The company's interests require, not simply top price or top volume, but top profit. Sometimes a larger profit contribution comes from a bigger volume at lower price; sometimes it is the other way around. With this method, sales units will have the knowledge, the authority, and the incentive to sell the product at prices that will produce the greatest profits for themselves and therefore for the company. These advantages in turn will put the units in a better position to develop and attract men who are competent merchandisers.

CONCLUSION

Difficulties of installation and operation *can* be overcome; questions of criticism and skepticism *can* be met. Management will do well to make the necessary effort in view of the deficiencies of existing transfer pricing systems:

1. Economically indefensible methods of intracompany pricing are widely used in American industry.

2. Losses sustained from bad transfer prices do not show up on any set of books, because what would have happened under economically correct transfer prices will never be known. Anyone who has tried to restate in terms of correct transfer prices what has been reported in terms of wrong ones will testify to the practical impossibility of measuring the foregone profits. In other words, whatever losses result from noneconomic transfer prices are well and forever hidden.

3. Bad transfer prices do not necessarily lead to losses; but if they do not, it is because no attention is paid to them in making decisions. In some companies the critical decisions concerning flow of product, degree of processing, and channels and geography of distribution can be made without reference to any internal costs or prices. In such companies bad transfer prices may do no harm—they also do no good. And if the operations of these companies do not require an economically correct system of transfer prices, they probably require no intracompany pricing at all.

As a practical matter the chances are strong that an unsound system of transfer pricing *will* cause harm. For a large integrated organization with a diversified product line which is sold to a variety of industrial, commercial, and consumer market levels, the only system which will accomplish the needs of management is one based on negotiated competitive prices.

23. On the Economics of Transfer Pricing*

JACK HIRSHLEIFER

In order to achieve the benefits of decentralization in decision making, many corporations have developed divisional organizations in which some or all of the separate divisions are virtually autonomous "profit centers." This paper is concerned with the problem of pricing the goods and services that are exchanged between such divisions within a firm and with how these prices should be set in order to induce each division to act so as to maximize the profit of the firm as a whole. The problem is an important one, because the prices which are set on internal transfers affect the level of activity within divisions, the rate of return on investment by which each division is judged, and the total profit that is achieved by the firm as a whole.

Two papers which have drawn attention to the crucial importance of transfer-price policies have also discussed alternative approaches to the problem.[1] The paper by Cook recommends the use of market-based prices, at least as an ideal, while Dean favors "negotiated competitive prices." Such brief description does not, of course, do justice to either of the articles, both of which were more concerned with drawing attention to the importance of decentralization and transfer pricing than with rigorous determination of optimal transfer-price rules. The argument made in the present paper is that market price is the correct transfer price only where the commodity being transferred is produced in a competitive market, that is, competitive in the theoretical sense that no single producer considers himself large enough to influence price by his own output decision. If the market is imperfectly competitive, or where no market for the transferred commodity exists, the correct procedure is to transfer at marginal cost (given certain simplifying conditions)

---

*Journal of Business, vol. 29, no. 3 (July 1956), pp. 172–84. © Copyright 1956, The University of Chicago Press.

[1] Paul W. Cook, Jr., "Decentralization and the Transfer-Price Problem," *Journal of Business*, vol. 28 (April 1955), pp. 87–94; and Joel Dean, "Decentralization and Intracompany Pricing," *Harvard Business Review*, vol. 33 (July–August (1955), pp. 65–74.

or at some price between marginal cost and market price in the most general case.[2]

A. CONDITIONING OF THE ANALYSIS

For the sake of precision, we shall somewhat more formally restate the problem under investigation. A firm sets up two or more internal profit centers. Each of these is to maximize its own separate profits, possibly subject to restraints or rules imposed by overall management. Exchanges of goods may take place between two such centers. At what price should the unit of commodity be valued for the purpose of computing the "profits" of the selling and buying centers? The goal, for the present theoretical analysis, will be to establish that mode of pricing which leads the autonomous profit centers to make decisions resulting in the largest aggregate profit for the firm as a whole.

As a concrete case, let us take a firm with two such centers: a manufacturing unit (the seller division) and a distribution unit (the buyer division). The commodity exchanged—called the "intermediate product"—is the commodity as it leaves the manufacturing unit. There is also a final product to be sold by the distribution unit.

Unless stated otherwise, we shall assume that both *technological independence* and *demand independence* apply between the operations of the two divisions. Technological independence means that the operating costs of each division are independent of the level of operations being carried on by the other. Demand independence means that an additional external sale by either division does not reduce the external demand for the products of the other. Demand independence is a more special assumption than technological independence. The latter, we might expect, would apply at least approximately to a wide variety of practical situations. In general, however, we would expect there to be at least some demand dependence—for example, additional sales of the final product by the distribution division would tend to reduce external demand for the intermediate product. This point will be discussed in more detail later.

B. TRANSFER PRICE FOR BEST JOINT LEVEL OF OUTPUT

Suppose that a single joint level of output is to be determined for the two divisions; the distribution division will handle exactly as much product as the manufacturing division will turn out. A common level

---

[2] This statement is itself an oversimplification, since pricing at marginal cost is a necessary but not a sufficient condition. What is involved is a whole mode of procedure, described below, for finding the optimum price from the point of view of the overall interests of the firm.

of output might rationally be required by central management under either of two different sets of circumstances: (1) there might be no market for the intermediate product at all, in which case there is no way for the manufacturing division to dispose of a surplus or for the distribution division to make up a deficiency, or (2) there might be a strong relation of technological dependence between the operations of the two divisions, such that marginal costs for either division jump sharply in shifting to dealings with the outside market. For example, imagine an integrated steel mill, with two divisions exchanging molten iron. Shipping excess iron out of the mill could involve high handling costs to the selling division, and purchasing iron outside could involve high reheating costs to the buying division so that trading on the external market might rationally occur only under very unusual conditions. (This point will be alluded to again in Section F, which discusses technological dependence.)

The determination of the best joint level of output is shown in Figure 1. In this diagram quantity of output is measured along the horizontal axis for both divisions, q_m representing output of the manufacturing division and q_d of the distribution division. (We assume that the units of the intermediate and the final commodities are commensurate. In some cases there will be an obvious natural unit: e.g., pairs of shoes exchanged between a shoe-manufacturing and a shoe-retailing division. Sometimes, as when the intermediate product is copper and the final

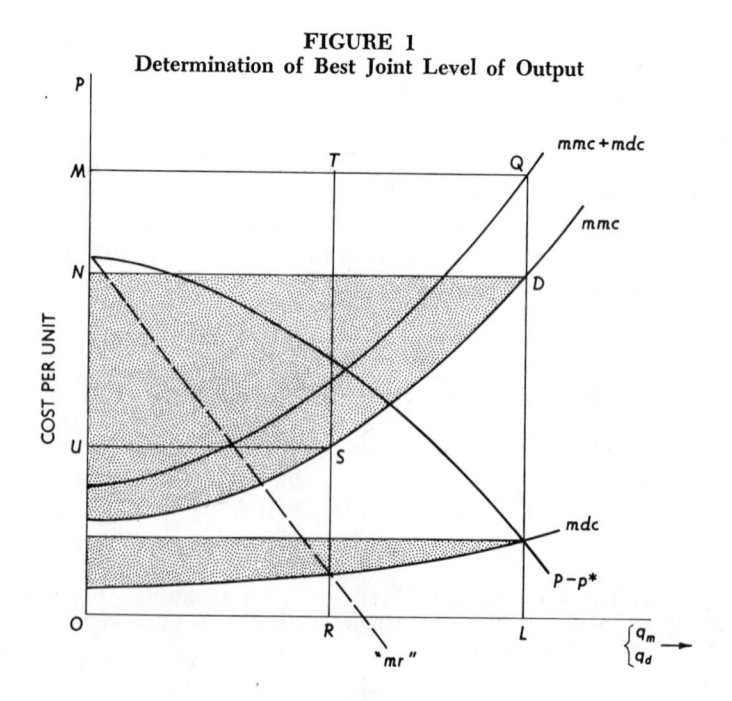

FIGURE 1
Determination of Best Joint Level of Output

product copper wire, it may be necessary to express the quantities of the latter in terms of some transformed unit like pounds of copper contained.) Prices and costs per unit of output are measured vertically. The curves labeled mmc and mdc represent the marginal manufacturing cost and the marginal distribution cost, respectively, each as a function of output.

Assuming that there is a competitive market for the final product, the distribution division will face a ruling price P. The best solution for the firm as a whole is to set the joint level of q_m and q_d at the output such that $mmc + mdc = P$—that is, where the overall marginal cost equals the price of the final product. If P equals the vertical distance OM in Figure 1, the optimum output is OL.

Such an output would be established by central management by adding the mdc and mmc curves of the separate divisions. It is simple, however, to devise a transfer-price rule which will lead the divisions autonomously to the same solution. Suppose that the distribution division calls for and secures from the manufacturing division a schedule showing how much the manufacturing division would produce (i.e., sell to the distribution division) at any transfer price p^* for the intermediate commodity. This schedule would, in fact, be the same as the mmc curve if the manufacturing division rationally determines its output to set $mmc = p^*$.[3] With this information, the distribution division can then determine a curve showing the difference or "margin" $(P - p^*)$ between market price and transfer price for any level of output which it might set. The distribution division then finds its own output where $mdc = P - p^*$ at OL and establishes the transfer price $LD = ON$. Evidently, the manufacturing division will then also produce at OL, since that is where $mmc = p^*$. The upper shaded area in figure 1 represents the separate profit of the manufacturing division, and the lower shaded area that of the distribution division. One condition must be stipulated: the distribution division must not be permitted to increase its separate profit by finding a quasi-marginal revenue curve *marginal* to $P - p^*$ (the one labeled "mr") and establishing an output of OR and a transfer price of $RS = OU$. This would amount to the distribution division's exploiting the manufacturing division by acting as a monopolistic buyer of the latter's product, in which case the gain to the former would be more than offset by the loss to the latter, and so the firm as a whole would lose thereby. The net loss is evident from the fact that firm output would be set at OR rather than at the optimal level of OL.

In the current discussion the distribution division has been given the dominant role in decision making. This could be reversed without any

---

[3] Technically, this statement is correct only over the range where mmc exceeds average variable cost.

essential change; instead of the distribution division working with the supply function of the manufacturing division, the latter could work with the demand function of the former. A parallel stipulation would also apply: the manufacturing division must be prevented from exploiting the distribution division as a monopolistic seller. Incidentally, bilateral bargaining might lead to a rather poor solution in these circumstances.

The solution remains essentially unchanged if the market for the final product is not perfectly competitive. In that case, a sloping demand curve and marginal revenue curve could be constructed instead of the horizontal demand curve MTQ used in figure 1. The process is exactly as before, except that what corresponds to the curve labeled $P - p^*$ in figure 1 would be $MR - p^*$, where MR is marginal revenue for the final product.

The result in this section may be considered marginal-cost pricing for the intermediate product, since $p^* = mmc$. We shall find, in fact, that marginal-cost pricing in this sense is a quite general answer for transfer pricing under conditions of demand independence. It is, however, marginal-cost pricing only in a special sense, where the rules of procedure described above are set up. These rules are designed so as to correspond to the solution that a centralized management would arrive at with full information—namely, to set the sum of the divisional marginal costs equal to price (in the perfectly competitive case) or marginal revenue (in the imperfectly competitive case) in the final market.

C. TRANSFER PRICE WITH COMPETITIVE INTERMEDIATE MARKET

We shall now drop the assumption that a single joint level of output must be established for the two divisions together. Instead, each division is assumed to be free to determine its own output, with the manufacturing division selling its excess production, if any, on the intermediate market, and the distribution division similarly calling on this market to supply any excess of the quantity it desires to handle over that available from the manufacturing division. For the present, we assume that the intermediate market is competitive, so that a price p for the intermediate commodity exists. The final market is also assumed to be competitive. It then follows from the assumption of technological independence that each of the divisions is indifferent between trading the intermediate commodity within or outside the firm.

In figure 2a, manufacturing cost per unit is measured *upward* along the vertical axis, and distribution cost per unit is measured *downward*. If $p = OH = BC$, then the manufacturing division should produce the output OC. If $P - p = EF$, the distribution division should handle the

FIGURE 2
Best Divisional Levels of Output, Competitive Intermediate Market

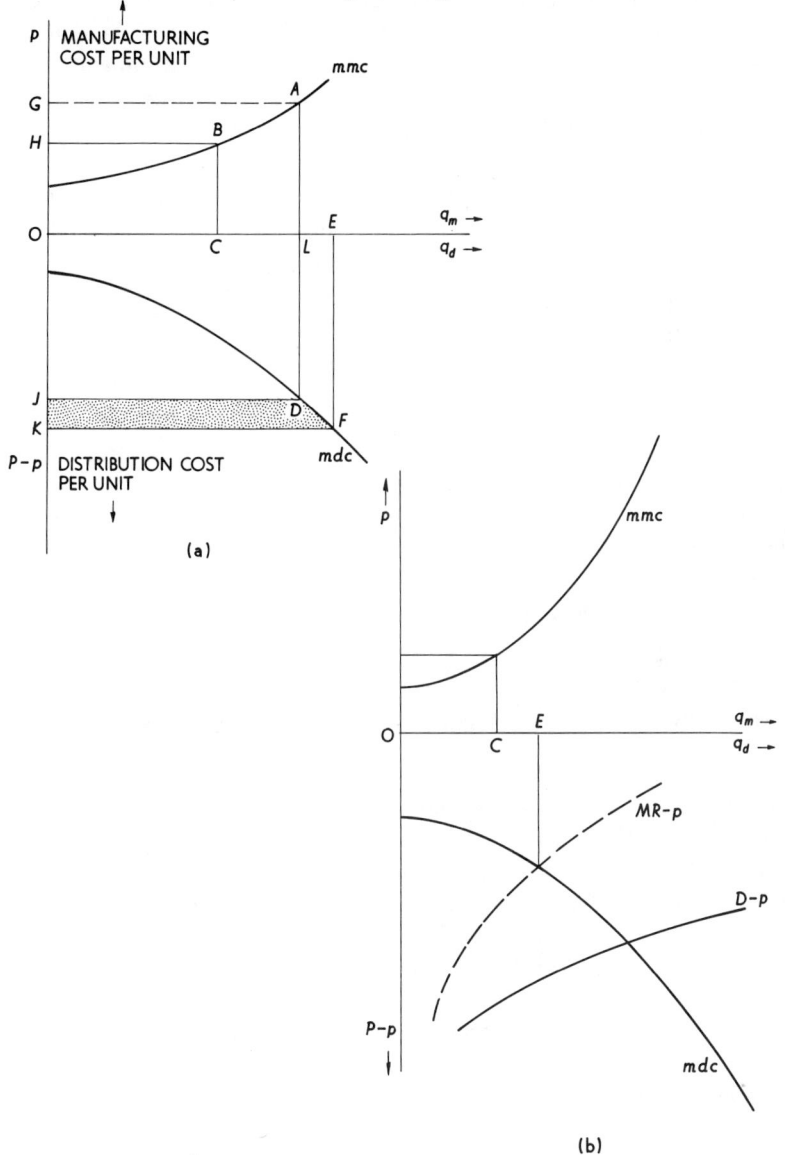

(a)

(b)

output OE. If both are required to set a best joint level of output, however, that output is OL, which is where $mmc + mdc = P$. Here P is measured by the vertical distance AD, which is constructed so as to equal $BC + EF$ (i.e., $p + [P - p]$). Evidently, the requirement of a single joint level of output led to the manufacturing division's producing too much and the distribution division too little. The net increase in profit over the solution is measured by the excess of the area $JKFD$ over the area $BHGA$ in figure 2a. Since $GH = JK$, it is evident from the geometry that the excess must be positive. This argument assumes technological independence.

If a transfer price p^* is to be established in this case, clearly it should be equal to p, because at any other p^* one of the two divisions will refuse to trade. Actually, under our assumptions there is no particular need for internal trading at all, since the divisions are effectively independent firms with common ownership. On the other hand, there is no objection to internal trading, and this can only take place if $p^* = p$.

The assumption of a competitive market for the *final* commodity is not essential for this result. If we assume that the distribution division faces a sloping demand curve as in figure 2b,[4] we merely substitute marginal revenue MR for P in making our output decision. In figure 2b the distribution division produces at OE where $mdc = MR - p$. The correct transfer price remains $p^* = p$.

In general, then, if the intermediate market is competitive, the transfer price should be the market price irrespective of the competitiveness of the market for the final product. For this case, however, p also equals mmc, so our earlier contention that marginal-cost pricing is the more general solution is not refuted by this result.

D. TRANSFER PRICE WITH IMPERFECTLY COMPETITIVE INTERMEDIATE MARKET

We now turn to the substantially more difficult case where the market for the intermediate product is not perfectly competitive, so that—setting aside the demand of the distribution division itself—the external market for the intermediate product facing the manufacturing division has a sloped demand curve. However, we assume demand independence, that is, sales made by the manufacturing division in the intermediate market do not reduce the demand for the final product sold by the distribution division, and, conversely, internal sales to the distribution division do not reduce external demand. In general, we would expect some demand dependence. For example, if the manufacturing division sells shoes both internally and externally, one would expect that each additional sale to the distribution division would reduce the final market demand for shoes sold to independent distributors, and this demand reduction would soon be reflected in the intermediate market demand for external sales of the manufacturing division. Nevertheless, we can imagine reasonable

---

[4] The demand curve is labeled $D - p$, representing the quantity demanded in terms of the net-back to the distribution division after subtracting the transfer outlay of p.

cases where the internal and external sales would have substantially independent demands. For example, our shoe firm could distribute its manufactured products solely through independent distributors in the domestic market, its own distribution division being limited to sales in the foreign market. Or a copper concern might use some of its copper internally only for a wire-fabricating division, while selling externally only to producers who make pots and pans or any copper products other than wire.

Under these conditions the firm is in a position akin to that of a discriminating monopolist; it sells the output of its manufacturing division in one market and of its distribution division in another.[5] We shall first derive the overall solution for the firm and then find that mode of transfer pricing which will permit autonomous realization of this solution. The overall solution is to equate the joint marginal cost of production with the net marginal revenue in each separate market. The word "net" means that we must adjust the market marginal revenue by the incremental cost of delivering to the market concerned.[6] In this case, we assume no delivery cost to the market for the intermediate product, so the relevant marginal revenue is simply that derived from the external demand for the intermediate product. In the case of the distribution division, however, marginal distribution cost must be subtracted from market marginal revenue to derive net marginal revenue for the firm's output of the final commodity.

The solution is illustrated in figure 3. Figure 3a shows the demand curve d and the marginal revenue curve mr for the intermediate product. Figure 3b shows the demand curve D and the marginal revenue curve MR facing the distribution division in the final product market. The mdc curve is as before, and the net marginal revenue curve nMR is the vertical difference between MR and mdc. In figure 3c the two curves mr and nMR are plotted, together with their horizontal sum mr_t. The maximum profit solution is to establish the output q_m of the manufacturing division by the intersection of the mmc and mr_t curves at Q. The amount sold on the intermediate market is OM (shown also in fig. 3a), and the amount sold by the distribution division is OD (shown also in fig. 3b).

The solution just discussed would be arrived at directly by a central decision agency with the appropriate information. We have not yet discussed the pattern of transfer pricing which would lead to the optimal result, given autonomous decision making by one or both divisions. It

---

[5] The firm need only have the power to separate its markets and to face imperfect competition in the intermediate market. The final market may be perfectly competitive.

[6] This point is neglected in standard economic textbooks but usually is of great importance in applied economic problems.

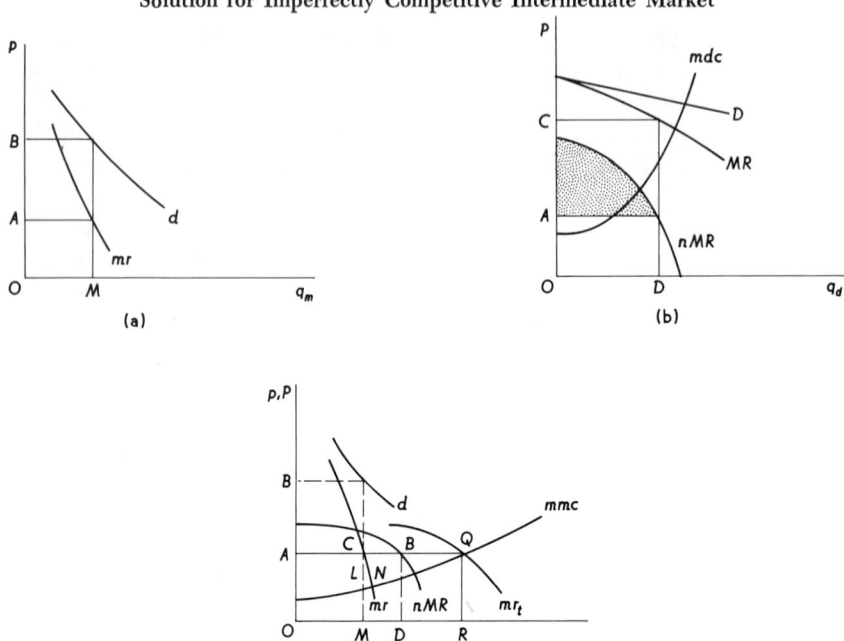

FIGURE 3
Solution for Imperfectly Competitive Intermediate Market

can be seen immediately, however, that the correct transfer price to achieve the maximum-profit result is $p^* = OA = mmc$. In figure 3b setting p^* equal to OA would lead the distribution division to handle the correct amount OD. It would arrive at this by setting p^* equal to nMR, which is equivalent to setting $mmc + mdc$ equal to MR. This suggests the rule that marginal-cost pricing (i.e., setting the transfer price equal to mmc) be adopted for the conditions examined here. However, we do not know quite enough to assert this yet, because the level of mmc is a function of q_m, and q_m itself is dependent upon q_d. This difficulty, however, is not hard to resolve. All that is required is that the distribution division indicate to the manufacturing division its demand for the intermediate product as a function of p^*—namely, the curve nMR. The manufacturing division, incidentally, must be instructed to accept this curve as a marginal revenue curve to be added to mr to get mr_t. This stipulation, analogous to those made in section B, is necessary, because there might otherwise be an incentive for the manufacturing division to treat the demand curve of its affiliate on the same par as an external demand curve, which would lead to constructing a curve *marginal* to nMR for adding to mr to get mr_t, with a view to charging the affiliate a transfer price higher than mmc. This would be equivalent to using the monopoly power of the manufacturing division to exploit the internal as well as the external market for the intermediate commodity; the effect of doing so would be to increase the apparent profit of the manufacturing division separately but to depart from the over-all optimum for the firm by imposing a greater loss of profit upon the distribution division.

Our transfer-price rule, then, for the case where demand independence with technological independence apply, with the market for the intermediate commodity imperfectly competitive (the market for the final product may be perfectly or imperfectly competitive), is to establish the price at marginal manufacturing cost—or, more generally, at the marginal producing cost of the seller division. This is to be understood, however, as a shorthand statement for following the rules indicated in the previous paragraph, which we may state more formally as follows:

Distribution divisions:
1. Determine the nMR curve and convey the information to the manufacturing division.
2. Given the transfer price p^*, produce where $p^* = nMR$.

Manufacturing division:
1. Determine mr and sum mr and nMR to get mr_t.
2. Produce where $mmc = mr_t$.
3. Establish p^* at the mmc determined by (2)—OA in Figure 3c.
4. Establish p at the price along the demand curve d corresponding to the output reserved to outsiders—in Figure 3c OM is sold to outsiders at the price OB. Evidently, p always exceeds p^*.

One defect of this analysis is that the divisional "profits" determined by the transfer price established as here advocated do not provide an unequivocal answer as to whether or not to abandon a subsidiary. (This was also true in the analysis of sec. B.) Turning again to figure 3b, the shaded area represents the profit of the distribution division before allowing for any separable fixed costs of that division. Suppose that the separable distribution fixed costs are such as to exactly equal the shaded area and that it is possible to avoid these costs by abandoning the distribution operation. The implication, then, is that we are indifferent as to having the distribution subsidiary. In fact, however, we are not, because, with the mmc curve as drawn, the distribution division is being charged a transfer price p^* which is contributing to the "profit" of the manufacturing division. In figure 3c the quantity OM is sold directly by the manufacturing division, and the quantity $OD = CQ$ is transferred to the distribution division. The total manufacturing cost for the items transferred is $MLQR$, while the aggregate transfer payments are $MCQR$. The incremental advantage to the manufacturing division of the internal market is the area LCQ less the small triangular area CLN, the latter representing the additional profit on external sales of the intermediate commodity which would have been made had there been no transfers to the distribution division.

Unfortunately, the true profitability to the firm of having a distributing division is not always greater than the profitability of that division alone. A differently shaped mmc curve yielding the same marginal solution—in particular, a **U**-shaped curve with most of the area above OA—can lead to the distribution division's being, on balance, a negative contributor to the profits of the manufacturing division. We may summarize the present point by saying that the transfer-price policy indicated gives the correct solution for firm operations in terms of autonomous determination of marginal levels of operations. For nonmarginal adjustments like abandoning a subsidiary, the autonomous calculations based on the transfer-price rule discussed will not generally be correct, and a correct decision requires an overall examination of the cost and revenue functions of the firm as a whole.

E. DEMAND DEPENDENCE

The analysis to this point has assumed demand independence—that the markets for the intermediate commodity and for the final commodity are entirely independent. Generally speaking, the firm's two markets will be connected in that an additional internal sale to a distributing subsidiary would be expected to lead to some reduction of external demand on the part of purchasers of the intermediate commodity who compete with the distributing subsidiary in the market for the final good. However, demand dependence is a matter of degree. For the instance already cited of a firm making an internal transfer of copper to be used only for wire, and external sales of copper to be used only for pots and pans, our demand independence model of section D would apply in all substantial respects. If, however, both the internal and the external demands were for copper to be used for wire, demand dependence would probably be too strong to be ignored.

For analytical purposes it is convenient to define a category of "perfect demand dependence," which is a situation in which customers in the final product market are perfectly indifferent between purchasing the product of the distributing subsidiary or of its competitors, perfect competition being assumed, and where all the competitors as well as the distributing subsidiary secure the intermediate product solely from the manufacturing subsidiary of the firm studied. For this case, the following points briefly summarize the results of a somewhat complex analysis which is not reproduced here.

1. In long-run equilibrium, as defined in economic theory, enough firms enter any industry so as to eliminate economic profit in that industry; that is, what is eliminated is any economic surplus over and

beyond the normal return to factors employed in the industry, plus rents accruing to unique factors (such as unusually favorable location) responsible for reducing the cost functions of particular firms below the general level of the industry. Under these conditions, and assuming that there are no unusual features about the cost function of the distributing subsidiary which distinguish it from the outside competitors, there is no advantage to be gained by granting the distributing subsidiary any lower price for the transferred commodity than the price charged to outsiders. The manufacturing unit can, by its monopolistic situation, essentially secure all the surplus available to the industry, and so there is no point in attempting to get more by artificially expanding the output of the distributing subsidiary—in fact, this can lead only to a net loss for the firm as a whole.

2. In the short run, however, all the economic profit in the industry may not have been eliminated by changes of scale of plants or entry of new competitors. In these circumstances the monopolist of the intermediate product can capture some of this economic surplus by selling at a subsidized price to a subsidiary operating in the final product market. It follows from the above that, if a monopolist in the intermediate market does not have such a subsidiary, he will in general be able to gain by buying out an independent distributor at the value of the latter's economic surplus—which will be less than the net advantage of the subsidiary to the manufacturing unit.

The case for a subsidized price can be illustrated in terms of a numerical example. Suppose that there are a hundred firms in the final product market, that Q_e is the quantity being distributed by outsiders, q_d is the quantity distributed by the subsidiary in the final product market, and P is the price of the final product.

Let the demand for the product be given by the equation

$$P = 100 - \tfrac{1}{100}(Q_e + q_d),$$

let the marginal manufacturing cost be given by $mmc = 0$,[7] and let the marginal distribution cost be given by $mdc = 20 + 2q_d$ for each of the independent distributors as well as the distributing subsidiary.

Given these relations, it can be shown that the optimal market price p (assuming no subsidy) is equal to 40. However, if a subsidy is permitted, it can be shown that the optimal transfer price p^* is approximately $13\tfrac{1}{3}$. Since mmc is zero throughout, this result for the optimal transfer price falls between the market pricing of section C and the

---

[7] This assumption is made only to simplify the analysis. It could occur in a real situation if, for example, the branch of the firm here called the "manufacturing division" (but actually simply the selling division in an internal exchange) was engaged solely in licensing use of a patent in exchange for a royalty on each unit of output produced by the licensee.

marginal-cost pricing of sections B and D. While this is a special case, it reveals the nature of the general solution.

3. The analysis of this section has, up to this point, assumed perfect demand dependence. More generally speaking, a degree of demand dependence may exist somewhere between perfect dependence and absolute independence. Perhaps the most likely situation is that in which the product of the distributing subsidiary is differentiated, to some degree, from that of its competitors. Still, there may be some demand dependence in that additional sales of the distributing subsidiary would have some adverse effect on outside sales. Partial demand dependence might also occur if the firm we are considering is not a sole monopolist in the intermediate market but shares the market as an oligopolist with one or a few other firms. In this case an additional sale of the distributing subsidiary might lead to losses of sales for all the oligopolists together, but the manufacturing branch of the firm subsidizing its subsidiary might not bear the full impact of the loss. (This argument assumes that the oligopolists in the intermediate market jointly establish the optimum monopoly price for the group, each taking a certain fraction of the market.) In general, the solution for partial demand dependence will lie somewhere between the solutions discussed in section D and in the earlier paragraphs of this section.

F. TECHNOLOGICAL DEPENDENCE—SOME COMMENTS

Technological dependence may affect, in more or less complicated ways, the indicated optimum output for the firm as a whole and therefore the transfer-price rule which determines the optimum output for the divisions operating separately. The level of operations in division A may raise or lower the marginal cost function of division B, and vice versa.

We shall not attempt an analytical solution of the overall problem here. A formal solution for optimum behavior of the firm would run in terms of the economic theory of multiple products, but this would only be a first step to the solution in terms of transfer price. We shall, instead, make only some general comments.

1. In the typical firm producing more than one product, it seems likely that additional production in any one line will tend to reduce the average and the marginal costs of producing the other. The existence of such complementarities in production (i.e., the ability to produce the products jointly more cheaply than if they were produced separately) is a common reason for producing a secondary product, and, even if a secondary product were produced for other reasons, it would be unlikely to be retained by a firm if its adverse effect on the other products were serious.

2. It appears that a beginning approach to the problem of transfer pricing under conditions of technological dependence would involve establishment of an internal "tax" or "subsidy" to make the autonomous calculations of the separate division take into account the effects on the margin of impaired or enhanced productivity in the other divisions.

3. Fairly frequently, a vertically integrated firm will not trade outside the firm on an intermediate market at all but will instead establish a level of joint output at which the selling division and the buying division will both produce. Under technological independence, such behavior is difficult to explain (see sec. C above). With technological dependence under conditions of complementarity, however, such behavior becomes more understandable. When any division produces beyond the level which keeps it in step with the other vertically integrated divisions, the excess units are more costly to produce than if all the divisions had increased output together.

G. CONCLUSIONS

1. If a single joint level of output is to be determined (because no market for the intermediate commodity exists, or for any other reason), this output should be such that the sum of the divisional marginal costs equals the marginal revenue in the final market. To achieve this result by internal pricing, the transfer price must equal the marginal costs of the seller division. This is only a necessary condition, however, and not a sufficient one. The full solution involves one of the divisions presenting to the other its supply schedule (or demand schedule, as the case may be) as a function of the transfer price. The second division then establishes its output and the transfer price by a rule which leads to the optimum solution specified above for the firm as a whole.

2. Given technological independence and demand independence, if a perfectly competitive market for the intermediate commodity exists, transfer price should be market price. If the market for the intermediate commodity is imperfectly competitive, transfer price should be at the marginal costs of the selling division. The latter is the more general solution. In the general case of imperfect competition, the price of the intermediate commodity will exceed the marginal cost of the seller division. Transfer pricing at the market will then lead to excessive output by the seller division and insufficient output by the buyer division—in comparison with the optimum solution.

3. Where technological dependence exists, the situation is so complex that we have not been able to indicate even the nature of the general solution. We suspect that the prospects for divisional autonomy may be poor under these conditions.

4. Where demand dependence exists, the analysis is rather complex.

Generally speaking, the solution falls between market price and marginal cost.

5. Even under the assumptions of demand independence and technological independence, the optimal rule for transfer price leads to correct output adjustments only on the margin. It does not follow that, if an autonomous division is apparently losing money at the established transfer price, the firm would really increase its profits by abandoning the operation concerned.

We may close with some remarks about the practical implications of the foregoing analysis. Most commonly, divisional autonomy is probably desired not so much to rationalize interdivisional trading as to create incentives for the separate "profit centers" which will lead to improved internal efficiency within each. Nevertheless, cases may arise in which the former objective is the dominant one, and even where the latter is dominant some of the potential gains may be lost by an improper transfer-price rule or policy. In practice, the rule of pricing at the market is apparently the one most frequently adopted, and there are circumstances in which that rule is appropriate. Where it is not, however, the consequences of adopting it may be serious. Perhaps even more serious are the possible consequences of the error warned of in paragraph 5 above—evaluating the overall operations of a division (with a view toward either expanding or abandoning it) on the basis of its separate "profit" calculated from the established transfer price, whether correct or incorrect. When nonmarginal decisions like abandoning a subsidiary are under consideration, a calculation of the incremental revenues and costs of the operation as a whole to the firm should be undertaken.

part SIX
Capital Budgeting

INTRODUCTION

Capital budgeting is one of the main topics of managerial economics. Known also as investment decision making, equipment replacement analysis, and the analysis of capital expenditures, it is concerned with choices among the investment alternatives available to the firm, with the goal of accepting the most profitable alternatives and rejecting the others.

The main parts of capital budgeting concern (a) the cost of capital, (b) replacement policy and the estimation of useful life, (c) ranking criteria, and (d) uncertainty. Work on the cost of capital has grown so technical in recent years as to be largely inaccessible on the introductory level. Until the results and controversies associated with the names of Modigliani and Miller are synthesized, they must be ignored here.

Estimating the useful life of an investment implies something about its depreciation—not a part of the subject investigated much by economists. In most decisions one cannot find an opportunity cost to match the imputed "depreciation cost." But in questions of replacement policy and investment timing generally, the economic basis of depreciation—decline in market value—is obviously relevant. Vernon Smith takes a strictly economic approach to this question in the article reprinted here. His results give unexpected support to some common methods of depreciation.

The part of the capital budgeting literature not concerned with the cost of capital and uncertainty tends to dwell on ranking criteria, especially the "theoretically correct" methods of present value and internal rate of return. But there appears to be little evidence that actual firms are influenced much by the results. Warren Haynes and Martin Solomon argue that current capital budgeting theory fails to cover enough of the decision-making process. The struggle for continued existence by small firms in highly competitive markets, for example, may be more important than the refinements of theoretically sound capital budgeting techniques.

Martin Weingartner investigates some properties and advantages of the usually maligned payback period, the criterion most commonly used in business. Weingartner recognizes that the payback concept is an oversimplification in every case. But the problems that lead managers to its use, e.g., uncertainty, will not disappear simply because academicians call the payback approach unscientific.

The problem of uncertainty is in many ways the most interesting part of capital budgeting and has received some of the best work in the field. But attacks on it at present take such a multitude of approaches that the form of a new synthesis, if it ever occurs, cannot be foreseen. That the problem is so serious as to raise doubts about the attention paid to refined ranking criteria based on certainty assumptions is shown nicely in the article by Martin Solomon.

Joel Dean's article is concerned with the extension of capital budgeting into the field of advertising. It argues that so long as responses to advertising occur with a delay, advertising expenditures are a form of capital investment and should be treated as such.

24. Depreciation, Market Valuations, and Investment Theory*

VERNON L. SMITH

A voluminous literature exists on various aspects of the so-called "depreciation" problem, what it should or should not measure for different purposes, and how to compute it. The present paper does not propose to review, repeat, or add to this literature, but rather to discuss depreciation within the context of investment decision theory. In short, we ask, "What does investment decision theory have to say about the depreciation problem?"

To obtain some perspective for this purpose, it should be emphasized that the salient feature of capital goods in production is the fact that such goods have only to be present as physical stocks in order for the typical modern productive process to operate. They do not necessarily require it, but in fact it often pays to provide such capital goods with varying degrees of logistic support in the form of maintenance, servicing, adjustment, attending, and so on. Sooner or later, no matter how great the physical durability of a capital good, it usually pays to discard it. Also, from time to time it pays to acquire new units of such assets for the purpose of maintaining, increasing, or altering the structure of output. These considerations lead, then, to the necessity of making capital goods investment and discard decisions.

But in choosing a criterion for making such decisions we cannot use profit maximization in the ordinary sense of current profits, because if capital goods are durable, and required only to be present, there is no currently incurred cost associated with capital to be deducted from short-term cash flow earnings to arrive at profits. In recognition of this, investment decision theory is traditionally formulated as a problem of maximizing the present worth of the revenue-outlay stream associated with maintaining the physical presence of capital goods in production. The mathematical formulation of the problem thus preserves this empiri-

---

* *Management Science*, vol. 9, no. 4 (July 1963) pp. 690–96.

cal feature of capital goods by admitting only to lum-sum capital outlays, current outlays for operating purposes, and current receipts from sales.

Now, where in this theoretical picture do we fit the so-called depreciation problem? To begin with, it must be emphasized that the depreciation problem arises for one major reason: It arises because someone—management, the stockholders, the government—wants the answer to an ambiguous question. Someone wants to know what are the firm's net earnings or profits for an interval of time, such as a year or a quarter, which is very short compared to the investment period of capital employed by the firm. But, as is well known, there is no completely unambiguous way to allocate to a current period costs which have not been incurred during that period for inputs used in the process of production. All we really know is that the firm has certain receipts from current sales and certain out-of-pocket expenditures for current inputs during the year. The difference is a sum which can be divided in any arbitrary manner between something which is called "profit" for the year and something which is called "depreciation" for the year. The road is thus opened for disagreement and bargaining, which fact surely helps to guarantee full employment for economists, accountants, and lawyers in industry and government.

The economic theorist has generally recognized this ambiguity, and has preferred to employ concepts of opportunity cost, involving market alternatives, to permit depreciation and other valuations to be made for decision making purposes where they do not exist in ordinary clerical reality. Such concepts arise naturally in the simple Preinreich-Lutz-Terborgh theory of investment timing, and can be related directly to the depreciation problem, which is the objective of this discussion.

According to this theory, the present value of an incumbent asset and the chain of future assets to be held after the existing asset is discarded can be expressed

$$V = \int_0^{L_0} R_0(t)e^{-rt}\,dt + M_0(L_0)e^{-rL_0} + V'e^{-rL_0} \qquad (1)$$

where $\int_0^{L_0} R_0(t)e^{-rt}\,dt$ is the present worth of the net revenues (gross receipts minus out-of-pocket operating expenses) expected over the remaining life, L_0 of the present asset, $M_0(L_0)$ is the market value of the asset as a function of the additional years it is held, and $V'e^{-rL_0}$ is the present worth of the future chain of assets to be acquired after the existing asset is sold off. V' is given by

$$V' = \sum_{k=0}^{\infty} e^{-rkL} \left\{ \int_0^L R(L_0 + kL, t)e^{-rt}\,dt - C + M(L)e^{-rL} \right\} \qquad (2)$$

24. Depreciation, Market Valuations, and Investment Theory 379

where $R(L_0 + kL, t)$ is the net revenue of the $k + 1^{\text{th}}$ member of the future asset chain, C is its investment cost, and $M(L)$ is its market value after L years of service. We assume that the future chain of investments are to be equally spaced every L years. If V is to be maximized, the present asset should be retained for a period $L_0 \geqq 0$, such that

$$R_0(L_0) + M_0'(L_0) - rM_0(L_0) + \frac{\partial V'}{\partial L_0} \leq rV' \qquad (3)$$

or

$$H_0(L_0) = \frac{R_0(L_0) + M_0'(L_0) + \dfrac{\partial V'}{\partial L_0}}{r} - V' \leq M_0(L_0), \qquad (4)$$

where $L_0 = 0$ if $<$ holds, and V' is now evaluated at L such that $\partial V'/\partial L = 0$.

The inequations in (3) and (4) provide two alternative but equivalent forms for the investment decision rule. The less familiar form (4) can be expressed verbally as follows:

Discard an incumbent asset in favor of the most attractive alternative commitment (the "challenger" asset, to use Terborgh's phrase) if the net contribution to the present worth of the enterprise due to holding the asset an additional year does not exceed the external market value of the asset. The complement of this rule is to hold the asset an additional year if the resulting contribution to net worth exceeds the market value of the asset.

In this form the rules are intended to reflect the emphasis of modern programming-decision theory. According to this theory, the maximizing firm should adjust its utilization of each resource until the marginal internal value of the resource to the firm no longer exceeds the market value of that resource. In the present investment theory context, "adjustment" means holding an asset. An asset is held until its marginal internal value to the enterprise from another year's service no longer exceeds its external market value.

This decision rule is illustrated in Figure 1. In the illustration, $H_0(L_0)$ is the net contribution to the present worth of the enterprise of holding a sunk investment L_0 additional years, while $M_0(L_0)$, the market value (salvage or resale) of the asset at L_0, is the contribution to present worth that will result from sale. As indicated in (4), $H_0(L_0)$, is composed of the capitalized value of the asset's expected net earnings in year L_0, $(R_0(L_0))/r$, plus the capitalized value of the asset's expected decline in market value that year (this component is algebraically negative), $(M_0'(L_0))/r$, plus the capitalized value of the expected technological change benefits obtained by delaying reinvestment an additional year (such a delay permits the purchase of a more "profitable" asset in a

FIGURE 1

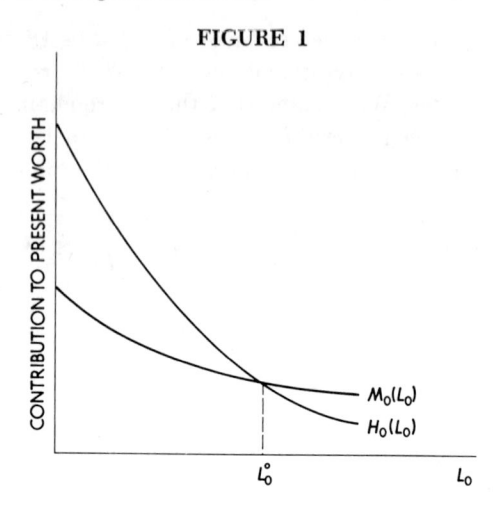

[Figure 1: Graph with vertical axis labeled "CONTRIBUTION TO PRESENT WORTH" and horizontal axis labeled L_0. Two downward-sloping curves labeled $M_0(L_0)$ and $H_0(L_0)$ intersect at L_0^0.]

world of technological improvement), $(\partial V'/\partial L_0)/r$, less the present worth of the expected future net income stream of the reinvestment asset and its chain of replacements, V'. The first three enumerated components of $H_0(L_0)$ provide the gross contribution of the asset to the firm's present worth. From this is subtracted V', which is an opportunity cost of not reinvesting at L_0, to arrive at net present worth contributed. When the internal worth contributed by holding the asset no longer exceeds its market value, the asset should be replaced, as indicated at L_0^0 in figure 1.

What all this theory means is that the astute enterprise will constantly review its investment program, comparing each asset's internal contribution to the net present value of the firm with the asset's market value. If such procedures are used consistently and the rules followed, then within the accuracy limits of the firm's data and the assumptions of the model, capital will be allocated so that the firm's net worth is at all times as great as possible. Note also that this procedure not only allocates capital efficiently, but also allocates management to its most efficient ends. Since the net revenues obtained from an asset depend vitally upon its propitious management, those assets which a given management can organize most effectively will show the highest present worth.

It is worth noting that this interpretation leads naturally to a theory of second-hand markets. If a capital good has only one homogeneous use to an industry composed of identical firms faced with the same external conditions, then no second-hand market would develop for the capital good. But the moment one recognizes different uses for the same capital good, or the existence of firms operating under different environ-

24. Depreciation, Market Valuations, and Investment Theory

mental stimuli, the stage is set for the emergence of a second hand market. The economic function of such a market is to allocate the units of a capital good in each age or "condition" class to its most important (highest present worth) use. Thus, the rational line-haul trucking firm will offer a unit to the used truck market whenever its resale value equals (or exceeds) its contribution to the firm's net worth. The unit may in turn be purchased by a maximizing firm specializing in local service, who finds the used unit its most attractive alternative to replace a still older unit that is being sold to a junk dealer.

This downgrading function performed by the market mechanism is illustrated in figure 2. We assume only two classes of firms with different

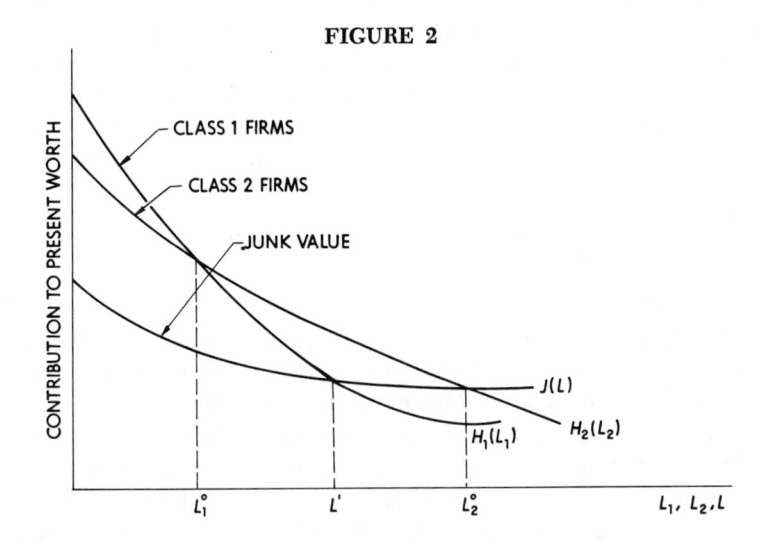

FIGURE 2

employment for the same capital good (such as over-the-road and local uses for trucks). The typical firm in class 1 finds that a unit of equipment contributes an amount $H_1(L_1)$ to the firm's present worth, while the firm in class 2 has a marginal internal worth function $H_2(L_2)$. A third use of the equipment is for junk, and this value is given by the function $J(L)$. From the illustration it is seen that firms in class 1 will buy new equipment, and replace every L_1^0 years. Firms in class 2 will buy used units L_1^0 years old, and replace every $L_2^0 - L_1^0$ years, selling their discarded units to the junk market. If this second hand market were organized one would observe new units being sold at a price $H_1(0)$. Quotations on units falling in the age interval between zero and L_1^0, would be $H_2(L_2)$ bid, $H_1(L_1)$ asked. Since $H_1 > H_2$ on this interval there would be no exchange contracts. At L_1^0 an exchange would occur between the two classes of firms, and quotations on the age interval between L_1^0 and L_2^0 would be $H_2(L_2)$ asked, $H_1(L_1)$ bid, with no exchanges. The going bid price at all ages from the junk yard would follow $J(L)$, and this bid would not exceed both the next best bid, $H_1(L_1)$, and the best (and only) offer until age L_2^0. Hence, the market value function $M_0(L_0)$, in the sense of best bid would have the form:

$$M_0(L_0) = \begin{cases} H_2(L_0), & 0 \leq L_0 < L_1^0 \\ H_1(L_0), & L_1^0 \leq L_0 < L^1 \\ J(L_0), & L^1 \leq L_0 \leq L_2^0 \end{cases}$$

Returning now to the depreciation problem, we see in figure 1 and in the decision rule (4), two interpretive concepts of depreciation—market value, $M_0(L_0)$, and contribution to internal worth, $H_0(L_0)$. Still a third concept of depreciation appears most obviously in inequation (3), the more common current-income form of the decision rules. Thus we note that one of the components of the discounted net income of the replacement asset, rV', is the discounted current account equivalent of its capital investment cost plus that of its future replacements, i.e.,

$$r \sum_0^\infty C \exp(-rkL) = rC/(1 - \exp(rL))$$

This latter concept of depreciation is simply the annuity method of allocating the investment cost of an asset to current account.[1]

Now, if the purpose of depreciation accounting is to develop data and records suitable for investment decision making, then all three of these concepts of "depreciation" are relevant. Estimates of capital cost plus interest expressed on current account are necessary for the purpose of computing $H_0(L_0)$ (a "subjective" value concept of depreciation), which in turn must be compared with the declining market value of an asset to determine optimal investment timing. It seems to me that the question of whether or not these concepts provide "true" measures of "depreciation" in some sense such as capital consumption—whatever that means at the firm decision making level—is neither relevant nor interesting.

---

[1] As I have indicated elsewhere, this popular straight-line method of depreciation can be rationalized as a rough approximation to the annuity method, since $rC/(1 - e^{-rL}) \cong C/L$, if rL is small. This approximation is satisfactory only for relatively short-lived capital goods and/or low rates of discount and has the effect of understanding the allocation of cost to current account.

25. A Misplaced Emphasis in Capital Budgeting[*]

W. WARREN HAYNES and MARTIN B. SOLOMON, JR.

This article is based on detailed research on small business investments. Our findings are somewhat opposed to the usual emphasis in the literature on capital budgeting. We believe that the three most promising areas for the improvement of managerial performance, especially in small firms, are the search for investment opportunities, the search for information about each of the discovered alternatives, and the careful estimation of the incremental gains and costs that will result from investments. The literature, however, stresses an entirely different step in the decision-making process: the precise computation of the relative worth of investment alternatives. It is contended here that management would be mistaken to devote so much attention to refinements of computation that it neglects the really important, more basic steps in the investment process. Perhaps such a neglect is less likely in large firms which have definite procedures for finding investment opportunities and developing information. But the evidence in this study is that small firms often do neglect the early stages of the decision-making process.

One case in the study illustrates a main theme of this article. The owner of a small, two-year-old chemicals firm was neglecting the refinements of investment analysis. His funds were in short supply. His investment opportunities were numerous. His problem was one of keeping up with his most urgent needs, to keep his operation going, and to make as full use of his plant as possible. He believed he knew what the most urgent investment needs were; he relied on a subjective evaluation, sometimes supported by a rough payback computation.

This chemical manufacturer was unusual among our managers in that he was somewhat familiar with the theory of investment. He knew about the discounted rate of return and present value. He was somewhat confused by this knowledge. He was apologetic for his crude decision-making

---

[*] *The Quarterly Review of Economics and Business*, vol. 2, no. 1 (February 1962), pp. 39–46.

processes and claimed that "as soon as things settled down" he would use more refined criteria.

We believe that this manager would be mistaken to devote much attention to the usual refinements of investment theory. His time (and the time of his staff) is more valuable in other occupations, such as improving the working capital position and stimulating sales. We shall present other case illustrations to support this viewpoint and to indicate important improvements some managers can make in investment decision making.

THE EMPHASIS IN CURRENT LITERATURE

Three recent publications are representative of current capital budgeting literature: *The Management of Corporate Capital,* edited by Ezra Solomon; *The Capital Budgeting Decision,* by Harold Bierman and Seymour Smidt; and George Terborgh's *Business Investment Policy: A MAPI Study and Manual.* The Ezra Solomon volume is a collection of somewhat technical articles, written primarily by economists concerned with the investment problem. Of the 22 articles, 8 are concerned with measuring investment worth, giving attention to present value and rate of return computations. Six articles are concerned with the difficult problem of measuring the cost of capital. Only two short articles devote much attention to the administrative and organizational aspects of decision making, though there are passing references to such matters in other parts of the volume.

The Bierman-Smidt volume is similar in its relative emphasis, devoting the majority of its space to measures of investment worth and to the cost of capital. The MAPI volume quite naturally is also concerned primarily with the arithmetic of evaluating and ranking projects, with a great deal of technical explanation of the MAPI formula. Somewhat surprisingly the MAPI volume gives proportionately greater attention than is usual to the other steps in the investment decision-making process. It gives attention to organizational and informational problems, including the maintenance of records, the systematic use of the records already in existence, and the need for "enlightened judgment" in addition to formulas. But the major stress in the MAPI volume is on the computation and use of formulas.

The refinements of analysis contained in these and similar books obviously represent an advance in knowledge. We now know more about the implicit assumptions underlying each formula. We know the conditions under which the payback reciprocal will give a close estimate of the discounted rate of return. We know how little we know about the cost of capital. Further advances in the computation of investment worth are desirable, but not to the neglect of the other steps in investment decision making.

WEAKNESSES OF THEORETICALLY CORRECT METHODS

Two formulas are generally accepted as "theoretically correct" when dealing with investment decisions. In spite of controversy about which of the two is superior, there is general agreement that one or the other is the standard by which all other formulas are to be judged. The two methods are present value analysis and computation of the discounted rate of return.

These formulas will not be discussed in great detail. They appear in most discussions of capital budgeting and even in elementary textbooks.[1] The main point to stress here is that while these methods may be theoretically correct, they are not widely used in actual investment decisions. Not one of the 50 small firms included in this study used either of these methods; and other surveys suggest that their use is exceptional even in large firms. This raises the question of whether management is remiss in failing to apply refinements that have received attention for over a decade. Can management justify its continued use of qualitative and crude quantitative methods?

A further development of this issue requires a discussion of the weaknesses of the theoretically correct methods so far as practice is concerned. Four central weaknesses receive attention here: (1) the reduced productivity of refinement in the face of the uncertainty involved in investment

---

[1] The simplest formula for the present value is

$$V = \frac{Q_1}{1+i} + \frac{Q_2}{(1+i)^2} + \cdots + \frac{Q_n}{(1+i)^n} + \frac{S}{(1+i)^n}$$

where V = present value,
Q_t = after-tax cash flow in year t (t is the year in which the cash is received),
S = terminal salvage value,
i = rate of interest, and
n = useful life of asset.

The formula for the discounted rate of return is closely related to that for the present value. The discounted rate of return is the rate of discount which when applied to the future cash inflows will equate them to the supply price of the investment. The formula is

$$C = \frac{Q_1}{(1+r)} + \frac{Q_2}{(1+r)^2} + \cdots + \frac{Q_n + S}{(1+r)^n}$$

where C = the supply price or installed cost of the asset, and
r = the discounted rate of return.

decisions; (2) conceptual difficulties in determining what the actul theoretically correct criterion is; (3) the difficulty of educating management in the use of the refined methods; and (4) the misdirection of managerial attention that the stress on refined calculations may entail.

The Problem of Uncertainty

While traditional managerial and economic literature has recognized the usefulness of the present value method under conditions of certainty, it has generally neglected to point out its limitations under conditions of uncertainty. The businessman cannot assume conditions of certainty when he is faced with the problem of ranking a set of investment proposals in order of profitability. He is uncertain about the annual costs and revenues resulting from each proposal, the length of life of each proposal, the possible salvage values, the opportunity cost of capital, competitors' retaliatory actions, availability of capital, actual interest rates, reinvestment opportunities, and the supply price of the proposal under consideration. The uncertainty involved in each of these categories is a matter of degree. Usually the investor is not completely ignorant of what the future holds but at the same time he cannot derive mathematical probability distributions concerning these variables.

One case is selected to illustrate the uncertainty connected with capital investments. A diversified investor was considering a proposal to open a coin-operated laundry. The total investment was estimated at about $40,000. He was highly uncertain about annual revenues. After months of careful study he estimated that revenues would range from $30,000 to $60,000 annually. He was also uncertain about the life of the equipment involved; estimates ranged from two to six years. The discounted rate of return for this investment ranged from negative figures to more than 60 percent. When he narrowed down the possible revenues-life combinations that he thought were most likely the discounted rate of return ranged from negative figures to about 30 percent.

How could refined investment formulas help such a businessman? They would probably confuse him rather than aid in a logical decision-making process.

As mentioned before, most businessmen do not use the theoretically correct methods. They prefer alternative methods that are simpler, more direct, and involve fewer hidden assumptions. Alternative methods deserve greater attention in investment literature than they have usually been given and are more useful than has been generally recognized. In many cases these alternative methods provide close estimates of the discounted rate of return and, what is more important, they seem to have the ability to rank investments in about the same order as theoretically correct methods.

To illustrate the use of an alternative method, we return to the laundry case discussed earlier. This businessman simplified his decision-making problem by using the payback criterion. While losses were possible, he was pretty certain that the investment would pay off in one year and much more certain that it would pay off in less than two years.

Since estimates about years beyond the second became extremely uncertain, it is not surprising that this investor should focus on the payback criterion. If profitability depends heavily on returns beyond the payback period, there is a natural unwillingness to take chances on the investment. The payback criterion acts as a "go-no-go" gauge which may at first seem crude but which may actually be a sensible way of dealing with the problem of uncertainty.

In this respect, payback analysis is analogous to break-even analysis. Both are simplified treatments of the outcomes of decision making. Both may represent reasonable compromises with uncertainty. In break-even analysis, the manager can concentrate on the probability that sales and output will exceed the break-even point, without having to specify the exact level of future output. In payback analysis, the manager can focus attention on the probability that the life of the investment will exceed the payback period, without having to make exact estimates of how profitable the investment will be. Both methods provide the manager with shortcuts to decision making that are often satisfactory substitutes for refined analysis.

Conceptual Difficulties

It is often assumed that discounted rate of return and present value are theoretically correct criteria for evaluating alternative formulas. The two methods may, however, give a somewhat different ranking of investment proposals. The difference between the present value method and the discounted rate of return arises from a difference in the implicit assumptions about the reinvestment of the returns from the initial investment. Present value analysis assumes that earnings will be reinvested at the discount rate used. The discounted rate of return rests on the assumption that returns can be reinvested at the same rate as the proposed investment.

A purist on investment theory might insist on the "chain of machines" formulation. It seems certain that most firms that *do* use the present value or discounted rate of return do not make use of this refinement. Managers normally make a rough estimate of length of life. In some cases they include an estimate of the salvage value at the end of this life, but they avoid the problem of explicitly determining how the inflow of funds will be reinvested. The theoretical issues at that point are too abstract and complex for most managers.

The Problem of Education and Communication

Even if it were clear that the use of theoretically correct methods is helpful under conditions of uncertainty, it is unlikely that managers of small firms will take the time to understand the formulas and their interpretation. No doubt the difficulty of communicating the meaning of the refined methods is a major reason for their unpopularity. Even for large firms it would be a mistake to conclude that the answer is to delegate investment decisions to the specialists; general management normally has much to contribute to the evaluation of investments that the specialists may overlook.

A Possible Misdirection of Managerial Attention

The obvious reply to the position just taken about the difficulty of communicating with managers unfamiliar with the refined formulas is that they should *take* time to learn and to apply these methods. But this depends on whether management can afford the time required. To use the language of economics, there must be a comparison of the marginal product of refinement in measuring investment worth with the marginal product of other allocations of management time. The argument so far has been that in many cases, and almost always in small firms, the marginal product of refinement is low, especially under conditions of uncertainty. The remainder of this article is concerned with demonstrating that other uses of management time, even in the sphere of investment decision making, are likely to be more productive.

OPPORTUNITIES FOR IMPROVEMENT OF CAPITAL BUDGETING

Capital budgeting involves much more than the careful computation of the worth of a project and its comparison with a norm. Capital budgeting requires, first of all, the search for and discovery of investment opportunities. Second, it requires the collection of information about alternatives, such as estimates of the resultant changes in revenues and costs. Third, it requires the application of incremental reasoning to the collected information, to ensure that the relevant estimates are used and irrelevant considerations are ignored. In our opinion, these are the areas in which a great improvement in practice is possible, especially in the small businesses which are the object of our research. Each of these opportunities for the improvement of capital budgeting deserves special attention.

The Search for Alternatives

The best way to indicate the importance of the search for alternatives is to cite some cases from our study.

A wholesale liquor dealer devotes most of his time to the search for and evaluation of alternatives. After years of routine work, he decided he was not moving forward. He hired a sales manager to relieve him of routine work and turned to larger issues. He built up a file of ideas for investment which he reviewed periodically with the addition of new schemes. He now keeps his time free to search for new and better investments. He applies unsophisticated methods to his selections.

The backlog of investment opportunities built up in this firm helps assure that unprofitable alternatives will not be selected. The backlog contributes to a high "aspiration level," leading to rejection of less profitable proposals without a refined evaluation of the relative profitability of alternatives.

As a contrast to this case of the active search for investment opportunities, take the case of a wearing apparel firm. The president admits that "only one investment opportunity seems to come up at a time." No search for alternatives is undertaken. As a result, when a proposal is evaluated, the president has few if any other investment opportunities with which to compare it. It seems likely that the engineering department of this company could discover internal improvement in such areas as materials handling and purchasing. The failure to seek such alternatives appears to reduce the profit potential of this firm.

Other cases in the study reveal a similar inattention to new investment opportunities. They also illustrate a failure of management to set aside time for search activity. It is our impression that the distinction between firms that are actively engaged in search and those that are not is a major factor in determining small firms' success or failure in sound, imaginative investment programs.

The Search for Information

Great differences exist among firms in the devotion of managerial time to the search for information about alternatives, once these alternatives are discovered. Again two cases illustrate these differences.

One successful manager and his associates were considering investment in a bowling alley. They had opportunities to invest in other activities: an expansion of their manufacturing activities (the production of wooden parts), or of the advertising business in which several of them were engaged. The outstanding feature of the decision-making process in this case was the long perod of time devoted to the collection of information about the alternatives. The manager and his associates interviewed the owners of bowling alleys in other parts of the country; they collected operating statements for bowling alleys of a size similar to that of the one under consideration; they obtained statistics from a national accounting firm on bowling alley financial results. In addition, they sought the opinions of business associates. They made estimates of volumes of business that could be expected and of potential costs. They projected income statements and source and application of funds statements for three years of bowling alley operation. They made up break-even charts based on several sets of assumptions and considered the probabilities of being above the break-even point and the prospective profits at various volumes. They compared their estimates and had business associates make independent estimates.

In the meantime these businessmen were gathering similar information on the advertising alternative. It seems highly unlikely that they would invest in an unprofitable venture after such careful collection and evaluation of information; the information and the existence of alternatives were more certain guarantees of profitable decisions than any mechanical formulas could be.

In contrast to this case are the firms that make investments on the basis of "hunches" or extremely limited information. Some managers fail to take advantage of investment opportunities because of inadequate information or the pressure of routine duties.

The president of a small tire company was thinking of opening a branch retail store. Because he was busy with more routine work he neglected the collection of information about this opportunity; he let the idea drop. A little study on the part of the interviewer revealed that the president had probably passed up an extremely lucrative opportunity. The president, at the request of the interviewer, estimated that revenues (in a particular location) would range from about $48,000 to $80,000. An analysis of *incremental* costs indicated that annual pretax profits of from $750 to $12,000 were likely. The entire investment amounted to only $2,000. The careful collection of data about this alternative would have revealed its hidden potential.

The accumulation of information must take priority over refinement in computation. It is not particularly helpful to apply a theoretically correct formula to the wrong information.

Correct Incremental Reasoning

The collection of information is not enough. It is necessary to separate relevant information from the irrelevant and to organize the data in a meaningful form. For example, many managers are confused about the costs that should be considered in an investment decision. In particular, they are not clear on the treatment of overhead costs.

One case from a large firm illustrates this type of confusion. A manufacturer of rubber and plastic products utilized more elaborate decision-making procedures than the firms cited so far. The firm required a 30 percent return on investment despite the fact that it was in a highly liquid position, with a current ratio of 7 to 1 and several million dollars of low-yield government bonds. The rate of return was based on first year performance. But in obtaining the first year performance the firm not only charged depreciation against the new investment, it also charged depreciation on a "capital corollary," which was considered to be 70 percent of the investment. This analysis was based on the assumption that each new machine required space involving an average investment of 70 percent of the machine cost. The analysis ignored the possibility of idle space. It neglected the probability that some labor-saving or capital-saving equipment might not take up additional space or might even save space.

Similarly this firm charged overhead and selling and administrative expenses against the returns on a new investment. Again predetermined averages were used. It appears that the overhead allocation duplicated the depreciation charges already mentioned. In addition, it is not at all clear that each new investment would result in the same proportional change in selling and administrative expense.

The method used by this rubber and plastics firm violates the canons of incremental reasoning in several ways. It ignores the fact that each investment will affect overhead costs in a different way, so that overall averages are inappropriate. It fails to recognize that many overhead costs may be "fixed" for a particular decision. This company substitutes predetermined allocations for "tailor-made" estimates of the impact of investments on costs.

Other cases in this study reveal a similar confusion about the correct treatment of depreciation and overhead costs. The result may be a 50 percent or even 100 percent error in the estimates of cash inflows. No formula can overcome fundamental errors in the collection and evaluation of data. If there is to be education of managers for improved decision making, it might be best to concentrate on the incremental reasoning that will help them make correct estimates of cash inflows and outflows.

CONCLUSION

The need, especially in small business, is not for further refinement in the application of formulas for investment worth, but for greater attention to the other steps in the decision-making process.

Capital budgeting consists of at least five managerial functions: (1) continuous and creative search for investment opportunities; (2) forecasting the supply and cost of funds for investment purposes; (3) estimating each project's cash flows and other benefits; (4) ranking and choosing among competing projects; and (5) post-auditing already committed investments.

The literature has devoted primary attention to the fourth function (ranking and choosing) and considerable attention to the second (forecasting the cost of funds), but has usually neglected the others. Our case studies suggest that the highest priorities should be assigned to the search for alternatives, the search for information, and the correct processing of the available data *before* ranking formulas are applied. Precise computations applied to the wrong information cannot result in correct measurements of investment worth.

We do not consider our position to be antitheoretical. Advances in the theory of capital budgeting are to be welcomed. The difficulty is that the currently publicized theory is too narrow to cover the entire decision-making process. As is natural, the theory has concentrated on those phases that are most amenable to systematic analysis and to quantification. The theory has stressed the fine points that require clarification when one constructs a precise model. The need is not for less theory but for more and broader theory. Important phases of capital budgeting cry for research and for theoretical generalization. For example, there are questions of motivation involved in investment decisions: why are some managers and some subordinates more effective in the search for alternatives? There are problems of measuring the productivity of search. There is a need for the empirical measurement of the increased profits resulting from refinement in ranking. It is interesting that the literature stressing the quantification of evaluations of investment worth is so vague on the rate of return on refinement itself.

Thus, Walker's stress on managerial judgment that goes beyond the technical computations of investment worth is welcome.[2] But, as Simon has stated, the word "judgment" is a challenge to the scientist, who must feel the urge to identify the characteristics of sound judgment. We have suggested that judgment on investment decisions may frequently require more attention to the less developed phases of decision making, even if this requires reduced attention given to the refinements of ranking and measurement of investment worth.

---

[2] Ross G. Walker, "The Judgment Factor in Investment Decisions," *Harvard Business Review*, vol. 39, no. 2 (March–April 1961), pp. 93–99.

26. Some New Views on the Payback Period and Capital Budgeting Decisions*

H. MARTIN WEINGARTNER

While academic writers have almost unanimously condemned use of the "payback period" in capital budgeting, it continues to be one of the most widely applied quantitative concepts in making investment decisions. It must be conceded that the payback period, i.e., the time it is expected for an investment project to recoup its initial cost, is hardly a tool which can provide the decision maker with all the information he needs. As most textbooks correctly point out, the time value of money via discounting of future cash flows never enters into its calculation. Nevertheless, a serious question must be raised and answered: why is the payback period so ubiquitously used, despite its universal critics? It may be the case that the problem which managers are seeking to solve by use of payback is not, in fact, handled by the tools many textbook writers espouse.

This paper seeks to provide a better understanding of the capital investment problem by carefully analyzing the payback concept. Given the complexity of the problem of capital investment decisions and our state of knowledge with respect to the economic, psychological and organizational bases for current practice, it must be admitted that what follows should more properly be labeled as a set of conjectures. Although the plausibility of the arguments will be supported wherever possible, the objective here is to widen the perspective within which much of the discussion of investment decision methods takes place. By following an encyclopedic approach in the paper, it should not be assumed that all or even most of the suggested rationales for the use of payback are operative at the same time, or within the same individuals, parts of the organization or even firms. Rather, it is suggested that all of them are considerations at one time or another, and that the variety of problems which the payback concept attacks helps to reinforce the

*Management Science, vol. 15, no. 12 (August 1969), pp. B594–B607.

appeal which businessmen profess for this measure of investment value. In the course of the analysis which follows we shall discuss payback as a criterion versus payback as a constraint, liquidity of capital assets versus liquidity requirements of the firm, payback as a break-even concept and finally, payback and the resolution of uncertainty.

One point should be emphasized at the outset. *We shall not end by rehabilitating payback*, for more sophisticated and precise methods are available or can be developed to deal with the issues to be raised below. Hopefully, however, we shall have learned something about the nature of the investment problem and encouraged development of alternatives.

One disclaimer seems appropriate at the outset. In seeking to analyze the capital investment decision within firms, one ought to include also a variety of aspects whose origin lies entirely within the organizational process of decision making. On the descriptive side, this would include preparation of the underlying data for a project, its review at higher levels, etc. These considerations will not be our concern here. Nevertheless, it would be useful to point out the immense difference between a single figure of merit which is attached to a proposed project for purposes of *communication* as opposed to use of that same figure as the *sole basis* for making the accept/reject decision. At various levels of the organization a hierarchy of different considerations is brought to bear on the problem, while other aspects are presumed to have been dealt with before a proposal has reached that stage. The need to communicate explicit information between groups and levels is a function of the nature of the organization and its past. When a single figure of merit is cited as being "used" by a firm in its capital investment process, care must be taken to distinguish its use as a communications device from its application as a decision criterion. While these remarks apply to all the common textbook criteria for capital budgeting decisions, they apply with special emphasis to the payback period.

PAYBACK AS A CRITERION VERSUS PAYBACK AS A CONSTRAINT

Some writers have interpreted the payback period as an indirect though quick measure of return. Given a uniform stream of receipts, the reciprocal of the payback period is the discounted cash-flow rate of return for a project of infinite life, or a good approximation to this rate for a long-lived project. Alternatively, using annuity tables one can translate the payback period directly into the correct rate of return given the project life, again if the inflows are uniform during this life.

When the scale of the investment is itself a decision variable, the above interpretation of payback has also erroneously led to its advocacy as a criterion for optimization. We refer once more to investments of the "point-input, stream-output" type, and assume a perpetual stream of receipts whose level is a function of the amount of investment, exhibiting the usual property of decreasing returns to scale. Under these assumptions, the scale of investment which maximizes the internal rate of return also minimizes the payback period. Unfortunately, maximization of the internal rate of return is not an appropriate criterion. The scale must be decided upon by reference to economic variables external to the investment, viz., the interest rate. For present purposes this implies that the optimal scale is achieved by maximization of the net present value, and is given by the point at which the marginal rate of return equals the interest rate. This, in turn, is equivalent to the point at which the payback period is equal to the reciprocal of "the interest rate" or cost of capital.

Before income taxes played an important role in investment decisions, one also could see a direct similarity between the payback period and the price/earnings ratio. Taking once more a uniform stream of receipts as the first approximation for an investment project, the ratio of cost to annual receipts, which is the payback period, is of the same form as the price of earnings per share multiple for common stock. Projecting earnings to be uniform for the foreseeable future, one may interpret P/E for a company's stock as a payback period, or, alternatively, the payback period may be regarded as the project's cost expressed as a multiple of earnings (receipts). Judgment as to whether specific numerical values associated with particular alternatives are "reasonable" or desirable is made in the same way, though obviously with different numerical standards.

Such use of payback as a figure of merit may describe business practice during the last century and perhaps the early decades of the present one. It is, however, difficult to believe that these plausible reasons plus a general cultural lag explain this tool's still current popularity. Careful consideration of the effect of taxes and depreciation rules requires distinguishing between cash flows and the more general earnings concept represented in the firm's income statement.

It is not clear that payback is used as a direct figure of merit, i.e., that it is applied to choose that project among mutually exclusive alternatives which minimizes the payback period. It *is* often (and perhaps more properly) used as a constraint: no project may be accepted unless its payback period is shorter than some specified period of time. Furthermore, not all projects satisfying the payback constraint are automatically accepted. They must satisfy *additional* criteria as well.[1] The foremost among those concerns the interrelationships which exist between

---

[1] Even when payback is cited as the sole quantitative concept applied to investment decisions, it does not follow that desirability is expressed in qualitative

projects because of the use they make of resources that are of limited supply in the short run, such as, especially, managerial manpower. Handling such problems formally requires sophisticated methods, as discussed in the references cited.

Assuming that the desirability of projects is judged on an individual project basis, perhaps by application of an appropriate discounted cash flow (DCF) measure, the question we wish to answer is, what does the payback period tell? To answer requires taking a step backward and glancing briefly at the framework of certainty within which the common DCF criteria are usually derived.

Under the assumption of certainty and perfect capital markets, the investor may be shown to be better off whenever he commits his funds to an undertaking which yields a positive net present value after allowance for all costs. The discount rate or rates which are applied to the venture's cash flows are also the market determined trade-offs between present and future consumption, which allows the investor to choose the timing of his consumption independently of the timing of his investment. Under conditions of uncertainty, the cash flows generated by the investment as well as all other claims the investor has on future benefits are subject to random fluctuations. The appropriate discount rates themselves are uncertain and these rates might be expected to change due not only to changes in market rates for risky investments, but also because the uncertainty of the cash flows of the particular investment most probably will change over its life. It is the latter notions that need to be unravelled to make sense out of the payback period.

There is one other item in the theoretical ancestry of DCF analyses which needs to be raised in these preliminaries. Basically, it is that capital goods of which economists traditionally speak are assumed to have a market value reasonably close to their depreciated cost, so that investment is essentially a reversible process. Accordingly, at any time a firm finds changed conditions which indicate future profitability of some investments to be impaired, the firm is assumed to be able to sell the assets at prices which, while affected by these new conditions, nevertheless are not too far from original cost less allowance for wear and obsolescence. (Put in different terms, the return to capital called rent in such a situation is at most a minor component of the total

---

terms such as "strategic" value, while payback is utilized in the form of a constraint as just described. Reading of much of the literature would lead one to believe that investment decisions should always be made on the basis of some single figure of merit, such as the present value or the discounted cash-flow rate of return. When the decision is placed into its organizational setting, it should become clear that no single number can answer all the questions which need to be raised concerning the commitment of the firm's resources.

return. While this method may hold for reasonably competitive industries, firms which make careful evaluations of their capital expenditures generally believe that they face falling demand curves, in which environment selecting the best level of output in the short run and capacity in the long run are among the most important managerial problems, along with choice of the best production function.)

If the investment implies potentially substantial returns to the combination of managerial or entrepreneurial skill in the form of marketing, production or other know-how; or, alternatively, if it requires substantial nonrecoverable outlays such as for site preparation, etc., the "going concern value" of the assets of the project far exceeds their market value at all times of the project's existence. Such an investment does not fit the model of completely reversible investment.

It is the case that common, though incomplete analysis of investment projects using the present value criterion is subject to the myopia problem. That is, a project usually has as one alternative its own postponement, with consequential changes in payoffs and costs. When measured from the present it is by no means always true that the highest discounted value is associated with the earliest starting date. Application of the present value criterion here, viz., the selection of that project which has the highest net present value from among the set of mutually exclusive alternatives, would still be appropriate within this framework.

The imposition of constraints on capital expenditures invalidates the present value apparatus. That is, when the expenditure of funds on capital projects has been limited to an amount not explicitly based on the investment opportunities, it is no longer true that the present value criterion satisfies a more basic objective of investment in terms of the investor's utility and consumption possibilities. Here the myopia problem of constructing an investment project too early becomes more important in that the timing of expenditures and revenues requires internal valuation, e.g., in terms of the alternatives they open up and/or foreclose because of the capital constraints. In either of these instances the payback period contains information (in the form of a single number) regarding the timing of the inflows, which could be a warning against early commitment of funds if without its use the only choice evaluated is to accept the project now or not at all.

PAYBACK AND LIQUIDITY

One consequence of insisting that each proposed investment have a short payback period is that, in some sense, the investments made are relatively "liquid." Deferring more careful analysis of this statement for a moment, it would seem to imply that this early repayment of the invested funds is desirable in and of itself, specifically apart from the desirability measured by some DCF figure of merit. Payback is sometimes applied as a constraint across all investment opportunities simultaneously, and not on a project-by-project basis, and also in a probabilistic way.

This use of payback does raise some question about traditional project evaluation. For one thing, the investment opportunities which would have to be foregone were it not for the funds generated by the new projects, as implied there, are usually assumed to have been evaluated using an appropriate discounting rate or its equivalent. That is, if the cost of capital has been estimated, and the prospective investment yields a positive net present value after discounting at this rate, then, presumably, future investments offering a positive present value will still be available: they will yield more than they cost in terms of the combination of debt and equity capital and retained earnings which will be required to finance them. When this is not the case one might presume that the cost of capital had changed *as a result* of making the investments, in which instance this change should have been anticipated and taken into account in the computation of present values currently.

Put somewhat differently, the assumption of competitive capital markets, plus, perhaps the assumption that the expectations of the capital market regarding the firm's new investment are substantially the same as those of the managers of the firm itself, would guarantee that future opportunities must not be foregone for lack of funds. Additionally, growth by *internally* generated funds is by no means the only path for rapid growth. It would seem, therefore, that in this use of payback the motive of providing for the internal generation of funds from investments for future, as yet undetermined, additional investment is based more on an implicit or explicit spending limit than on an explicit limitation of risk. More directly, the usually designated speculative and/or precautionary motive of firms to hold liquid or near liquid funds in order to seize upon unexpected opportunities is a *different* motive from that which requires each new investment separately to recover its original cost within a short time. Unless we assume that firms cannot plan for the generation of funds from operations generally, and from the investment program taken as a whole, we are forced to conclude that this use of payback is for purposes different from those related to an individual project payback constraint.

PAYBACK AS A BREAK-EVEN CONCEPT

The payback period appears to be one of a common type of break-even notions frequently employed by businessmen. Generally, the break-even point is a point of indifference—with qualifications—beyond which an accounting profit is expected to be generated by the operation under analysis, and below which loss is expected. The qualifications come from use of accounting profit rather than some more meaningful economic measure which would attach a cost to the use of funds and to the application of managerial effort.

Once again, under certainty there is no significance to the break-even point. Under uncertainty, estimation of the break-even point serves to reduce the information search for resolving choices in allocation problems. The risk against which the profit potential is to be evaluated is the risk that the firm will not be "made whole again" as a result of undertaking some operation. The fact that this standard for comparison, the firm as it was before, is not the correct measure of foregone opportunities serves only to point out that the break-even measure is an oversimplification.

Indeed, some writers suggest that the payback period should be computed to include not only recovery of the original outlays, but also the foregone interest on the amount of capital committed to the project. Doing so would, to some degree, give expression to the requirement that under normal circumstances the firm would not stand still but would earn some "normal" rate of return. However, the essential differences between the ordinary cost-volume break-even point and the payback period as a break-even point must also be considered.

In the usual break-even analysis, the evaluation made implicitly concerns the chances that the firm would incur a loss as opposed to the chances that the particular undertaking would result in gains of varying amounts. Viewing the decision from the point of view of the decision maker, the asymmetry between payoffs and penalties can, to a first approximation, be represented by a two-by-two payoff matrix which

	Success	Failure
Accept	+	−
Reject	0	0

divides the world into two states, success and failure, and two actions, accept the project and reject it, as in the figure. Assuming that similar choices must be made with sufficient frequency so that *some* projects are likely to be accepted, the rejection of a particular one by the decision maker is probably neutral.

If degree of success is a refinement which plays a role secondary to the *counting* of successes in the evaluation of a manager's performance, his initial view of the decision has having two outcomes *for him* (in contrast to the outcomes for the firm) makes some sense. The question of interest then is the meaningful line of separation between success and failure.

The least ambiguous, even if not the most appropriate, dividing line, as already discussed, is whether the firm is ahead or not by doing the project. It is not necessary to suggest that decision makers accept a minimax strategy with respect to such decisions. It is probably sufficient to say that unless the probability of "at least breaking even" is sufficient, the decision maker is likely to reject the project. Such a procedure appears to be a crude substitute for a computation which goes beyond merely the *expected* profit (in the statistical sense) to a consideration of some aspects of the *distribution* of outcomes and their consequences for the decision maker. In such a simplified shortcut procedure, the means of judging the distribution are combined with the measure itself. This is intended to take the place of a much more elaborate, if correct, two-step procedure in which the distribution is first generated, then evaluated. The probability of failing to reach at least the break-even point (the area under the density of outcomes up to a zero accounting profit), is compared with the probability of making a profit (the area to the right of the break-even point).

By contrast, the payback period is a point in *time* at which the firm expects "to be made whole again" (except for foregone interest) after making an investment. When the life of the project's stream of revenues is subject to substantial uncertainty, the payback period focuses on the period of time over which the project is expected to generate a "profit." That is, assuming for simplicity that net revenues are constant through time and only the project's life is a random variable, the aggregate (undiscounted, i.e., accounting) profit is proportional to the life of the project after the payback period has elapsed. Prior to then the stream of net revenues has been used to offset the original cost.[2]

A measure of undiscounted profit is then the project life after the payback period, and the conditional probability distribution of the

---

[2] The proportionality is only approximate because of the depreciation expense deduction for reporting profit. The effect of taxes has also been ignored here. Project life, unfortunately, enters here in two distinct ways. Aside from the above remarks that profitability depends on the project's life (especially after payback), accounting profit depends also on the rate at which depreciation expense is charged against the project's revenues. Thus a longer anticipated life yields a higher initial profit, other things remaining equal, because depreciation expense will be lower. Indeed, the life of the project may be overestimated by the proposer not only to enhance its total profitability, but also to reduce the payback period on the accounting profit basis. A bias countering this one may arise in the selection of the shortest project or asset life which the tax authorities permit to improve the actual after-tax cash-flow profitability. Cash-flow payback, the usual concept, is less affected since depreciation enters only as a tax shield. (The above qualifications to the statement in the text were suggested by Sidney Davidson.)

project's life, given that it has reached the payback period, becomes a measure of the distribution of project profitability. In the same sense as for break-even analyses in general, the decision maker than is presumed to weigh the probability that the project's life lasts longer than its payback period to make it worthwhile for him. For a given distribution of project lives, under the assumption of uniform flows, the longer the payback period the greater are the chances of incurring an accounting loss on the project. However, a short payback period would mean a higher probability of profit, and hence the project would be more attractive.

One additional observation seems still to be in order. The shorter the payback period, given the net present value (or internal rate of return) of the project, the sooner its profitability would become known.[3] A manager therefore could also reasonably expect that his wise decision would show up early enough for the rewards (e.g., in the form of a bonus or advancement) to be received when they still do him some good, given his high personal rate of discount. If the forecast turns out, ex post, to have been too optimistic after a number of years have elapsed, the possibility for alibi in the form of higher future returns yet to come is not lost, a circumstance which makes risk and reward in this situation once more asymmetric for the manager.

STABILITY OF THE PAYBACK MEASURE

An interesting observation regarding the payback period may also reinforce the basis for some of its appeal. This concerns its relative stability under random variation in the cash flow. Projection of cash flows is, at best, an imprecise art, and the ex post results are unlikely to have been included among the projections made in advance. The correctness of the decision will be somewhat more easily assessed after the fact, since the outcomes will have turned out to have been favorable or not when compared against alternatives thought to have been available. Hence the ex ante measure of project worth should be "robust," in analogous fashion to the concept as used by statisticians. The internal rate of return, for example, is quite sensitive to variation in the underlying cash flows. By contrast if it is possible to generalize from results which use the simplifying assumptions analogous to those made earlier, the payback period appears to be relatively constant.

---

[3] Given the net present value, a short payback period implies that early cash flows are expected to be high relative to later ones, and/or to the investment. Actually, of course, neither cash flows nor accounting profit will be easily attributable to a given project, and initial accounting profit may, in any case, be a loss due to heavy initial depreciation expense.

To illustrate, we assume that net revenue is normally distributed at each moment in time, with constant expectation and constant variance over time. Under these assumptions the probability distribution of the payback period can be obtained from the following expression:

$$f(T) = \frac{I}{T} \frac{1}{(2\pi kT)^{1/2}} \exp\left[-(I - cT)^2/2kT\right]$$

where I is the initial investment, $c(t) = c$ is the uniform stream of net revenues, with variance $\sigma^2(t) = k$, and T is the payback period.

A few sample computations have been carried out using this formula, and the results are presented in the table below. In the examples the

Table of Payback Periods (in Years) Exceeded with Probability P, for Three Values of Cash Flow Variance k, Given Investment I = 10, Average Annual Cash Flow c = 4

P	k		
	1	2	5
.05	3¼	3½	4¼
.10	3	3¼	3¾
.33	2¾–	2¾–	2¾
.50	2½	2½	2½
.67	2¼+	2¼–	2
.90	2	1¾	1½

amount invested, I, was assumed to be $10. The expected cash inflow, c, assumed to be received continuously, has an expected value of $4 per year, with three different values of the variance, k:1, 2, and 5. The table gives six points on the right-tail cumulative distribution of payback periods for each of the three values of cash-flow variance, from the 10 percent point to the 95 percent point.

The expected payback period of 2½ years appears for each of the values of k, the variance, in the row indicated by $P = 0.50$; i.e., 50 percent of the time one would expect the mean value of $T = 2½$ years to be exceeded, while the other half of the time it would not be expected to be this high. Approximately one third of the time the payback period here would be as high as two and three-fourths years or higher, and this quantity is about the same for all three values of cash flow variance. Ten percent of the time it would be as large as three years when the variance is one, three and one-fourth years when the variance is two, but three and three-fourths years when the variance is as high as five.

PAYBACK AND THE RESOLUTION OF UNCERTAINTY

In addition to the fact that the return on capital investment projects includes substantial rewards for good management of the project and related activities (economic rent), capital investments differ in the course of action afforded to those making the investment in contrast to the alternatives facing investors in other assets. To bring the differences into sharp relief it may be useful to compare "investments" or gambles at a roulette table, investments in bonds and stocks which are traded in a market, and capital investments.

Gambles on a roulette wheel have the characteristic that, once the wheel stops spinning the payoff has been determined and settlement is made. The outcome of subsequent spins is (presumed to be) independent of earlier outcomes. Also, the bettor's wealth has already been determined at the end of a spin, and in making his next bet he can take his new wealth position into account. Put more directly, the bets are made sequentially with the state of information the same at the beginning of each bet.

An investor purchasing marketable securities is essentially in the same position as the gambler at the roulette table. At any moment in time his decision to leave funds in an investment may be interpreted to be a reinvestment of the funds which the market value of his securities represents. The fact that the variability of outcomes is smaller for shorter intervals of time than for longer ones is unimportant here. The only significant discontinuities in this investment-disinvestment decision process are introduced by brokerage costs which are avoidable by leaving funds invested in the same securities. Another, though minor qualification, is that outcomes are not precisely known until the decision to liquidate the investment is actually carried out. However, since a market price is quoted at all times, an investor knows his wealth position with only a small degree of uncertainty and can take this into account in making decisions with respect to the continued commitment of his funds. Additionally, the decition to make the commitment does not affect the outcome in a noticeable way. Given a reasonably broad market, an individual investor's decision to make a transaction does not affect the price of the security more than trivially. Thus it is not surprising that no one computes a payback period for, say, a bond, which is expected to generate a known income stream when held to maturity.

An extreme contrast with the preceding situations would be an investment in a space flight which is expected to last several years, and which is expected to bring back valuable objects from another planet. The space ship is presumed to be the first of its kind, and to be on a mission the scope of which had never before been attempted. It is assumed to be unable to communicate with the earth (or its outposts) during almost the entire duration of its voyage. Thus the outcome of the investment will not be known until some substantial time after the original commitment of funds, and little if any additional information is assumed to be generated in the interval to alter the subjective probabilities of the recovery of the spacecraft, or its success in bringing back the valuable cargo.

Under these rather extreme assumptions the investor in this venture has tied up some of his capital for a potentially long time, with the interval to the time when the returns come in being itself a random variable. To analyze the investor's attitude to such an investment, we see that it can be broken down into two distinct components which, in turn, may be clarified by referring back to the roulette wheel.

First, suppose that the investor could place a bet today on one of two roulette wheels, the first being spun today, while the second is not spun until one year from today. If the odds were the same for the two wheels, a risk-averting bettor would prefer the first wheel to the second, assuming only that the availability of gambles next year is not expected to be curtailed or yield less favorable odds. (It is important that in either case the bet is made today, and the chips are paid for today.) Reasons for preferring the present over the deferred payoff would include a) the bettor might not be alive next year, and his utility for a bequest may not be the same as his utility for consumption while alive; b) until the outcome is known, the bettor's wealth is uncertain and he cannot adjust to the preferred consumption based on his wealth *during* the year with the second wheel; and c) even if the gamble is for an objective in the distant future, e.g., retirement, by repeating similar gambles to the first wheel, the bettor can achieve the same expected payoff, but with a lower variance of payoff. Selection of the second wheel would generally require more favorable odds.

Suppose now alternatively that the first wheel is still one which is spun today, but that a third wheel, physically identical to the second one, is not spun until some randomly selected time interval has passed, as might be determined by an auxiliary process. If the *expected* outcome of the auxiliary process, which determines the timing of the spin of the third wheel, were exactly one year, would the investor be indifferent between this deferred spin or the earlier one (the second wheel) for which the spin is slated to take place one year from now? Most likely not. Obviously, the nature of the auxiliary process would enter into the choice between the second and the third wheel.

The space venture resembles the third wheel here, since both the payoff and its timing are uncertain. The investor's consumption decisions until the return of the space craft are constrained in the following sense. The investor may be able to sell some or all of his shares in the venture, and, indeed, a market for them may exist. Prices for the shares may fluctuate in response to changes in expectations regarding the final outcome, its timing as well as its amount. For any given set of expectations regarding the amount of payoff, the elapse of time would presumably result in an increase in the price of the shares since the actual payoff is then closer.

Alternative to selling his shares, the investor may prefer to borrow against them. While he could always lever himself generally, by pledging his other assets or earning power against a loan, the shares themselves do not lend themselves to bank borrowing in the form of the common demand note with the shares as collateral. From the nature of the probability distribution of outcomes facing the *lender*, the latter would find himself in a position with more than trivial risk. Of course, such a risk may fit the portfolio of some lenders, so that at some high enough rate of interest (contingent upon there being a payoff at all) the lender would advance some or all of the required funds. To make a loan attractive to both borrower and lender requires their utility functions to be of different shape, assuming that their expectations of the outcome are the same and the composition of their portfolios is otherwise similar. The size of the residual risk, however, precludes banks operating with the funds supplied by depositors from making loans of this type.

In the preceding example the uncertainty arising from the delayed knowledge of the outcome is resolved all at once, at the end of the venture. The only time of relevance is the interval until the voyage is over. Capital investment projects of the ordinary kind represent a situation between the simple roulette wheel or security and the space venture with respect to the resolution of uncertainty. Cash flows are projected at the time the investment is first contemplated, and at least implicitly, the cash flows are considered to be subject to random deviation from their expected values. As time passes and some of the anticipated cash flows are realized, information is generated thereby as to the subsequent outcomes of the whole project. Each time such information is received, the "investor" may take any corrective managerial action he deems necessary to realize his expectations. For example, he may commit additional resources in the form of advertising, further product or process development, and especially assign additional or different managerial supervision to the project. More important, however, he is in a better position to make decisions with respect to his current consumption and with respect to other investment alternatives which present themselves. Thus the evolving information on the project's outcome is extremely valuable to him for making subsequent decisions.

A natural scaling of the importance of the information content of the initial cash inflows might be the size of the original commitment of funds. In looking at the investment entirely *ex ante*, the rate at which the uncertainty devolving around the outcome is expected to be resolved may be measured, at least crudely, by the relation between the series of cumulated expected cash inflows and the amount of the investment. In terms of a standardized measure, the time interval required for the cumulated expected inflows exactly to equal the original investment is a measure of the rate at which the project's uncertainty is *expected* to be resolved. But this measure is precisely the payback period.

CONCLUSION

In this review of different ways in which the payback period can be interpreted, we have seen that only the first, the payback reciprocal as a measure of the rate of return of a project, had significance in the context of certainty. Even with this interpretation it is more appropriate to regard payback as a constraint which a project must satisfy than as a criterion which is to be optimized. The use of payback as a measure of the "liquidity" of an asset, essentially as the reciprocal of the capital turnover ratio, but computed separately for each proposed project, was found to be substantially different from a liquidity requirement for the firm as a whole.

Payback was seen to imply a form of break-even analysis, which makes no sense in a world of certainty, but which can function like many other "rules of thumb" to shortcut the process of generating information and then evaluating it. Thus it was shown that payback reduces the information search by focusing on that time at which the firm expects to "be made whole again" in some sense, and hence it allows the decision maker to judge whether the life of the project past the break-even point is sufficient to make the undertaking worthwhile. The fact that this break-even notion is both naive and incorrect does not alter the fact of its use in the absence of other simple measures which serve the same purpose. To this must be added the appeal of payback for the decision maker, rather than for his firm, in that it indicates how rapidly he can expect confirmation that he has made a good choice, and for which he can expect to benefit personally.

Finally, the paper discussed some of the inherent differences between financial investments and investments in capital projects by firms. While the choice of the investor in the former case revolves purely around the decision to withdraw the funds from an investment or to leave them, the situation is different with investments in physical assets. Not only is the market value of the assets substantially below the "going concern" value of the project at almost all times during the life of the project, but the range of alternatives available with respect to the project are quite different. Additional resources can be committed to alter the outcome of a project after it has been initiated, or less funds can be devoted to it than was originally contemplated. The randomness of both the size and timing of the outcomes themselves focus on the financial restrictions within which the firm is forced to operate. For both these reasons, information of a certain kind is extremely important to the decision maker. This is the rate at which he can expect the uncertainty devolving around a project to be resolved. While once more no single number can convey the necessary information, the payback period does provide some idea of the relevant data.

As the detailed discussion above makes abundantly clear, the payback concept is an oversimplification in each case. However, the problems which managers seek to attack by its use will not disappear simply by arguing that payback is not meaningful. Rather, it is necessary to face up to these problems, and to employ methods which solve them.

27. Uncertainty and Its Effect on Capital Investment Analysis*

MARTIN B. SOLOMON, JR.

This article is concerned with one specialized aspect of capital budgeting: the usefulness of "theoretically correct" choice criteria[1] in real-world investment decisions.

There are other areas of capital budgeting that are surely much more important; but this one deserves special attention because so many recommendations, explicit and implicit, based on these criteria have bombarded the businessman. Before we assail the business practitioner for his crude and unscientific methods, we should be sure that our theory will provide better total results than his unsophisticated decision rules.

There is general agreement that if investment parameters such as costs, revenues, salvage values, and interest rates were amenable to accurate prediction, theoretically correct methods could be used to great advantage in most firms. But all capital investments involve uncertainty in one form or another. The contention of this article is that theoretically correct choice criteria have *limited practical value due to the uncertainty involved in the estimates required for the analysis.*

A GENERAL ANALYSIS OF ESTIMATING ERRORS

Two types of investments are considered: investments with constant annual returns and investments with declining annual returns. The discussion centers on two hypothetical illustrations that have been purposely framed for easy calibration of errors. We ignore errors in salvage values.

Proposals with Constant Annual Returns

Suppose we estimate that an investment will yield $1,000 annual pretax returns[2] for seven years. Assuming the supply price of the asset

---

* *Management Science,* vol. 12, no. 8 (April 1966), pp. B334–B339.

[1] Without entering into a unnecessary debate, present value and the discounted rate of return are simple defined for the purposes of this article as "theoretically correct" criteria.

[2] Returns is used here to mean the excess of revenue over out-of-pocket cost.

is $4,000, a 32 percent tax rate, straight-line depreciation over the life of the asset, and no terminal salvage value, the posttax discounted rate of return would be 11.6 percent. Now if the proposal lasts only six years, all else remaining equal, the discounted rate of return is 9.1 percent. This means that the actual return is 2.5 percentage points less. On the other hand if the proposal lasts for the predicted seven years but returns $800 per year (before taxes) instead of $1,000 the discounted rate of return falls to 6.5 percent which is 5.1 percentage points less than the estimate. There is a plethora of possible combinations of returns, lives and rates of return. The simplest way to illustrate these relationships is to graph them as in figure 1. Shown are lines connecting the discounted rates of return for proposals with the same life and different pretax annual returns. The line labeled "7 years" shows the discounted rates of return for all investments with a life of 7 years. As the pretax returns decrease, the discounted rate of return declines. For this reason the lines slope downward to the left.

In evaluating the effect of uncertainty, we can use figure 1 to determine the possible variations in the discounted rate of return when uncertainty exists. (The data used to construct figure 1 are shown in table 1.)

How much variation then in the discounted rate of return could we

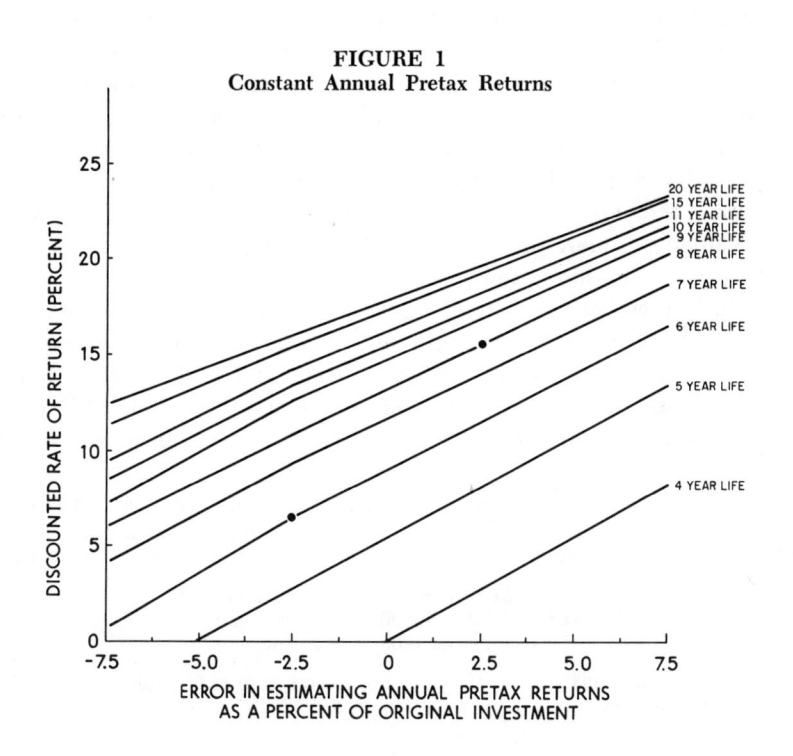

FIGURE 1
Constant Annual Pretax Returns

TABLE 1
The Effect of Estimating Errors on the Discounted Rate of Return—Constant Annual Pretax Returns

Life of the Proposal (years)	$700	$750	$800	$850	$900	$950	$1000	$1050	$1100	$1150	$1200	$1250	$1300
20	.122	.132	.142	.151	.161	.170	.180	.189	.198	.207	.216	.225	.234
15	.112	.123	.134	.144	.154	.165	.175	.184	.194	.204	.213	.223	.232
11	.092	.104	.116	.127	.139	.150	.161	.172	.182	.193	.203	.213	.223
10	.083	.096	.108	.120	.131	.143	.154	.165	.176	.187	.197	.208	.218
9	.072	.085	.097	.110	.122	.134	.145	.156	.168	.179	.190	.200	.211
8	.057	.071	.083	.096	.109	.121	.133	.145	.156	.168	.179	.190	.201
7	.037	.051	.065	.078	.091	.103	.116	.128	.140	.152	.163	.175	.186
6	.010	.024	.038	.052	.065	.078	.091	.104	.116	.129	.141	.153	.165
5	*	*	.010	.015	.028	.042	.055	.068	.081	.094	.107	.119	.131
4			*	*	*	*	.010	.014	.027	.041	.054	.066	.079
3							*	*	*	*	*	*	*

* Indicates negative discounted rate of return.

expect with this amount of error? If the returns of this estimated 7-year $1,000 per year investment are subject to an error of plus or minus 2.5 percent and plus or minus one year, the maximum and minimum rates of return are 15.6 percent and 6.5 percent (as shown in figure 1 by the X's).[3] This is a variation of about 9 percentage points. If we extended the possible error to plus or minus two years, the maximum and minimum rates are 16.8 percent and 2.8 percent, a variation of 14 percentage points. Errors in estimates of these magnitudes do not appear at all unlikely. This much uncertainty would seem to discourage the use of theoretically correct rationing methods for ranking investment proposals. There may be no significant difference among proposals' rates of return if they are nearly equally profitable; and if one or more proposals are obviously more profitable than the others, "alternative" methods[4] provide the same information with less cost.

Another interesting feature of figure 1 is that it provides some insight into the effect of errors in length of life versus error in returns. The relationship between annual pretax return and the discounted rate of return is close to linear with a slope of about .02 to .03. This means that an estimating error of about 1 percent results in an error of about

---

[3] In figure 1, —7.5 percent represents annual pretax returns of $700; —5.0 percent represents returns of $800; —2.5 percent represents returns of $900, etc. The percentage errors are percentages of the original investment. ($4,000). That is,

($700–$1000)/$4000 = —7.5 percent
($800–$1000)/$4000 = —5.0 percent
($900–$1000)/$4000 = —2.5 percent

[4] Alternative methods such as the payback period, rate of income on investment, or MAPI urgency rating.

2 to 3 percentage points in the discounted rate of return. This relationship is fairly constant throughout. On the other hand, the relationship between discounted rate of return and length of life is not stable. As the life becomes shorter, an error of one year in the estimated life becomes more critical; the relationship is curvilinear. The difference in the rate of return between a life of 20 years and 15 years is only about one half of 1 percentage point when pretax profits = $1,000 (zero or horizontal axis). The difference of only 2 years between a life of 4 and 6 years (with $1,000 returns) results in a change of more than 6 percentage points in the discounted rate of return. Perhaps this is a good reason for businessmen being particularly cautious about making length of life estimates.

The conclusions here are that standard formulations of theoretically correct rationing methods have limited usefulness when dealing with uncertainty.

Proposal with Declining Annual Returns

To make the analysis more complete, the case of declining annual returns is included.[5]

The results are shown in figure 2. There is much similarity between figures 1 and 2 as most everything that has been said applies to both. The conclusions about uncertainty seem to apply equally to both constant and declining return investments.

Unless an investment will continue for a long period, a relatively small positive miscalculation in the estimate of length of life (two to three years) can result in a serious overstatement of profitability.

---

[5] An investment's estimated pretax returns are: $2500 the first year, $2400 the second year, $2300, $2200, $2100, $2000, $1900. The estimated life of the investment is therefore seven years. Errors in length of life are handled the same as before, that is, if the estimated life overstates actual life by one year, the actual investment would return $2500, $2400, $2300, $2200, $2100, $2000, or an actual life of six years instead of the estimated seven years. This estimate, although in error as far as length of the life is concerned, is correct concerning the returns (0 on the horizontal axis). Errors in pretax returns indicate an error in the initial annual returns. For example, a −2.5 percent error in estimating returns represents an investment that actually returns $2300 the first year instead of the estimated $2500. The annual decline in returns ($100 per year) remains constant. Thus an investment whose life was correctly estimated as seven years but whose returns were overstated by 2.5 percent would return $2300, $2200, $2100, $2000, $1900, $1800, $1700 (before taxes). In figure 3, zero on the horizontal axis represents an investment with an actual initial return of $2500 and a $100 annual decline in pre-tax returns. A +3 year error in length of life (ten-year life) and a −8.75 percent error in estimated pretax returns would designate an investment that actually returns $1800 the first year, $1700 the second year, $1600, . . . , $1000. The cost of the investment is $8000, the tax rate is 32 percent, and straight-line depreciation is used over the life of the asset with no terminal salvage value assumed. As before, errors are computed as a percentage of the original investment ($800 in this case).

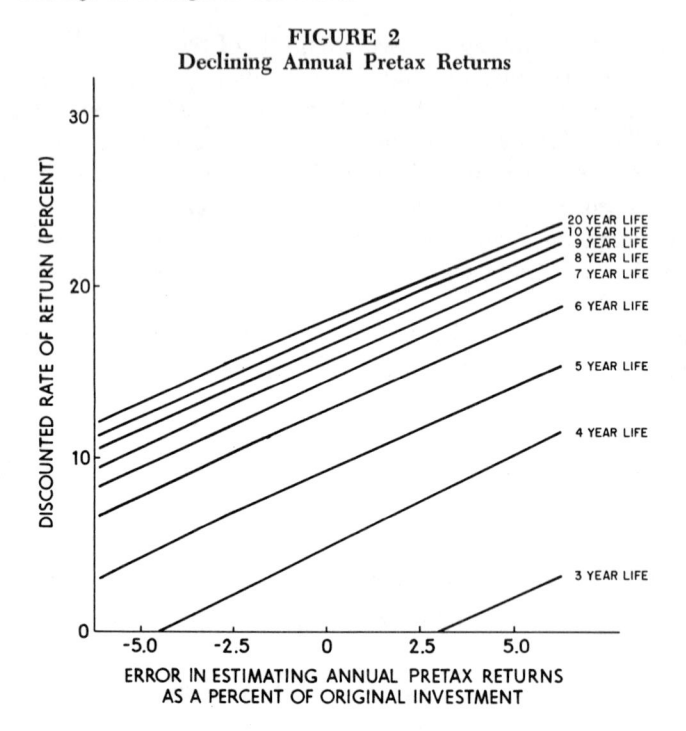

FIGURE 2
Declining Annual Pretax Returns

[Graph showing discounted rate of return (percent) on y-axis from 0 to 30, and error in estimating annual pretax returns as a percent of original investment on x-axis from -5.0 to 5.0, with lines for 20, 10, 9, 8, 7, 6, 5, 4, and 3 year lives]

The Effect of Technological Change

Because errors in returns are linear and errors in life are curvilinear, errors in estimating annual returns may average out over a large number of investments, whereas errors in length of life will not. Proposals that last less than the estimated life lower the average discounted rate of return for the firm more than proposals lasting longer than the estimated life raise the average.[6]

Today, with technological advancement so rapid and innovation so frequent, it seems logical to assume that many capital investments will be subject to extremely high rates of obsolescence. Businessmen do not usually know which of their investments will become obsolete soon; they are understandably worried about proposals that require ten years to pay for themselves. The farther into the future one predicts, the more uncertainty of obsolescence he is subjected to and the more unsure he is of the prediction.

---

[6] This curvilinear phenomenon occurs whether we plot present values or discounted rates of return. It may, however, be more apparent than real. It stems from an assumption underlying the discounted rate of return: proceeds are assumed to be reinvested at the rate of return for the original project; there is a cumulative effect of a high return project. If proceeds are not reinvested at this high rate but placed into low yield investments, this assumption does not hold and the curvilinear phenomenon is not operative.

By insisting upon proposals that pay back quickly, or by using a higher discount rate, within the realm of feasible prediction, the businessman is providing greater flexibility for himself and, in a rough way, taking into account the effects of uncertainty. He is in a better position to maneuver and change his plans when necessary but will accept fewer projects. His hope is that those projects that are rejected (that otherwise might be accepted) will become obsolete before earning a return.

Technological change is one difficulty in estimating length of life. Businessmen can search for information about the expected annual returns from a proposal, but it is generally much more difficult to do research on the length of a proposals life. In addition, figures 1 and 2 suggest that errors in length of life may be more serious. Use of the short payback period or higher discount rate tends to reduce errors of this type. The old saying about one in the hand being worth two in the bush is quite descriptive of business behavior in relation to projects in danger of obsolescence. It may be more worthwhile to invest, receiving a small quick return, than to take a chance on a larger return or obsolescence.

Simple (or even simple-minded) methods of investment ranking may not be as absurd as some of the literature would lead us to believe if used in a careful way by clever people; and although no one claims superiority for a payback method, it appears that in investment decisions confounded by large amounts of uncertainty, the present value and discounted rate of return rankings are so sensitive to estimating errors that the payback criterion may provide results that are about as good as any. The main point of this paper is to point out the sensitivity is discounted rate of return results and not to recommend alternative methods.

28. Measuring the Productivity of Investment in Persuasion[*]

JOEL DEAN

I. PROLOGUE

My starting point in this article is ten propositions, which are debatable, at least as boldly stated here:

1. Much advertising (and other corporate persuasion) is in economic reality partly an investment. The investment mix varies over a wide spectrum.

2. Investments in promotion are different from conventional capital expenditures, but their peculiar traits do not disqualify promotion from investment treatment.

3. Profitability must be the basic measurement of the productivity of capital invested in promotion. Despite the multiplicity of conflicting corporate goals, the overriding objective for decisions on investment of corporate capital should be to make money.

4. The main determinants of profitability of an advertising investment that need to be estimated are the amount and timing of added investment and of added earnings, the duration of advertising effects, and risks.

5. The measurement concepts of capital productivity that must be estimated are future, time-spotted, incremental, after-tax cash flows of investment outlays and of added profits from added sales.

6. Discounted cash-flow analysis (DCF) supplies the yardstick of investment worth which is most appropriate for promotional investments. By comparison, payback period, though widely used, has no merit.

7. Advertising belongs in the capital budget. Promotional investments should be made to compete for funds on the basis of profitability, i.e., DCF rate of return.

8. The criterion for rationing scarce capital among competing investment proposals should be the DCF rate of return. The minimum acceptable return should be the corporation's cost of capital—outside market cost or internal opportunity cost, whichever is higher.

[*] *Journal of Industrial Economics,* vol. 15, no. 2 (April 1967), pp. 81-108.

9. Plopping advertising into the corporation's capital budget will not perform a miracle. The most that it can do is to open the way for a research approach which is oriented to the kind of estimates that are relevant and that will permit investment in promotion to fight for funds on the basis of financial merit rather than on the basis of personal persuasiveness of its sponsor. Judgment cannot be displaced by DCF analysis and computers. But judgment can be economized and improved.

10. To make this investment approach produce practical benefits will require an open mind, fresh concepts, substantial research spending, and great patience.

Readers who find these propositions unacceptable as a point of departure should stop here. Right-thinking readers who persist are warned that the analysis is necessarily technical, studded with charts and culminated by mathematics.

My paper has two interrelated parts: theory and measurement. It is primarily concerned with the conceptual framework for deciding how much to invest in promotion. Measurement problems are examined only incidentally and mechanics of application not at all. The analysis is presented in terms of advertising; but is equally applicable to all forms of promotion. Advertising is used because it is the purest and most indisputable form of persuasion cost and for many firms also the largest. For clarity, the analysis is narrowed to one product and one medium. In principle, however, it is extensible to all forms of corporate persuasion. Allocation of the advertising budget among media and among products is not formally tackled but the decision-making apparatus could be logically extended to these problems. The interplay of promotion with other ways of getting business such as product improvement and pricing is, for simplicity, bypassed.

My approach, blushingly labeled "profitometrics," can be previewed thus: because most advertising is in economic essence a capital expenditure, the question of how much to invest in advertising (and other forms of persuasion) is a problem of investment economics. A new approach is therefore required: economic and financial analysis of futurities. This approach focuses on future aftertax cash flows, centers on the profit productivity of capital and relies on quantitative estimates.

II. THEORY OF OPTIMUM PROMOTIONAL OUTLAY

A. Two Time Horizons

Strictly and elegantly, all promotion can be viewed as investment, since there is some time lag in its benefits, even though short. Nevertheless, the problem of determining optimum persuasion outlay can, in principle, be solved in two separate time-horizon settings: (1) immediate-impact promotion, where most of the benefits come soon; and (2) Delayed-impact promotion, where benefits are deferred and often cumulative.

Pure forms of either are rare or nonexistent. Most promotion brings about some benefits quickly and others spread out into the future. The proportion accounted for by either kind depends on the product, the nature of the promotional benefit, and perhaps the character of the media. The controlling determinant is the anatomy of the purchasing decision, which differs greatly among products.

Pure types are nevertheless notoriously appealing for developing principles. As a first approximation, therefore, we shall examine each category separately. The immediate-impact case will be studied first.

B. Two Decision Increments

Two kinds of decision increments in promotional investment need to be distinguished: (1) intensity increments and (2) project increments.

The first kind, intensity increments, are small increments of additional depth of investment in a single advertising submedium. The intensity increment of investment is pertinent (a) when outlays can be varied by small additions, and (b) when the decision is to select, by examining this growing edge, that amount of advertising outlay which would maximize the rate of return from this investment project.

The second kind, project increments, are pertinent when the incremental unit of decision is the entire advertising project. The choice (because of indivisibility or other restraints) is to take it or leave it. Under these circumstances, we do not have the choice of a panorama of outlay amounts. Consequently, optimization of the advertising amount is not the problem. Instead, what is at issue is acceptance versus rejection of the entire project. The total advertising outlay of the project is, therefore, in this case, the pertinent increment of investment. And the question is whether the added profits from resultant sales as they spread through time will or will not produce a rate of return greater than the cost of capital.

In both situations the basic concept is incremental. In the intensity-increment case, we use profitometrics analysis at the margin to select, from a gradation of alternative outlays, that investment amount which is optimum. Hence, small increments are the vehicle of decision for optimizing the size of this investment project. In the project-increment case, lacking this fluidity of choice, we use the profitometrics method to stack the entire project against alternative uses of capital, so as to make it fight for funds in rate-of-return rationing of the corporation's scarce capital.

Both kinds of increments are normally needed. Optimization of some sort (within the restraints) may be presumed to have taken place before a project of the all-or-none sort comes for capital-rationing decision. The intensity-increment analysis leads us to an optimum depth of advertising investment. But the entire project might nevertheless fall short of the minimum profitability requirement, e.g. cost of capital. To find this out we need to estimate the capital productivity of the project increment.

The two kinds of decision increments are, for illustrative purposes, examined separately for the two kinds of time horizons in the analysis which follows. For the first time-horizon, namely immediate-impact advertising, intensity increments are alone used. For the second time-horizon, namely delayed-impact promotion (investments), both kinds of decision increments are needed. For one-shot investments, intensity increments are examined for one treatment and project increments for another. For spread-out investments, both are needed, but the analysis is in terms of project increments only.

C. Immediate Impact Promotion

The basic tenet of the profitometrics approach to decisions on immediate-impact advertising outlay is simple common sense: advertising expenditures are justified to the extent that they cause increases in sales which add enough to corporate profits to warrant the outlay. To determine if this is the case, we must measure two things: (1) the effect of advertising on sales, (2) the effect of sales on profits.

To illustrate these ideas in simple terms, I have a series of charts and tables relating to direct-mail promotion of a book. In our example, we have assumed that the price will remain the same at all rates of sale considered, and, further, that the added cost of production and physical distribution per copy—which we call the incremental production cost—will also not change. These assumptions are realistic for a surprisingly wide range of commodities.

Exhibit 1 shows the kind of relationship we can reasonably believe exists between advertising and sales and which in fact has been found to exist when measurements have actually been made. You will observe that the increase in sales attributable to advertising becomes less and less as more and more advertising is used. That is, the increase in sales resulting from spending $9000 on advertising rather than $8000 is less than the increase in sales attributed to the expenditure of $2000 rather than $1000. This conforms to common sense: initial advertising attracts the most susceptible customers and subsequent advertising must be more and more intense to induce the less susceptible to become customers.

As an example, consider the response to successive mailings of adver-

EXHIBIT 1
Effect of Advertising on Sales

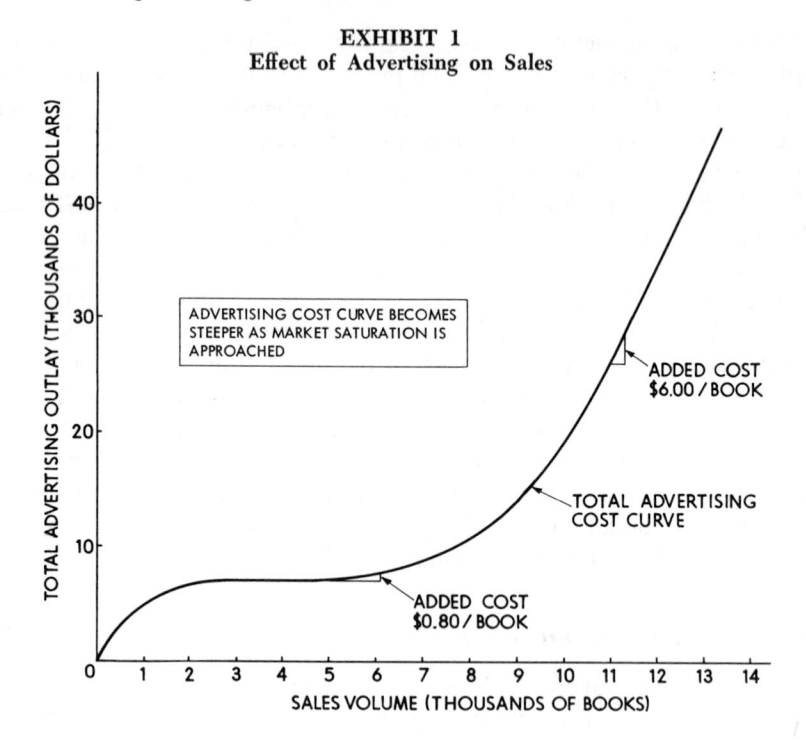

[Graph: Total Advertising Outlay (Thousands of Dollars) on y-axis (0–40+) vs. Sales Volume (Thousands of Books) on x-axis (0–14). Annotations: "ADVERTISING COST CURVE BECOMES STEEPER AS MARKET SATURATION IS APPROACHED"; "ADDED COST $6.00/BOOK"; "TOTAL ADVERTISING COST CURVE"; "ADDED COST $0.80/BOOK".]

tisements for the book. The initial mailing will bring in the customers while subsequent and more intense persuasion may be required to induce recipients of other mailings to become customers. As a result, the added advertising outlays required to sell one more copy increases from $.80 to $6.00 in our example. (The curve in Exhibit 1 traces total costs. The slope of this curve, that is the rate of climb, indicates added cost of selling one more book.) The same form of relationship is found when single mailings are made to lists that differ in susceptibility.

Exhibit 2 shows the same basic relationship restated in terms of the added advertising outlay required to produce added units of sale—a relationship that might be called the incremental advertising cost curve.

The second measurement that this approach requires is the relationship between sales and profits. Exhibit 3 shows the relationship following from our assumptions that the price is independent of promotional outlays and that incremental production costs remain the same over the range of variation in sales that it seems relevant to consider. Because price stays the same and incremental production cost is constant, the incremental prepromotional profit remains constant. That is, leaving advertising costs aside for the moment, each additional book that is sold results in a constant increase in profits—$6.00 in our example.

EXHIBIT 2
Added Advertising Cost Necessary to Make An Added Sale

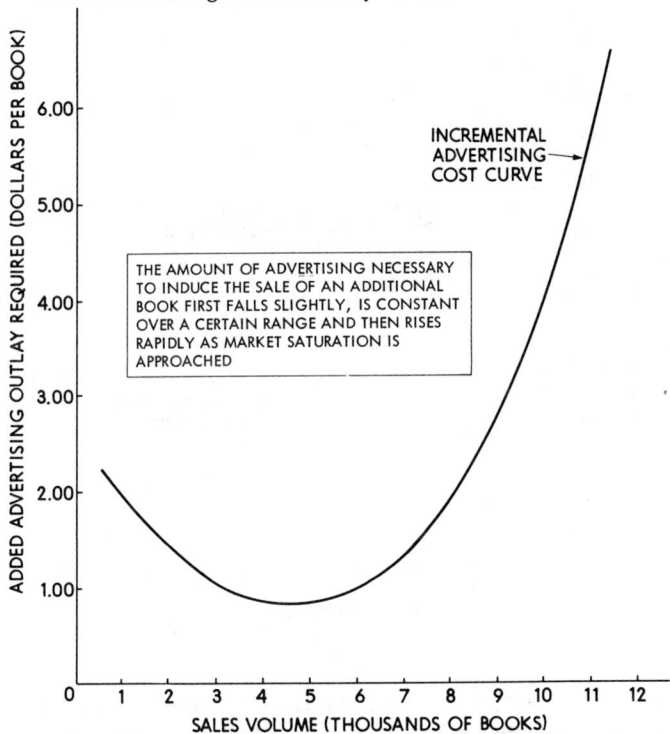

Incremental Advertising Cost Curve

THE AMOUNT OF ADVERTISING NECESSARY TO INDUCE THE SALE OF AN ADDITIONAL BOOK FIRST FALLS SLIGHTLY, IS CONSTANT OVER A CERTAIN RANGE AND THEN RISES RAPIDLY AS MARKET SATURATION IS APPROACHED

(Y-axis: ADDED ADVERTISING OUTLAY REQUIRED (DOLLARS PER BOOK), X-axis: SALES VOLUME (THOUSANDS OF BOOKS))

We can now combine the two measurements to see how large the advertising outlay should be. In exhibit 4 we superimpose the curve representing the relationship between advertising and sales of Exhibit 2 on the chart representing the relationship between sales and profit. We can see that advertising beyond the intersection of these two lines results in an absolute reduction in profits. That is, beyond the point of intersection it costs more than $6.00 to increase sales by one book whereas the increase in sales by one book adds only $6.00 to our profits.

Exhibit 5 summarizes in a table the analysis of immediate-impact one-shot advertising outlays charted in Exhibits 1, 2, 3, and 4.

D. Delayed Impact Advertising

Most advertising is an investment, in essence, since it has delayed as well as immediate impacts. This kind of advertising requires a different kind of economic analysis from that described above. The appropriate analysis is directed at the productivity of the capital tied up in a promotional investment measured in terms of rate of return.

EXHIBIT 3
Effect of Sales on Profit

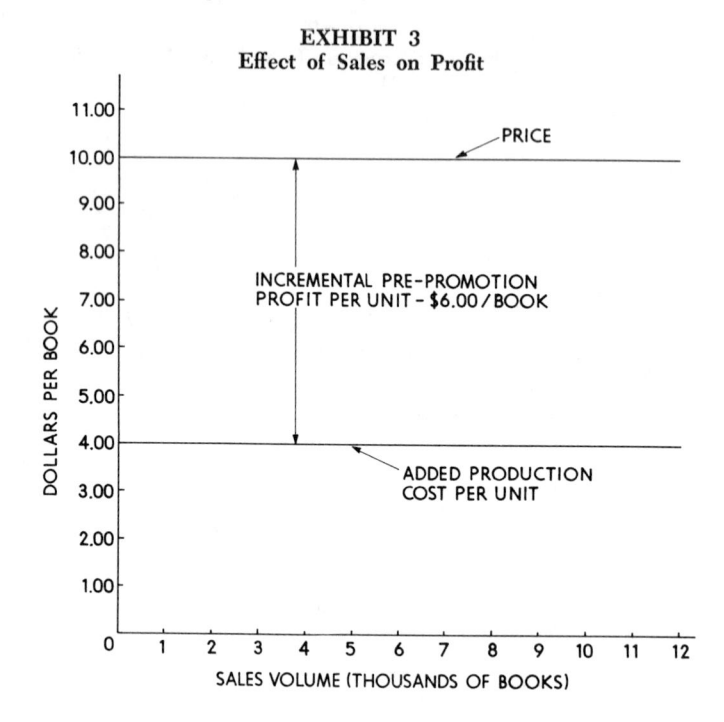

[Chart: Dollars per book (y-axis, 0 to 11.00) vs Sales Volume in thousands of books (x-axis, 0 to 12). PRICE line at $10.00. ADDED PRODUCTION COST PER UNIT line at $4.00. INCREMENTAL PRE-PROMOTION PROFIT PER UNIT - $6.00/BOOK shown between the two lines.]

In measuring capital productivity it is convenient to classify promotional investments into two categories: (1) one-shot promotions, where all or most of the outlay is made all at once; and (2) spread-out investments, where outlays are sprinkled over a period of years.

1. *One-Shot Investments.* For one-shot investments in advertising there are two alternative attacks. One is a simple extension of the preceding analysis of immediate-impact advertising. The second is a pure-investment approach which, though compatible with the first, gets at the problem in a different way, namely through DCF measurements of capital productivity. Incidentally, this second attack is alone suitable for spread-out investments.

(a) *Patch-on Analysis.* Exhibit 6 illustrates how the analysis of immediate-impact advertising which is summarized in Exhibits 1, 2, 3, and 4 can be patched up to account for the follow-on effects of a one-shot advertising investment. Essentially the process is: (1) estimate the incremental per-unit profits (or other benefits) from follow-on sales in each follow-on year; (2) find the present value at the corporation's cost of capital of each year's profits; (3) sum them as a single figure of present worth of incremental profit from follow-on sales; and (4) add this sum to the incremental prepromotion profit from immediate sales. This present-value sum in our illustration is $14.24 a unit. The

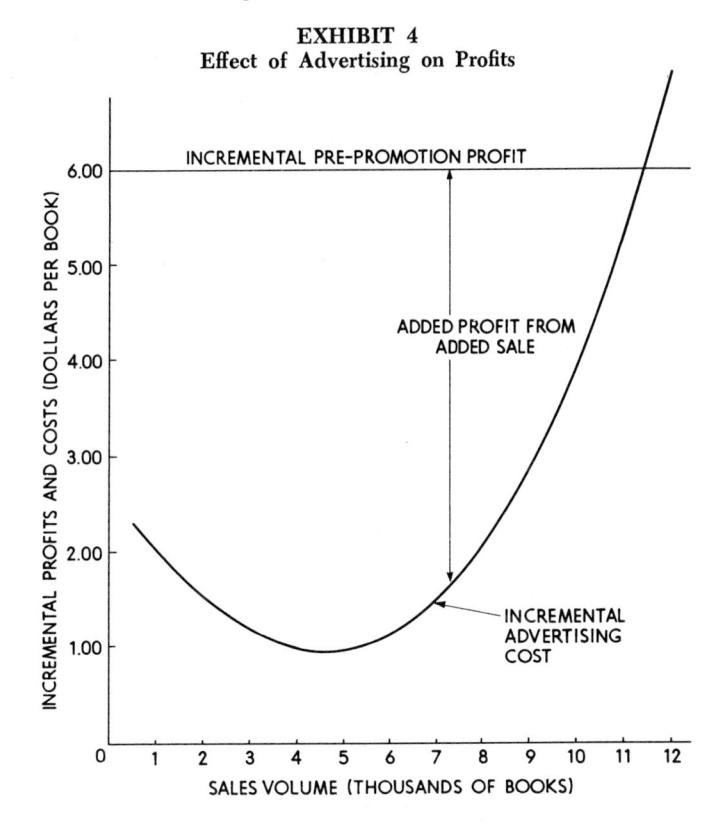

EXHIBIT 4
Effect of Advertising on Profits

[Graph: x-axis "SALES VOLUME (THOUSANDS OF BOOKS)" from 0 to 12; y-axis "INCREMENTAL PROFITS AND COSTS (DOLLARS PER BOOK)" from 0 to 6.00. Horizontal line at ~6.00 labeled "INCREMENTAL PRE-PROMOTION PROFIT". U-shaped curve labeled "INCREMENTAL ADVERTISING COST". Vertical arrow between curve and horizontal line labeled "ADDED PROFIT FROM ADDED SALE".]

resulting aggregate of incremental profit from immediate plus follow-on sales supplies a cutoff criterion identical in concept to that illustrated in Exhibit 4.

Exhibit 6 indicates quite plausibly that the amount that it is economic to spend on a one-shot advertising outlay is greater when it has follow-on effects than when it does not.

This simplified solution presumes that the corporation's overall cost of capital has been measured, that it is used as a cutoff for rate-of-return rationing of funds for other capital expenditure, and that the corporation's internal opportunity cost of funds is not significantly higher than this market cost.

How the add-on for follow-on sales that is diagrammed in Exhibit 6 is computed is shown in Exhibits 7 and 8. Exhibit 7, like Exhibit 5, examines six alternative levels of advertising outlay. It goes further by also considering the effects upon sales and profits in the second year. Exhibit 8 is derived by extending Exhibit 7 in that it shows several follow-on years. Exhibit 8a shows how we calculate the present value of immediate and follow-on effects of the sale of one additional book.

EXHIBIT 5
One-Shot Advertising Outlay with no Follow-on Effect

	Advertising Outlays ($1000)		Effect on Sales (1000 units)		Effect on Prepromotion Profits ($1000)		Effect on Net Profit per Unit of Added Sales ($ per unit)		
	Altern. Total Advt'g Outlays	Differential Advt'g Outlays	Total Sales	Differential Sales	Total Profits	Differential Profits	Increm. Pre-prom. Profits	Increm. Advt'g Cost	Added Net Profit from Added Sales
A	5	5	1.7	1.7	10.2	10.2	6.00	2.94	3.06
B	10	5	7.8	6.1	46.8	36.6	6.00	.82	5.18
C	15	5	9.0	1.2	54.0	7.2	6.00	4.17	1.83
D	20	5	10.0	1.0	60.0	6.0	6.00	5.00	1.00
E	25	5	10.9	.9	65.4	5.4	6.00	5.56	.44
F	30	5	11.6	.7	69.6	4.2	6.00	7.14	-1.14

EXHIBIT 6
Effect of Advertising on Profits: One Shot with Follow-on Effects

[Chart: Y-axis "INCREMENTAL PROFITS AND COSTS (DOLLARS PER BOOK)" from 0 to 15.00; X-axis "SALES VOLUME IN YEAR 1 (THOUSANDS OF BOOKS)" from 0 to 14. Labels on chart: "DISCOUNTED SUM OF INCREMENTAL PRE-PROMOTION PROFIT FROM FOLLOW-ON SALES", "INCREMENTAL PRE-PROMOTION PROFIT FROM FIRST SALES YEAR", "ADDED PROFIT FROM ADDED SALES", "INCREMENTAL ADVERTISING COSTS".]

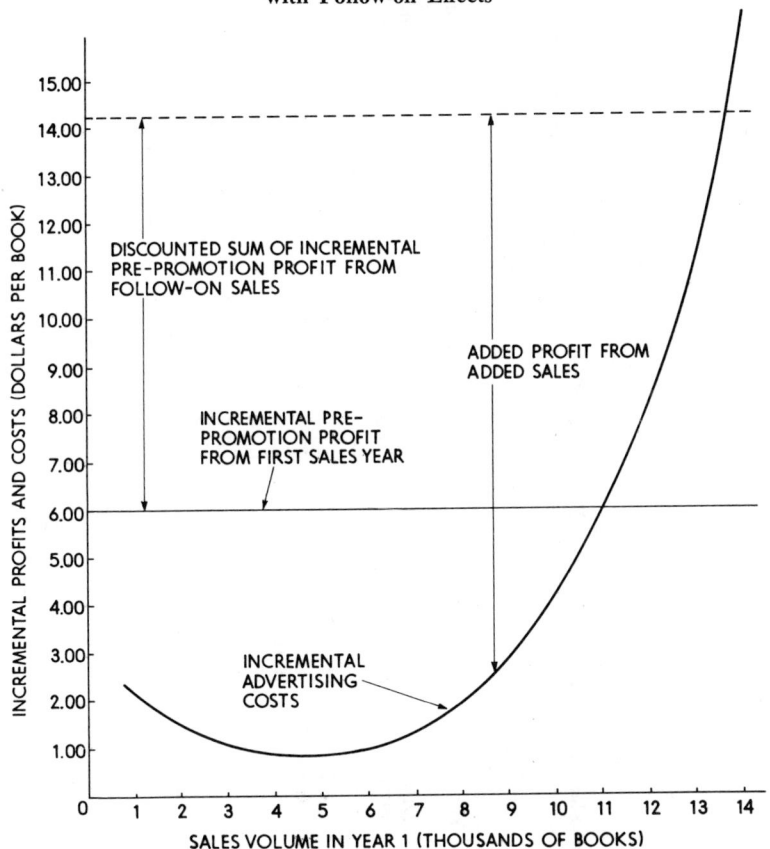

Follow-on profits are discounted to a present value at 10 percent and then added to the immediate profit to give a total present value of $14.24. Exhibit 8b shows this present value stacked up against incremental advertising costs to provide a net incremental profit figure.

(b) *New-Cloth Analysis*. There is an alternative but intellectually compatible attack on the problem of a one-shot advertising outlay with follow-on effects. It is to treat the entire outlay as an investment by starting anew and measuring directly the capital productivity of the immediate, together with the follow-on, benefits. The investment profile of a one-shot advertising outlay which has follow-on effects is diagrammed in Exhibit 9. The outlay is portrayed in the negative section of the chart as a down-bar. The whole-life incremental prepromotion profits are depicted for each year in the positive section of the diagram as bars of diminishing length. This illustrates the kind of timetable used for DCF calculation of the rate of return for such an investment.

EXHIBIT 7
One-Shot Advertising Outlay with Follow-on Effects

	Alternative Advertising Outlays ($1000) Total	Differential	Sales (1000 units) First Year Total	Differential	Second Year Total	Differential	Profits ($1000) First Year Total	Differential	Second Year Total	Differential	Face Value of Differential Profit Sum
A	5	5	1.7	1.7	1.1	1.1	10.2	10.2	6.6	6.6	16.8
B	10	5	7.8	6.1	5.2	4.1	46.8	36.6	31.2	24.6	61.2
C	15	5	9.0	1.2	6.0	.8	54.0	7.2	36.0	4.8	12.0
D	20	5	10.0	1.0	6.7	.7	60.0	6.0	40.2	4.2	10.2
E	25	5	10.9	.9	7.3	.6	65.4	5.4	43.8	3.6	9.0
F	30	5	11.6	.7	7.7	.4	69.6	4.2	46.2	2.4	6.6

EXHIBIT 8A
Follow-on Effects Due to One-Shot Advertising Outlay

Year	Incremental Prepromotion Profit*	Present Value at 10 percent
1	6.00	5.71
2	3.99	3.44
3	2.65	2.06
4	1.76	1.24
5	1.17	.75
6-10	2.02	1.04
	Total	14.24

* Assumes that quantity sold during year n due to promotional outlay at time o is $Q(.665)^{n-1}$ where Q is quantity sold during year 1.

EXHIBIT 8B
Added Net Profit Per Book from Added Sale Due to One-Shot Advertising Outlay with Follow-on Effects

Alternative Advertising Outlays Total ($1000)	Incremental per Book	Present Value of Incremental Prepromotion Profit per Book from 8a ($)	Added Net Profit per Book from Added Sale ($)
5	2.94	14.24	11.30
10	.82	14.24	13.42
15	4.17	14.24	10.07
20	5.00	14.24	9.24
25	5.56	14.24	8.68
30	7.14	14.24	7.10
35	10.00	14.24	4.24

The calculation format is illustrated in Exhibit 10. The investment amount ($200,000) is shown as a negative value. For convenience it is put in the column entitled *Incremental Prepromotion Profits,* where the incremental prepromotion profits estimated for each year are shown as positive amounts. In the next four columns these face-value amounts are translated into present value by discounting each at four trial rates of return: 30, 20, 18, and 17 percent.

The mechanics of the DCF method of measuring the productivity of capital consists essentially of finding that interest rate which discounts the future earnings of an advertising investment to a present value precisely equal to the investment outlay. This rate (roughly 18 percent

EXHIBIT 9
Investment Profile of One-Shot Advertising Outlay with Follow-on Effects

ADVERTISING OUTLAY (THOUSANDS OF DOLLARS)

PRE-PROMOTION PROFITS DUE TO ADVERTISING OUTLAY (THOUSANDS OF DOLLARS)

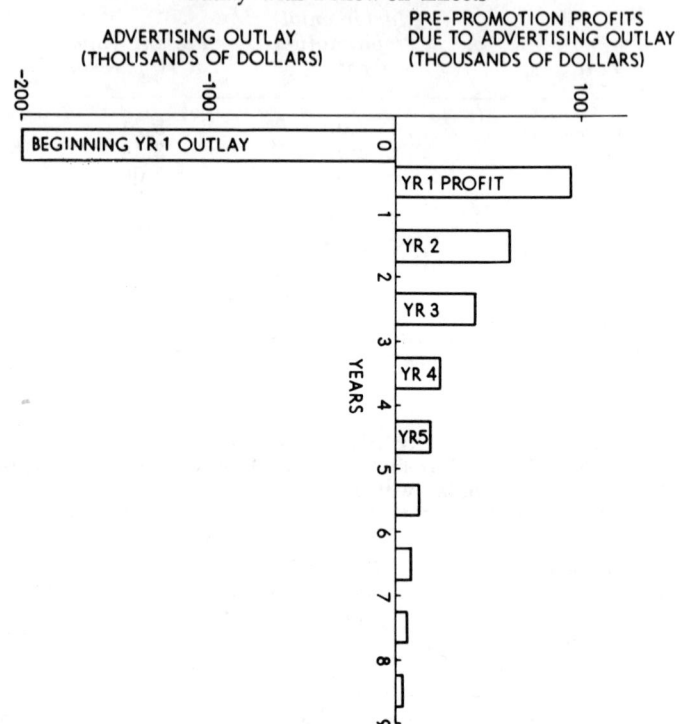

BEGINNING YR 1 OUTLAY

YR 1 PROFIT
YR 2
YR 3
YR 4
YR 5

YEARS

EXHIBIT 10
Discounted Cash-Flow Method of Computing Rate of Return from One-Shot Advertising Investment with Follow-on Effects

Year	Added Pre-promotion Profits (face value) ($1000)	Present Value Discounted at 30 percent	20 percent	17 percent	18 percent
0	(200)	(200)	(200)	(200)	(200)
1	96	83	87	88	88
2	64	41	47	50	49
3	43	20	26	28	27
4	29	10	15	16	15
5	19	5	8	9	8
6	13	2	4	5	5
7	9	1	2	3	3
8	6	1	1	2	2
9	4	—	1	1	1
10	3	—	—	—	—
	Net present value	(37)	(9)	3	(1)

in our illustration) is the true rate of return on that investment. It is the highest rate of interest that could be paid to an outsider to whom you turn over all the earnings of the project to pay back the loan and still come out with a zero balance at the end of the project's economic life (i.e. its stream of incremental earnings).

The source of the typical time shape of follow-on incremental profits is shown in Exhibit 11, which charts profiles of follow-on incremental sales obtained by an added dollar of advertising. Plausible profiles of

EXHIBIT 11
Profiles of Follow-on Incremental Sales from an Added Dollar of Advertising Outlay at Beginning of Year 1

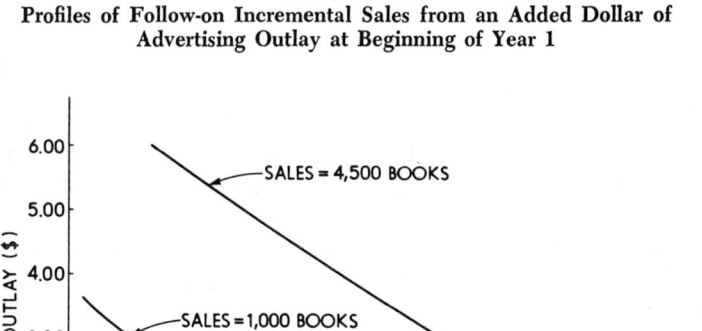

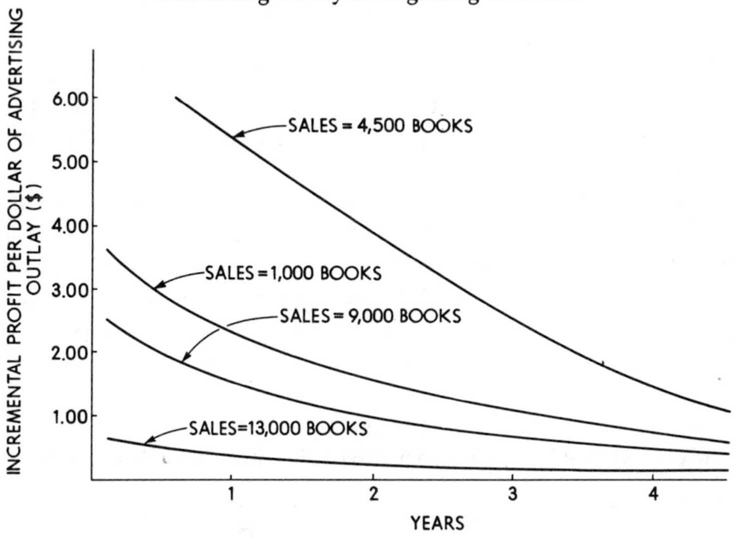

follow-on incremental sales from an added dollar of advertising indicate that the impact of a one-shot promotional outlay does not die—it just fades away. If, as we have assumed, marginal production costs are constant with output rate and if prices are independent of promotion, then incremental prepromotion profits would follow the same pattern. Exhibit 7 shows how these would be derived, and Exhibit 8 shows their time shape.

The present-value variant of DCF analysis provides an alternative route to measurement of investment profitability. Instead of computing the individual rate of return for the promotional project it applies a "go, no-go" gauge to promotional investments. It does so by merely computing the present value of time-spotted incremental profits discounted at the corporation's cost of capital. If this present value is greater than the face value of the one-shot advertising outlay, then the promotional investment should be made (assuming an adequate allowance in the estimates for any above-average risk this particular project may entail). Unless the corporation's opportunity cost of capital is significantly higher than its market cost, the promotion investment should be made, since the productivity of capital exceeds its price.

This DCF variant is illustrated in Exhibit 8, where the present value of incremental prepromotion profits is stacked up against the incremental advertising outlay to produce a net present increment profit per book. This net present value decreases as the level of output increases and will eventually become zero at the maximum-profit advertising outlay.

To summarize, in measuring the productivity of one-shot promotional investments (i.e. outlays which have follow-on effects), we can use three kinds of economic techniques:

1. Patch-on analysis: graft a summary figure of the present value of follow-on benefits on to the value of first-year incremental profits, which is the criterion of optimum outlay for immediate-impact advertising.

2. New-cloth analysis of the DCF rate of return: treat the initial year of benefits as earnings of the advertising investment as well as all the follow-on years. Compute DCF project rate of return, after allowing for any unusual risks of the advertising investment as compared with rival corporate investments. If its DCF return is higher than the

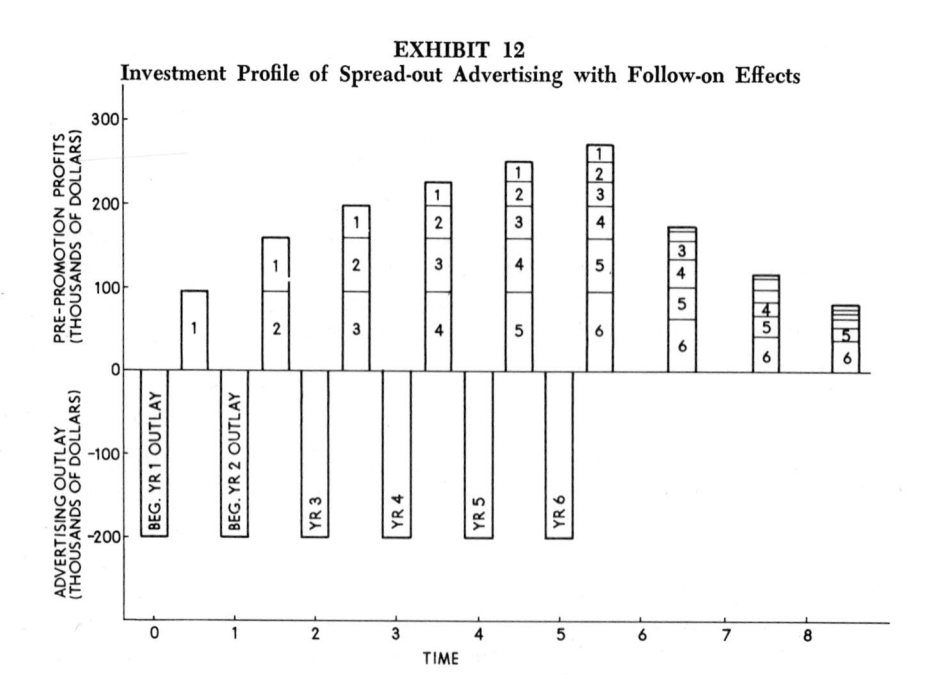

EXHIBIT 12
Investment Profile of Spread-out Advertising with Follow-on Effects

corporation's market or opportunity cost of capital, the project should be accepted.

3. Present-value version of DCF analysis: simply find the present worth of the entire stream of incremental prepromotion profits (adjusted for risk) using a single discount rate, namely, the corporation's cost of capital. If this is bigger than the outlay, accept the project.

2. Spread-Out Investments. So much for one-shot outlays. Now we turn to the second and more common category of promotional investments, namely those spread out over a number of years. For spread-out investments, several analytical treatments are possible; modern investment-economics practice has, however, narrowed them to the two variants of DCF analysis: (1) individual project return, and (2) present value at cost of capital.

The investment profile of a spread-out advertising investment is shown in Exhibit 12. Diagrammed by down-bars in the negative section is the advertising investment of $200,000 each year for six years and then none for four years. The incremental prepromotion profits caused by each year's advertising trail off over a six-year period following the pattern suggested in Exhibit 9. For each year they are identified with numbers corresponding to the year of advertising outlay which caused them.[1] Profit bars are slightly offset, primarily for clarity, but also to indicate some time lag.

The net balance of cash flows from spread-out advertising investment with follow-on effects is illustrated in Exhibit 13. It is derived from Exhibit 12 in a manner diagrammed for the first year where the down-column is the net balance of an advertising outlay of $200,000 and an incremental profit of $96,000. This balance each year is shown in black and traced by a solid line. It is this net balance which is fed into the DCF computation to save arithmetic.

Exhibit 13 also shows the cumulative balance of outlay and inflow for each year. This cumulative balance is shown by crosshatched columns. The dotted line which hooks up these columns indicates that after the fifth year, in terms of face (not discounted) value cash flows, the advertiser has got his bait back in incremental profits. But he has not yet any return on his investment, and the only thing that matters for such a return is what happens after he gets his bait back. Productivity of capital is *not* measured or even indicated by how *soon* he gets back his advertising investment (payback period).

---

[1] The cumulative impact of this time pattern can be seen most clearly by tracing the effects of year 1, diagrammed at the pinnacle of the profit bar for successive years. By year 7 the effects of the first year's advertising have disappeared; by year 8 the effects of the second year's advertising have, too, and so on. After advertising ceases at the end of year 6, the follow-on benefits of this and previous years continue for several years but trail off in aggregate.

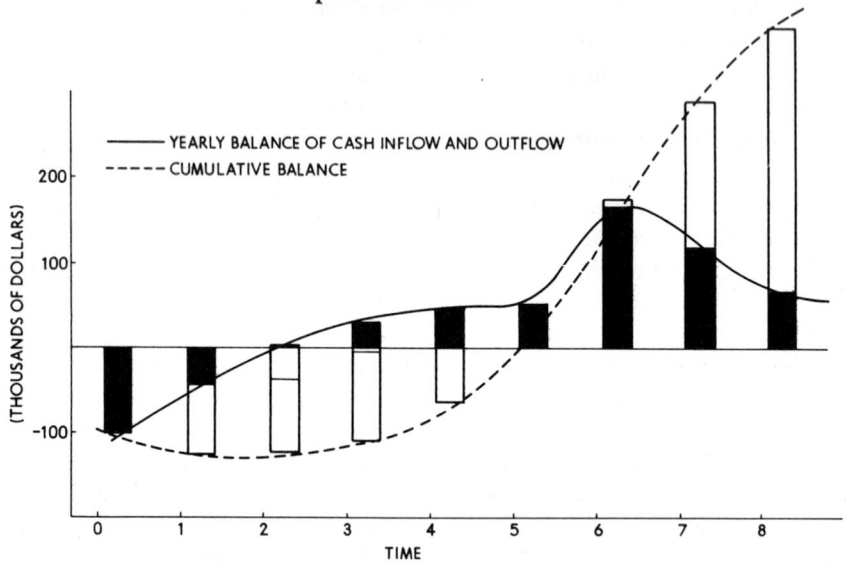

EXHIBIT 13
Profile of Net Balance of Cash Flows from Advertising Outlays
Spread Over Six Years

The mechanics of applying both variants of the DCF measurement of the productivity of a promotional investment are illustrated in Exhibit 14. For each year the advertising outlay and the prepromotion incremental profits of Exhibit 12 are shown and are netted as in Exhibit 13. The DCF project rate of return is computed from continuous discount tables; it is found to be 18 percent. The present-value variant of DCF is also applied, with cost of capital assumed to be 10 percent. With this value of money the advertising investment promises plus values, since discounted incremental profits when summed are bigger than the present value of the advertising outlays by $1140.

Hence we see that for promotional investments of the spread-out type, DCF measurement of the productivity of the capital that is tied up gives management an engine of analysis which can cope with a stream of future investment outlays forecasted to produce a fluctuating, delayed, and cumulative stream of prepromotional incremental profits. This analysis makes it possible for promotional investments to compete for corporate funds on an objective rate-of-return basis of economic merit, and for investments in persuasion to become an integral part of the firm's planning and rationing of capital.

Thus, there are at least two decision edges for each medium. For example, in direct-mail advertising of a book one decision is where to cut off in working down candidate mail lists which have been laddered as to productiveness. The other decision is where to stop in progressively more intensive promotions of each mail list thus selected.

EXHIBIT 14
Discounted Cash Flow Method of Computing Return for Spread-out Investment

Year	Net Cash Flow ($1000)	Present Values* at 10 percent	18 percent
1......	(104)	(109.0)	(112.0)
2......	(40)	(41.0)	(45.0)
3......	5	(7.7)	(12.0)
4......	30	4.0	6.2
5......	50	25.0	17.7
6......	65	32.0	18.0
7......	175	91.4	54.0
8......	115	54.3	30.0
9......	75	32.1	16.3
10......	50	19.3	9.1
11......	25	8.8	1.3
12......	15	4.8	.6
Net present value		114.0	(6.0)

*Since continuous discount tables are used, each year's net cash flow must be separated into beginning year outlay and "through year" inflow before being discounted.

For immediate-impact advertising the criterion is the same for decision edges. It is the point where incremental costs of advertising equal incremental profits.

For delayed-impact advertising, the investment decision can be all or none, in which case the cutoff criterion is where the rate of return equals the cost of capital.

The concept that a corporation's investments in promotion should be made to compete with traditional capital expenditure proposals for scarce investable funds is illustrated in Exhibit 15, where the rate-of-return ladder for capital rationing is portrayed.

The idea is simple and plausible. Investment proposals should be ranked on the basis of productivity of capital. In rationing capital, the corporation should work down the rate-of-return ladder until its investable funds are exhausted, if it is unwilling to go to market for additional capital and if the rate of return on the least profitable project thereby accepted is higher than the corporation's market cost of capital. If, on the other hand, the corporation is willing to secure additional capital which can be profitably invested then it should work down the rate-of-return ladder to its market cost of capital (e.g. 10 percent,) accepting all projects above that cutoff and rejecting all below it.

DCF analysis has three variants. The project rate-of-return variant is that illustrated in Exhibit 15. The present-worth variant has also been discussed and used in the preceding analysis. By computing the

EXHIBIT 15
Rate-of-Return Ladder for Capital Rationing

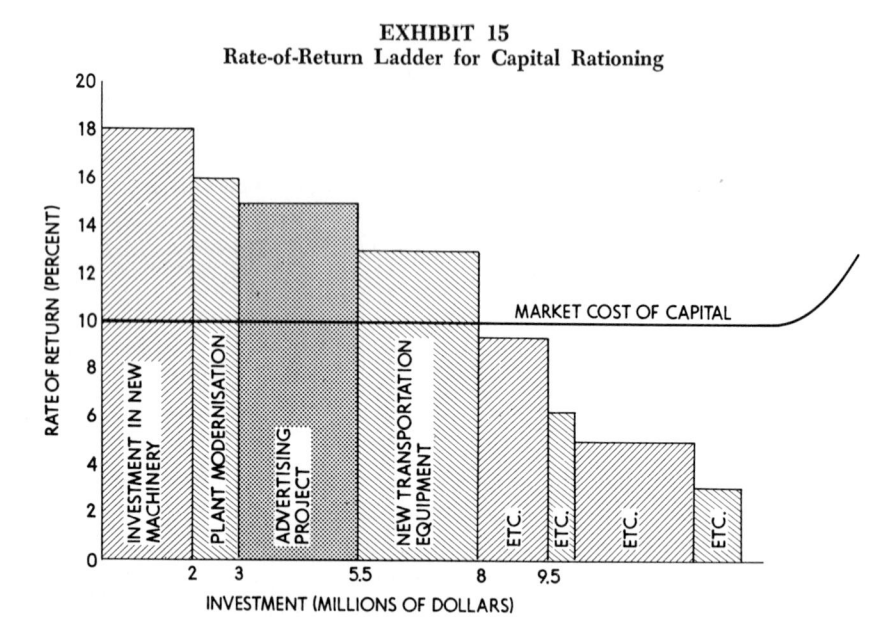

present worth of the benefits of a project at the corporation's cost of capital, all projects on the rate-of-return ladder whose profitability is greater than cost of capital are implicitly accepted by this "go, no-go" gauge and all below it rejected. The third variant, labeled "profitability index," is simply the ratio of the present-worth variant to the amount of capital tied up. If this profitability ratio is greater than 1, the project has a DCF return which beats cost of capital and is implicitly accepted. The profitability-index variant differs from the present-worth variant only in expressing results as a ratio rather than in terms of subtraction.

III. MEASURING THE EFFECTIVENESS OF PROMOTION

Measuring effectiveness of advertising is a big subject, contentious and technical. It would go beyond the scope and space limitations of this paper to do more than touch on a few aspects of it which relate most closely to measuring the productivity of investments in persuasion.

Measurement of the effects of advertising has two dimensions: kinds of effects, and techniques of measurement.

A. Kinds of Advertising Effects

There are basically four kinds of advertising effects that can be measured: (1) effects on behavior (sales), (2) effects on attitudes (usually brand preferences, but sometimes attitudes toward the company), (3) effects on intentions to buy, and (4) effects on the level of knowledge (usually brand awareness, but sometimes knowledge of product characteristics or uses).

Sometimes the explicit purpose of advertising is to change people's attitudes quite apart from the effect of those attitudes on sales and profits. This paper is, however, restricted to a consideration of the effect of advertising on profits. We shall therefore judge the four kinds of advertising effects in terms of the light they cast on advertising's effect on profits.

Clearly the most direct relationship is between profits and sales. If we can measure advertising's effect on sales, we have all the material necessary to measure profitability. We must, of course, take account of the effect of advertising not only on present but also on future sales. For example, the value of a new customer depends on his "loyalty-life" expectancy as well as on his emulation value.

To measure all *other* kinds of effects of advertising, it is usually necessary to translate observed changes in attitudes, intentions, or levels of knowledge into changes in sales. This is usually difficult. The translation can be avoided only when the findings are negative. Sales could not have been favorably affected by advertising if there was no improvement in brand preferences, intentions to buy, brand awareness, etc.

To interpret positive findings, however, it is necessary to know how much sales will increase because of a given improvement in consumer attitudes, intentions, or knowledge. Although the relationship between changes in these indirect effects and changes in sales can sometimes be estimated at given points in time by making both direct and indirect measurements, there is no assurance that the relationship will be stable through time. This basic fact limits the usefulness of measurements of these indirect effects in determining the optimum size of the advertising budget. Therefore, direct measurement of the effect of advertising on sales is usually the only firm basis for the application of the profitometrics approach.

B. Measurement Techniques

Just as there are different kinds of effects that can be measured so there are different techniques for measuring them. Techniques can be put in two groups: (1) controlled experiments, and (2) nonexperimental techniques.

1. *Controlled Experiments.* By far the most powerful technique available for measuring the effect of anything—be it chemical compounds or advertising—is the designed experiment. No other technique provides such precise information with so little ambiguity. Controlled experiments deserve to be better understood. There is ample evidence that businessmen have failed to appreciate and utilize fully this very powerful technique for providing useful information.

These are three basic principles to designed experiments: (1) The factor being investigated—whether it be advertising or penicillin—must be administered to identifiable subgroups of the entire group in which you are interested. If you are interested in all consumers in the United States, you must administer your advertising to only a portion of these consumers. (2) The subgroup exposed to the facts being investigated must be representative of the entire group which is of interest. (This means that the subgroup must be selected by some random process, defined in its technical, statistical sense.) (3) The difference between changes in the subgroup and the rest of the group (or some portion of it) must be measured before and after the factor being investigated is administered. (This means that controlled experiments on the effects of advertising would involve measuring the rates of sale before and after the advertising in groups which had been exposed to the advertising and groups which had not.)

Many businessmen fail to realize that experimentation, which has been so productive in the natural sciences, can be used with equal validity in business and advertising research even though the subject investigated is the uncontrollable behavior of people. The designing and interpretation of experiments is a technical process to be performed by trained statisticians, but businessmen should understand the potential value of such experiments to all executives responsible for the control of substantial discretionary expenditures.

It is much easier to carry out controlled experiments of this sort in some advertising media than in others. For example, it is very hard to conduct a controlled experiment for a promotion that uses mass media like television or radio, since we cannot isolate randomly selected groups only one of which was exposed to the promotion. Radio and TV promotions have an impact on all households in a specifiable geographic area that own receiving equipment. Thus, it is necessary to match up groups of geographic areas rather than groups of individual households, and random selection is not usually feasible.

In contrast, a promotional campaign conducted by mail is ideally suited for a carefully controlled scientific experiment aimed at gauging the effectiveness of the promotion quickly and accurately. A process of selecting every *nth* household or of sampling candidate mailing lists presumably produces a random group within the mailing-list population. And two such groups constitute a matched pair of random samples with all the characteristics required for comparison. Thus, the main problem with measuring the effectiveness of a mail promotion is obtaining data on sales to individual households in each of the matched groups.

Even for mass media, where matched random-sampled groups cannot in general be obtained, there are statistical procedures capable, in principle, of producing reliable results. Instead of comparing sales in perfectly matched (randomly selected) groups, one can compare sales in areas exposed to the promotion with sales in areas not exposed, adjusting the comparison statistically for whatever differences exist between buyers in the two areas. That is, while the groups are not matched in the sense of being the same in all respects except exposure to the promotion, the effect of the differences between the groups on sales can sometimes be independently estimated, and consequently we can estimate the net effects of the promotion. Whether this procedure will produce reliable results depends on the adequacy of the adjustments for differences.[2]

Painful experience with the practical difficulties of developing controlled experiments in this area make me recognize that competitors can sometimes, without making the outlays, learn much about research findings and even, under some circumstances, distort results. I am aware that the variables that determine a product's sales are numerous and hence that it is impossible to control all variables except the one under study. But this impossibility exists in the physical sciences, too, and it has not prevented the enormous productivity of the controlled experiment here. The variation caused by factors other than the one examined is usually greater in the social sciences. But because we know it is bigger we can sometimes design the experiment so as to show us how much of the variation comes from these irrelevant factors.

2. *Nonexperimental Techniques.* When the measurements ideally called for in the profitometrics approach are not feasible, it is sometimes possible to obtain, by inferior means, suggestive indications of the effect of advertising. Information about changes in consumer attitudes, buying intentions, and levels of product and brand knowledge can sometimes provide valuable negative information about advertising effects. However, for positive usefulness it is necessary to measure the relation between sales behavior and these indications of buying conditioners. Bridging this gap metrically is difficult indeed.

An inferior technique of measurement is that involving information gathered in a nonexperimental situation. Data can often be obtained

---

[2] Ideally, if we know that two areas are matched in all critical respects except that household income is higher in one area (the one receiving the promotion) than in the other, and if we know the true relationship between household income and sales, we can obtain an accurate estimate of the promotion's influence on sales by a simple comparison of sales adjusted for the known income difference. But in the real world, groups of people in "matched" areas differ in a variety of subtle ways that we do not fully understand and cannot adequately measure. As a consequence, we can only approximate the true effects of a promotion on sales, and the measurement is subject to a good deal of uncertainty.

with less planning, cost, and technical knowledge than is required for experimentation. The basic and inevitable deficiency of nonexperimental data is that it is never possible to be sure what they mean. There is an inherent ambiguity in all nonexperimental data which makes it impossible to identify and measure causal relationships with certainty and precision. If you are interested in measuring the effect of advertising on sales with the use of historical data relating to advertising and sales, you will always run the research risk that any observed correspondence between increases in sales and advertising is the result of something other than the effect of advertising on sales. For example, when the advertising budget is set as a fixed percentage of sales, the research risk is that sales have determined advertising rather than vice versa. Or conceivably, both advertising and sales increased during periods of rising national income and prosperity and decreased during periods of declining national income, correlation being partly spurious. Under these circumstances, it would be hard to isolate and measure the effect of advertising on sales. The picture gets even more confused when one recognizes the important effects of concurrent changes in competitors' advertising and product policies during the period.

No amount of data can prevent the possibility of several different and perhaps equally plausible interpretations of the results. Under such circumstances the interpretation often chosen is one which conforms to preconceptions or prejudice. This, of course, largely destroys the function of the measurement.

To sum up, profitometrics requires the measurement of the effects of advertising on sales and the effects of sales on profits. These effects ideally should be measured by means of controlled experiments. Delayed and cumulative impacts should be analyzed in terms of the investment return produced by the stream of incremental profits over the loyalty-life expectancy of the customers acquired by the advertising investment.

IV. SOME IMPLICATIONS

There are some interesting implications of this analysis and its underlying postulates:

1. Most promotional outlays are in economic reality (even though not for bookkeeping, for taxpaying, or for conversation) largely investments.

2. Although most companies have multiple objectives the overriding corporate goal for the decisions on investment of corporate capital should be to make money. The basic measurement of the productivity of capital invested in promotion must therefore be profitability.

3. For immediate-impact advertising in principle, profits can be maximized by pushing spending up to the point where the added adver-

tising cost of increasing sales by one unit just equals the incremental prepromotion profit which the additional sale will create. For advertising whose significant effects are "quick and dead," the incremental profit obtained from the sale adequately measures worth.

4. For advertising whose impact is delayed and cumulative and whose results may create a stream of repeat sales, a more complex measure of worth is needed. Because such advertising is really an investment, purchasing customers by promotion is like purchasing annuities. The value of a customer, like the value of an annuity, is the present worth of the stream of future profits he will produce. How long this stream will last has a profound effect on customer worth. It is partly determined by gestation period, partly by the new customer's loyalty life.

5. The investment-profitability yardstick that is realistic and economically appropriate for promotional investments derives from discounted cash-flow analysis (DCF). It has three variants: (a) project rate of return, (b) present worth at cost of capital, and (c) profitability index.

6. Because much promotion is really an investment (happily expensable for tax purposes), it should compete for funds with alternative ways of investing them. This rivalry for capital should be on the basis of profitability. The present worth of the stream of profits which the promotion can yield should be compared with the cost of funds and with the present worth of the stream of profits which could be obtained by the best alternative use of funds.

7. In rationing scarce capital among competing investment proposals, the cutoff or minimum acceptable rate of return should be the corporation's cost of capital—outside market cost or internal opportunity cost, whichever is higher.

8. The estimates necessary for practical application of discounted cash flow analysis *can* be made:

(a) Incremental production cost and prepromotion profit per unit can be predicted cheaply with adequate precision for most massproduced products.
(b) The effect of advertising on sales is far more difficult to estimate. Yet progress must be and is being made here. Of the various kinds of estimating techniques, the controlled experiment is by far the most precise and powerful means of measuring advertising's effect on sales.
(c) The cost of its equity capital can, with modern techniques, be measured and predicted with sufficient precision so that no corporation is today justified in refusing to use it in sourcing and rationing its capital.

(d) The cost of direct-debt capital is easy to measure with precision. The cost of indirect debt, such as lease debt and oil payments debt, is harder to measure, but workable approximations can be made.

(e) The mix of equity and debt capital that is economic for each corporation can be estimated with adequate accuracy. The mix that is probable for the future (which often differs from the existing mix) is all that is needed to complete the estimate of the corporation's combined cost of capital.

9. There are a number of reasons why the profitometrics approach has not been widely used in determining the advertising appropriation. The basic explanations for this oversight are, I think (1) lack of a determined desire to find the most scientific solution for this intricate management problem, (2) ignorance of the potentialities of modern research techniques for this problem, and (3) quite normal distrust of practically any sort of analysis which is not easily understood by the untrained layman. Economic analysis, even in its most managerial applications, sounds academic, and a DCF investment approach to the advertising budget sounds formidable as well as being unfamiliar.